UNIVERSITY CLASSICS
WALTER HENDRICKS, *General Editor*

MACHIAVELLI

THE PRINCE
AND OTHER WORKS

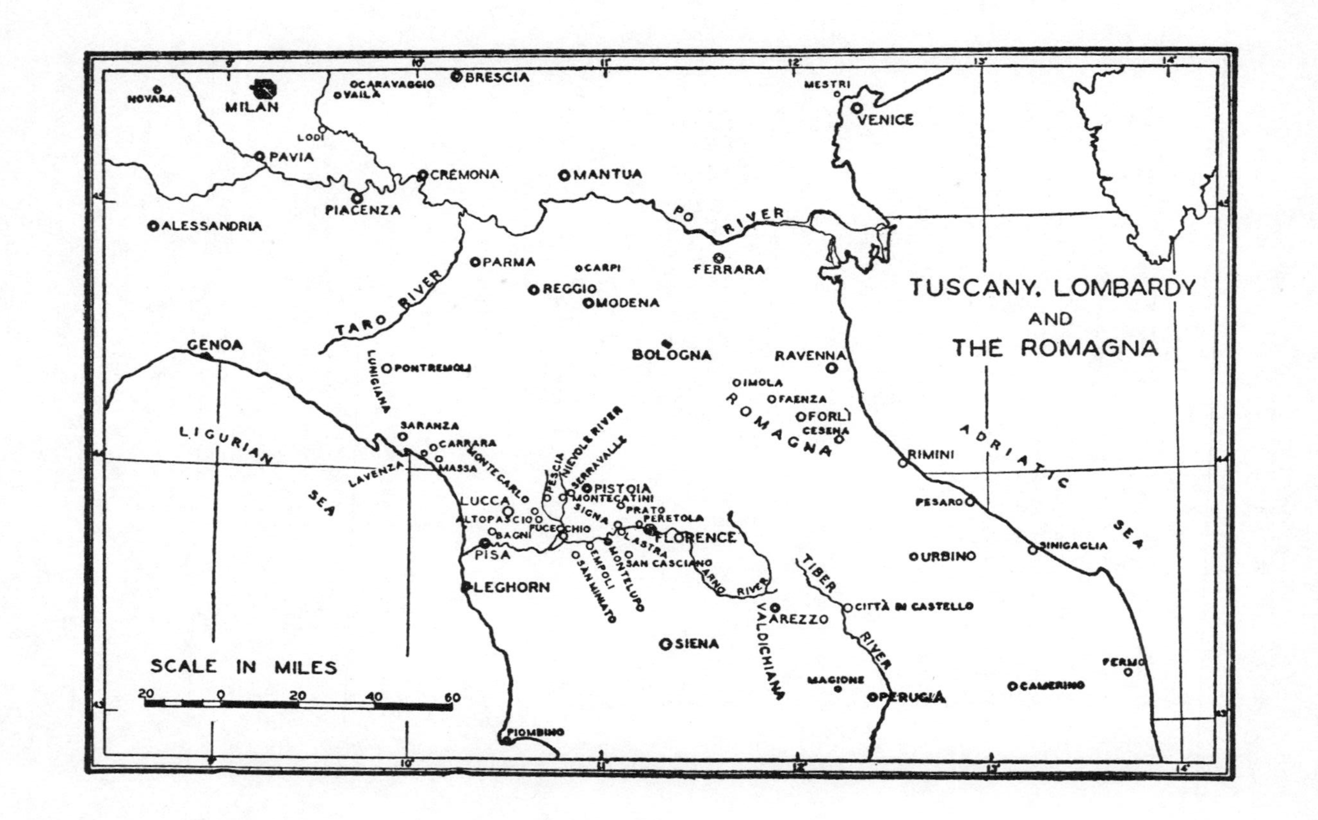
TUSCANY, LOMBARDY
AND
THE ROMAGNA
NOVARA
MILAN
CARAVAGGIO
VAILÀ
BRESCIA
LODI
PAVIA
CREMONA
MANTUA
PIACENZA
ALESSANDRIA
MESTRI
VENICE
PO RIVER
PARMA
CARPI
FERRARA
TARO RIVER
REGGIO
MODENA
GENOA
BOLOGNA
RAVENNA
LUNIGIANA
PONTREMOLI
IMOLA
FAENZA
FORLÌ
CESENA
ROMAGNA
SARANZA
CARRARA
MASSA
LAVENZA
LIGURIAN SEA
ADRIATIC SEA
RIMINI
MONTECARLO
PESCIA
NIEVOLE RIVER
SERRAVALLE
PISTOIA
MONTECATINI
PRATO
PERETOLA
SIGNA
LUCCA
ALTOPASCIO
BAGNI
FUCECCHIO
FLORENCE
LASTRA
PISA
EMPOLI
MONTELUPO
SAN CASCIANO
SAN MINIATO
LEGHORN
ARNO RIVER
AREZZO
VALDICHIANA
TIBER RIVER
CITTÀ DI CASTELLO
PESARO
URBINO
SINIGAGLIA
SIENA
MAGIONE
PERUGIA
CAMERINO
FERMO
PIOMBINO
SCALE IN MILES
20
0
20
40
60
9°
10°
11°
12°
13°
14°

MACHIAVELLI

THE PRINCE

AND OTHER WORKS

TRANSLATION, INTRODUCTION
AND NOTES BY ALLAN H. GILBERT

HENDRICKS HOUSE INC., NEW YORK

PRINTED IN THE UNITED STATES OF AMERICA

In his HISTORY *and* DISCOURSES ON LIVY, *Machiavelli in every word and thought breathes liberty, justice, prudence, truth, and the most lofty spirit. Hence whoever reads carefully and understands well, and takes the author to his heart, cannot at the end be other than a fiery enthusiast for liberty and an enlightened lover of every political virtue (Alfieri,* OF THE PRINCE AND OF LETTERS, *II, 9).*

PREFACE

The purpose of the editor is to present Machiavelli as political thinker and political artist so far as one small volume allows. The first necessity is that he be made to speak English as clearly as possible. At the same time I have endeavored to keep something of the effect of the original, though the sentence-structure of *The Prince* has been usually abandoned in deference to modern expectations. No attempt has been made to improve the style, as by using synonyms where the same word is repeated in the Italian, for Machiavelli wished his book to be ornamented by its ideas rather than by its elaborate language. All available translations into English, German, and French have been consulted.

There has been no English version of the *Discourse on Reforming the Government of Florence* since the Eighteenth Century, and the Familiar Letters here presented make their first appearance in English as independent units. The same is true of the *Capitolo on Fortune*. The *Life of Castruccio Castracani* is more fully annotated than any other edition of it known to the editor. Some of the *Discourses on Livy*—too few—have been selected for their value in illuminating *The Prince,* or for their application to contemporary affairs; among the latter are those on the dictatorship and on the faith to be placed in exiles. This is, I believe, the first English translation of any of Machiavelli's works since the publication of the text of his historical and literary works by Mazzoni and Casella.

The notes and tables supply a minimum of information on the history of Italy in Machiavelli's time, but since the purpose of the volume is to present the author of *The Prince* as one who has something to say to the present age, the number of facts not demanded for explanation of his ideas has been kept as low as possible. The topical index will, I hope, assist the reader in gaining a view of Machiavelli's ideas, as well as guide him to explanations given in the footnotes and introduction.

My chief obligations, not otherwise apparent, are to the Research Council of Duke University, Professor Ben Lemert, Professor Raven I. McDavid, Professor Arpad Steiner, Mrs. Freda Townsend, Miss Barbara Sopp, Miss Dixie Swaren, Miss Lucetta Teagarden, and Mr. John L. Stender.

TABLE OF CONTENTS

INTRODUCTION

MACHIAVELLI IN OUR TIME

1 No one can read many pages of Machiavelli without feeling that the questions he discusses are those of our own time, and without asking how many of his ideas are still applicable. The Florentine Secretary would have welcomed such a question, for he had a strong belief in the practical value of ancient wisdom. History is useful, he holds, because it can help us with our own problems. Yet so great are the variations in human affairs and so difficult is the estimate of both past and present that Machiavelli admits that he may himself have fallen into error, as he observed that men did even in their attempts to compare the times of their youth with those of their old age. Nevertheless, he holds that with all its changes the world is essentially the same, for though in one age a people may be strong and in another weak, the passions of men do not vary.

2 Yet a reader disposed to allow that the nature of mankind has not altered since the sixteenth century may still fear that there is insuperable difficulty in applying to the recent world ideas developed in the limited sphere of Florence, or even the Mediterranean area, with England and Germany, that chiefly concerned our author. There are, however, aspects of the present century in which it resembles the sixteenth. Both are periods of restless activity of the human spirit, in the Renaissance especially in art, in our day in the natural sciences. Both are highly developed in commerce. Italian cities had long been rivals for commercial and financial supremacy in great foreign areas; Venice still held an Eastern empire based on trade. The nations of Europe were attempting to expand at the expense of their neighbors. France and Spain were continually in rivalry on their own borders and in Italy; armies from beyond the Alps—Swiss, German, French—repeatedly descended on hapless Italy; Henry VIII of England had designs on France; the Turk pressed in from the East. Italy, as the focus of much of the world's movement, was a land of political change. No state was stable. Any small city was liable to attack by some more powerful neighbor, such as Venice or Florence; some successful mercenary general might decide to make himself its ruler, after a massacre of the leading citizens; the strife of political parties within the walls might lead to riot, plunder, and flight. The exiles, such as the Florentine Medici, then intrigued with friends within the city and foreigners without, until they were able to return for the overthrow of their opponents. The present age has likewise shown desire for expansion, commercial and territorial, resulting in warfare that has shattered the stability that seemed near establishment in the first years of the twentieth century. Such turmoil as Italy showed during the lifetime of Machiavelli is that of the whole world since 1914. Russia has completely changed its government; Germany has twice fallen in ruin; Japan has changed its allies, developed an empire greater than Venice dreamed of, and lost it utterly; the United States has undertaken violent interference in European affairs; England has lost the rule of the waves and the ability to defend her empire. If the nature of men is still the same, the present century has sore need for wisdom developed in a time of political confusion. Can moderns learn how to approach their problems by observing the political thought of Machiavelli?

3 In the Third and following Chapters of *The Prince,* Machiavelli discusses the administration of newly conquered regions. Since 1914 this has been a persistent problem. Russia has seen parts of her territory under alien rule and then has herself come to play the part of a foreign administrator. Germany has twice been subject to the rule of strangers and yet has had the task of controlling France, Denmark, Norway, and the Low Countries. In these countries some of the methods discussed by Machiavelli have been employed. In Chapter Five, for example, he recommends government by quislings. This advice has been justified by much other policy since 1900, such as English rule in South Africa and that the United States in the Philippines. On the other hand, the Secretary points out that those who have enjoyed independence do not soon forget it—something that all the conquerors of recent times are witnesses to. These lovers of freedom, moreover, have always found that the foreign enemies of their would-be rulers were glad to make use of them.

4 At the end of the Eighth Chapter of *The Prince* appears the topic of conferring benefits in time of adversity, when, as forced by need, they are unlikely to be permanent. The history since 1918 of Palestine and the surrounding Arab lands would have interested Machiavelli as an illustration of this topic.

5 The Tenth Chapter is on the strength of nations, or true independence. No state is strong that cannot get together an adequate army and fight a battle with whosoever comes to attack it. When this assertion is taken from its limited Italian setting and applied to our day, its light on England and France is startling. In 1914, the two countries qualified for Machiavelli's approval, fighting on something like equality with their enemy. In the Second World War, neither could provide the adequate army Machiavelli demands. England, being the fortress necessary to a weak combatant, was able to hold out until aid came, using all the methods indicated as those of the besieged prince. The siege, as *The Prince* suggests might happen, proved too difficult for the enemy. But the rescue brought with it another Machiavellian difficulty. To some extent in World War Number One and to a great extent in Number Two, there was invited into Europe "the powerful foreigner" of the Third Chapter, to wit, the United States, able to take from England and France the influence they had hitherto wielded. Russia too gave up the possibility of immediate and sole dominance over Germany by summoning that powerful foreigner, who was still lingering in the island fortress. As King Louis XII of France did not realize that a strong Venice would keep other powers out of Lombardy, so in 1946 the United States failed until after the destruction of Japan to see that a barrier against Russia in the Orient would be removed.

6 Living in an age of warfare, Machiavelli had meditated on problems that the present age has been obliged to consider. *The Art of War* is one of his longer works and many parts of his *Discourses* are on the same theme. His demand that a state defend itself by means of its own citizens has become the norm of military practice. But he did not condemn mercenaries merely because they were foreigners. His objection was to a class that made war its profession, its "art," as he puts it. He wished for soldiers who even in time of war were primarily citizens. This he asked for "the great as well as the small"; the chief speaker in *The Art of War* protests that his king does not reward and honor him because of his understanding of war so much as because he can give good advice in time of peace. The professional soldier whom, in Machiavelli's belief, no well-regulated republic ever allowed among its citizens, has much to answer for in this century. He is blamed for German action in 1914 and for Fascist rule in Spain. In America he has been heard demanding and securing power over the individual and over the economic and foreign policy of the nation such as the Founding Fathers did not dream of. Like Machiavelli, such writers as Liddell Hart have told us, moreover, that the professional soldier is often not very forward-looking in his business. So we can ponder the Florentine's belief that a class whose glory and profit comes from war is not likely to treat the world as a place where peace is to be sought for.

7 As my final illustration, Machiavelli turned from the character of the professional soldier to war itself, even to the details of armament. In his lifetime military methods were in flux, partly as a result of the application of gun-powder, as they have shifted in the twentieth century because of further inventions. In his search for better ways he turned both to antiquity and to the battles of his own day, striving to combine what could be learned from Romans, Swiss, and Spanish. Though not infallible, his judgments are often excellent. He realized what the "fury" of artillery could do to fixed targets, whether city walls or bodies of troops long standing in one position, as at Ravenna. Likewise he realized the comparative ineffectiveness of field artillery against troops in rapid motion. In dealing with the smaller firearms, he judges them according to their value when he wrote; later in the century his opinion would have been modified by the facts. His characteristic point of view is shown in his treatment in the *Discourses* of the problem whether artillery will not make impossible the exercise of the highest qualities of the soldier. His answer is that men are still superior to machines, that the intelligent soldier will change his methods but not his courage.

8-11 This suggests that Machiavelli can do much more for us than make suggestions which, translated into terms of the present, bear on our troubles and dangers. He does not so much give the right solution as, with political and poetic genius, show us how the difficulty is to be met. His precept and example are for labor unceasing, for much reading in antiquity and observation of the world around us, for faith in the common good of man, for the belief that human intelligence is not exerted in vain.

MACHIAVELLI'S REPUTATION

12 The fame of Machiavelli has passed through many vicissitudes. Perhaps he has hardly appeared worse than in the

Elizabethan drama. In Marlowe's *Jew of Malta* he enters to speak the prologue in person:

> *Machiavel.* I am Machiavel,
> And weigh not men, and therefore not men's words.
> Admired I am of those that hate me most.
> Though some speak openly against my books,
> Yet will they read me, and thereby attain
> To Peter's chair: and when they cast me off,
> Are poisoned by my climbing followers.
> I count religion but a childish toy,
> And hold there is no sin but ignorance.
> Birds of the air will tell of murders past?
> I am ashamed to hear such fooleries.
> Many will talk of title to a crown:
> What right had Caesar to the empery?
> Might first made kings, and laws were then most sure
> When like the Draco's they were writ in blood.

Barabas, the villain of the play, and supposedly a follower of the Florentine, is grotesquely wicked:

> I walk abroad o'nights
> And kill sick people groaning under walls:
> Sometimes I go about and poison wells;
> And now and then, to cherish Christian thieves,
> I am content to lose some of my crowns,
> That I may, walking in my gallery,
> See 'em go pinioned along by my door.
> Being young, I studied physic, and began
> To practice first upon the Italian;
> There I enriched the priests with burials,
> And always kept the sextons' arms in ure
> With digging graves and ringing dead men's knells:
> And after that was I an engineer,
> And in the wars 'twixt France and Germany,
> Under pretence of helping Charles the Fifth,
> Slew friend and enemy with my stratagems.
> Then after that was I an usurer,
> And with extorting, cozening, forfeiting,
> And tricks belonging unto brokery,
> I filled the jails with bankrupts in a year,
> And with young orphans planted hospitals,
> And every moon made some or other mad,
> And now and then one hang himself for grief,
> Pinning upon his breast a long great scroll
> How I with interest tormented him.

But mark how I am blest for plaguing them;
I have as much coin as will buy the town (act 2, sc. 3).

13 When Marlow and his collaborators were setting this conception of Niccolò before the public, it is no wonder that he became the symbol of all wickedness. The genuine knowledge of his works possessed by such Englishmen as Sir Philip Sidney, Sir Walter Raleigh, Lord Bacon, and the poet Francis Quarles could not make headway against a popular conception favored by the stage. No wonder that his name Niccolò or Nicholas has been connected with the Devil's pet name, Old Nick, or Nickieben, as Burns has it. The word *Machiavellian* came to mean the unscrupulous intriguer, characterized by cunning, duplicity, and bad faith for the most selfish reasons. Such is the word and such its meaning is likely to remain, without much regard for historical verities.

14 Obviously such a reputation did not grow from nothing. Its root is found, apparently, in the attacks of clergy and other moralists, such as Cardinal Pole, Possevino the Jesuit,[1] and Gentillet the Huguenot, whose *Contre-Machiavel* was translated into English by Simon Patericke.[2] In 1564 the Council of Trent confirmed a papal decree of 1559 which placed the works of Niccolò on the Index of Prohibited Books. Among later opponents is to be reckoned Frederick the Great of Prussia, who wrote a work called *The Antimachiavel or The Examen of the Prince of Machiavel.*

15 On the other hand, defenders appeared. Spinoza thought Machiavelli a very acute and prudent man, who perhaps intended to show how careful a free people ought to be about entrusting its welfare to a single person, because a tyrant, unless he was so vain as to think he could please everybody, would always fear plots against himself, and therefore would look out for himself and plot against the multitude rather than work for their advantage.[3] Rousseau is said to have held the same view. The dramatist Alfieri, a great admirer of his countryman, wrote as follows:

From *The Prince,* alone among his works, it is possible to gather here and there some immoral and tyrannical maxims;

[1] Antonius Possevinus, *Iudicium de Nicolao Machiavello,* Rome, 1592. He calls Machiavelli "a wicked instrument of Satan" (p. 158).

John Case in his *Sphaera Civitatis* (Oxford, 1588) says that he detests Machiavelli as an object of hatred to God and men, like the dog and the serpent (p. 2). I owe this reference to Professor Don Cameron Allen.

[2] See Mario Praz, *Machiavelli and the Elizabethans,* London, 1928. Napoleone Orsini, "Elizabethan Manuscript Translations of Machiavelli's *Prince,*" in *Journal of the Warburg Institute,* I (1937), 166-9.

[3] *Political Tractate,* Chap. 5, sect. 7.

and they are written down by the author (as is clear to anybody who thinks clearly) for the purpose of unveiling to the people the ambitious and crafty cruelty of princes, and surely not to teach princes to practice it; for they always do employ it, have employed it, and will employ it, more or less according to their need, genius, and skill.[4]

16 From failure to recognize the qualities of Machiavelli, and yet a perception of his greatness, rose the belief that he is a character of mystery, fascinating in wickedness, and yet with a message for mankind; on the one hand he condemned tyrants, yet he taught them the way of oppression. Carlyle could do no better than call *The Prince* a "perverse little book."[5]

17 Study of Niccolò by professional scholars of various nations began more than a century ago, but its progress was relatively slow. What a highly intelligent man of strong political interests could do in 1897 is shown by John Morley's *Romanes Lecture* on Machiavelli. This member of Parliament rejects the notion of Machiavelli as a scientist, and therefore supposedly uninterested in good and evil for themselves, and incapable of emotion. According to this common theory, the Florentine had looked on the world and described it, without interest in its moral condition or in the possibility of its improvement. But Morley still unconsciously retains much from the old views. He seems astonished, for example, that the last chapter of *The Prince* "flowed from the deeps of what was undoubtedly sincere and passionate feeling" (p. 31). But if here and elsewhere Machiavelli can "glow," he generally writes in "iron harshness." In conclusion Morley can only write:

> Machiavelli and his school saw only cunning, jealousy, perfidy, ingratitude, dupery, and yet on such a foundation as this they dreamed that they could build. What idealist or doctrinaire ever fell into a stranger error? . . .
>
> It is true to say that Machiavelli represents certain living forces in our actual world; that Science, with its survival of the fittest, unconsciously lends him illegitimate aid; that 'he is not a vanishing type, but a constant and contemporary influence' (*Acton*). This is because energy, force, will, violence, still keep alive in the world their resistance to the

[4] Alfieri, *Of the Prince and of Letters*, II, 9.

[5] "And as to the other question, 'Was the Signor Niccolò serious in this perverse little Book; or did he only do it ironically, with a serious inverse purpose?' We will leave that to be decided, any time convenient, by people who are much at leisure in the world" (*Frederick the Great*, bk. 10, chap. 6). To alter a name in Carlyle's paragraph, "What is the use of arguing with anybody that can believe in Frederick the Great?"

control of justice and conscience, humanity and right. In so far as he represents one side in that eternal struggle, and suggests one set of considerations about it, he retains a place in the literature of modern political systems and of European morals.

Something is doubtless to be pardoned here to the necessary clap-trap of a member of parliament, the verbal insistence on morals that practical politicians (Morley would not have had to go to the eighteenth chapter of *The Prince* for it) deem necessary; but at least Gladstone's friend does recognize that "you will hardly find in Machiavelli a good word for any destroyer of free government" (p. 28). Yet over his words the shadow of Niccolò the bogey man is still dark; stripped of much of his mystery, he is still sinister.

18 As the process of attempting to see Machiavelli in the setting of Medicean Italy has gone on, as his words have been considered by scholars who have as their ideal, at any rate, the discovery of the truth, a wise and admirable Machiavelli has more and more clearly emerged.[6] Not that the scholar of the present is wholly independent of even the misinterpreters of the past. The response of a violent opponent of *The Prince* who, like many violent opponents, has never read a word of the book, is yet originated by something in Machiavelli; men do not become symbols without a reason for it. The scholar of the present, however honest he may be, however properly determined to judge his author first from what is written in the *Complete Works,* is still able to learn something from the reaction of the past. It can at any rate assure him that something more than commonplace resides in the pages of *The Prince.* In our zeal we have sometimes forgotten this. In one of the most recent works on the subject—and one worthy of commendation—we read:

> Antagonists and apologists arose; analysts, critics, philosophers, casuists and political economists of every shade of opinion seized upon the work and either tore it to shreds in their rage or lauded it so extravagantly that in comparison with his work its author appeared puny. What was there in this book to occasion so much feeling and controversy? A modern writer hardly dares answer the question except in the stereotyped manner; can scarcely trust himself to confess it; fears an accusation of unforgivable heresy;

[6] Mr. Roswell G. Townsend calls to my attention an analogous change in the reputation of Hobbes, once a champion of tyranny, now a lover of justice. See Sterling P. Lamprecht, "Hobbes and Hobbism," in *The American Political Science Review,* XXXIV (1940), 31-53.

> —but the answer to the query now, as it always has been in reality, is—*Nothing.* There is nothing in *The Prince* to justify the hatred, the contempt, the loathing and horror that it called forth, just as there is nothing in it to merit the praise awarded it by enthusiasts who have read into it an interpretation of their own deeds or ideals. Does it not always remain true that a book written in a certain century must be judged according to the conditions and requirements of that century? *The Prince* does nothing more than tabulate the various species of principalities, the different kinds of rulers, and the methods to be employed in maintaining their rule. . . .
>
> In their ardent desire to prove Machiavelli a man of the deepest and darkest villainy, or a demigod of wisdom, the writers of more than three centuries have read into *The Prince,* and out of it, far more than its author ever knew. More than from any other injuries, *Il Principe* has suffered from "interpretation" and over-interpretation. There is nothing in the work that calls for interpretation; the plain text contains all that is necessary for a perfect understanding of its meaning; Machiavelli said exactly what he meant to say, and meant just what he said. . . . When the judicious Burd writes (*Cambridge Modern History*) that Machiavelli's works "are not intelligible except when considered in relation to the historical background of his life and to the circumstances in which they were written," is it not time for us to say that we have no room for the nebulous imagings of abstract philosophy, the anachronistic censures of moralists who look for greater virtues at the Renaissance than they find in the Bible, and the hair-splitting arguments of economists without historical knowledge—and recommend all who would know what Machiavelli aimed at for his own and the succeeding generation *to go and read his book.*[7]

The oft-reiterated *nothing* of this assertion is the very word recently heard used by a highly intelligent young woman in speaking of *The Prince* after her first reading. It is the right word if we have gone to the little book expecting to find it a manual of secret perfidy for all the relations of life.

19 Yet we still do find in *The Prince* the reason for all that has been said against it, for all the false interpretations, for all the praise. The modern reader who finds nothing to justify the critics is right, provided he goes on to find everything to justify them. The truth about the work must be derived in part

[7] Jeffrey Pulver, *Machiavelli,* pp. 227-9.

from its history, even though that history avails little without the text itself, read not with the eyes alone but with the mind. Nor is the past valuable merely because of flashes of insight by great men, as when Bacon said that Machiavelli told what men do, and not what they ought to do, or Spinoza that he was surely a friend of liberty and gave excellent advice on protecting it,[8] or Voltaire's paradox that the first thing for a Machiavellian prince to do is to take in hand the refutation of *The Prince*. When the Church forbade the reading of Machiavelli it did more than emphasize his belief that the corrupt papal court had corrupted Italy, as we read in the *Discourses*, I, 12; it led a reader to ask whether Niccolò does not represent the layman in his conflict with the cleric for the rule of the world's affairs. When the liberators of Italy exalted Machiavelli because he believed in Italian unity, they suggested that we look for a pervading patriotism not confined to the last chapter of *The Prince*. Considered in this way the reputation of Machiavelli is the interpretation of his work.

TRADITION AND ORIGINALITY

20 Like most great books, *The Prince* enjoyed the advantage of a great body of predecessors.[1] The book of advice to rulers was one of the established medieval types, to which some of the most important thinkers of the period contributed. St. Thomas Aquinas, Vincent of Beauvais, and Petrarch are the most striking. The most important medieval work of the sort is probably the *De regimine principum* of Aegidio Colonna. The Renaissance was equally active: the poet Pontanus wrote on the subject, and perhaps in the very year Machiavelli was writing *The Prince,* Erasmus was composing his work on *The Instruction of a Christian Prince*. Savonarola touched on some of the topics usual to such writers in his *Tractate on the Organization and Government of the City of Florence*.

21 Machiavelli was conscious of this body of material and recognized his own relation to it in the first sentences of the Fifteenth Chapter of *The Prince*: "It now remains to see what should be the methods of a prince in dealing with his subjects and his friends. And because I know that many have written on this topic, I fear that when I write too I shall be thought presumptuous, because, in discussing it, I break away com-

[8] *Political Tractate,* Chap. 5, sect. 7.

[1] See Allan H. Gilbert, *Machiavelli's "Prince" and Its Forerunners.*

pletely from the methods of my predecessors." Superficially, Chapters 15 to 23 are the most conventional in the work. No one familiar with books of advice to princes can look at their headings without a feeling of familiarity; in particular, liberality, love and fear, the keeping of faith, the king's ministers, and flattery are oft-discussed headings, as doubtless Machiavelli supposed his readers would recognize.

22 But deeply indebted to the past as Machiavelli was, the thing that counts is the power of his own product. No familiarity with tradition would have made *The Prince* one of the books that everybody must pretend to know, the only one of the many works on the conduct of princes of which that is true. One matter scarcely touched by the older writers but dominant in Machiavelli is that of the new prince. This comes from his hope that Italy is to be redeemed from the foreigners by such a monarch. A political scientist would have been less concerned with the first appearance of a sovereign, but Machiavelli is patriot before he is scientist. In details also he departed from the tradition, as in suggesting that liberality might sometimes be unwise.

23 But above all he abandoned the norm in his attitude to morality. The earlier works generally had a most pious flavor, and bristled with references to the Bible and the Fathers of the Church. After the discovery of Aristotle, his theories, as sanctioned by the Church, were heavily drawn on. Of the first type, Vincent de Beauvais' *De morali principis institutione* is a good example; of the second, the *De regimine principum* of Aquinas. Yet whatever their intellectual basis, they demanded in common that the good ruler be the good man, the full example of moral virtue to his subjects. Machiavelli also wished his ruler to be a good man, able to furnish them examples, as he suggests near the beginning of Chapter 24 of *The Prince*. Yet his standard is different. The earlier writers take an absolute ecclesiastical standard. Machiavelli takes as his the well-being of the people of the country. To this the ruler is to devote himself with the fullest willingness to sacrifice his personal comfort and pleasure. To be sure, this will include the observation of many common rules of morality. For example to be licentious with respect to women is, as we read in Chapter 17, to overthrow one's government. The good prince is chaste, then, rather to benefit his people than to obey the law of God.

24 The moral rules of the older writers tended to be absolute. They often insisted, for example, that the king's faith should be wholly reliable. But Machiavelli, in his Fifteenth Chapter, explained that human conditions must be regarded, that the morality of the king must be based on the practical truth of affairs, and not on abstractions. The moral conduct that fits the conditions is the one to be advised. For that reason the prince who does his duty by his people will learn how to act contrary to the precepts of the moralists, when necessity requires it. Goodness may require him to be not good, in the conventional sense.

25 But even such unconventional though not wholly unprecedented ideas could not have given *The Prince* its great reputation. Nor is it that it represented the ideas of its age; they are expressed elsewhere in volumes known to but the few. But to all of this he added the intense feeling of the patriot and the skill of the artist. In both what the author says and how he says it, the greatness of the book resides. Its final originality is in its touch with the realities of the world seen through the eyes of the artist.

WHY DID A REPUBLICAN WRITE *THE PRINCE?*

26 "Cola Montano spoke with loathing of life under a prince who is not good, and called those glorious and fortunate to whom Nature and Fortune had granted the privilege of being born and living in a republic. He demonstrated that all famous men were brought up in republics and not under princes, for the former nourish able men and the latter destroy them, because republics profit from the capacities of men, but princes fear their abilities."[1] These words are attributed by Machiavelli to one of his characters, but it is difficult to feel that they do not express the belief of the historian himself. Certainly it is impossible to read Machiavelli's works other than *The Prince* without concluding that he was a republican. The *Discourses on Livy* not merely deal with republics but show their author's sympathies. Brutus is his hero and Caesar, destroyer of the liberties of Rome, his villain.[2] The common good is attended to in a republic, rather than under a prince. Something of this sort is said in most of the selections from the *Discourses on Livy* given in this volume; he who turns to the complete work will find that its whole spirit is republican, as it is founded on the history of free Rome, great Rome as distinguished from degenerate imperial Rome.

27 But Machiavelli was not a frenzied republican. He could

[1] *History of Florence,* VII, 33; cf. also the *Art of War,* book 2, p. 301.

[2] *Discourses on Livy,* I, 10, par. 3, below.

see advantages in constitutional monarchy. Good government was possible under a prince. France is cited as a country to be envied by Italians because unified under a wise monarchial constitution.[3] Machiavelli can discuss princely rule as a possible government for Florence.[4] Moreover, there are circumstances when only a monarch can rule, as when reform is needed and the people are too corrupt to bring it about for themselves; the kingly hand alone can be effective.[5]

28 Such was the state of Italy when *The Prince* was composed. It was useless to dream of unified Italy under a republican government. There must be a prince or nothing. The rule of almost any prince would be superior to the chaos on which Niccolò looked. To be sure, he hoped for a monarch who would devote himself to the common good of Italy. To such a ruler anything to accomplish his purpose would be permitted. When the security of Italy is in the utmost danger "there can be no consideration of just or unjust, piteous or cruel, praiseworthy or shameful; every other consideration can be laid aside and without question the plan adopted that will save the life and preserve the independence of the country."[6]

29 In practice, such a guiding conviction would often be necessary. Not every Italian would accept the notion of a united Italy, if it seemed to infringe on his own liberties. Machiavelli had himself confronted such a problem. Pisa had been a free city; it had fallen under the Florentine dominion; it had rebelled with success; one of Machiavelli's important official tasks was to aid in bringing the stubborn Pisans again under Florentine rule. Yet he knew that the yoke of a republic was heavier than that of a prince.[7] Moreover, there seems to be some sympathy in his references to their liberty, not only in *The Prince,* Chap. 5, par. 2, but in the *Historical Fragments,* where he writes: "Entraghes, the French officer, came out of the castle with the keys in his hands and knelt before the image of Our Lady, asking her favor for the liberty of Pisa and expressing his loathing for the tyranny of the Florentines. He declared with tears that he restored that castle into the hands of the Pisans because he was moved by the justice of their cause and the wickedness of their adversaries."[8]

30 But for all that, Machiavelli did move against the Pisans with vigor, and nowhere suggests that his conscience troubled him for doing so. Perhaps he looked on the expansion of the

[3] *The Prince,* Chap. 19, par. 6; *Discourses on Livy,* I, 12, last par., below.
[4] The *Discourse on Reforming the Government of Florence,* par. 13, below.
[5] *Discourses on Livy,* I, 9, below. [6] Ibid., III, 41.
[7] *Discourses on Livy,* II, 2, par. 9, below. [8] *Opere,* II, 294.

Florentine dominion as a blessing. Certainly he admired the growth of the Roman state, through its conquest of neighboring peoples, for he devotes to the expansion of that republic the second book of his *Discourses on Livy*. There is no question that he hoped for the establishment of his prince in Italy as a great blessing. A high price can properly be paid for delivering Italy from the barbarian and uniting her warring states in internal peace. Part of that price would be restriction of local independence,[9] yet firm but foolish patriots might refuse to pay it. The prince then would have no choice but to act as Machiavelli did toward Pisa, or as Rome did toward the Samnites. To the common good of Italy, all lesser respects must yield.

THE RELATION OF *THE PRINCE* TO ITS AUTHOR'S OTHER WORKS

31 Students of Machiavelli have often remarked that if *The Prince* is to be properly understood, it should be read in connection with its author's other writings, particularly the *Discourses on Livy*. They are right. The whole long misapprehension of *The Prince,* such as the view that it is a textbook for the tyrant, may be assigned to the reading of the little work in isolation from its background. Possibly this very incompleteness, allowing the mystery of wickedness to brood over the book, has had something to do with its wide circulation, though hardly with its genuine reputation. On the other hand, in view of the place of *The Prince* among the world's books, it is hardly possible to say that greater intelligibility would have made its fame greater, or even added to its true stature.

32 It is a highly practical book in the strictest sense of the word *practical;* it tells what the ruler is to do, but does not detail the ultimate reasons for his actions. He must be a sympathetic reader indeed who can from *The Prince* alone deduce the full theory of its author. Something of this sympathy has been furnished by the Italians of the Risorgimento, who saw in Niccolò one of their own predecessors because they caught the spirit of the last chapter of *The Prince* and with it illumined the whole work. Students not thus attuned to sympathy turned, as might be expected, to the theory that the last chapter had nothing to do with the remainder, and in

[9] See *Discourses on Livy,* I, 12, last par., below.

general that the work had little life and less nobility. Lacking the sympathy of the patriots of the Risorgimento, or wishing to show its rational basis and perhaps to correct its excesses, the student must turn to the bulk of Machiavelli's writings for the explanation of the higher reasons why the prince is to act as he does.

33 For this purpose the *Discourses on Livy* come first. They were written at leisure, with no immediate and pressing occasion. Time and space were available for the author to say what he would. Any restraint from Livy, freely chosen by Niccolò for comment, was slight, for the text was quite to the mind of the commentator, and a mere hint was enough to allow the comment to turn where the feelings of its writer directed. From the *Discourses,* then, Machiavelli's dominating ideas can best be learned.

34 They appear also in the *History of Florence,* but are recovered with more difficulty than from the *Discourses,* being somewhat more thinly and less directly stated. Relatively more importance must be given to the spirit of the work than to specific and obvious statements. The *Art of War* is replete with special details, but it too is dominated by principles of society and even states them directly. The personal letters of Machiavelli are invaluable in giving direct expression of his personal convictions.

35 The chief of his political ideas is to be found in the traditional political conception of the common good;[1] which he shared with many thinkers of his time and the preceding ages. A typical passage is that in the dedication of the *Art of War,* where he speaks of "the arts which in a well-organized state are properly disposed for the sake of the common good of the inhabitants." In *The Prince,* however, this expression does not occur, nor does any synonym appear except in the last chapter, where, as has been suggested, it is likely to be least effective for ordinary readers. It sometimes seems as though he were deliberate in leaving out such references. For example, in the *Discourses on Livy,* III, 34, he says: "Nothing makes a prince so much esteemed as to give a striking instance of the use of some exceptional action or saying, in harmony with the common good, which shows that the ruler is magnanimous or liberal or just, and is such as to become a proverb among his subjects." Much the same thing is said in *The Prince,* Chapter 21, but the clause "in harmony with the common good" does not appear. The reader of *The Prince* alone cannot know that the good of the whole is its author's chief concern.

[1] See also the *Introduction,* pars. 39-51, below.

36 Why is this? *The Prince* is, as it were, a sort of excerpt from the great body of Machiavelli's thought at the time, of which the *Discourses on Livy*, the *Art of War*, the *History of Florence*, the *Discourse on Reforming the Government of Florence*, and other works also form parts. From this mass *The Prince* was detached for the purpose of giving practical advice to a new prince on how he was to conduct himself. It is so thoroughly practical that it neglects general assumptions on the purpose and value of government; matters which might have had a higher tone appear merely as devices. For example, in the *Art of War*, citizen soldiery appears as a means for securing the well-being of the country, but in *The Prince*, until the last chapter, citizen soldiers may be externally interpreted as nothing but a better device for the prince than mercenaries. It is true that they are a better instrument, and for the moment the author needs to say nothing more.

37 It is possible that Machiavelli himself hardly realized how barren most of his little work was of the higher ideas that filled his mind. But his situation must be taken into account. As appears elsewhere, *The Prince* has many of the features of the type of works on the conduct of princes. These had as their common foundation the doing of justice to men as the first duty of the ruler. Machiavelli could assume that every reader would take for granted that it is the business of the king to rule well, that, as Isidore of Seville had said, he gets his name from ruling well, *rex a bene regendo vocatur*. Niccolò did not imagine readers who were innocent of medieval and Renaissance theory. Moreover, his mind was filled with the notion of the common good of Florence, the basis for the *Discourse on Reforming the Government of Florence*, and the good of Italy, dominating the Letter to Vettori of August 26, 1513. He may scarcely have realized that so little on justice and the public good was to be found in *The Prince*. But if he said little, he implied the more. What other could he have in mind than the best for Italy? Why say it, when practical knowledge on how to proceed was a *desideratum? The Prince* is, then, dominated by what is the more important as it is but implied. The full statement is to be found in the other works, above all in the *Discourses on Livy*.

38 It is, then, to be taken for granted by a reader of *The Prince* that the ruler is to fulfill the function urged on the Medici in the *Discourse on Reforming the Government of Florence*, and that he is to strive to bring Italy to the condition of Rome under the best emperors.[2] Machiavelli's prince is but a means for securing the common good.

[2] *Discourses on Livy*, I, 10, par. 5, below.

MORALITY AND RELIGION

39 Machiavelli lived within the frame of human society; not Heaven or Hell, but the earth was his center. Much concerned with religion, he subordinated it to human affairs; its purpose is not so much to carry the soul to future bliss as to make man happier here and now. This happiness is not limited and selfish; it is the common good—an expression that runs through Niccolò's writings and sets forth the object of his devotion. To Machiavelli the founder of Christianity is important primarily because his principles of life, retained as he established them, would have made states and Christian republics more united and much more prosperous than they are. If ecclesiastics had followed in the footsteps of St. Francis and St. Dominic, Italy would not have owed its ruin to the corruption of the Church.[1] No faith can be put in soldiers or citizens who are without religion and the fear of God.[2] It is the duty of the prince to furnish his subjects an example of moral goodness and patriotism.[3]

40 Though looking beyond Italy to admire the government of France or the German cities, Machiavelli did not develop the imperial vision of Dante. With the difficult problem of Italy under his eyes, he had no energy for what was beyond. The good of humanity in the peninsula was concern enough for one practical man. Indeed in the political confusion of the sixteenth century, practical concern with all even of Italy—a mass without unity—was difficult enough. The common good must be sought in a still smaller territory.

41 The *patria,* the native city of Florence, then, is in practice sometimes the object of Machiavelli's religion. Such a unit can at least express in concrete form the highest good, that of men united. In the *Discourse or Dialogue on Our Language,* he affirms that man has no duty more important than that to his native city, and when he writes on the proper constitution for Florence he asserts that the greatest good within man's power, and the most pleasing to God, is what he does for the sake of his native land.[4] As a higher thing than the individual, the common good, represented by the city, can properly be the object of sacrifice. Machiavelli himself loves his country more than he does his soul.[5] No higher praise, he declares, can be

[1] *Discourses on Livy,* I, 12, pars. 3, 4, below.

[2] *The Prince,* Chap. 12, par. 2, below. See also the *Art of War,* book 7, near the end.

[3] Cf. *The Prince,* Chap. 24, par. 1, and footnote 5.

[4] *Discourse on Reforming the Government of Florence,* par. 29, below.

[5] Letter of April 16, 1527, par. 2, below.

given to Cosimo Rucellai than to say that no enterprise, even involving the loss of his soul, would have made him tremble, if it were for the good of Florence.[6] The citizens of the good old days deserve commendation because they loved their country more than their souls.[7] They had the courage to act against papal censure, even though they believed that Florentines who died when the city was under interdict would not go to heaven. Patriotism overcame desire for salvation.

42 Such a conflict brings Machiavelli's position into clear light. Not merely the rites and ceremonies of the church must yield to a higher good, but all morality must be adapted to it. Hence the assertion that when the safety of the country absolutely depends on one's decision there should be no thought of what is just or unjust, humane or cruel, praiseworthy or shameful; the citizen should lay aside every consideration except that of finding a plan that will save the life and maintain the liberty of his country.[8] The same attitude is that of the Eighteenth Chapter of *The Prince*. The ruler is bound by a higher law than the particular precepts of the moralists.

43 Yet it must not be supposed that these precepts are of no moment; on the contrary they form the general rule for life, and should be observed. Early in Chapter 15 of *The Prince* Machiavelli distinguishes between the way men live and the way they ought to live; the latter is in itself good. Proceeding in the chapter he gives a list of virtues and vices, and then continues: "I know that everybody will admit that it would be very praiseworthy for a prince to possess all of the above-mentioned qualities that are considered good." The Eighteenth Chapter, on the faith of princes, opens thus: "Everybody knows how laudable it is in a prince to keep his faith and to be an honest man and not a trickster." And in the *Discourses on Livy*, III, 40, he asserts that the general use of fraud is "detestable." These statements are not to be passed over lightly, but mean quite what they say. The principles of morality and

[6] *Art of War*, book 1, beginning.

[7] *Florentine History*, book 3, chap. 7, end.

In his *Dialogue on the Government of Florence*, book 2, Guicciardini refers to Gino Capponi's saying that the Ten of War should be persons who loved their country more than their souls because it is impossible to regulate affairs of state and governments according to the precepts of the Christian law.

This is an intensification of the belief of Savonarola that "everybody ought to love the common good more than his private good" (*Tractate on the Organization . . . of Florence*, book 3, chap. 1), and that "it is necessary that the citizens love the common good of the city, and that when they belong to the governing boards and hold other offices, they should lay aside every private interest and all partiality for their relatives and friends and fix their eyes solely on the common good" (Ibid., chap. 2).

[8] *Discourses on Livy*, III, 41.

religion are not toys, but realities.

44 How is it, then, that Machiavelli allows his prince not merely to violate moral laws but praises him for doing so? The answer is to be found in Machiavelli's conception of a complex and difficult world, where things are not always what they seem. At the end of the Fifteenth Chapter he writes: "If everything is considered, it will be seen that some things seem to be virtues, but if they are put into practice will be ruinous to the prince; other things seem to be vices, yet if put into practice will bring the prince security and well-being." Virtues and vices, then, masquerade in each other's garments. How can they be distinguished? The answer is furnished by the sentence just quoted, but not with full clarity. As has been explained, Machiavelli did not present his ultimate principles in *The Prince,* but expresses in terms of the ruler alone what he intends to apply to the whole people. He means, then, that vices masked as virtues will ruin the people, and that virtues, though disguised as vices, will bring about the common well-being. There are open to a prince two courses: one, devotion to the principles of morality; the other, devotion to the good of his people. In the imaginary kingdoms of the moralists the two are one; Machiavelli wishes they were one in actual life. But they are not. The prince, then, must choose. Shall he save his own soul? Shall he ruin his people? For Niccolò there is no debate. The duty of the prince is to his people. Only the tyrant prefers his private good to that of his subjects. He who saves his own soul, and destroys his people, may be masked as a saint, but he is really a tyrant. What the prince does for the sake of his people is in itself virtuous, however masked; what he does against their interest is wicked, even though he appears like an angel.

45 Niccolò's morality is sometimes thought to depend on justifying the means by the end, doing evil that good may come. In explanation, it may be said that the end to be attained is clear, the common welfare of the people. No worldly success is excuse for unworthy conduct. Only the unthinking mob approve mere success as justifying any means. In condemnation of their short-sighted view, Machiavelli wrote: "A prince needs only to conquer and to maintain his position. The means he has used will always be judged honorable and praised by everybody, because the crowd is always caught by appearances and the outcome of events, and the crowd is all there is in the world; there is no place for the few when the many have room enough."[9] Here the end is nothing but the main-

[9] *The Prince,* Chap. 18, par. 6.

tenance of the ruler's personal position—the end not of the good prince but of the tyrant. Niccolò's sense of the difficulty of the problem of the means and the end appears in a discussion of the attitude of a strong man to reforms indispensable to the life of his country:

> The necessary changes cannot be brought about by normal methods, because ordinary means are bad [because inadequate]. It is necessary to resort to extraordinary means, such as violence and arms, and above all to become prince of that city, and to be able to fashion it to one's mind. And because the reorganization of a city according to the best republican principles presupposes a good man, and the becoming prince of a republic by violence presupposes a bad man, it will be found to come about very infrequently that a good man, even though his end be good, wishes to become prince.[10]

46 Machiavelli never gives ethical approval to tyrannical conduct on the part of republic or prince. The bad ruler is condemned as such. The question is this: May a good ruler, for good purposes, break his word, or engage in acts usually thought of as immoral? That, and only that, is Machiavelli's ethical problem. But this assumption of a perfectly good ruler can be made only for the sake of clarifying a position. Its practical application is not easy. Was Florence right in taking away the independence of Pisa? Were the Romans justified in their conquest of the other states of Italy? A possible reply is found in Dante's belief that the progress of the Roman arms was divinely appointed, and the generals of the Republic divine agents. Conquest was justified by the principle of St. Thomas Aquinas that "they who wage war justly do it for the sake of peace."[11] It is now almost universally admitted that Lincoln was right in fighting to preserve the Union, because its preservation was necessary to lasting peace; yet South Carolinians have been long in coming to such a view. There has been debate about many wars, such as Britain's Boer War and America's Spanish War. Both sides in the World War of 1914-18 were loud in proclaiming their righteousness. So it was in 1940. Clear decisions of right and wrong in such matters are made only by partisans, until many years have elapsed, and perhaps not then. But however difficult the application, Machiavelli's principle still is that no action of the prince is praiseworthy except as directed to the common good.

47 Hence, the habitual conduct of the prince is not crooked; he breaks faith only when it is necessary to the good of his

[10] *Discourses on Livy*, I, 18. [11] *Summa theologica* 2, 2, 40, 1.

people; that is, he deceives only their enemies.[12] But does he owe faith to enemies who, Machiavelli says, will not observe it to him? Milton, in his treatise *On Christian Doctrine,* quotes the "trite" saying: *Cui nullum est ius, ei nulla fit iniuria* (If a man has no right, to him no injury is done). Continuing, Milton says that a lie occurs "when anybody by a malicious trick perverts the truth or says something false to someone, whoever it may be, to whom it is his duty to tell the truth." [13] If the crafty enemy has no right to verity, the prince who deceives him has no need for apology. Machiavelli may be said to be explaining ethics to a prince, to make him see that he need not deliberate anxiously or feel morally pained when he considers deceiving his enemies. If he cannot lie freely in case of need, he can hardly get the proper results from his deception; simulation and dissimulation cannot succeed when practised with obvious reluctance.

48 In a perfect world there would be no problem. The virtuous act would appear as immediately good, and never wear the garb of malice. If the principles of Christ had been observed from the beginning, all nations might live as ideal commonwealths. But states are cursed with parties thinking only of their personal good and not of the people as a whole. Even if there could be a perfect community, it would have crafty enemies seeking to devour it. The ruler who will protect his state must acknowledge the necessity of adapting himself to things as they are. As Guicciardini has one of his characters say, "He who plans to live entirely according to the law of God, can hardly do it unless he removes himself entirely from the life of the world, and it is hardly possible to live in accord with the world without offending God."[14] The practical lawgiver, Machiavelli admitted, must assume that all men are bad and "will always employ the malice of their spirits whenever they have a good chance to do so." [15]

49 In such a world a man gifted with the perceptions of the comic poet of the *Mandragola* could not overlook the incongruity between life as it is and the assertion that a ruler must act as though in a paradise of all the virtues. On perception of this incongruity is based Machiavelli's censure of the effects of the Christian religion.[16] Forgetting that meekness seldom is a

[12] Obviously such deceptions as those of an army by a general about the numbers of an opposing force are permitted. But such deceptions of friends are in a different category from the breaking of faith.

[13] John Milton, *De doctrina christiana,* II, 13.

[14] *Dialogue on the Government of Florence,* book 2.

[15] *Discourses on Livy,* 1, 3. Obviously this is no denial of the existence of virtue; see, e.g., the *Introduction,* pars. 96-9, below.

[16] *Ibid.,* II, 2, pars. 5 and 6, below.

defense against the insolent and rapacious,[17] men have given Christianity a slothful and not a vigorous interpretation, says Machiavelli, and have thought more of patient endurance than of vengeance. Hence they have given the world over as a prey to the wicked. But they should realize that religion permits the exaltation and defense of our native land, and intends that we should love and honor it, and fit ourselves for its defense.

50 But to individual advancement nothing can be allowed. Men can rise to high places by wickedness, but they cannot gain the true fame that results from such service to the city as Niccolò urged on the Medici. Agathocles gained the lordship of Syracuse by killing his fellow citizens, betraying his friends, abandoning faith, piety, and religion; but he acquired only rule, not glory.[18] Philip of Macedonia was ruthless in establishing himself. Such methods as his are "thoroughly cruel, and hostile to every kind of life that can be called human, not to mention Christian. Every one ought to avoid them, and prefer to live in a private station than to be a king with such injury to men." [19] The ruler is worthy of detestation, then, who resorts to wickedness for selfish purposes, just as he is to be condemned for folly who fails to see that the highest good, as represented in the well-being of his native land, demands the sacrifice of all conventional notions of morality.

51 The patriot who puts first the good of humanity, as expressed in his own country, thereby acquires the glory impossible to tyrannical rulers such as Agathocles or the bad emperors of Rome,[20] but deserved by the good, such as Marcus. No more glorious way can be trodden than that of the prince who makes his people happy with good government; he secures an immortality of fame,[21] such as St. Thomas imagined for his ideal ruler:

> Since it is the duty of the king to seek the good of the multitude, the office of king would be too wearisome unless

[17] *Ibid.*, II, 14.

[18] *The Prince,* Chap. 8, par. 3, below.

[19] *Discourses on Livy,* I, 26.

[20] *The Prince,* Chap. 8, par. 3; Chap. 19, pars. 9, 11, 18; *Discourses on Livy,* I, 10, pars. 1, 4, 6, below.

[21] *Discourse on Reforming the Government of Florence,* par. 29, below.

In Guicciardini's *Dialogue on the Government of Florence* we read: "Glory and true honor consist altogether in doing noble and praiseworthy deeds for the benefit and advancement of one's native land and the good of the other citizens, without regard to labor or danger" (book 2). "Certainly if men knew in what consists praise and true glory, many princes would be found to do it [i.e., lay down their crowns], for I do not know how a man could leave a more honored memory of himself than to do such an admirable deed showing his goodness and his great love for his country, because he would obviously set the good of his country ahead of his own greatness and that of his house and his descendants" (*Ibid.*).

some individual good came to him from it. Hence it is well to consider what reward is fitting for the good king. Certain men have thought that this is nothing other than honor and glory. . . . But nothing earthly is a sufficient reward for the king. . . . God alone can quiet the desire of man and make man happy, and become the reward suited to a king. . . . So it can be established that the reward of the king is honor and glory. For what worldly and fading honor can be like this honor, namely that a man be a subject and servant of God, and counted among the sons of God, and should obtain the inheritance of the celestial kingdom with Christ? [22]

MACHIAVELLI'S PERSONAL CHARACTER

52 The reproaches directed against Machiavelli have been primarily because he wrote *The Prince* and was willing to serve the Medici; charges against his private life have resulted from his reputation as author. The more violent accusations have died a natural death. It seems possible that his relations with women were not always above reproach, though apparently he never engaged in anything the age considered scandalous. A number of his own letters are supposed to sustain charges against him, but some of them are obviously exaggerated for comic purposes and others are perhaps more imaginary than real. Nor does there seem to be anything of reproach for his financial dealings; his poverty indicates that he was not clever in getting money.[1]

53 One of the sins charged to him is the ingratitude he condemned when he wrote of the man "who does not remember nor return the favors that are done him, but to his utmost rends and bites his benefactor." [2] Piero Soderini, gonfalonier in Florence from 1502 to 1512, presided over the most important years of Niccolò's public career. Without Soderini the formation of the Florentine militia and the capture of Pisa, the most striking of the Secretary's accomplishments, would have been impossible. The relation between the two men seems to have been close. In the light of Machiavelli's subsequent fame and Piero's failure, it is easy to think that the *gonfaloniere* was indebted to the secretary rather than the reverse. Yet Niccolò's talents and rank were not such as to enable him to gain the independent place

[22] From St. Thomas' *De regimine principum* (*On the Conduct of Princes*) 1. 7-8, one of the most important works of advice to rulers that preceded *The Prince*.

[1] See the Letter of December 10, 1513, par. 7.

[2] *Capitolo on Ingratitude*, 52-4.

in public affairs that his friend Guicciardini was able to attain; he was always the subordinate in active life, and seems to have realized it, without underestimating his own capacity as a thinker. To the world he appeared as Soderini's puppet,[3] at least in 1507. Possibly a little later, when organizing the militia, he appeared more independent. To Soderini most of one of the *Discourses on Livy* (III, 3) is devoted. He is made an instance of the man who failed to act with sufficient ruthlessness; nevertheless he is called prudent, and the reasons for his fatal hesitation are judged "wise and good."

54 Against this extended and deliberate judgment is to be set the famous epigram, in the form of an epitaph, which has made Soderini an immortal symbol of governmental imbecility.

> The night when Piero Soderini died,
> His soul went to the mouth of Hell.
> Pluto yelled: "What the Hell? silly ghost!
> Go up to Limbo with the other babies."

With this epigram, says Prezzolini, "Machiavelli gave him second burial."[4] Schevill asserts that "it breathes such withering contempt that it must have scorched the dead man in his grave."[5] Even Villari is disturbed by its "bad taste," though he admits, as though unwillingly, that its authenticity can hardly be denied. He excuses it partly because it has "a certain foundation of truth," and partly by quoting Machiavelli's grandson, who said: "Machiavelli wrote this epitaph in a poetic spirit, since whenever he spoke seriously and not in jest of Soderini, he always praised him and held him in high esteem."[6]

55 Still more distressed is Janni, who begins by calling the epigram "ferocious," and continues to say that if it is to be given importance equal to its fame, an unfavorable judgment must be pronounced on the spirit of its author. After some pages on the intimacy of the two men, he comes to the official condemnation of Piero's memory by the Medici party, and continues:

> As herald of this "condemnation" of his memory, there was hurled at the dead man the famous epigram, so ferociously reviling him in its bitterness. If we can suppose that in that period of new persecutions, of imprisonments, tortures, and punishments that brought vividly before him his own woes at the time of the other conspiracy, Machiavelli thought of

[3] Villari, *Machiavelli*, I, 429 (English trans.).
[4] Giuseppe Prezzolini, *Nicolo Machiavelli*, p. 130.
[5] Schevill, *History of Florence*, p. 470.
[6] Villari, *Machiavelli*, II, 35.

saving himself, and, in order to make himself obvious to the Medici party as wholly unconnected with the conspirators with whom he had been found in the Orti Oricellari, hurled his personal "condemnation" at the republican who had remained faithful to the principles of the old government of Florence, no view of the conditions could keep one from considering him as at that moment worthy of the utmost contempt.[7]

Rejecting this possibility as too shocking for belief, Janni goes on to attempt to excuse Niccolò, suggesting that the epitaph was not written at the time of the gonfalonier's death, but years before, "at a moment when he was exasperated by the memory of the errors of Soderini's government." If written on the announcement of Piero's death, it must show the mordant spirit of Machiavelli carried to excess. Possibly the best explanation, continues Janni, is that it is a *bon mot* such as the age delighted in, though a very bad one considering the moment and its tone.

56 Such suggestions, I believe, are evidences of the persistence of the old notion of Machiavelli as the arch-cynic. "Give a dog a bad name, and hang him." If the Secretary's name had never been a synonym for wickedness, he would not have been supposed ungrateful enough to tear to pieces the reputation of his old friend.

57 The explanation is probably that hinted at but not understood and developed by Villari and Janni. I believe that the epigram is a *bon mot,* that it was composed years before Soderini's death, and that it was written in jest. Somewhat similar epitaphs are not unknown. While Mabilius was still living, Politian wrote the following:

> Flecte, viator, iter; foetet: nam putre Mabili
> Hac fovea corpus conditur atque animus.[8]

Less bitter is the interchange of epitaphs between Paolo Giovio and Pietro Aretino; the first wrote:

> Qui giace l'Aretin, poeta Tosco,
> Che d'ognun disse mal fuorchè di Christo,
> Scusandosi col dir: Non lo conosco.[9]

[7] Janni, *Machiavelli,* pp. 65-6. But my quotation is from the Italian edition.

[8] *Prose Volgari inedite e Poesie Latine e Greche,* Florence, 1867, p. 140. "Turn aside your steps, traveler; what a stench! for the rotting body of Mabilius, and his soul too, are lying in this pit." I owe this and the following epitaphs to the kindness of Professor James Hutton.

[9] L. DeMauri, *L'epigramma italiano,* Milan, 1918. "Here lies Aretino, a Tuscan poet, who spoke ill of everybody except Christ, excusing himself by saying: I don't know him." For variants, some of them in Latin, see Pietro Aretino, *Opere,* Milan, 1863, pp. 94-5.

And the reply was:

> Qui giace il Giovio, storicone altissimo;
> Di tutti disse mal, fuorchè dell'asino,
> Scusandosi con dire: Egli è mio prossimo.[10]

The same type was later known in England, as when Ben Jonson, "being merry at a tavern," began his own epitaph and gave it to Shakespeare to complete.[11] We may, then, imagine Florentine officials enjoying themselves when off duty, as at a celebration of the triumph of Soderini's government over Pisa. One amusement is that of making epitaphs for one another, and above all for the Gonfalonier himself. Machiavelli, with his sense of the comic, is the leader, and his epitaph, with its tempting rime *Soderini-bambini* (babies), was preserved, to become an example of fleeting comedy turned by posterity into biting satire.

58 It has also been held against Machiavelli that he was willing to serve and did serve the Medici government of Florence, that he dedicated his *Prince* to a representative of that house. Part of the belief that such conduct is most reprehensible comes from the time when *The Prince* was looked on as a frightful and mysterious work giving tyrants directions for carrying on their worst oppressions. When this was believed, its author was primarily one who strove to aid the tyrannical Medici to fasten their yoke on Florence. But since it is now generally accepted that the little book has much in common with other treatises on the conduct of princes,[12] and that its principles are also those its author presented when he wrote the *Discourses on Livy* with republics in mind, such a view falls of itself. It could never have arisen at any time when *The Prince* and the other writings of its author were carefully read. Yet the conduct of Machiavelli should be explained.

59 He came to public office as a young man, at a time when Florence was governing herself. He continued for fourteen years in the service of the city, with increasing influence and responsibility. Because the continuance of the administration he served depended on the exclusion of the Medici, he necessarily acted against that powerful family. The Florentine soldiers who were set to defend Prato, and failed, were from the militia that owed its being to Machiavelli's labors. When the

[10] "Here lies Giovio, a great big history-writer; he spoke ill of everybody, but not of the ass, and excused himself by saying: He is my neighbor."

[11] Herford and Simpson, *Ben Jonson* (Oxford, 1925), I, 186. For Jonson's own account of a comic epitaph on himself composed by a companion, see Ibid., p. 149.

[12] See the *Introduction*, pars. 20-25, above.

Medici appeared in the city, he made no effort to escape; he seemed even to hope he could retain his position, as some other officials did. So mild was the new regime that he did hold his office for nearly two months after the setting up of the *balìa*, or committee with power, through which the Medici exercised their authority over a government outwardly little changed. For some two months, then, he actually did serve as a Medicean official. Then he was dismissed, under a decree that confined him to Florentine territory, but forbade his entrance into the government building. Even this decree was officially suspended, to permit him to clear up the business of his office. Obviously he felt under no more inclination to leave his position than now would be felt in America by a zealous Democrat in the post-office department on the election of a Republican president.

60 It must be observed that the Medici did not come as tyrants enforcing their military despotism on a perfectly free people. On the contrary, they were traditional rulers of the city, who had been expelled only eighteen years before, after a long period of rule. Their departure had been regretted by many, and their return was desired by an important part of the population. In fact their re-entry had been a matter of negotiation, since there had been no attack on the city. Giovanni de' Medici was escorted by four hundred lances when he made his entrance, and other soldiers were smuggled in, but there was no military occupation. If the Spanish forces had not come to Prato, Soderini would not have fled when he did, but it seems not impossible that feeling in Florence might have brought the Medici party into power again without the help of foreign arms. Soderini had never been without political opposition.

61 Moreover, Machiavelli had always been dissatisfied with the Florentine system of government. He well understood that Florence had never been a republic in the full sense of the word.[13] The government of Soderini was much more to his mind than that of the Medici, but the choice was not between a true republic and an absolute tyranny, but between two governments not wholly dissimilar. The Medici were acceptable on the ground that no other administration was then possible. After the flight of Soderini, who had been requested to resign not by a popular tumult, but merely by five young men, the state of affairs, even of public opinion, was such that a freer government than that of the Medici was impossible in the city.

62 Meanwhile, Florence must be governed; papers requir-

[13] *Discourses on Livy*, I, 49, par. 3, below.

ing the attention of a secretary piled up in the offices in the Palace of the *Signoria.* Why should not Niccolò continue to read them? To do so was to give the city, to the utmost of his powers, the best government she could have. At least he could carry out the policy of the administration well; possibly he could even, as of old, in some ways influence it for the better. For example, though the militia he formed was abolished when the Medici returned, it was soon restored. Who so well experienced in administering it as Niccolò?

63 Such was the direction of Machiavelli's conduct when later he was to some extent employed by the Medici administration. He was twice requested to prepare suggestions for a new constitution for Florence. In 1519 he turned out his *Discourse on Reforming the Government of Florence,* and in 1522 a similar work. He frankly accepts the rule of the Medici as a monarchy, but prepares for a republican administration of the state after the deaths of the members of the House, Leo X and Cardinal Giulio, later Clement VII. Its author does not specifically state that the Pope or the Cardinal is to hold the position of the man who must stand alone in reforming the constitution of a weakened state,[14] but it surely is implied: "No man is so much exalted in any of his actions as are those who have reformed republics and kingdoms with laws and institutions."[15] The Medici, then, have an opportunity to benefit their city and to appear as its second founders, on a level with Romulus, Lycurgus, or Solon. Carrying out this idea, Niccolò suggests a constitution for Florence that will secure it permanent good government. For that city a long-continued absolute regimen is not possible; hence the constitution set up by the Medici must be republican. Their absolute power is but a temporary device to secure that end.

64 Given Machiavelli's presupposition, then, he is the best of patriots in assisting Pope Leo and Cardinal Giulio toward such an accomplishment. His position can obviously be attacked. It may be supposed the Medici, when they requested plans for the government of Florence, were less serious in their desire to give the city a good constitution than the enthusiastic Machiavelli hoped. Possibly he overestimated republican sentiment in Florence. Yet the terrible siege the city endured in 1529-30 indicates that there was a great deal of spirit to be broken before the tyranny of the dukes could be accepted without protest. It is not unlikely that the interest of Leo X and Clement VII was much more in their own family than in the

[14] *Discourses on Livy,* I, 9, below.

[15] *Discourse on Reforming the Government of Florence,* par. 29, below.

city, and that their requests for proposals on an improved Florentine constitution were intended only to conciliate the republican faction. Machiavelli was probably led by his enthusiasm to hope, perhaps even to expect, more of both patriotism and ability from the Medici than either of them possessed. The career of Giulio before he became Clement VII permits a more favorable judgment than do the later events of his life. It is now easy to disparage all the Medici who can be connected with Machiavelli. But in 1519 that was more difficult. The tremendous prize of the Papacy had fallen to them. Moreover, a Florentine, however broad his outlook, could hardly escape some exaggeration of the importance of the family of Lorenzo the Magnificent.

65 But even though Machiavelli's hopes did urge him on to overestimate the Medici, the spirit of his plan for the reform of Florence is not thereby altered. It is, as his leading biographer says, "the distilate and final extract of all those other *Discourses* of his on Livy. He who reads through it finds them there complete; he perceives in it the aura and the pen-stroke of the old chancellor of the republic." [16] So in his service of the Medici, the Florentine patriot is still his old self. The spirit of this work done at their request is that of the most republican of his writings. The same is true of the *Florentine History* subsidized by Pope Clement.

66 This is enough to decide the problem of *The Prince*. Though preferring republics, he recognized the kingdom as a legitimate form of government, sometimes the only possible one. Even for Florence it is a possibility, inferior to republican government, but not beyond consideration.[17] As to the dedication of the work to the Medici, the considerations suggested above apply with equal force; the Medici prince is an instrument for the good of Florence and Italy, not an end in himself.

67 Typical of his life-long attitude is one of his last public services for the Medici, that on the walls of Florence. There can be no doubt that he preferred Medicean rule to Barbarian invasion, and wished walls that would keep the foreigners out even though they kept Alessandro and Ippolito in. But at the same time he labored against such a plan as to permit the fortifications to be used against Florentine liberty. So he opposed the papal notion for fortifying San Miniato.[18] Better sacrifice part of the city than build a possible stronghold for a tyrant!

68 After whatever changes, Florence still existed both as an

[16] Tommasini, *Machiavelli*, II, 200-1.

[17] *Discourse on Reforming the Government of Florence*, par. 13, below.

[18] Letter of June 2, 1526, par. 2, below.

object of devotion and a corporation whose affairs, small and great, required daily attention. There was a difference between Florence enslaved and Florence free, but not an absolute antithesis. Machiavelli, moreover, was by temperament not inclined to see things as absolute whites and blacks; observing men with the clear vision of a comic poet, he was prepared to find defects and virtues everywhere, and to take them just as they were. There is seldom a choice between the perfect and detestable; men usually have to choose between ills,[19] and must do the best they can. Not the most heroic attitude, but one that keeps the world moving.

CESARE BORGIA

69 An estimate of Cesare Borgia, Duke Valentino, obviously is beset with difficulties, not the least of which are the frightful stories circulated for many years about Cesare and his father, Pope Alexander VI; this scandal still circulates in such volumes as *The Incredible Borgias,* by Alfred Henschke. About this side of Cesare nothing is found in the pages of Machiavelli.

70 There are varying estimates of Cesare's political activity. Some recent writers, such as the Italian senator Gaetano Mosca, have minimized his capacities and importance. William H. Woodward, the author of an elaborate biography, is nearer to Niccolò's judgment, and the latter not only proposed Cesare as a model in *The Prince,* Chapters 7, 13, and 17, but wrote to Vettori that if he were a new prince he should steadily imitate the deeds of Duke Valentino.[1] This opinion of 1514, seven years after the death of the Duke, is late enough to have given Niccolò time for reflection. In the still later *Art of War,* he expresses his admiration for one of the military movements of Cesare.[2] Machiavelli's opportunity to observe had been good; he had been Florentine agent to Cesare in the Romagna, and he had been in Rome and had talked with Cesare after the election of Pope Julius II.

71 The main passage in question is the Seventh Chapter of *The Prince,* where it is asserted that Cesare had done all a prudent and strong man could do to fix his roots in the state given to him by the arms and fortune of others. It is true that

[19] Cf. *The Prince,* Chap. 21, par. 7, below.

[1] Letter of January 31, 1514-5, par. 7, below.

[2] *Art of War,* book 7. In the letter of August 26, 1513, par. 5, below, he is mentioned as a typical able general.

he fell, but his fall was not his fault; it sprang from the unusual and excessive malice of Fortune. The Duke's problem was, moreover, an exceedingly difficult one. Machiavelli gives the first part of the chapter to making clear that power bestowed by others is most uncertain; the first adverse wind is enough to overthrow it. Of all the types of princedom that which Cesare strove to hold offers the most difficulty.

72 These difficulties fall into two classes, here indicated as those of the present, and those of the future. The first class embraces two groups, made in the Nineteenth Chapter of *The Prince,* namely the conduct of the ruler to his subjects, and to other rulers. For Cesare's administration of his realm, Niccolò has nothing but praise. About the middle of the chapter he calls special attention to it, saying: "This part [namely, his gaining of the Romagna mentioned in the preceding sentence], deserves special notice and is worthy to be imitated by others." The Duke also succeeded in his relations with other rulers, especially the king of France. Summing up what Cesare had done in these two things, Machiavelli makes them exemplify wise conduct for a ruler. But there was a third group of difficulties for Valentino, namely those at Rome, which Machiavelli divides into four parts. Of these Cesare settled three, and part of the fourth. In the fourth, the acquiring sufficient territory to make him independent of the papal power, he had made great progress, but had not completed what was needed. His failure was not in any of these as a whole, but in his use of one of them, namely his party in the College of Cardinals. He should have kept the papal crown from going to any candidate who might have cause to fear him. His foundations were, then, good; it was a specific piece of bad judgment, not part of his general policy, that undid him. Even that might not have been fatal if he had not been sick almost unto death when his father died. According to Niccolò's analysis, then, Cesare's failure was in none of the normal duties of a new ruler, but in a matter that only a ruler in his exceptional circumstances as to the papacy would have to deal with. Though he came to his throne through Fortune, he had yet been able to overcome all the difficulties in laying foundations that resulted from such an origin. A still further difficulty was required for his ruin.

73 Machiavelli's interest, then, is not primarily in Cesare's ultimate success or failure; Fortune, indeed, might have given him success with small desert, as on the other hand she overthrew him by an almost incredible exercise of her malice. What interested Niccolò was the fundamental correctness of the Duke's conduct, which almost brought him success in the most difficult of situations for the new prince. Perhaps in some sense Machiavelli was even more pleased to take an instance of a man who did the right thing and still failed. It worked into proof of his theory of Fortune, or his notion that there are situations, such as that to be faced by the hypothetical conqueror of France mentioned in *The Prince,* chapter 4, where no amount of ability is equal to the task proposed. The view of the world as uncertain and as presenting insoluble problems satisfied his feeling for the *verità effettuale,* the practical truth. Still further, an unsuccessful hero as an example satisfied the comic poet's fondness for the contradictories of life. But indeed in this instance one may recall that he once signed one of his letters Niccolò Machiavelli, *Istorico, Comico e Tragico*; the life of Cesare is almost an Aristotelian tragedy, with the hero's tragic fault his failure in choosing the right pope. As Florentine agent in Rome, our poet wrote to his employers that Cesare seemed to be slowly sinking into his grave.

74 It is probable that in the mind of Machiavelli, Cesare did not remain the absolute historical Borgia. The conqueror lost some of his human imperfections as he gave hints of the ideal of the new prince. Like Machiavelli's own Castruccio or Xenophon's Cyrus he glowed with a brighter light than the mere earthly. If it is unusual for a man with whom a writer has often talked to become so rapidly transfigured, it may be answered that Cesare was a figure calculated to strike the imagination of a poetically minded politician, an admirer of prowess, energy, and clarity of mind. In fact the change worked in Cesare seems to have been rather a slight one. Guicciardini was not inclined to favor the Borgias, and as president of Romagna under Clement VII, he had opportunity to learn the truth. His opinion is that after the election of Julius II, "the states of the Romagna stood firm for Cesare, and if he had been in good health he could certainly have found refuge there, because he had set in authority over those peoples men who had ruled with so much justice and honesty that Cesare was greatly loved by them." [3] Since Guicciardini wrote later than Machiavelli, and had no hesitation in differing from him, this may be taken as pretty good evidence. The judgment of Cesare as successful in making himself loved at home and feared abroad is apparently a correct one.

75 Some of the hesitation in accepting Niccolò's picture of the Duke is apparently based on the assumption that a potential saviour of Italy is being placed before us, and that the rôle is too heavy for the actor. The Seventh Chapter is, how-

[3] *History of Florence,* Chap. 27.

ever, in the less obviously patriotic part of *The Prince,* for in the first eleven chapters there is little overt concern with Italy as an object of devotion, and the author is influenced by his intention of analysing the various types of principate. There is no suggestion in Chapter 7 that Cesare might have been the deliverer of Italy. One later reference is less complimentary, for he is spoken of as an instrument of his father, Pope Alexander VI.[4] He is, however, usually thought of as one of those mentioned in the last Chapter, par. 2, who showed signs that they were divinely chosen for the redemption of Italy, but were abandoned by Fortune in the midst of their careers; certainly the emphasis on Fortune in Chapter 7 strengthens the opinion that he is one of those apparently but not really chosen. That, then, is the most Machiavelli says for him. Whether or not he had the ability and the moral capacity to unite Italy against the barbarian, he is not represented as attempting to play such a part.

THE STRUCTURE OF *THE PRINCE*

76 When Machiavelli wrote to Vettori of the little book he was composing,[1] he referred to it as *De Principatibus, On Principalities,* or *Principates.* Similarly in the *Discourses on Livy,* II, 1, it appears as a tractate *De' Principati,* later as "the other tractate" (III, 19), and still later as *De Principe* (III, 42). The references are to the Third, the Nineteenth, and the Eighteenth Chapters of *The Prince.* Some significance has been seen in this change of name. At any rate the first eleven chapters of the work often use the word *Principate,* fulfilling especially three of the purposes laid down in the letter to Vettori, namely, to tell what a principality is and what its species are, and how they are gained. The other two purposes, namely, to show how principalities are kept and lost, also appear in the first eleven chapters. This is especially true of Chapter 3, which is chiefly concerned with holding acquisitions, Chapter 5, Chapter 7, which shows how Cesare strove to keep his place, Chapter 9, which exhorts the prince to gain the people, and Chapter 10, on defending a besieged city. These chapters may have been greatly changed in the process of enlarging and polishing that Niccolò mentioned to Vettori. Yet as they stand, they may be considered adequate to fulfil the description

[4] Chap. 11, par. 3.

[1] In the Letter of December 10, 1513, par. 5.

given in the letter. Chiefly for this reason, it has often been said that the original treatise consisted of only eleven chapters, and that all the latter part is an afterthought, not contemplated by the original plan and not wholly in harmony with it.

77 There is, however, some danger of pushing too far the concern of these early chapters with the principate rather than the prince. Even in the letter to Vettori, the work is said to deserve the attention of a prince, especially a new one, and to be therefore dedicated to Giuliano. Niccolò begins to speak of the prince in the Second Chapter. In the Third he begins his use of the second person, as though addressing a ruler directly, and gives the advice: Go to your province to live, and don't let your officials fill their pockets with your subjects' money. The conduct of King Louis as a representative prince takes up much space. The faith of princes is touched on, with a reference to the later discussion in Chapter 18. Chapter 3 ends with a warning to princes not to aid others to become powerful. At the beginning of Chapter 6, Machiavelli says he is treating of "principalities wholly new and of the prince and of government," and a little further he speaks of "principates wholly new, where there is a new prince." He then discusses not so much the nature of principates as the conduct of a prince. The Seventh Chapter is entitled *Of New Principates*, etc., but it deals essentially in advice to the new prince, with emphasis on Cesare Borgia. Chapter 8 deals not with principalities occupied by means of wicked deeds, but "with those who have come to the position of prince through wickedness." The following chapter is entitled *On the Civil Principate;* it again does not discuss a country ruled by a citizen, but the conduct of a citizen who comes to rule his own country. The same is true of Chapter 10; the topic is not the strength of a country, but "a prince who has a strong city and has not made himself hated."

78 With this in view, we may ask what Machiavelli meant by his words *principatus* and *principato* (principate, principality). It is true that the Italian word *principato* sometimes indicates *the territory ruled by a prince,* but this it seldom signifies in Machiavelli. It frequently means *the office of a prince,* or *government by a prince.* The first chapter begins, in the most literal translation possible: "All the states, all the dominions, which have had and have rule over men, have been and are either republics or principates." The word *state* in Machiavelli has been much discussed.[2] It often means *ad-*

[2] Orazio Condorelli, *Per la storia del nome "stato" (il nome "stato" in Machiavelli)*, Modena, 1923.
Francesco Ercole, *La Politica di Machiavelli,* Rome, 1926, pp. 65-96.

ministration, government (as in the phrase *Churchill's government*), even *party*; it does not usually signify *state* in the present sense of nation as a whole, though at times it can be so rendered. Hence the sentence just quoted means: "All the types of administration and forms of government that control men are either republican administrations or princely administrations."[3] As to the Latin word *principatus*, in classical usage it never means the totality over which a prince rules. Harper's *Dictionary* gives as a general meaning *first place*, etc., and more particularly, (1) *the chief place* (in the state or army), *the post of commander in chief*, and (2) *reign, empire, dominion, sovereignty*.[4] Machiavelli need not be held to classical usage, and may be allowed to have thought of the Latin word as meaning at times the territory ruled by a prince, but he must also have had in mind the classical meaning in such a passage as Tacitus, *Agricola* 3: "Nerva res olim dissociabiles miscuit, principatum et libertatem" (Nerva mingled things formerly separate, the principate and liberty). The title *De principatibus* means, then, something like *On the various kinds of princely administration*, as well as, sometimes, *On countries with princely government*. The boundary between the two is not firmly fixed and the ideas mingle, just as St. Thomas' work *De regimine principum* (On the conduct of princes) is also known as *De rege et regno* (On the king and the kingdom). Machiavelli did not need, then, to set a fixed limit for his words *principato* or *principatus*, or to oppose them to *prince*; in Chapter 15, for example, he speaks of "imaginary principates," and then in a few lines: "Laying aside what relates to an imagined prince," as though equating *principate* and *prince*. Apparently he felt much less difference between the two words than modern readers do. Certainly he was willing to let the complete manuscripts of *The Prince* bear the title *De principatibus*; at least that is the title preferred by the most accurate editors. It seems, then, that belief in the separateness of the first eleven chapters can derive little support from the use of one word instead of the other, or from the supposition that the primary concern of the early part is the country ruled rather than the individual ruling.

79 It may also be observed that the subject of how principates are gained, kept, and lost is not confined to the first

[3] Note also the employment of *principato* in *The Prince*, Chapter 19.

[4] There is apparently no reason to suppose that the meaning changed in the Middle Ages, unless the use of the Italian *principato* to mean the *Prince's territory* is evidence. The classical meanings of *principatus* are also among the present meanings not merely of *principato* but of *principality* or *principate*.

eleven chapters, but also is treated later, where the chief emphasis is on how they are to be kept; governing and maintaining are prominent in Machiavelli's statement of purpose in Chapter 2. Various other topics suggested in early chapters are later developed. For example in Chapter 7 the theme of Duke Valentino's use of his own arms is touched on, and in Chapter 13 it is developed. The theme of cruelty is discussed in Chapter 8 and again in 17. The later chapters are not excluded from the purpose expressed in the letter to Vettori.

80 The first eleven chapters furnish two or three references to later parts of the work. In Chap. 3, par. 14, the clause "what I shall say later about the faith of princes" indicates Chapter 18. In Chap. 10, par. 1, is a more general reference to placing an army in the field as a topic to be further dealt with "as it is required." This perhaps indicates Chapter 13, and Chap. 24, par. 2. In the same paragraph of Chapter 10 he indicates that the management of subjects is to be later discussed; this may allude especially to Chapters 17, 19, and 20. Though not a specific reference, it indicates that a section following Chapter 11 is contemplated. Various other passages where there are no cross references also look forward.[5] For example, the summary of Duke Valentino's admirable actions in Chap. 7, par. 10, looks forward to the later discussions of the qualities he exhibited, as is indicated in the notes.

81 The break at the end of Chapter 11 is, however, clear and intentional, since the beginning of the next chapter is a transition from one section to the next. The earlier part considered the causes why principates are well off or badly off, and the methods by which many have striven to get and hold them. Machiavelli now intends to discuss generally the injuries to which these governments are subject and the methods of protection against them. Military defence, the most important of these, is taken up as a development of the idea of foundations, considered in Chapter 7, and occupies Chapter 12 and the two following it.

82 At the beginning of Chapter 15 is another deliberate transition, with announcement of the subject now to be pursued as the conduct of the ruler to his subjects and his allies, that is, domestic and foreign policy. Liberality, the subject of the Sixteenth Chapter, is chiefly directed to those within the state, as is the cruelty and mercy of the next. The dissimulation of

[5] Cross references from later chapters to earlier ones, as that to Hiero (Chap. 6, last par.) in Chap. 13, par 5, only indicate that later chapters were written with earlier ones in mind.

Obviously references to following chapters may have been inserted in the last revision.

Eighteen is largely a matter of foreign policy. Contempt and hatred, next treated, are developed primarily as to internal affairs, though external relations are also mentioned. The following chapter, with its assertion that the best fortress is the love of the people, deals mostly with domestic policy; thus it is unlike Chapter 10 in point of view, though like it in asserting that the people must be so treated as to keep them loyal. In fact, a reference in the earlier chapter to a treatment of the subject below doubtless refers to that in Twenty. The Twenty-first Chapter is about equally concerned with the king's reputation at home and abroad. Twenty-two and Twenty-three deal with the king's advisers.

83 At the beginning of Chapter 24 is another transition to the effect that the things presented will, when prudently carried out, make a new prince appear like an old one, and enable him to get the double glory of founding a new state and making it prosperous; at the same time the hereditary prince who fails to observe them and loses his state is doubly disgraced. This recurs to Chapter 2, and to the various discussions of the new prince in the first eleven chapters. The purpose of Twenty-four is evidently to apply what has been said to Italian princes. Hence there are various other passages that echo earlier opinions. For example, mercenary arms are referred to as discussed at length above, that is, in Chapters 12 and 13. The friendship of the people and the making sure of the upper classes go back to Nine. The last words of the chapter, that a ruler must depend on himself and his own prowess, go back to Six, Seven, and Seventeen, among others.

84 Chapter 25, on Fortune's power, takes up the argument of its predecessor that the fall of the Italian princes was inavoidable by human efforts, and endeavors to show that prudence and labor can exert great influence, even though Fortune's power cannot be denied. As is explained below (*Introduction,* par. 115), *The Prince* from beginning to end is permeated with the concept of Fortune; it occurs in seven of the first eleven chapters, being especially important in Seven, and equally often thereafter. An idea vital to the whole work should somewhere be set forth at length.

85 The final chapter forms still another section. "The structure of *The Prince* has always been examined in the hope of finding a solution to the much debated question whether the Italian nationalism of the last chapter formed an integral part of Machiavelli's political outlook or whether it was merely a decorative conclusion." [6] One answer is that "the last chapter,

[6] Felix Gilbert, "The Humanist Concept of the Prince and *The Prince* of Machiavelli," in *The Journal of Modern History,* XI (1939), 483.

which is not prepared for by any hint in the preceding sections of the book, stands by itself, mainly intended as a concluding rhetorical flourish."[7] On the other hand, it is asserted that "the last chapter, which has been regarded by many critics as a later addition, forms in reality the necessary conclusion of the whole work, and may be described as the appeal of enthusiasm in favor of the demonstrations of logic."[8]

86 First, the chapter gives a sentence of transition: "Having considered all the matters dealt with above, and thinking whether at present in Italy the circumstances of the time were united in offering the chance of honor to a new prince," etc. This follows easily from the reference to the new prince in the letter on *De principatibus*, just as the choice of a Medici prince fits with the dedication to Giuliano there announced. The new prince has been Niccolò's chief concern throughout the tractate, for the hereditary ruler almost disappears after the short second chapter.[9] Such excessive concern with the new ruler is unjustified in a work merely of a general sort. It may be accounted for by plans, known in 1513, for making Giuliano a new prince, or by such a function for a new ruler as appears in the final chapter. A general treatise on the prince, such as that of Erasmus, properly gives little attention to the special case of a new government, but if from the beginning a writer is thinking of a sweeping change, he will concern himself with the man who is to administer it. *The Prince* is from the beginning appropriate for the new ruler of the final chapter.

87 To the right conduct of a prince, new or old, something must be added if he is to succeed. Fortune must favor him, the conditions of the age must be such that prudence and energy have proper opportunity, for there can be difficulties beyond the power of the greatest men. The question, then, is whether what has been discussed in general, though with a strong Italian cast, is now workable. Niccolò answers in the affirmative. The very corruption of the time gives the new prince an opportunity for the double glory mentioned in Chapter 24, that of founding and administering a new state, for one who seeks glory "should long for a corrupt city, not to ruin it as did Caesar, but to reform it as Romulus did. For of a truth the heavens are not able to give a man a greater opportunity for glory, nor can men desire a greater one."[10] Next, Machiavelli asserts that there have been indications that certain

[7] Ibid.

[8] L. Arthur Burd, edition of *Il Principe*, p. 30.

[9] But see Chap. 14, par. 1; Chap. 19, pars. 9, 15, 18; Chap. 24, par. 1.

[10] *Discourses on Livy*, I, 10, par. 6, below.

men have been ordained by God for the redemption of Italy, yet in the full flood of their careers they have been rejected by Fortune. Is this a reference to Cesare Borgia, who, as we read in Chapter 7, was overthrown by a extraordinary and excessive malice of Fortune? The times are fit for action, yet God has not done everything, but prefers to leave something to man's efforts, in order not to take free will away from us. This echoes Chapter 25, where we are told that Fortune governs but half our lives, "in order that free will may not be destroyed." If no Italian has thus far been successful in delivering Italy, it is not strange, because military virtue is lacking, as has been made clear in Chapter 12. The remedy is to be found in proper training, such as Cesare Borgia introduced, according to Chapter 7. Continuing, Niccolò explains that the trouble lies largely with the heads; they have not applied themselves to military affairs, as is advised in Chapter 14, or gone to war in person, according to Twelve. Using words applied to Cesare in Chapters 7 and 13, Machiavelli explains that the true "foundation" of the prince is to provide "his own arms." He then turns to military details that seem a brief summary of his *Art of War,* and out of place near the end of a concluding chapter. Even this, however, he turns back to his main theme by saying that such military measures give great reputation "to a new prince." The last paragraph declares that the "occasion," the right time marked by Fortune, has come, and turns to exhortation such as has no precedent in *The Prince,* though such a sentence as the last of Chapter 12 indicates that the author had been moving toward it. While the tone of earlier parts of the chapter rises above what is normal, yet the reputation of Machiavelli as an enthusiastic lover of Italy may, with little exaggeration, be said to depend on this short paragraph, with the patriotic prophecy of Petrarch as its last words.

88 That it gives Machiavelli's sentiments cannot be doubted. A few months before he wrote of composing the little book, he concluded a letter: "Our ruin and servitude may not come today or tomorrow, but they will come in our days. And for this ruin Italy will have to thank Pope Julius and those who make no provision against it—if now it can be provided against." [11] When he wrote the last chapter of *The Prince,* the doubt had become a hope, and he felt that a Medici prince at that hour had an opportunity to deliver Italy, if, as he says in the same letter, Duke Valentino or any other good leader with fifteen thousand men could do as much as a king of France. His letters a year later than that on *The Prince* show him intent on the foreign

[11] Letter of August 26, 1513, last par., below.

relations of Italy,[12] and in the spirit of "This barbarian rule stinks in every nostril," he wrote in May 1526: "Free Italy from constant care; extirpate these horrible beasts, which have nothing human about them except their faces and voices." As to the eloquence of the passage, one needs but to compare his words on Julius Caesar,[13] or the speech of the Florentine exiles to the Duke of Milan.[14]

89 Some of the difficulty comes from a defective view of the preceding parts of *The Prince* itself. Critics who acclaim Niccolò as a patriot see in the last paragraph the dominating idea of the whole work, and assert the unity of the whole. On the other hand, those who think of him as a scientific student analyzing without emotion the deeds of men, come to the last chapter as something quite out of the key of the remainder. Machiavelli obviously was fascinated by political ideas and their exemplification anywhere and at any time; he was, moreover, capable of views detached from an immediate partisan or patriotic feeling; some of the qualities of the scientist were his. But still stronger were his emotional and poetical qualities; even his detachment is rather that of the artist than of the curious student.[15] In proportion as readers are familiar with the other works of Niccolò they realize his patriotism and his artistic and poetical tendencies. On a lower plane the mixture is seen in his *Discourse on Reforming the Government of Florence,* where practical details about the various councils do not suppress his patriotic and artistic delight in the figure of the beneficent ruler. The last chapter of *The Prince* is not only in harmony with the earlier parts of the work in its matter, but is Machiavellian in the sense that it expresses the temperament and feelings of its author as poet and patriot.

90 But in spite of a total effect of unity, there is something to justify those who feel some difference between the earlier and the later chapters. The Fourth, for example, mentions the plan of habitation in his new territory by a prince as a good one. Now the Italian prince of the last chapter, dominant over the whole peninsula, would obviously live in Italy, but his new acquirements would be so various that he could hardly live in one of them as distinguished from another. He could, it is true, carry out the spirit of Niccolò's advice by giving much of his personal attention to the peculiarly difficult new province discussed in Chapter 5, namely, the district accus-

[12] Letters of December 20, 1514, below.

[13] *Discourses on Livy,* I, 10, par. 5, below.

[14] *History of Florence,* V, 8.

[15] See the *Introduction,* pars. 95-114, below.

tomed to free government. His advice seems, however, more suitable to a prince in the position of Giuliano, as set forth in the letter of January 31, 1514-5.[16] Certain cities are to be bestowed on him as a new prince, and Machiavelli thinks it the part of wisdom for him to go to them to live. Such conditions had evidently been in the mind of Machiavelli when, in the letter of December 10, 1513, he announced his work as suitable to a new prince, and therefore dedicated to Giuliano. Did he begin the little book as a study of the new prince and his government, having practical application only to the princedom the Pope might hand over to Giuliano?

91 At any rate, the beginning of *The Prince* is not especially felicitous. Even with its Italian examples and the idea of the new ruler, it opens rather like a dry analysis. The Second Chapter shows some warmth over the Duke of Ferrara, but still preserves the suggestion of a merely systematic treatise. In dealing with mixed principates, Niccolò really lets himself go, to conclude with the story of his answer to Cardinal Rouen. After that the work is never really in danger of dryness, though the illusion of systematic treatment of the varieties of new princely governments is still kept up, to break down entirely with the Eleventh Chapter. Then the author goes freely on his way, though with the friendly support of those who have written books called *De regimine principum*.[17]

92 My analysis of the connections between the parts of the book and of their bearing on the last chapter indicates that from the beginning Niccolò was essentially ready for the kind of thing he wrote. But early he seems to have been ready spiritually rather than intellectually, and only later did he discover that he was writing for the liberator of Italy. Whether he came to that consciousness after laying the work aside for a time,[18] whether he arrived at it as he completed the Tenth Chapter, whether it was not fully clear until he had written the Twenty-fourth—this makes little difference. In any case the treatise he was not well fitted to write became the work of art suited to his genius. Yet the earlier plan left its marks of uncertainty on the finished product—such marks as his lesser but longer

[16] Given below; see pars. 5-7.

[17] See the *Introduction*, pars. 20-25, above.

[18] Some students allow two or three years for the completion of *The Prince*. A late limit is February 1516, when news of the death of King Ferdinand, referred to as alive at the end of Chapter 18, could have reached Tuscany. Those who hold to composition within a few weeks or months can point to the enlarging and polishing mentioned in the Letter of December 10, 1513, par. 5, as opportunity enough for anything the author did.

As believing in essential but not absolute unity, I occupy a place between the extreme unifiers and the fractionalists, but nearer the first than the second.

works, begun as what they were to be, do not show. How strange that when he acted as an artist should he was less successful than when he set out to do what an artist shouldn't!

93 As a work of art, *The Prince* inclines in nature toward the informal essay or the letter. Its affinity with its author's familiar letters on politics is close. Niccolò recognized this when in the Dedication he said he had not adorned his work with full periods, swelling and magnificent words, and other extrinsic ornaments. He wished its decoration to be the variety of the matter and the importance of the subject; a reader can but add the tone of animated personal exhortation that pervades the whole. The construction according to sense, the shift from one person or number to another, the piling of clause on clause that are so difficult to the translator—all make part of the informal character of the whole. Similarly, the theme is not treated rigidly, but scanted where it interests the writer, and developed, above all in the examples, when it pleases him. Hereditary princes are dealt with in a brevity that is almost contempt, and the mixed principate and the prince who owes his state to the aid of others greatly expanded; the latter has in it the romance of Cesare Borgia and the suggestion for the Medici who came to their place of power in 1512 by the aid of foreign arms. In the long Chapter 19 he runs into an excursus on satisfying the soldiers that obviously belongs with his treatment of military affairs, and he breaks off by saying: "Let us return to our subject." The *Discourses on Livy* show the method he liked. He takes a passage that pleases him, elaborates what it suggests to him, and supplies modern parallels. So in *The Prince* the same spirit is at work. Niccolò recognizes the logical structure and continually returns to it, but he has to return because he has previously run away. That is the sort of artistic work *The Prince* is.

94 Does the little book owe its quality to a sudden burst of composition under pressure? Did it come from a long labor of the file that deliberately made the language, as one student puts, it, "a snake that with its rolling coils enwreathes its prey until it crushes his bones, a tiger that leaps more and more furiously on its adversary, grips him, drags him, rends him?"[19] But the method of composition is not what counts. What is *The Prince* as we have it? The reader may judge for himself whether it is a congeries of treatises or a work of art dominated by the Spirit of free Italy.

[19] Mazzoni and Casella, *Opere*, p. L.

NICCOLÒ CHARACTERIZED AS A COMIC ARTIST

95 In temperament Machiavelli seems to have been a blend of idealist and realist. The first quality is generally the dominating one; certainly it gave much of the power to his ideas. The other was a balancing force, and is responsible for much of the opprobrium that has been poured on his head.

96 As an idealist, the Secretary believed in the power of mankind to manage its affairs well. This good conduct was often secured through the action of men of great ability—Romulus and Solon—able to secure willing support from the masses. St. Francis was another who had shown men how to live. Such will and power to benefit mankind on a large scale was a permanent human characteristic that Machiavelli had seen himself. Cesare Borgia gave the Romagna a government so good that the people awaited his return for a month after his power had really been overthrown. Even in the younger Lorenzo de' Medici, Michelangelo's Thinker, Niccolò thought he discerned this quality indispensable to the best life of man in society; he hoped he saw it in Pope Leo X and the Cardinal Giulio de' Medici, when they seemed to plan for settled good government in Florence. Since without men great and good there can be no secure and happy life, and since Italy as he saw her was in dire need of reorganization, Machiavelli's faith made him prone to hail a savior with what now seems faint justification. But a belief that the order of the world permitted happiness for Italy, and that human nature was equal to producing the leader, led him to see possibilities for leadership where cooler heads could hope for nothing.

97 His faith in human capacity did not embrace merely leaders. The Roman people, in the great days of the Republic, were able to furnish intelligent and patriotic support for their statesmen. He who builds on the people does not build in the mud; let him do his part, said Machiavelli, and he will find the people worthy of his reliance. This belief in generally diffused goodness, wisdom, and unselfishness sometimes, though not often, led the Secretary too far. He actually supposed that the common people of the papal dominions administered by his friend Francesco Guicciardini could be formed into an army to fight for the benefit of their own land. The less enthusiastic Guicciardini had his doubts, which seem to have been justified. Niccolò's confidence in this type of soldiery is the more striking after the citizens his own faith and hope had organized failed at Prato.

98 Over against this idealism that anticipated deliverance for Italy, as Dante had expected it from Henry VII or the mysterious Veltro, Machiavelli had another side, more frequently observed by his critics. This is the belief that men are bad, as it is put in *The Prince,* Chapters 18 and 23. When carefully considered, both these passages are seen to be qualified. Yet his advice as a whole is intended to enable a ruler to survive in the midst of corruption. If all men were good, the prince could be faithful in all his dealings; only because of the wicked, must he learn not to keep faith when the interest of the state requires it. Because he seldom finds the unselfish, the prince cannot trust his ministers singly, but must finally act as his own adviser. Niccolò insisted that since a ruler is dealing with persons of all sorts, he must fit his conduct to the *verità effettuale*, the practical truth.

99 In this consists Machiavelli's realism, and chiefly for this reason he is sometimes called a scientist; he did endeavor to see things as they are, to get down to brass tacks. Instances from history, ancient and modern, and from his own observation, formed the basis of his conclusions. Florence and Siena, France and Germany, were the countries he looked at, not Utopia or Atlantis or the City of God. But though these things are part of the method of the scientist, Niccolò did not possess an essentially scientific mind. Facts did not always remain facts to him. For example, his biographer Villari shows that he had before him accounts of the battle of Anghiari giving the number of the killed and wounded; yet the account in the *Florentine Histories* says that only one man died, as the result of a fall from his horse.[1] He is, says Villari, "carried away by his desire" to speak ill of mercenary soldiers. Now the objection to mercenary soldiers was founded on Machiavelli's personal observation of them, but his belief has become a conviction to be proclaimed with zeal, not a hypothesis to be supported scientifically. His example gives the illusion of scientific quality, but is not used in the manner of the accurate historian; he closes his eyes to the reality that the field is scattered with corpses. As in his *Life of Castruccio Castracani,* the detail yields to the dominating idea.

100 But if he is not primarily the political scientist, what is he? For the answer we may turn to one of his letters to Guicciardini, which he signs "Niccolò Machiavelli, istorico, comico e tragico,"[2] historian, comedian and tragedian. The preceding sentences say that he has just received another hun-

[1] *History of Florence,* V. 33. Villari, *Machiavelli,* II, 425-6.

[2] Lesca, in his edition of the *Lettere,* p. 257, interprets *comico* and *tragico* as adjectives relating to *istorico.*

dred ducats for the *History of Florence* and has commenced to write again, "and I relieve myself by accusing the princes, who have, all of them, done everything to get us where we are." Not exactly the impartial historian. The tragedy of Italy was biting enough to Niccolò, yet his mood was not always tragic; indeed in this same letter he speaks of the possible presentation of his *Mandragola*. If he is one thing more than another, he is a comic poet.[3]

101 An artist he has been called,[4] and properly enough. His mystery may be explained by asserting that he is not primarily a *politico*—whether political theorist or crafty politician—but rather an artist in politics. If the *Life of Castruccio Castracani* and even *The Prince* itself are imaginative creations, if the structure of *The Prince* is determined less by considerations of political science than by those of art, the clue of the labyrinth is perhaps in our hands. Yet such a characterization is but vague. What sort of artist is he?

102 If his *Mandragola* is the greatest of Italian comedies, he must be the greatest of Italian comic writers. Such a genius does not lay aside his nature when he turns to another type of art or half art, for at first appearance *The Prince* is a political rather than a primarily artistic work. A Machiavelli carries the comic spirit wherever he goes.

103 As Meredith has shown in his *Essay on Comedy and the Uses of the Comic Spirit*, that spirit is so far from being a vain or light thing that it is one of mankind's most precious possessions. Paradoxical as it sounds, one of the comic poet's first qualities is gravity and seriousness. He must have the sound and not the frothy mind, for he must observe long and steadily, must relate what he has seen at different times, and must form judgment on the whole—not things to be done by one unaddicted to contemplation. This piercing observation is not to be carried on by those who stand coldly aloof. The observer mingles with men while he observes them, and without sympathy he does not see into their hearts. With both their virtues and defects plain before him, he knows what they are likely to do and does not expect too much. Niccolò prepared

[3] It seems that every great poet or philosopher, in fact every wise man, must have something of the comic gift. A comic basis even for Hegel's attack on delusion and folly has been suggested by Mr. J. Lowenberg (*Hegel, Selections*, New York, 1929, pp. xxi-xlii). The comparison of Hegel with Machiavelli is the more suitable in that both have been connected with the totalitarian state. The *Discourse on Reforming the Government of Florence* and the selections from the *Discourses on Livy* show what sort of totalitarian Niccolò was; for Hegel I shall not attempt to speak.

[4] See, e.g., Marianne Weickert, *Die Literarische Form von Machiavelli's "Prince,"* Würzburg, 1937; Luigi Russo, "L'Arte nel *Principe*, e la *Mandragola*," in his edition of *Il Principe*, Firenze, 1931, pp. LXI-LXXIII.

his prince to deal with evil subjects and evil advisers. On the other hand, the comic artist is not a cynic who expects too little; sometimes he sees that he can demand a great deal. An anti-social spirit is not that of comedy, for the comic muse lives in society. A proper estimate of virtue small and great is the result of the sober wisdom of the observer, for comedy is "a fountain of sound sense." If ever Machiavelli—being human—fails to show this sense, it is when his patriotism overwhelms it, but that does not happen often. The Comic Spirit loves men who are honest,

> and whenever they wax out of proportion, overblown, affected, pretentious, bombastical, hypocritical, pedantic, fantastically delicate; whenever it sees them self-deceived or hoodwinked, given to run riot in idolatries, drifting into vanities, congregating in absurdities, planning short-sightedly, plotting dementedly; whenever they are at variance with their professions, and violate the unwritten but perceptible laws binding them in consideration one to another; whenever they offend sound reason, fair justice; are false in humility or mined with conceit, individually, or in the bulk; the Spirit overhead will look humanely malign, and cast an oblique light on them, followed by volleys of silvery laughter (Meredith, *Essay on Comedy,* p. 142).

104 If, however, social insanities go too far, tragedy takes the place of comedy. Indeed it is difficult to deny tragic power to a great comic writer, though Aristotle thought the finished dramas the productions of different men. Comedy wholly apart from pity and fear is but froth. On the other hand, the tragic plot grows heavy and the tragic speech bombastic if the poet has no spark of comedy. After reading the speech of Rinaldo degli Albizi and the account of the conspiracy at Milan in 1476,[5] one easily believes that Niccolò, had he attempted tragedy, would have succeeded as well as did his friend Giovanni Rucellai, even though his gift was not intense enough for the highest tragedy.

105 It seems, too, that his age was not altogether propitious for comedy. Plautus and Terence reigned supreme. No man could escape them when even the author of the *Orlando Furioso* yielded to their power. Nor did Machiavelli escape. He translated the *Andria,* and imitated the *Casina* in his *Clizia.* Yet the reader of the *Mandragola* all but forgets Plautus and Terence. Essentially Machiavelli has emancipated his Muse; plot and characters are of the Florence around him, not of ancient Rome.

[5] *History of Florence,* V, 8; VII, 33-4.

Yet there were limits beyond which even the politically-minded Secretary could not go. If ever a man has lived whose gifts and interests fitted him for political comedy, it was Machiavelli, yet the *Mandragola* is a play of private life, with only touches that suggest the author of *The Prince*. Italy has been ruined by King Charles (I, i); war and peace in Italy must be the meditation of an Italian in Paris (I, i); a man not in the government of Florence is nobody (II, iii); "it is the act of a prudent man to choose the better of two evils" (III, i); good and ill are balanced in the world (IV, i); Fortune rules (I, i; II, 6); the reputation of Father Timoteo's image of the Virgin must be kept up (V, i). But these bits do not take the play from private life. Plautus had dealt with the lives of citizens; the Renaissance had taken to heart the idea that comedy could have no other subject. The dead hands of the Latins withheld the independent Machiavelli from composing political comedy on a grand scale.

106 Yet even the Romans could not keep him from writing as one who looked on Florence as a political organism dependent finally on its individual units. The qualities of his characters are those of the Florentine citizens who made it impossible for the city ever to gain and keep the government Niccolò longed for; they are the persons before his mind's eye when he wrote the *Discourse on Reforming the Government of Florence*. Dr. Nicia is the eternally gullible man of position. Father Timoteo is the preacher who will show Florence the way to hell;[6] he can be influenced by any reasons sufficiently gilded, and even admires the skill of the trickster who tests him with an unreal situation. Callimaco is willing to attain his end by any trick; if he cannot plan for himself he can, as one of the second type of intellect in *The Prince,* chap. 22, use the plans of the clever Ligurio.[7] In a desperate situation he will act and risk loss rather than remain supine. Machiavelli attempts no moral solution. The enterprise of Callimaco gets its reward, for Lucrezia, overcome by circumstances, becomes his mistress without reserve, yet not wholly as a fatalist, for sensual pleasure has touched even her. Such is the Florentine scene. These are the persons the prince must understand, placate, master, if he is to hold his position. Their good is overcome of evil; they are avaricious, selfish, easily deceived. When measured by a standard derived from the common good they fall far short. Yet life must be lived with such as they.

107 To know what Machiavelli might have been, we must

[6] Letter of May 17, 1521, par 1, below.

[7] Ligurio suggests the Plautine parasite.

turn to Aristophanes, a writer of comedy who would have been capable of a serious state-paper on the politics of Athens. Of his deep seriousness there can be no doubt. The mistaken foreign policy of his country mattered tremendously to him. He hated the demagogues that controlled the city because they were bringing on national ruin. His ridicule was not enough to sober the mob, yet he presented the great idea of the firm and prudent citizen as the basis of the state, and the only security for the common good. If the Italian Renaissance had looked with favor on Aristophanes as a model, we might have seen Dr. Nicia as a gullible prior, Ligurio as a clever political manager, and Callimaco as the rich young man determined on office at all costs. But there was little room for such comedy in the theories of Renaissance critics or in the practice of Renaissance poets, and the Florence neither of Soderini nor of Pope Leo offered a stage for it.

108 Nevertheless it appears that Machiavelli actually attempted such a play in imitation of the *Clouds* and other comedies of Aristophanes, entitled *Le Maschere, The Masks*. His grandson, who had a fragment of it, spoke of it as "lacerating and maltreating under feigned names many of the citizens living in 1504." [8] Would that it had survived!

109 Machiavelli's comic abilities appear in his other works. The *novella* of *Belfagor* has even something of the comedy of government. Satan speaking to his princes in the rôle of clement tyrant is for an instant the comic predecessor of Milton's ruined archangel before his infernal council. But the private tone of the story is again resumed. The Familiar Letters also offer a little political comedy. The solemnity of Machiavelli at Carpi, receiving from Guicciardini's sweating archer a missive of no great import as though it concerned the fate of Italy,[9] is perhaps not unlike what he had seen in the Palace of the *Signoria* in Florence. The tone of the letter on the mistakes of Clement VII has the comedy of accumulation in it, and as details the Pope like a baby in Rome, the Florentine Contessa sacrificed to Aeolus, and the Spaniards coming to keep All Saints' Day with the Italians.[10]

110 There are touches of laughter in *The Prince* itself. The Venetians made the French king master of a third of Italy that they might gain two cities in Lombardy (Chap. 3, par. 10). Machiavelli made a sharp answer to the Cardinal of Rouen, (ibid., par. 14). There is grim humor in the assertion that the

[8] Tommasini, *Machiavelli*, II, 305.

[9] Letter of May 17, 1521, par. 2, below.

[10] Letter of November 1526, pars. 4, 5, below.

prince can make sure of the upper class, because they are few; he must always live with the same people, but he can get on without the same aristocracy (Chap. 9, par. 2). In the early part of Chapter 11, Niccolò first speaks of the difficulty of gaining an ecclesiastical state, and then of the churchly rulers as "exalted and maintained by God." He knew how Julius II bribed his way to the papal throne. In discussing auxiliary arms, he remarks: "He, then, who wishes not to be able to conquer should make use of such forces" (Chap. 13, par. 2). "Fortune is a woman and, if you wish to keep her down, you must beat her and pound her. . . . Like a woman, she is always the friend of young men" (Chap. 25, end).

111 Yet the prevailing tone of *The Prince* is serious; not, however, with the seriousness of a scientist, but with that to be found in the character of a great comic artist, Rabelais or Cervantes. The book is dominated by the artist even when it seems to follow more prosaic methods. Although the Fifteenth and a few following chapters, for example, give the superficial appearance of a work *de regimine principum*—and there is no question Niccolò had the type in mind as he wrote—[11] he cannot keep to the method of the erudite. Long before his own list of virtues and vices is exhausted he remarks, at the beginning of Chapter 19, that he has dealt with the more important ones, and will now put the rest under the generality that the prince should see to it that he is not hated and despised. Francesco Patrizi would have labored uncomplainingly through the whole list, but Machiavelli prefers to turn to the vivid and personal; the Emperor Severus was both a fox and a lion; Maximinus was despised because he had kept sheep in Thrace; the Countess of Forlì, after her husband's death, held her castle against her subjects. As he composed *The Prince* he thought of Italy, with its divers peoples and governments, as the theatre in which his new prince is to play his part; similarly he says of the stage in the prologue of the *Mandragola:* "This is your Florence; next time it will be Rome or Pisa." From this imaginative concept comes the episodic quality of the whole. In comedy a character can pause to say something not demanded by the plot but fitted to the character and interesting in itself, as when in the *Mandragola* one of Father Timoteo's worshippers asks: "Do you believe the Turks will land in Italy this year?" And he answers: "Yes, if you don't attend to your prayers." So in *The Prince* he can give a chapter to Liverotto of Fermo and the other rascals, though it interrupts his plan. So Hannibal and Scipio in Chapter 17, though they are not princes, appear because the

[11] See pars. 20-25, above.

theme of cruelty allows him to say something on their generalship.

112 Machiavelli wished to write on the practical truth, and he does it as a dramatist. Valentino, Rouen, Pope Julius are real to him as were the comic men and women he saw in Florence, and perhaps as easily modified and shifted and given permanence by the imagination. They are immediate and living, not bookish illustrations of principles. His apparent low estimate of men also derives from his comic perception; he took men as they were, expecting something, but not too much, from their philanthropy, and accepting their selfishness as normal. Their lack of public spirit is to be condemned but is not personally offensive to Niccolò; the comic spirit is not that of moral indignation. Yet he loves mankind and wishes for its improvement in no ordinary way, as he sees its defects more clearly than most of us can. Moreover, he has standards for judging humanity, and sees heights to which he believes it can attain.

113 The concluding paragraph of *The Prince* has been so lauded that we may suppose it of a higher note than the comic, and the work of Machiavelli the tragedian. Yet even here, though Hope and Justice come forward, the Tragic Muse does not ascend her throne. In the center stands the sentence: "This barbarian rule stinks in every nostril." Certainly not gorgeous Tragedy in sceptered pall.

114 Such a genius as Niccolò's is not an obvious one to be easily circumscribed with a formula, and the classes to which it has been hitherto assigned are not satisfactory. If *The Prince* is to be explained as an intelligible unity deserving the place assigned to it through the ages, if the remainder of his work is to be grouped around a center, some new expression for its entirety is needed. Whatever the ultimate decision on Machiavelli's personality may be, it cannot, I believe, be one that does not envisage his passion for politics as modified by his comic endowment.

TIMES AND THE MAN; FORTUNE

115 As one gifted with the powers of the comic poet, Machiavelli was keenly aware of the frequent incongruity between men and their surroundings. When acted on by powers of generalization, this incongruity became one of the chief factors of his view of the world, namely that success or failure of men depended largely on their power of adaptation to circumstances. This is immediately related to the theory of Fortune, on which he wrote one of his poems,[1] and to which he devoted the Twenty-fifth Chapter of *The Prince*. But one chapter is far from indicating the importance of the theme in the work. It would still be prominent if this chapter were lacking, for the word *Fortune* occurs in fifteen of the other twenty-five, and the idea is found in still others.

116 The theory of Fortune's power over worldly affairs was shared by Machiavelli with all other men of the Renaissance; scarcely any other extra-Biblical belief was more widely diffused. To tragic poets it was a commonplace, for they dealt with the fall of kings from their high estate to the dust. This was expressed when the Elizabethans called one of their theatres the Fortune, and put a figure of the goddess of Fortune over the door. The statute and the picture of Fortune were everywhere to be met. She often poised herself on a globe to denote her movement hither and thither without evident cause. She carried a sail or her garments were billowed out by the wind to indicate that she could send favorable breezes to waft men on prosperously, though these winds were also uncertain. She had two faces, to indicate that she could look either favorably or unfavorably on human actions. Her best-known attribute was the wheel, ceaselessly moving, carrying to its summit the king, who there sat proudly erect, but who also could be carried along to the bottom to become "the lowest and most dejected thing of Fortune." Change is of the essence of the goddess; if she could stand firm she would cease to be Fortune. She expresses, then, the Renaissance view of the uncertainty of life, to be set over against the post-Darwinian theory of Progress. As Machiavelli says, he was inclined to belief in Fortune by the great variations in human affairs he had seen and that were to be seen daily around him. The events of the second quarter of the present century have in them some of the same quality. The rise of an Austrian paper-hanger to power such as perhaps no emperor has ever wielded, the unimaginably rapid overthrow of France, the imminence of invasion of England, the financial depression, all these lead one to think of the uncertainty of human affairs. But Machiavelli lived in a world where changes were so many and rapid that no order could be called permanent. The government and foreign affairs of Florence alone furnished him instances enough.

117 The individual ruler or republic has some protection against the attacks of Fortune. First of all is the defence from within. Fortune has no power over the spirit of man, but only over material concerns, over that part of the world not con-

[1] The *Capitolo on Fortune*, given below.

trolled by nature and personal ability and vigor. Fortune may deprive a hero of all external goods, but she has no further power; he can preserve the same mind in adversity as in prosperity. If he but holds out spiritually, and does not yield to despair, Fortune may at any moment turn her wheel further and restore him to his former station. Mere courage, however, can do nothing but enable him to hold out against unfavorable chance and await the return of prosperity. In order actually to deal with Fortune, prudence and forethought are required. The ruler who has wisdom to see dangers in his state while they are still small can provide against them; if, for example, a discontented aristocracy is plotting with a foreign government, he will execute the leaders and remove the reasons that have caused the discontent of the followers. He will be a good analyst of the times and their relation to his capacity. If, like Castruccio Castracani, he has the gift for warfare, he will fight his Florentine enemies; but if, like Castruccio's protégé Pagolo, he has little warlike capacity, he will depend on negotiation. If he is still more wise and skilful, he will employ warfare when it makes for his advantage and will turn to other means when hostile military forces are too strong for him. But very few men have minds so flexible and powerful as to enable them to choose the right moment for a change of method and then to carry on the new policy with success. Most are too well satisfied with the habits that have won them position to suppose that any change can be required; or they are too hardened in their ways to be capable of variation.

118 Such disharmony between the conduct proper to the world as it is and the world as the unwise prince would have it, could not but be striking to Machiavelli's perception of incongruity. Pope Julius, rushing to success while the slow-witted looked on in amazement, or entering the city of Siena with all the cardinals and so astonishing the tyrant that wickedness failed him, made comic figures of those he overreached. But if Julius had dealt in this fashion with some cool and prudent man, the Cesare Borgia of Sinigaglia, Louis XI, Oliver Cromwell, or a prince "of our times whom it is good not to name," the fiery Pope would have shifted his rôle to that of the man incongruous with his surroundings. Machiavelli was not himself always able to apply his perceptions; to us at least the spectacle of Lorenzo de' Medici, Duke of Urbino, as the liberator of Italy is comic; we think Niccolò's wishes overcame his judgment. Yet even here the hopes of the patriot are those of a man who lives in society, not in some outer sphere. He does see that Italy can expect no republican deliverer; if she is to rise at all, she must have the aid of some great authority, such as the house of the Medici. Likewise Machiavelli's sense of the times kept him from opposition to the Medici in Florence. Republican government had been possible, but that day had passed. The social sense of the comic poet tells him that the overwhelming absurdity is to struggle against the times. Even a prophet, however pure his zeal, must still adapt himself to surroundings; if he fails to take up arms at the right hour, he too will be a subject for laughter. No man, however, can be perfect in his adaptation; that is beyond human nature. So the perfectly fortunate man is but an idea. This Machiavelli expresses in his poem on Fortune by saying that the perfectly happy and successful man would be able to leap from one of Fortune's wheels to another, but this feat of the juggler is beyond human powers.

119 The secret of success in the world lies in adaptation, in defending oneself against the "slings and arrows of outrageous Fortune" by prudence and foresight, in showing such prowess that Fortune will yield before it. Yet man is not wholly master. Lest he grow too sure of himself, he must remember that Fortune still retains her power over half his actions.

ITALY IN MACHIAVELLI'S TIME

120 The main powers in Italy were the king of Naples, the Pope, Florence, Milan, and Venice.

121 The kingdom of Naples included southern Italy but not Sicily, which belonged to Ferdinand of Spain. Much of its political interest derived from the claim laid to it by the French and Spanish royal houses. Charles VIII marched through Italy to Naples in 1494-5, meeting so little resistance that, according to Philippe de Commynes, Pope Alexander VI said they came with spurs of wood and with chalk in the hands of their quartermasters to indicate their lodgings, and needed no other weapons. After the departure of Charles from Naples, Ferdinand of Spain sent there Gonsalvo of Cordova, known as "the Great Captain," who expelled the French. Later Ferdinand and Louis XII agreed to divide Naples between them.[1] This led to war, and the expulsion of the French. Naples then remained in the hands of Ferdinand and of his successor, Charles V, who was Emperor as well as king of Spain. Hence one of the strongest of the European rulers was firmly fixed in southern Italy.

122 The temporal power of the pope was also great, since he

[1] See *The Prince*, Chap. 3, par. 11.

ruled over a considerable territory in central Italy, extending from Rome to the Adriatic and including Ravenna. The effectiveness of papal authority depended on the character of the pope, who might or might not have immediate and compelling authority over the cities and baronies subject to him.

123 North of Rome was Tuscany, dominated by the Florentine power, which had for centuries been gradually extended by conquest. The center was the wealthy manufacturing, commercial, and banking city of Florence. Florence had never been able to annihilate the fierce spirit of independence that inspired many Tuscan towns and made them unwilling subjects. Pisa, for example, freed herself from Florence by the assistance of Charles VIII in 1494 and sustained her liberty with arms until 1509. Siena was independent.

124 In the north-west was the city of Milan, claimed by the Sforza family. They were, however, driven out by another claimant, Louis XII, and the French occupied the city, except when temporarily dispossessed by Ludovico Sforza or the Swiss, until 1523. In the next year the citadel was retaken by the French, to fall again in 1526. At its greatest extent, under Galeazzo Maria Sforza, its territories included much of Lombardy and even Genoa.

125 Venice owed her wealth primarily to her maritime trade, indicated by such signs as her rule of Cyprus, mentioned by Shakespeare in *Othello*. In the Italian politics of the time her land dominion was more obvious; this extended over much of northern Italy, as far west as Brescia. Venice was an oligarchy, one of the most celebrated and administratively efficient governments in the Renaissance world. Nevertheless the territory of Venice on the mainland, resulting from conquest by mercenary troops and depending on them for defense, was never thoroughly consolidated. Machiavelli speaks of her losing in the battle of Vailà what she had gained in eight hundred years. Yet after this defeat Venice remained a powerful state, able to suffer further defeat (Vicenza, 1513), and still keep a prominent place in Italian affairs.

126 In addition there were small states not generally included in any of these, such as Lucca, Mantua, and Ferrara.

127 The picture is complex enough, with five large states and various small ones in Italy. But the complexity has then but begun. These states had various close relations with those outside Italy, which quite changed their standing within the peninsula. Naples as part of the dominions of Charles V, King of Spain and Holy Roman Emperor, was quite different from Naples under a king limited to southern Italy. The pope too was a disturbing factor, because he could bring spiritual pressure to bear, as by interdict, and drew his income from all the Christian world. Moreover the frequent changes from pope to pope were greater than those normally occurring in the kings of other lands. Alexander VI, for example, did all he could to assist his son Cesare Borgia, but a later pope, Julius II, was utterly hostile to him. A pope's term of office, too, was normally short, because he came to the tiara when well on in years. On the other hand, Charles V came to the throne of Spain at sixteen, and to the Empire at nineteen, and reigned over Spain forty years. Maximilian was Emperor twenty-six years. Moreover, almost any Italian city was the possible prey of any ambitious citizen who could make himself prince, or of a leader of mercenary troops who could seize it. Milan came under the first Sforza in this way. Such a ruler, if he had a nominal overlord, acknowledged his power only as it was supported by armies and resolution. Moreover dependent cities were often willing to turn against their rulers when a favorable opportunity offered. Arezzo, for instance, which Florence acquired by purchase, made various attempts to regain its liberty. In addition to this, the Emperors of the Holy Roman Empire had still a claim to Italy and some right to meddle in its politics, though Maximilian never even took the trouble to be crowned. So far as the confusion of Italy in Machiavelli's time can be charged to the Imperial rule, as distinguished from meddling by the Emperor as essentially a German, it is derived from earlier times, when the Emperors were in process of withdrawing from Italy.

128 Under Charles V, Empire and crown of Spain were united, and he was also ruler of Naples. Consequently he was in a position to interfere in almost every part of Italy. For example, in 1527 Pope Clement VII, after fighting with the forces of the Emperor in the kingdom of Naples, made a truce with them, but the Emperor's northern army, made up largely of Germans, marched on Rome and sacked the city.

129 The Swiss were not merely northern neighbors but were actually in control of Italian-speaking peoples along their border. They figure in Italian history chiefly as mercenaries of high quality. Their worth was partly explained by the method of their recruitment, since they were often raised by their own cantons and hired out by the government; even when they were recruited directly by the ruler who desired their services, an arrangement had to be made with the authorities in Switzerland. Their quality as in some sense a citizen army was especially interesting to Machiavelli. Sometimes they came into Italy on their own initiative, and not as the mercenaries of France and

Germany. In fact, Machiavelli feared that they would actually be the conquerors of the land.[2] This view seems strange to us now, when the patriotism of the Swiss has long been idealized and they have for many years been a nation whose policy is neutrality. But it must be recalled that their history before and during Machiavelli's time was to a considerable extent that of conquerors. They did not incorporate their conquests in their own body, but kept them subordinate and apparently regarded them as a source of revenue. It may be observed that Machiavelli writes of them as likely to be masters of Italy after they had defeated the French at Novara, and were in control of Milan. Even after the battle of Marignano, in 1515, where the Swiss were badly defeated, Machiavelli's theory of combat-methods was such as to lead him to estimate the Swiss perhaps too high as soldiers. He put a low estimate on cavalry and artillery, and a high one on infantry. The Swiss had little artillery and less cavalry; they were a splendidly disciplined infantry. To be sure Machiavelli knew their defects, and suggested a method for correcting them in the *Art of War,* but he would have tended to some prejudice in their favor.

130 Another neighbor of Italy was Germany, ruled by the Emperor Maximilian until 1519 and then by Charles V. Maximilian made various moves against Italian states, especially that of Venice, and Charles V was still more concerned in Italian affairs. Imperial armies from Germany were also partly made up of admirable infantry, drilled in the same tactics as were used by the Swiss. These German spearmen also served as mercenaries.

131 France was very powerful in Machiavelli's Italy, and especially brought to his notice because his chief employer, Piero Soderini, gonfalonier of Florence, was a firm believer in the French alliance. The French claims on Naples and Milan, already mentioned, were also of great practical importance to all Italian states, for a French army might appear, at least in transit, at almost any time. These armies were formidable for their artillery and their heavy cavalry. The native French infantry was of small value, but a large number of Swiss and German spearmen were normally in French pay.

132 Spain perhaps would have played but a small part in Italian affairs if her kings had not also ruled Naples, Sicily, and Sardinia, and, under Charles V, Germany. However, as an important Catholic country, easily reached by water, she was always in the picture. Pope Alexander VI was a Spaniard. The Spanish infantry was somewhat superior to the Swiss and Ger-

[2] Letter of December 20, 1514, par. 7, below.

man, being equally well trained and having greater mobility. Some of them were equipped with spears like those of the northerners, so that they were able to hold their own in stand-up fighting, against either infantry or cavalry. Others, chosen for agility, were armed with shields and swords. Their function was to avoid the points of the spears and get so close to the spearmen that long weapons were useless. At the battle of Ravenna, as Machiavelli points out in the last chapter of *The Prince,* these methods almost won the victory, though the Spanish infantry were outnumbered and deserted by the remainder of their army. The Spanish also were enterprising in developing the use of fire arms.

133 To one who considers the political and military history of the age, it seems as though Italy were given over to warfare. How could there have been resources or time for any other activity? Yet the activity of Italy in other respects during that same era is one of the wonders of the world. The engineer who accompanied Cesare Borgia on his campaign of 1502 was Leonardo da Vinci, and the man in charge of the fortifications of Florence just after the death of Machiavelli was Michelangelo. Some of the plans he drew are still preserved at the Casa Buonarroti in Florence. To mention these two is to suggest the vast artistic works that were achieved in Italy. Nor were painting and sculpture the only arts that flourished. Machiavelli himself is one of the first of the dramatists of the period, for in his enforced leisure from political activity he wrote the *Mandragola.* In 1516 Lodovico Ariosto, envoy from Ippolito d'Este to Pope Julius II, published the *Orlando Furioso,* the greatest of Italian Renaissance poems, a work that speedily became known to Machiavelli. The Cardinal is said to have been peeved because Ariosto had neglected his secretarial and diplomatic duties to work on the poem.

134 It may be asked how artistic life was able to survive; why did it not share the fate of Michelangelo's bronze statue of Julius II at Bologna, which was thrown down and melted up as material for casting a cannon? The answer has various parts. For one thing, there were men of energy in the age; Julius II was not exhausted by his warlike efforts, but could still give thought to the plans for his great tomb, planned by Michelangelo to be the masterpiece of memorials. The artist himself had the power and versatility to turn from sculpture to fortification, and thence to poetry. Italy, too, was a rich country. The comparative poverty that everywhere appears to the visitor in this day should not mislead us. In the sixteenth century there was already practised the painstaking agriculture that still supports a large population by labor and care so excessive that an American cannot be quite happy in an Italian countryside. And in fifteen hundred the hand labor of the Italian farmer was not an anachronism. The sickle and the spade in the forms still employed in the country, crude as they seem to an American who knows the hand implements of the age before mechanized farming, were still effective in competition with any agriculture in the world. But Italy was also a great manufacturing country; Florence supplied a European market with silk. Italians were the carriers of the world; such wealth as England has derived from its carrying trade was then that of Venice. London as a banking center in the immediate past has brought the tribute of the world to the banks of the Thames. The Medici bankers brought the tribute of Europe to the banks of the Arno. Even the continual wars of Florence could not exhaust the wealth that poured into the city. Much of this wealth was spent for artistic purposes. The enormous expenditure of the present day for applied science was lacking. One of the things a wealthy man expected to do with his money was employ artists. There was travel, but not the purposeless and expensive running to and fro of the present. Men traveled when they had something to go for.

135 But with all this, there must have been also something in the nature of the wars themselves that rendered them less destructive than in later times. Destruction there was, but the mercenary soldier had no special hatred for the people whose city he captured, though he did want their portable property and had no scruples about methods of obtaining it. If by seizing their persons he could obtain ransom or the price of a slave, that also pleased him, but he had motives for keeping them alive rather than killing them. A town stripped of its movable wealth might be capable of another stripping, but a town destroyed would not furnish further opportunity for sacking. The interest of a leader was often to prevent sack if he could, as Cesare Borgia did in Sinigaglia; he wished to rule the town and derive income from it. Moreover the armies, though like enough to locusts, were relatively small. As Machiavelli pointed out in *The Prince*,[3] the mercenary leader did not employ a large force. The army led to Italy by Charles VIII is said to have consisted of 40,000 at least; perhaps its size accounts in part for his easy success. Apparently later armies did not equal it, though that of Francis I in 1524 approached it. Consequently the drain on the country of a Renaissance army was not like that of the huge citizen armies we have now become accustomed to. And such

[3] Chap. 12, par. 7.

drain as there was did not spread over the whole country. When Florence was not actively at war, her military expenses were relatively small, and so for many cities and districts of the peninsula. Moreover a large proportion of the armies was foreign. Of the battle of Ravenna, we are told that "on the French side there were French, Germans, Swiss, Navarrese, Italians, and Greeks; on the Spanish side there were Spaniards, Italians, Sicilians, Greeks from Naples and from across the Adriatic, Tyrrhene islanders, and Africans." Relatively few Italians were killed in such a conflict, and possibly Italians even had some feeling for each other against the barbarians. At the battle of Ravenna the cannon of Alphonso, Duke of Ferrara, cut down not only the Spanish infantry of his adversaries, but the German landsknechts in the service of his allies the French, as they mingled at close quarters. Alphonso is said to have encouraged his gunners to keep up their fire by saying: "You cannot make a mistake; they are all our enemies." Of course the Duke later denied this. However in one of the stories by Giraldi Cintio published in 1565, the Duke is represented as saving the life of the Roman leader, Fabricio Colonna, because of "the love that he always had for the Italian people." Fabricio surrendered to him, though he had determined to die rather than yield to the "barbarous people," the French who were attacking him. So while Italians were killed in the wars of Italy, many of them were still carrying on wealth-producing activity, and the loss of life fell on foreigners. Testimony to the power of the Italians to prosper in spite of war is given by the successive waves of "barbarians" who came to enjoy the plunder of Italy.

THE FLORENCE OF MACHIAVELLI

136 Of the famous cities of the world, none perhaps at the present more easily reveals its appearance in the year 1500 than does Florence.[1] If the visitor stands on the Ponte Vecchio, still covered with shops, he looks up the river at the very bridge known to Dante as Rubaconte. Crossing to the left or south bank of the Arno, he passes along the Via Guicciardini and soon comes to the house of Machiavelli. A little farther is the palace built by Luca Pitti, the rival of Lorenzo the Magnificent. The building was later much extended but even in the fifteenth century it was a vast mass, and the original portion still stands. Further along the street is the Porta Romana, the gate from

[1] See the Proem of George Eliot's *Romola.*

which one took the direct road south to Siena and Rome. This gate, built in 1326, has lost the outworks that made it defensible against sudden assault, and probably is lower than in its prime, but it still carries something of the air of the old city. If the visitor will pass a little further along the road he will find leading up the hill to his right the Via delle Campora, the Street of the Fields. Ascending almost to the summit, he can find a spot whence he sees only the city of Dante and Machiavelli. The hills and trees are so placed as to shut out the new Florence beyond the circuit of the walls, and give only that of the Palazzo Vecchio, Brunelleschi's dome, and Giotto's tower. When one looks on Florence from Fiesole or San Miniato, one becomes in large part a student of recent history as well, of the growth of Florence since that unification of Italy of which Machiavelli dreamed. The city of the Renaissance is still there, but surrounded with its recent fringe.

137 The circuit of the walls was about five miles. Their position is marked on the north side of the river by some of the gates still standing and by boulevards that encircle the older part of the city; the walls still stand on the south side of the Arno. Much new building is to be found immediately inside the circle of the boulevards, because the walls in Renaissance times included within them a considerable amount of space not occupied with buildings. Possibly there was some expectation that Florence would increase in size. If there had been an increase in population and further demand for building space, the vacant land would have been of high value. In fact in Machiavelli's time, when further extension of the walls to include San Miniato was debated, a certain Giovanni del Bene declared that the land included would increase in value by eighty thousand ducats. Machiavelli commented: "This is a myth, and he doesn't know what he is talking about, nor where this increase would come from; so everybody feels there is no use in thinking about it." [2] Machiavelli seems to have been right, for a picture of Florence a hundred years later shows open ground inside the wall that was built to include San Miniato. Even the open ground within the wall as Machiavelli saw it seems to have remained until the nineteenth century.

138 Within the fallacious security of the wall, causing the citizen to trust too much to brick and mortar rather than to men and iron, was gathered the enormous wealth gained from the manufacturing, commercial, and financial operations of the city, reflected in the churches and palaces still to be seen. But

[2] See the Letter of June 2, 1526, below. The quotation is from another of the same date, not here included.

if the city was rich, it had its poor. Struggles between workers and capitalists were as well known then as now, and wretchedness was crowded close to luxury. The rich Florentine could retire to his villa in the country, but for the poor there was no escape from the narrow lanes and dark rooms of the slums.

139 With the best-known expression of Florentine wealth, its achievement in painting and sculpture, there is no need to deal here. It is enough to say that two at least of the Medici owe their fame first of all to Michelangelo's figures for their tombs in San Lorenzo; the second reason why we know their names is that Niccolò Machiavelli planned to dedicate his *Prince* to one of them and did dedicate it to the other. But in thinking of the artistic riches of Florence in the sixteenth century, we must recall that Florence as a city of galleries was the work of the Medici grand-dukes. In earlier days works of art were not museum pieces but the decorations of homes and public buildings in which men lived, worked, and worshipped. Many great Florentine works are, fortunately, still to be seen in the places they originally adorned, and a few of them, happily, in buildings still in use for much their original purposes. Many of the buildings have, it is true, been converted into museums of a bare and forbidding sort. But this at least enables their decorations to be seen.

140 In the sixteenth century Florence not only had the works of art that were then being produced, but also enjoyed those of earlier days, still splendid. The doors of the Baptistery, designed by Ghiberti, which Michelangelo said were worthy to be the gates of Paradise, were when their admirer saw them by no means recent, having been completed in 1452, but they still must have been glorious in their gilding. But now traces of the gilding are to be seen only by those who look closely, and the whole is black with the grime of decades and gray with the dust of a motorized Florence. Yet these reliefs are among the best-preserved works in Florence that are still in their original position. How often the visitor sees but a pathetic wreck that hardly suggests the glories of the past! If modern Florence, even apart from its Uffizi and Pitti, is a delight to the eye, how much more in the day when many a work now ruined was fresh from the hand of the maker!

141 As everybody knows, the Florence of Machiavelli's youth was influenced by the humanistic tastes of Lorenzo the Magnificent, who patronized Politian and Ficino. This atmosphere was not strange to Machiavelli, who was somewhat of an Aristotelian, even though he could not read Greek. Latin he could read, well enough to permit him to carry volumes of the poets with him on early walks in the country, as he tells us in one of his letters.[3] The stamp of classical comedy is also to be seen in his *Clizia,* and even in his *Mandragola,* probably the greatest of Italian comedies. But if Florence had the greatest of comic authors, it had no stage in our sense of the word. Such productions as the *Mandragola* had but rare chances for exhibition, on some special occasion; his friend Guicciardini, for example, wished to arrange for a presentation of it during the carnival in Faenza, one of the towns he governed for the Pope. Names of poets and dramatists now well known to fame did not abound, even in the group that met at the Orti Oricellari, the gardens of the Rucellai family. Yet there was Giovanni Rucellai, author of the *Rosmunda,* one of the most important tragedies of the age, and Luigi Alamanni, author of various poems, one of which, *Girone il Cortese,* gained the approval of Tasso. A visitor in the gardens was Giangiorgio Trissino, critic, poet, and dramatist. From him better than from any other Italian, Machiavelli could have learned of the *Poetics* of Aristotle, then at the beginning of its long dominion over the poetry of modern Europe. Moreover, he justified his faith by a tragedy, *Sofonisba,* and a comedy, *I Simillimi.*

142 Of the historians whom Machiavelli knew, the most famous are Francesco Guicciardini and Francesco Vettori, with both of whom he exchanged many letters. There were also lesser historians who did not buttress their fame by correspondence with Niccolò, such as Bernardo Segni. Of the group including them a recent historian of Florence writes: "Whoever looks about to discover another city or nation which within the spread of approximately half a century harbored an equally brilliant array of historians will be put to a long and probably futile search." [4]

143 Religion occupied a great place in the life of the period. Ecclesiastical buildings were numerous and clergymen of various sorts were everywhere to be seen. The forms of religion were observed by virtually everybody, even the least pious. A large proportion of the artistic work of the period was ecclesiastical in some way or other. Nor was such expense confined to the cities; private chapels on country estates, such as the oratory of Santa Caterina dell' Antella with its frescoes by Spinello Aretino (about 1387), were splendid with decoration. The wealth of monastic foundations was great. If today Italy seems filled with clergy in spite of the comparative poverty of the Church, what must have been its appearance before various

[3] That of December 10, 1513, par. 4, below.

[4] Schevill, *History of Florence,* p. xviii.

governments seized ecclesiastical property! Today some work is being done on Italian churches, but it is mostly of a cold archeological character, having nothing to do with religion, and much of it consists in removing the elaborate barocco improvements of the sixteen hundreds. But before, during, and after the sixteenth century, men were willing to spend large sums on churches for religious reasons.

144 The great religious leader of Florence was the famous Savonarola. Machiavelli had little confidence in his piety, contrasting him with the sincere and admirable St. Francis.[5] Modern historians, such as Villari, have set him higher, so that to some at least he now appears as "one of the long succession of the saints and martyrs constituting the church militant of Christianity."[6] George Eliot (for this is a matter on which a novelist's testimony may be received) found his character mingled of good and evil; his consciousness one "in which irrevocable errors and lapses from veracity were so entwined with noble purposes and sincere beliefs, in which self-justifying expediency was so interwoven with the tissue of a great work which the whole being seemed as unable to abandon as the body was unable to abandon glowing and trembling before the objects of hope and fear, that it was perhaps impossible, whatever course might be adopted, for the conscience to find perfect repose."[7] Three chapters of the novel (LVIII-LX) seem in part founded on a passage in Machiavelli:

> After 1494 the government of Florence was reformed with the aid of Brother Girolamo Savonarola, whose writings show his learning, his prudence, and the high powers of his mind. Among other enactments to secure the safety of the citizens, he had a law made giving the power of appealing to the people from the sentences that were given by the Eight and the City Council in cases of offence against the state. He advocated this law often and obtained its enactment with great difficulty. Now not long after its enactment, it happened that five citizens were condemned to death by the Signoria for an offence against the government, but when these men wished to appeal, they were not allowed to do so, and the law was not observed. This injured the reputation of that Friar more than anything else that happened, for if that appeal was a

[5] See the Letter of May 17, 1521, below, and the Index. Machiavelli's most complimentary reference seems to be that in his first *Decennale*, where he speaks of him as the "great Savonarola, . . . inspired with divine power" (lines 157-8).

[6] Schevill, *History of Florence*, p. 454.

[7] *Romola*, Chap. LXIV.

good thing, he should have had the law carried out; if it was not good, he should not have secured its enactment. And this affair attracted the more attention in that the Friar, in all the sermons he delivered after this law was broken, did not condemn those who had broken it, or offer any excuse for them; he acted like one who did not wish to condemn their act because it was to his advantage, and was unable to excuse it. This lessened his reputation and gave him much trouble, because it made plain that his spirit was ambitious and partisan.[8]

Romola's faith in the prophet is shaken by his refusal to insist that the law be observed. Yet the novelist asserts none the less that "power rose against him not because of his sins, but because of his greatness; not because he sought to deceive the world, but because he sought to make it noble" (Chap. LXXI). But the correct estimate of Savonarola is perhaps of less moment than the realization that a friar who appeared as a moral reformer was for a time the chief political power in Florence.

145 Florence during Machiavelli's time is spoken of as a republic, but the word *republic* in that day often meant no more than organized state. It was also used in a narrower sense, as by Machiavelli at the beginning of the second chapter of *The Prince,* where he distinguishes republics from principalities. The difference seems to be merely that the republic is not ruled by a king or duke or similar great man. There is in the word *republic* no implication of general activity by citizens in the affairs of state. Venice, the most admired republic in the world, was an oligarchy. Florence was a republic for most of its history, but even there nothing like manhood suffrage prevailed. During Machiavelli's youth Lorenzo de' Medici was virtual ruler of the city. Yet he was not prince; he kept constitutional forms, and exercised his authority through his influence on the formally chosen officials, except in times of great emergency. In 1479 he made a spectacular voyage to Naples to make with King Ferdinand a truce that brought peace to Florence, but he did not appear as all-powerful in the ordinary routine of government. Such a system worked well enough when administered by Lorenzo, but was beyond the powers of his son Piero. It meant, too, that when the Medici were expelled in 1494, no immediate change appeared in the government, for theoretically Piero had no more influence than any other citizen.

146 Nevertheless it was felt that the system that had permitted Medicean rule by influence must be so modified as to

[8] *Discourses on Livy,* I, 45.

make individual domination impossible. The process of change was begun by the summoning of a parliament or popular assembly, a vestige of an earlier time in Florentine government. This assembly approved the putting of the government in the hands of twenty men called *accoppiatori*. This word means literally couplers, and is applied to professional match-makers, or go-betweens in arranging a marriage. These men were to appoint the governmental bodies for a year. The most obvious of these was the *Signoria*, a name which perhaps can be rendered as city council. It was composed of a *gonfalonier* (literally flag-bearer) and eight priors, who held office for two months only—an arrangement satirized by Dante in his time. As advisers they had the gonfaloniers of the sixteen ancient militia companies of the city, chosen twice a year, and twelve Good Men. A new feature now proposed was a Grand Council, to be made up of those whose ancestors for three generations back had held one of the regular magistracies. This Council would include some three thousand citizens, and would choose the magistrates and be the final power in the state. But even this group of three thousand in the great city of Florence—with a population estimated at 120,000—was by some regarded as dangerously democratic. So strong were the supporters of government by the very few, that the scheme for the Grand Council might not have been adopted without the support of Savonarola. The unwieldly size of the Grand Council made necessary a smaller council, that of the Eighty, as an executive body.

147 The councils of the period of Leo X appear in Machiavelli's *Discourse on Reforming the Government of Florence* (given below). His plan may be called an attempt to use the best features of the governments he had observed during his lifetime and to get rid of the worst ones; for the most part, his plan fits in with the governmental habits of Florence.

148 For the detailed business of government still smaller groups than the Councils were obviously needed. One of these called the Ten, was a permanent body having charge of war, of territory belonging to the republic, and of some diplomatic matters. Other executive bodies were created from time to time, such as the Nine in charge of the militia advocated by Machiavelli. Much of the business of this group seems to have been carried on by a secretary not a member of the body. There was, however, a great deal of business not taken care of by special bodies, and in charge of the *Signoria* or City Council. Hence the latter needed secretaries of various sorts. The first secretary, or secretary of the republic, was likely to be a humanist who could write good Latin orations. The secretary next in rank, in charge of the Second Chancellery, was apparently a busier official. His chief business was the home department, though he was liable for other service.

149 On the return of the Medici in 1512 the Grand Council was abolished, and a parliament, carefully selected and overawed by troops, approved a large committee of Mediceans, who chose the city officials as directed by the ruling member of the Medici family. It is obvious that Machiavelli had no experience with anything like democracy in Florence.[9] The government before the return of the Medici was so completely in the hands of the rich that Guicciardini has one of the speakers in his *Dialogue on the Government of Florence,* bk. 2, assert that Florence is essentially like Venice, a commercial oligarchy.

150 The task of the Florentine government was immensely more complex than that of any city rulers of the present. It discharged not only municipal functions as we now understand them, but also all the functions of county, state, and national government. For Florence was not merely a city but also an independent nation, with its foreign policy and its army. It is easy and proper to call the Florentine system inefficient, but the difficulties of the problem should be acknowledged. The mere administration of territory subject to Florence, such as the rebellious city of Pisa, or the fortresses that secured the road to Siena, was no trifling problem. One of the chief difficulties was evidently the lack of continuity in administration caused by the frequent changes in the executive. An attempt to remedy this was made during Machiavelli's term of office, when Piero Soderini was made gonfalonier for life instead of for the customary two months. Machiavelli labored devotedly in the various offices he held, but Florence could not sustain herself, and the reëstablishment of the virtual tyranny of the Medici was inevitable.

THE LIFE OF MACHIAVELLI

151 Niccolò Machiavelli was born in Florence in 1469. His family was not of the utmost importance, but had some claims to nobility in the region a few miles south of Florence. They were among those exiled from the city after the rout of the Guelfs at Montaperti. The houses of the family were in the Oltrarno, or part of Florence south of the Arno, not far from the Ponte Vecchio. Niccolò lived at what is now 16 Via Guic-

[9] *Discourses on Livy,* I, 49, par. 3, below.

ciardini. Virtually nothing is known of his early life. His education seems to have been adequate but not exceptional; he knew Latin but not Greek, though he read Greek authors in Latin translations. His activities immediately after he came to manhood can only be inferred from his subsequent career. Obviously he continued to study literature and history. He also may have had experience in some public office of a minor sort. At any rate he first appears in public life because of his choice to an office so important that he must in some way have demonstrated his fitness for it, or secured the support of the influential.

152 In 1498 the Council of the Eighty considered four names for the position of secretary to the City Council or *Signoria,* to have charge of the Second Chancellery. Niccolò Machiavelli was chosen. A few days later the choice was confirmed by the Grand Council. About a month later he was chosen in the same way for the position of secretary to the Ten in Charge of War. He is then variously mentioned as secretary of the Ten, of the Second Chancellery, and of the *Signoria.*

153 With these appointments Machiavelli began a period of activity that gave him an admirable knowledge of the internal and external affairs of his city. His duties frequently took him into various parts of Italy and even into France and Germany. He was never ambassador for the republic, but rather what might be called agent. He did what he could in behalf of his government, but if a treaty was actually to be ratified, he had to yield to some Florentine of higher dignity. In the course of his fourteen years of service he visited most of Italy from Rome to the northern boundary, was in Switzerland and the Tyrol, and four times in France, going as far as Blois. Even on his first journey he was able to speak the language. On all of his journeys he observed as much as possible, but was limited by his official duties to certain places, and never traveled freely for the sake of gaining knowledge. However, the slow methods then necessary, usually on horseback, gave opportunity for observation such as modern travelers do not know. Perhaps his most striking mission of this sort was that to Cesare Borgia in 1502. Cesare was carrying on the campaign in which he took Sinigaglia and by his "splendid deception" overthrew his false mercenaries. Machiavelli followed the course of Cesare, visiting Assisi, Perugia, Forlì, Sinigaglia, and of course intermediate places. This was Niccolò's best opportunity to observe an able leader in action, and colored his view of how war should be carried on. In 1506 he accompanied the fiery Julius II on a campaign in Umbria, where he found plenty to observe, though Julius did not touch his imagination as did Cesare.

154 In addition to such journeys as these, there was much travel in the Florentine territories. As secretary to the Nine in charge of the militia, Machiavelli had executive charge of the raising of the forces, though of course he had no military command. Much of his time in 1506 and 1507 was devoted to this duty, though in December he was sent to the Tyrol to treat with the Emperor Maximilian. Soon after his return he again was occupied with the war against Pisa. Though he was only secretary to the Ten, and not one of the responsible body, his duties were heavy; in fact the Ten wrote to him: "We have laid on your shoulders the whole charge of this affair." Even then, however, there was a commissioner who was technically his superior, and whom he was exhorted to treat with more respect. In his effort to carry things on, however, Niccolò seems to have continued to cut Florentine red tape. Other commissioners were sent, but the fall of Pisa in 1509 seems to have been to quite an extent the result of Machiavelli's labors.

155 Obviously he would not have been able to render so important a service if he had not gained the respect of the Florentine government, which put into practice one of his favorite ideas, that of citizen soldiery. This was not an invention of his, for it had been recommended to Florence before him, but he seems to have made it a measure of practical statesmanship.

156 Yet during these fourteen years of labor in Florentine government, Machiavelli had not wholly ceased to be a man of letters. Even when in attendance on Cesare Borgia he had attempted to get a copy of the *Lives* of Plutarch. He wrote, too, his first *Decennale,* or versified history of Italy from 1494 to 1504, and began his second, never finished. Otherwise his writings are those suggested by his duties, though some of them, as the *Description of the Affairs of France,* are not the work of an ordinary undersecretary. But the time had now come for a change. When the Medici returned to Florence after the sack of Prato by the Spanish and their advance on the city, the confidant of Soderini could hardly be kept in office, though Marcello Virgilio Adriani, the harmless humanist who was First Secretary of the republic, obtained the reward of his non-entity by retaining his office.

157 For some years to come Machiavelli spent much time at his farm near San Casciano, from which he could look down on the city that now owes part of her fame to the labors her ingratitude made possible. If he could not act in affairs of state, he could write on them. Ere long he tells Vettori that he is engaged on the work known to us as *The Prince*.[1] At the same time he seems to have been composing the *Discourses on the First Ten Books of the History of Livy*. The substance of these works had been growing in their author's mind for years, and some of it appears in the reports he sent to the Florentine government, but further reading, as well as the labor of development and arrangement, was demanded. His letters of the period would, if taken seriously, lead us to believe that he gave only his evenings to study. But the letters are often not to be taken too seriously, though doubtless the affairs of his farm did require some attention, and he did enjoy observing in the peasants the human characteristics he had formerly been able to observe in the courts of princes. Other works also came from his pen, such as the *Art of War*, his two comedies, *La Mandragola*, or *The Mandrake*, the *Clizia* (an imitation of the *Casina* of Plautus), the novella of *Belfagor*, called also *The Devil Who Took a Wife*, and works in verse, *The Ass of Gold*, the *Capitoli* on Ingratitude, Fortune, Ambition, and Opportunity, the Carnival Songs, and shorter poems.

158 When he was in the city he often would have been found with his literary friends at the Orti Oricellari, where he puts the scene of the *Art of War*, written in the form of a dialogue. One fruit of his discussions there is probably his *Discourse or Dialogue on Our Language*. In this work Niccolò examines the language of the great Italian authors to decide whether it is properly to be called Florentine, Tuscan, or Italian, and discusses Dante's *On the Ordinary Language*, which is concerned with Italian as a literary language. The great poet is represented as admitting that the Florentine language is the "foundation and fountain of literary Italian." Doubtless the matter was brought especially to the attention of Machiavelli by Giangiorgio Trissino, who first translated Dante's work from Latin into Italian. Not only is the conclusion of Niccolò's *Dialogue* fully Florentine, but it gives his most deliberate expression of patriotism, beginning thus:

> Whenever I have been able to do honor to my native city, even with difficulty and danger to myself, I have been glad to do it, because a man has no greater obligation in life than to his country, because he is indebted to her first for his being and then for everything good that fortune and nature have bestowed on him; and this obligation is greatest in those whose native city is most noble. Any man who acts as an enemy to his fatherland in heart and deed deserves to be called a parricide, even though he has been injured by his country. For if to strike one's father and mother, for

[1] Letter of December 10, 1513, par. 5, below.

any cause, is a monstrous act, it follows that to wound one's native city is a thing most monstrous, because you never can suffer from her any persecution by reason of which she deserves to be injured by you, because you must recognize that from her comes every good thing you possess. Hence if she deprives herself of part of her citizens, you are obligated rather to thank her for those she leaves than to defame her because of those she takes away. And because this is true (and it is very true) I am certain that I do not deceive myself when I defend her and strive against those who too presumptuously attempt to deprive her of honor.

This statement may be taken as the rule of Machiavelli's life. So far as I know, no writer has ever indicated that his personal conduct did not square with this statement. He had been injured by his Florence in various ways. Whether he felt that his ability and services were never rewarded by proper rank and salary—and this is the greatest injury the city did him—I do not know; he seems never to have complained of it. He did feel that the money he received when traveling for the state was inadequate and often said so, indicating that he was out of pocket. But this was partly because he felt that as Florentine agent he must make a proper appearance abroad. Still further, when an anti-Medicean conspiracy was discovered in 1513, he was imprisoned and tortured on the rack, but then released as wholly innocent. He knew what injuries from Florence were.

159 One short prose work, preserved in a manuscript in Machiavelli's own hand from the last years of his life, is the *Exhortation to Penitence*. It is highly devotional in tone, concerned largely with the vice of ingratitude and the virtue of charity. It serves to show that Machiavelli was capable of religious expression, and that his attacks on the wickedness of the Church did not mean he was personally irreligious.

160 In spite of the suspicions of anti-Medicean feeling that led to Machiavelli's imprisonment and torture, he was so secure of his own honesty that he did not cease to hope for such employment under the Medici regime as he had had under Soderini. Well-known evidence of this is his plan for dedicating *The Prince* to one of the Medici, and the exposition in its last chapter of the opportunity open to the family. But as rulers they were not disposed to take him into confidence, though not unwilling to recognize him. A sign of this is the commission to write the *History of Florence* given him in 1520 at a salary of one hundred florins a year. The work was assigned to him with the approval certainly of Cardinal Giulio de'

Medici, then head of the University of Florence and Pisa, and dedicated to him when completed, after he became Pope Clement VII. In 1525 Niccolò went to Rome to present it to the Pope, who received it graciously and continued his subsidy with a hundred ducats. A plan for some diplomatic function for Machiavelli did not, however, meet the papal approval. Nor had the *History* been the first Medici commission. In 1519 the Cardinal Giulio, visiting Florence for the funeral of Lorenzo, Duke of Urbino, asked Machiavelli for advice on the government of the city. Machiavelli produced his *Discourse on Reforming the Government of Florence,* addressed to Pope Leo X.

161 Certain other opportunities for activity also came to him, having faint resemblance to his old travels for the republic. In 1518 he went to Genoa on business for some Florentine merchants, and in 1520 on somewhat similar business to Lucca. The latter appointment came from the *Signoria* and Cardinal Giulio, but fell short of being a public commission. One result of this journey was the *Life of Castruccio Castracani* of Lucca. In the next year he went at the suggestion of the Cardinal to Carpi, to the meeting of the General Assembly of the Franciscans, with the mission of bringing about a separation of the Florentine monks from those in the remainder of Tuscany. He was also charged by the gild of wool-merchants to secure Friar Rovaio as their Lenten preacher. In 1525 he was sent on the instance of Clement VII to discuss with Guicciardini, papal governor in the Romagna, his old idea of an armed populace as a substitute for mercenary soldiers. In 1526 he was charged by the Florentines to see how matters were going in the war against Charles V. Soon he returned to the camp of the League, having as his chief duty to make clear to Guicciardini, the papal lieutenant, the military weakness of Florence. Then he went on a further mission to Guicciardini, this time in the region of Rome, to see if any aid could be given to the Pope.

162 In addition to these travels, another important commission was given to him, which made him once more a Florentine official. The dangers of attack on the city forced Pope Clement to consider its defense, and that meant attention to the walls of the city. Machiavelli discussed the matter with the Pope on his visit to Rome, and on his return inspected the walls with the engineer Pietro Navarro. In May, 1526, five Superintendents of the Wall were chosen, and Machiavelli was made their secretary and purchasing agent. He seems to have undertaken the work with zeal, but as was usual with those who were obliged to depend on Pope Clement VII, he could obtain neither clear decisions nor money, and little was done.

163 Then came another Florentine revolution, and Machiavelli, just reëstablished as an official, was thrown out because of his Medicean sympathies. Happily, perhaps, he was not obliged to go again through a long period of waiting, for he died in May, 1527, about a month after the revolution.

CHRONOLOGICAL TABLE

1469 Birth of Machiavelli.
Lorenzo de' Medici becomes virtual ruler of Florence.
1491 Savonarola preaches for the first time in the Cathedral of Florence; is elected prior of San Marco.
1492 Death of Lorenzo de' Medici.
Alexander VI (Roderigo Borgia) becomes pope.
1494 Charles VIII of France invades Italy.
The Medici are driven from Florence.
Charles VIII enters the city, passing on to Rome and Naples.
1495 Charles leaves Naples. The French are driven out by Gonsalvo of Cordova.
Savonarola forbidden to preach in Florence by the Pope.
1496 Florence begins war to recover Pisa, taken from her by Charles VIII.
1497 Savonarola excommunicated.
1498 Savonarola executed.
Machiavelli Chancellor of the Second Chancellery.
Machiavelli made Chancellor and Secretary to the Ten, a body in charge of war and foreign affairs.
1499 Louis XII of France invades Italy.
Machiavelli goes on a diplomatic mission to Caterina Sforza.
Cesare Borgia, Duke Valentino, begins his attempt to conquer the Romagna.
1500 Machiavelli goes on a diplomatic mission to France.
Louis XII and Ferdinand of Aragon by the treaty of Granada agree to divide the kingdom of Naples.
1502 Machiavelli goes on various missions to Cesare Borgia.
Piero Soderini made Gonfalonier (chief magistrate) of Florence for life.
1503 Machiavelli continues his mission to Cesare Borgia.
Death of Pope Alexander VI.
Election of Julius II as pope.
Fall of Cesare Borgia.
Machiavelli goes on a mission to Rome.

1504 Machiavelli goes on a mission to France. Earliest date for the composition of the *Mandragola*.[1]

1506 Machiavelli attempts to organize a militia for Florence.
Pope Julius II conquers Perugia, the Romagna, and Bologna.
Machiavelli goes on a mission to him.

1507 Machiavelli made chancellor of the Nine in charge of the militia.
Machiavelli goes on a mission to Maximilian, Holy Roman emperor.

1508 Formation of the League of Cambray by the Emperor Maximilian, Louis XII of France, Ferdinand of Aragon, later joined by Pope Julius II, the Duke of Savoy, the Duke of Ferrara, and the Marquis of Mantua. Its purpose was the overthrow of the Venetians.

1509 Pisa surrenders to Florence, June 8. Though neither general nor commissioner, Machiavelli seems to have been chiefly responsible for operations against Pisa for some months before the surrender.
The Venetians defeated by the Army of the League at Agnadello or Vailà (see *The Prince*, Chap. 12, par. 5).
Machiavelli is sent to make a payment of money to the Emperor to enable him to continue the war against Venice.

1510 Pope Julius II makes peace with the Venetians.
Machiavelli goes on his third mission to France. On his return he endeavors to raise cavalry among the inhabitants of Florentine territory.

1511 War between the Pope and the Duke of Ferrara, supported by the French.
Council of the Church at Pisa in opposition to Pope Julius II.
Machiavelli is employed in the Florentine opposition to the Council; goes on his fourth mission to France.
Formation of the Holy League, against France by Pope Julius II, Ferdinand of Aragon, the Venetians, and Henry VIII of England.

1512 The French are victorious at the battle of Ravenna.
A Swiss army enters Italy against the French, who are obliged to abandon most of their conquests.
Machiavelli busied in raising forces in Florentine territory.

[1] The latest date is perhaps 1512. See F. D. Colimore, "The Date of Machiavelli's *Mandragola*," in *Modern Language Notes*, LV (1940), 526-8.

Overthrow of Soderini.
Return of the Medici.
Machiavelli loses his government offices.

1513 Death of Julius II, Feb. 20.
Giovanni de' Medici becomes Pope Leo X.
Ferdinand of Aragon and Louis XII make peace, to apply only outside Italy.
Louis and the Venetians attack Milan but the French are defeated by the Swiss at Novara, and leave Italy.
The Venetians are defeated by the League (Emperor, Spain, Milan, Pope) at Vicenza.
Henry VIII of England invades France and lays siege to Terouenne.
Machiavelli retires to his villa near San Casciano and begins *The Prince*, and the *Discourses on Livy*.

1515 Death of Louis XII and accession of Francis I.
Francis I invades Italy, defeats the Swiss at Marignano, and secures Milan.

1516 Death of Ferdinand of Aragon and succession of Charles V.
Death of Giuliano de' Medici.
Francesco Maria della Rovere, Duke of Urbino, is driven out of his duchy and Lorenzo de' Medici becomes Duke.

1517 Beginning of the Lutheran movement in Germany.

1518 Lorenzo de' Medici marries a French wife, Madeleine de la Tour d'Auvergne, a relative of Francis I.
Machiavelli meets other literary men in the Orti Oricellari, owned by the Rucellai family.

1519 Death of Maximilian I. Charles V becomes emperor.
Death of Lorenzo de' Medici, Duke of Urbino.
Giulio de' Medici, now cardinal, takes over the rule of Florence, giving more liberty than had Lorenzo.
Machiavelli at the request of Giulio de' Medici writes his *Discourse on Reforming the Government of Florence*.

1520 Martin Luther burns the Papal Bull.
Machiavelli in Lucca as a business agent for Florentine merchants. While there he writes the *Life of Castruccio Castracani*.
Largely through the influence of Giulio de' Medici he receives a commission for writing the history of Florence.
Performance of Machiavelli's comedy, the *Mandragola* (possibly not this year but in 1521 or 1522). The date of composition is unknown (see 1504).

1521 Leo X and Charles V make a secret treaty against the French.
The city of Milan captured from the French, though the citadel holds out.
Death of Leo X.
Francesco Maria della Rovere recovers the dukedom of Urbino; the Florentines send an army to defend Perugia against him.
Machiavelli goes on a mission to the Franciscan assembly at Carpi.
Publication of Machiavelli's *Art of War.*

1522 Adrian VI made pope.
The Duke of Urbino captures Perugia. Giovanni de' Medici (of the Black Bands) fights for Florence.
An anti-Medicean conspiracy in Florence in which various of Machiavelli's friends take part. Machiavelli had no share in it.

1523 The citadel of Milan is surrendered to Prospero Colonna, general for the Pope and the Emperor.
Death of Pope Adrian VI, and accession of Clement VII (Giulio de' Medici).
Publication of Augustino Nifo's *De regnandi peritia,* a Latin work based on *The Prince.*

1524 Francis I invades Italy.
Giovanni de' Medici joins him.
Clement VII makes the Cardinal of Cortona, Silvio Passerini, governor of Florence.
Publication of the *Mandragola* (probably but not certainly in this year).

1525 Battle of Pavia. Francis I defeated and captured by the Imperial Army.
Machiavelli presents his *History of Florence* to Clement VII.
The *Clizia* performed in Florence (composed after the *Mandragola*).

1526 The treaty of Madrid gives Francis I his liberty on condition of giving Burgundy to Charles V, and abandoning his claim to Milan.
The treaty of Cognac between the Pope, Venice, the Duke of Milan, and Francis I.
Giovanni de' Medici killed in battle against the Imperial troops.
Machiavelli busy with plans for modernizing the walls of Florence.

1527 Pope Clement VII carries on war with the forces of Charles V in Naples.
Charles de Bourbon with the Imperial army marches on Rome. The leader is killed but the city is taken and sacked.
The Medici driven from Florence.
Death of Machiavelli.
1531 First publication of the *Discourses on Livy*.
1532 First publication of *The Prince* and the *Life of Castruccio Castracani*.
First publication of the *History of Florence*.
1537 First publication of the *Clizia*.

THE MEDICI

Cosimo, *pater patriae,* 1389-1464. The most important man in Florence from 1434 until his death. For much of that time virtual ruler of the city.

Lorenzo the Magnificent, grandson of Cosimo, 1448-1492. Essentially, though not nominally, prince of Florence from the death of his father Pietro in 1469 until his own death.

Giuliano, Duke of Nemours, son of Lorenzo, 1479-1516. In charge of Florence in 1512-3, then Gonfalonier of the Papal forces.

Giovanni, Pope Leo X (chosen in 1513), son of Lorenzo, 1475-1521.

Giulio, Pope Clement VII (chosen in 1523), illegitimate nephew of Lorenzo, 1478-1534. Cardinal from 1513 to 1523. Representative of Pope Leo X in Florence from 1519 until 1521; after that in control of the city as head of the Medici family.

Lorenzo, Duke of Urbino, nephew of Giovanni, grandson of Lorenzo the Magnificent, 1492-1519. Represented Pope Leo X in Florence from 1513 until his death. *The Prince* is dedicated to him.

Ippolito, Cardinal, illegitimate son of Giuliano, 1511-35.

Alessandro, illegitimate son of Giulio, 1511-37. Became Duke of Florence in 1532.

Giovanni delle Bande Nere, great-grandson of Cosimo's brother, 1498-1526. A mercenary soldier.

DISCOURSE ON REFORMING THE GOVERNMENT OF FLORENCE

INTRODUCTION

This work was composed in 1519 at the request of Pope Leo X and Cardinal Giulio de' Medici, later Clement VII. Various other students of government also contributed their opinions.

Machiavelli's usual impartiality appears in that he is willing to consider both princedom and republic as possible forms in Florence, though probably his feelings as well as his judgment had place in his decision for the republic. In his discussion he exemplifies one of the principles of his *Discourses on Livy,* III, 8, that "he who wishes to alter the government of a state, should consider the subject he has to work on." It is a perilous matter to attempt to impose servitude on a people that wishes to be free. Still further, he follows the principle that should be observed by all who wish to overthrow the ancient mode of life in a state and bring in a new and free one, namely that "you should see to it that those alterations retain as much of the old as is possible; and if the governing boards vary from the old ones in number and authority they should at least retain their old names."[1] Machiavelli keeps the Florentine system of councils, though attempting to make it effective. The Gonfaloniers of the militia companies are preserved in name, though their functions are changed. The Great Council which he brings back had been in operation until seven years before he wrote, and apparently was looked back on with longing by the people.

He adapts his scheme also to circumstances in his attitude to the Medici. He is respectful to the Pope and the Cardinal, and makes provision for keeping their power during their lives. This was indispensable, for no government that did not recognize them was possible; in fact the Medici were in the position of the strong man who reforms a corrupt state and sets it on the road to prosperity; such a ruler, Machiavelli held, must be absolute.[2] Moreover, he keeps in mind the partisans of the Medici, a strong party in the city, who should not be made inevitable rebels against any new government. But the attitude of the writer is not sycophantic. There is no flattery of the present Medici or of their ancestors.[3] The position of Pope and

[1] *Discourses on Livy,* I, 25. [2] *Discourses,* I, 9, below.

[3] Cf. the *Introduction,* par. 58, above.

Cardinal and the ability of Cosimo and Lorenzo are recognized, but the defects of Cosimo's government are not spared, and no suggestion is made that his successors may be capable of doing better than he did. The present administration is looked on as but temporary, to make room for a better, republican government. The chief flattery, if it be that, is to assume that the Medici are so disinterested and enlightened as to wish to found a republic. But perhaps Machiavelli, like Erasmus, was willing to assume in a prince virtues he did not possess for the sake of encouraging the prince to assume them. The Medici, however, doubtless appeared greater and nobler to Niccolò than they do to us.

As exemplifying parts of Machiavelli's theory of government, this *Discourse* has much in common with *The Prince*. It allows the necessity of a prince, but endows him with prudence, vigor, and the most disinterested love for his people. The ruler's aim is to provide a solid government in Florence, able to satisfy the people within and repel enemies from without, just as in *The Prince* he thinks of the same thing for all Italy. The dissimulation advised in *The Prince* is not found here, for the reason that foreign policy and dealings with enemies are not in question. There are only slight suggestions of ruthlessness, since the weight is on the other side; the prince of the *Discourse* is eager to win the support of both the people and the upper classes, as is urged in *The Prince,* Chaps. 9, 19, and 24. The Medici are so situated that it is wise for them to employ such virtues as that of pity. The Pope is to recognize in time, as is recommended in *The Prince,* Chap. 3, the danger in the desire of the people for a more liberal government, and to forestall it by setting up the Grand Council, doing it so early, one may assume, that it appears something to be grateful for, according to the suggestion of *The Prince,* Chap. 8. Warfare is scarcely mentioned, and other matters prominent in *The Prince* are not touched on, but in its more limited scope, the *Discourse* applies the principles of its famous predecessor.

DISCOURSE ON REFORMING THE GOVERNMENT OF FLORENCE

Written at the Request of Pope Leo X

1 The reason why the government of Florence has always changed so frequently is that there has never been in the city either a republican or a princely administration having the proper qualities; a principality cannot be called stable where things are done as one person wishes, but are decided according to the opinion of many; and it cannot be believed that a republic will last long if satisfaction is not given to the factions that must be satisfied if the government is not to fall. The truth of this can be established from the number of governments the city has had from thirteen hundred ninety-three to the present day.

2 If you begin with the reform made in that year by Messer Maso degli Albizzi you will see that he and his followers then intended to give Florence the form of a republic governed by the nobles, and that because of the many defects in their plan it did not reach its fortieth year, and would not have lasted so long if the war with the Visconti, which then took place, had not kept the city united. These defects were of various kinds. One of these was that the choice of persons eligible to office was made a long time in advance, so that fraud could easily be introduced and the choice could be other than good; on the other hand, because men change easily and the good become wicked, when the citizens are put on the list a long time ahead, it may easily happen that the choice is good and the drawing bad.[1] Moreover, no check was laid on powerful men to keep them from forming parties, which are the ruin of a state. Still further, the *Signoria* [2] had little reputation and too much authority, since it could decide on the life and property of citizens without any possibility of appeal, and was able to summon the people to parliament.[3] Hence the *Signoria* came to be not the defender of the state but an instrument to cause its destruction, whenever a citizen of high reputation was able to rule it or to deceive it. On the other hand it had, as I have said, little reputation. Since it had in it many young men of inferior position, and its term was short and it did not deal with important affairs, it could not have a high reputation. There was also in that form of government a de-

[1] The lists of persons eligible for office were made up in advance, and choice made when the proper time came by drawing from the lists by lot.

[2] The city council, composed of the Gonfalonier and Priors; usually there were eight of the latter.

[3] The *parlamentum* or popular assembly gave the appearance of popular government without the reality. Savonarola declared: "When you say *parliament*, you mean nothing else than taking the government out of the hands of the people" (Sermon of July 28, 1495, No. 26 on the Psalms). Troops were brazenly brought into the city to guard the meeting place, and only those were admitted who would vote in the right way. The assembly was usually asked to give power to a *balìa* or committee to make such changes in the government as it liked. A parliament, then, meant a violent change in the government, usually for the selfish interest of those powerful enough to control it. Such assemblies were held in 1433 (twice), 1458, 1466, 1495, and 1512. The constitutional change of 1480 was carried through without summoning a parliament.

fect of no little importance, namely that private citizens were employed to deal with public matters; this maintained the reputation of these private persons, but took away that of the public officers, and thus was gradually taking away the authority and reputation of the bodies of magistrates. Such a condition is contrary to all good administration. To these defects was added another that included all the rest, namely that the people did not have its share in the government. All these things together caused numerous disorders; and if, as I have said, external wars had not kept things quiet, that government would have gone to ruin more quickly than it did.

3 The next government was that of Cosimo, which inclined more to the principality than to the republic. If it lasted longer than the other, there were two causes for it: one was that it was established with the favor of the people; the other was that it was carried on by the prudence of two men, namely Cosimo and his grandson, Lorenzo. Nevertheless the necessity of deciding by the vote of a large number what Cosimo wished to carry out made it so weak that it was often in danger of overthrow;[4] from this resulted the many parliaments and the many exiles during that period; finally, on the accident of the invasion by King Charles, the government was overthrown.[5] After this, the city determined to take up again the form of a republic, but did not apply herself to establishing it in such a way that it would be durable, because the new administration did not satisfy all the factions among the citizens, and on the other hand was unable to punish them; it was so weak and so far from being a true republic that a gonfalonier for life who was prudent and wicked could easily make himself prince, but one who was good and weak could easily be driven out, and the whole frame of government would fall in ruin.[6] And because it would be a lengthy matter to give all the reasons for this state of things, I will give but one, namely that the gonfalonier had nobody at hand who could defend him if he was good, or restrain and correct him if he was wicked.

4 The reason why all these administrations in Florence have been defective is that reforms in them have been made

[4] Cosimo governed by influence, without holding offices that gave him great and immediate power. Hence, anything he decided upon had to be passed through the councils and other channels of the supposedly republican administration which he allowed to stand. Naturally his control varied in completeness from time to time.

[5] In 1494; see Chronological Table.

[6] One is tempted to make this a reference to Piero Soderini, who was driven out just before the return of the Medici. But there is no prudent and wicked gonfalonier to set against him, so that both cases must be taken as primarily hypothetical.

not for the fulfillment of the common good,[7] but for the strengthening and security of one party; yet this security has never been attained, because there has always been a discontented party in the city, which has been a splendid tool for anyone desiring revolution.

5 It now remains to consider what the government was from 1512 to the present, and what weaknesses or virtues it possessed,[8] but because it is recent and everyone knows about it I shall say nothing. It is true that, because of the death of the Duke, matters have now come to such a state that it is necessary to consider new forms of government; hence it seems to me that if I am to show my fidelity to Your Holiness I cannot err in saying what occurs to me. First I shall give the opinion of many others, as I understand it from their talk, and then shall add my own; if I err in it, I trust Your Holiness will excuse me as more loving than prudent.

6 I say, then, that some think it is not possible to set up a more solid government than that in effect in the days of Cosimo and of Lorenzo. Some others desire one more liberal. Those, however, who would like a government similar to that of Cosimo say that things easily return to their natural courses; since it is natural for the citizens of Florence to honor your House, to enjoy the favors that come from it, and to love the things it loves, and since moreover they have been in the habit of doing these things for sixty years, it is not possible that if they see the same ways of doing things they will not return to the same frame of mind. Those who hold this opinion believe that few would be of a contrary frame of mind, and these few would easily be nullified by those of the opposite habit. They add necessity to these reasons, showing that Florence is unable to exist without a head, and if she must have one, that he had much better come from a house she is accustomed to adore, than that she should not have one and live in confusion, or should have one obtained elsewhere, with the result that there would be lower reputation and less contentment all around.

7 Against this opinion one may answer that a government so formed is in danger just because it is weak; if the administration of Cosimo had in his times so many kinds of weak-

[7] The expression the *common good* is important in political theory before Machiavelli (Gilbert, *Machiavelli's "Prince," and Its Forerunners*, Index), and occurs often in his writings (e.g., *Discourses on Livy*, I, 9, pars. 2-5, below). The phrase does not occur in *The Prince*, but Machiavelli is too much concerned with the specific conduct of the ruler to set forth this generality. See the *Introduction*, pars. 39-51, above.

[8] The government introduced when the Medici returned in 1512, supervised first by Giuliano, Duke of Nemours, then by Lorenzo, Duke of Urbino (died in 1519), and Giulio, Cardinal de' Medici.

ness as have been indicated above, a similar administration in this time would have twice as many, because the city, the citizens, and the times are wholly unlike those of that age; it is therefore impossible to devise a government for Florence that can last, and have it like Cosimo's.

8 In the first place, that government had the friendship of the mass of the people, and this has their enmity; those citizens had never seen in Florence a government that gave more power to the people than Cosimo's did, and these have seen one there that appears to them more for the good of the citizens and that satisfies them better. In Italy there was then no army or power that the Florentines, even when alone, were not able to meet on equal terms, and now when Spain and France are there it is necessary for Florence to be the friend of one of the two; if it happens that her ally loses, she must immediately become the booty of the victor—something impossible in Cosimo's time. The citizens were then accustomed to paying large taxes; now through weakness and disuse they are weaned from it, and to attempt to accustom them to it again would be a hateful and dangerous proceeding.

9 The Medici who ruled then, since they were brought up and educated with the other citizens, conducted themselves with such cordiality that it gained them favor; now they have become so great that they are no longer on an equality with the citizens, and there cannot be the old intimacy, and consequently the same old favor. Hence, in view of the difference in times and in men, there cannot be a greater deception than to believe that on such different matter the same form can be impressed; if, as I said above, the Medici were then in danger of losing their position every ten years, now they really would lose it. It should not be accepted as true that men easily return to their old and familiar way of living; this belief is valid when the old way of living pleases them more than the new one; when it is less pleasing, they do not return except under compulsion, and they live in the old way only so long as the compulsion lasts.

10 Besides this, though it is true that Florence is not able to get on without a head for the government, and that if she has to choose between one individual head and another, she would prefer a head from the house of the Medici to one from any other house, yet if she can choose between an individual head and a public one,[9] she will always prefer the public head, taken from whatever place, to the individual head.

[9] The individual head would be a single man who had made himself master. The public head would be a group of officers legally chosen, such as the Sixty-five of Machiavelli's plan; see par. 17, below.

11 Some think that the government cannot be overthrown unless the city is attacked from without, and believe they can always be in time to make friends with the one who attacks it. But in this they are completely deceived, because friendship is generally made not with the man who has most power but with the one who has most opportunity to damage you, or the one whom your spirit and fancy most incline you to love. It can easily happen that your friend loses, and in his defeat remains at the discretion of the victor, and that the other does not wish to make a treaty with you, either because you do not have time to ask it or because of the hate he has formed against you, as a result of your friendship with his enemies.[10] Lodovico, the Duke of Milan, would have made a treaty with Louis XII of France if he had been able to. King Frederick of Naples would have made a truce with the same man, if he could have accomplished it. Both lost their thrones because they were not able to make truces, since a thousand hindrances come up to impede the making of such agreements. Hence, if everything is taken into account, such a government cannot be called secure or stable; it has so many causes for instability that it should not be considered satisfactory to Your Holiness or your friends.

12 As for those who wish the government to be more inclusive than that of Cosimo, I say that if it is not liberalized in such a way as to become a well-organized republic, such inclusiveness will make it fall more quickly. If they would state in particular how they wish it to be done, I would answer them particularly, but since they stick to generalities, I can only answer in generalities. I intend this to be answer enough. It is enough to disprove the arguments for the government of Cosimo to say that no government can have stability if it is not a true principality or a true republic, for all the constitutions between these two are defective. The reason for this is apparent: the principality has but one way toward its liquidation, which is to descend toward a republic; the republic also has one way of liquidation, which is to rise toward the principate. The states in the middle have two ways, for they are able to rise toward the principality and descend toward the republic; from this comes their instability.

13 Hence if Your Holiness wishes to set up in Florence a stable government for your glory and the safety of your friends, you cannot do other than set up a true principality or a republic having all the necessary parts. All other forms are vain

[10] Cf. the treatment of alliances in *The Prince*, Chap. 21, pars. 3-7, and in the two Letters of December 20, 1514, given below.

and can last but a short time. As to the principate, I shall not speak in detail because of the difficulty of establishing one and the lack of proper material in the city. Your Holiness must understand that in all cities where there is great equality among the citizens, a principality can be established only with the utmost difficulty; and in a city where there is great inequality among the citizens it is impossible to set up a republic without the greatest difficulty. For example, one who plans to set up a republic in Milan, where there is great inequality among the citizens, would have to get rid of all the nobility and reduce it to equality with the masses, because there are many in the city so powerful that the laws would not be enough to keep them down, but they can be held in check only by the authority of the king in person. On the contrary, he who plans a principality in Florence, where there is great equality, will find it needful to introduce inequality there, and set up many nobles, with castles and estates, who in company with the prince will suppress the city and all the province by their arms and their supporters. A prince alone, without a nobility, cannot support the weight of the royal office, but it is needful that there be between him and the masses of people a middle group who will aid him in supporting it. You see in all the states ruled by princes, and especially in the kingdom of France, how the gentlemen rule the people, the nobles the gentlemen, and the king the nobles.

14 But to set up a principality where a republic would work well, and to set up a republic where a principate would work well is a difficult thing, and because it is difficult, is inhumane and unworthy of anybody who wishes to be thought prone to pity and good.[11] Hence I will say no more of the principate and speak of the republic, both because Florence is a subject well-adapted to receive this form, and because I understand that Your Holiness is much inclined toward it. In fact it is believed that you defer putting it into practice only because you desire to find an organization such that you will continue to possess great authority in Florence and your friends will live in security.

15 Since it seems to me that I have thought the matter out, I wish Your Holiness to understand my conception, in order that if there is anything good in it, you may use it, and also by means of it may realize my desire to serve you. You will see that in this republic of mine your authority is not merely maintained but increased, your friends are respected and se-

[11] A similar unfavorable judgment is pronounced in the *Discourses on Livy* (I, 26) on such a policy carried out by Philip of Macedon.

cure, and the mass of the citizens has evident reasons to be contented. I beseech Your Holiness with reverence that you will not blame or praise this discourse of mine until you have read it through, and likewise I pray you that you will not be disturbed at some change in the governing councils, because when things are not well ordered, the less there remains of the old, the less there remains of the bad.

16 Those who plan a state ought to provide a place for three different sorts of men, such as are to be found in all cities, that is, the upper class, the middle class, and the lowest class. And though in Florence there is the equality of which I spoke above, nevertheless there are in that city some of lofty spirit who think they deserve to precede the others, and who must be satisfied when the government is organized. The earlier administration came to ruin for no other reason than that it did not satisfy this party. Men of that sort cannot be satisfied unless majesty is given to the highest offices of the state, and this majesty must be sustained by their persons.

17 It is not possible to give this majesty to the highest offices in the government of Florence if the *Signoria* and the Colleagues are kept on the same footing as in the past. Because of the method in which these offices are filled,[12] it is seldom possible to put in them men of weight and high reputation; hence it is necessary to put the majesty of the government on a lower plane, and in obscure places—something contrary to every political principle—or to turn it over to private persons. Therefore this method must be corrected, and along with such correction the highest political ambition in the city must be satisfied. This is the way to do it: Get rid of the *Signoria*, the Eight of *Practica*, and the Twelve Good Men, and as substitutes for them, to give dignity to the government, choose sixty-five citizens, at least forty-five years old, fifty-three for the major gilds and twelve for the minor gilds,[13] who should continue in the administration for life in the manner I shall now set forth. From this number a Gonfalonier of Justice should be chosen for two or three years, if it should

[12] That is, by lot from among those eligible.

[13] Possibly Guicciardini had in mind this passage when he wrote of the choice of his proposed council of five hundred: "*Bernardo del Nero*. . . . I should prefer that they be chosen not according to the quarters of the city but for the city as a whole, because in such matters the distribution according to quarters has no reason; it is important not that the quarters be equal, but that those of most merit be chosen. For the same reason I should not like to give its proportion to the minor Art, but rather to take from every group according to the quality of the men; it would be much better to get rid of this distinction for all offices" (*Dialogue on the Government of Florence*, book 2). I have preserved in the translation Guicciardini's singular for "the minor Art." Machiavelli uses both minor and major in the singular, and omits the word *Art* (or *gild*) as understood.

not seem well to appoint him for life, and the sixty-four citizens who remain should be divided into two groups of thirty-two each. One group should govern with the Gonfalonier one year and the other group the next year, and so they would change annually, in the order I mention. All together would be called the *Signoria*.

18 The Thirty-two should be divided into four parts, eight in each, and each group should reside with the Gonfalonier three months in the Palace; it should enter upon its term with the usual ceremonies, and should carry on all the business that the *Signoria* alone performs today. After that, with its remaining companions of the Thirty-two, it should have all authority and carry on all the business that at present is attended to by the *Signoria,* the Eight of *Practica,* and the Colleagues; all these, as I mentioned above, are abolished. This body of sixty-five, as I have said, would be the head and chief of the government and its leading member. If this plan is carefully considered, it will be seen to give dignity and high standing to the head of the government, and it will be seen that weighty and authoritative men will always hold the highest positions and that committees of private citizens will not be needed—I remark above that such committees are damaging to a republic—for the Thirty-two who are not that year acting as magistrates can serve for consultation and committee work. When the first choice is made, Your Holiness can appoint only your friends and supporters, as I explain below.

19 But now let us come to the second rank in the state. I believe, as I said above, that it is necessary, since there are three sorts of men, to have also three ranks in a republic, and not more. Therefore I believe that it would be well to get rid of the confusion of Councils that has existed for some time in our city. They have been set up not because they were necessary to civic well-being, but in order to feed the vanity of many citizens, and to feed it with something that in truth is of no value to the well-being of the city, because all of them can be corrupted by their parties.

20 Since I wish, then, to restore a republic with just three divisions, it seems to me good to abolish the Seventy, the Hundred, the Council of the People, and the Council of the Commune. In the place of these I wish to set up a Council of Two Hundred, with each member at least forty years of age. Forty of these would be for the minor gilds, and a hundred and sixty for the major gilds;[14] none of them could be of the

[14] This was the proportion between the Arts observed in Lorenzo's Council of Seventy, formed in 1480.

Sixty-five. They should hold office for life, and be called the Council of the Selected. This Council, together with the Sixty-five already named, should carry on all business, and have all the authority held today by the aforementioned Councils that have been abolished for the sake of these. This would be the second rank of the government. All should be chosen by Your Holiness. Hence to do this, and to maintain and regulate the offices mentioned above and those that will be mentioned below, and for more security of your authority, and that of your friends, Your Holiness and the Most Reverend Cardinal of the Medici, must obtain, for the life of both, by means of a Committee with Power, as much authority as is possessed by the people of Florence. The magistrates of the Eight of Guard and Authority should be personally selected by Your Holiness from time to time. For the further security of the state and the friends of Your Holiness, the organized infantry should be divided into two brigades, to which Your Holiness should every year on your authority assign two Commissioners, one for each brigade.

21 You may see that what I have indicated above will satisfy two sorts of men, and that your authority and that of your friends will be well established in the city, for you have the army and criminal justice in your hand, and the laws in your bosom, and the chiefs of the state are all yours.

22 It now remains to satisfy the third and last grade of men, which consists of the whole general population of the city; they will never be satisfied—and he who believes anything else is not wise—unless you restore or promise to restore to them their authority. And because to restore it to them all at once would not be for the security of your friends or the maintenance of the authority of Your Holiness, it is necessary in part to restore it and in part to promise to restore it, in such a way they may be fully assured that they are going to get it again. Hence I judge it will be necessary to reopen the hall of the Council of the Thousand, or at least of the Six Hundred Citizens, who should distribute in the same way as they formerly did all the offices and positions, except for the aforementioned Sixty-five, Two Hundred, and Eight of Authority, who during the life of Your Holiness and the Cardinal would be appointed by you. And that your friends may be certain that their names are in the ballot boxes,[15]

[15] According to the Florentine system, the names of all persons eligible to office were put in ballot boxes (literally *bags*) to be drawn out when a choice was to be made. Supposedly, then, any man whose name was put in the box might hope to be chosen for the office in question. The function of the Couplers was to see that the right names were drawn.

when the Council makes its choice, Your Holiness should appoint eight Couplers, who in secret would be able to give the decision to whom they wished, and would not be able to take it away from anybody. And in order that the people may believe that the names of anybody who is chosen were put in the boxes, the Council should be permitted to send secretly two citizens chosen by it to witness the putting of the names in the boxes.

23 Without satisfying the people in general, it has never been possible to set up a stable republic. The mass of the citizens of Florence will never be satisfied unless the Council-Chamber is reopened. Hence anybody who wishes to organize a state in Florence must reopen this hall and give over the distribution of offices to the mass of citizens. And Your Holiness should be aware that whoever thinks to deprive you of your position will attempt to reopen the Council-Chamber before he does anything else. Hence it is a good plan for you to open it with secure conditions and methods, thus taking away from any enemy the chance to open it against your will, and with the destruction and overthrow of your friends.

24 When once the government was so established, it would be necessary to make no other provision if Your Holiness and the Most Reverend Cardinal were going to live forever. But you have to depart, and you wish to leave a perfect republic, supported by all the proper parties, and desire everybody to see and understand that it is really such, in order that the body of citizens may be contented because of what is given to them and what is promised.

25 Hence it is necessary to arrange that the sixteen Gonfaloniers of the Companies of the People be chosen by the method and for the time customary up to the present,[16] either by their appointment on the authority of Your Holiness or by allowing the Council to choose them, according as you please; the number of those ineligible should be increased, in order that the Gonfaloniers may be more generally distributed through the city; it should be laid down that none of the Sixty-five citizens are to hold this office. When the Gonfaloniers are assembled, four head men should be chosen, who should hold office for a month, so that at the end of their term all would have been head men. From the four, one should be selected, to reside a week in the Palace with the nine resident members of the *Signoria*, so that by the end of the month all four would have resided there. The members of the *Signoria* residing in

[16] These men, numbered among the Colleagues of the *Signoria*, were the heads of the ancient militia companies of the city. Their term of office was four months.

the Palace would not be able to do anything if the head man were absent, and he would not have the right to vote, but would merely be witness of their actions. He could, however, stop them from deciding on a case and could ask judgment on it from all the Thirty-two together. So likewise the Thirty-two would not be able to decide anything without the presence of two of these head men, yet the two would have no other authority than that of delaying a decision which has been discussed before them and appealing it to the Council of the Selected. Nor would the Council of the Two Hundred be able to do anything unless at least six of the sixteen, including two head men, were present; yet the Gonfaloniers, provided three of them agreed, would have power only to take a matter from that Council and ask for action on it by the Grand Council. It would not be possible for the Grand Council to meet without twelve of the Gonfaloniers, including at least three head men, who would be able to give their votes like other citizens.

26 Such an arrangement of these Gonfaloniers is necessary after the death of Your Holiness and of His Reverence the Cardinal for two reasons. One is that if the *Signoria* or the high Council did not decide a matter because of lack of union, or did something against the common good through malice, someone would be at hand to take away their authority and ask for a decision elsewhere; it is not a good thing that one kind of governmental body or council should be able to decide on any action without having at hand someone able to check them. Nor is it good that the citizens should not have someone to watch them and make them refrain from actions that are not good. The other reason is that, since the abolition of the *Signoria* as it is today takes away from the mass of the citizens the possibility of belonging to it, an office that resembles what is taken away must be provided for them. My substitute is such that it will be greater, more useful to the state, and more honorable than the older one. For the present it would be well to summon these Gonfaloniers in order to get the city properly organized, but they should not be permitted to exercise their functions without permission from Your Holiness; you could make use of them in order to have the actions of these governing bodies properly managed, so far as they involve your authority and position.

27 Besides this, in order to give perfection to the republican government after the death of Your Holiness and of His Reverence the Cardinal, and to be sure that nothing is lacking, it is necessary to add to the Eight of Guard and Authority a Court of Appeal made up of thirty citizens whose names are drawn from the ballot box of the Two Hundred and the Six Hundred together. This court would be able to summon the accuser and the accused within a certain time, but during your life you would not allow it to act without your permission. This Court of Appeal is very necessary in a republic, because a few citizens do not have courage to punish great men,[17] and therefore it is essential that many citizens agree on such an action, in order that the judgment may be concealed, and since it is concealed, each man may be able to excuse himself. This Court of Appeal will also be useful during your lifetime to cause the Eight to accelerate law cases and do justice, because in their fear that you would permit the appeal they would judge more justly. In order that not everything may be appealed, it is possible to order that there could be no appeal in cases pertaining to fraud unless they amount to at least fifty ducats, or in matters of violence if there is no breaking of bones or effusion of blood, or if the damage does not reach the sum of fifty ducats.

28 It appears to me that when this government is considered as that of a republic and without your authority, nothing is lacking, according to what has been debated and examined at length above. But if it is considered while Your Holiness and His Reverence the Cardinal are living, it is a monarchy, because you command the armies, you command the criminal judges, you have the laws in your bosom. I do not see what more a single person can ask for in a city. Nor do I see what your friends, if they are good and wish to live on their own property, have to fear, since Your Holiness has so much authority and your friends hold the first offices of the government. Moreover I do not see how the body of the citizens can fail to be contented, for they will see that part of the public offices are already given to them and that the others will gradually fall into their hands, because Your Holiness would sometimes be able to allow the Council to choose some of the Sixty-five when there were vacancies, and in like manner for the Two Hundred, and sometimes you would choose them yourself, according to circumstances. I am sure that in a little while, through the authority of Your Holiness, who would guide everything, the present government would be so changed into the one I propose, and the latter into the present one, that they would come to be the same thing,[18] and a single body, to the peace of the city and the perpetual fame of Your

[17] Cf. *Discourses on Livy*, I, 49, par. 4.

[18] Perhaps the example of Rome led Machiavelli to believe in the possibility of such a change. Cf. the *Discourses on Livy*, I, 9, pars. 3 and 4, below.

Holiness, because your authority would always be able to remedy any defects that might arise.

29 I believe that the greatest honor men can have is that which is willingly given them by their native lands.[19] I believe that the greatest good that can be done, and the most pleasing to God, is that which is done to one's country. In addition to this, no man is so much raised on high by any of his acts as are those who have reformed republics and kingdoms with new laws and institutions. After those who have been gods, such men get the first praises; and because there have been few who have had the opportunity to do it, and still fewer who have known how to do it, the number of those who have done it is small. This sort of glory has been so highly esteemed by men, who have never sought anything except glory, that those who have not been able to set up a state in reality have done it in writing; for Aristotle, Plato, and many others have desired to show the world that if they have not been able to found a commonwealth as did Solon and Lycurgus, they have not failed from ignorance but from lack of opportunity to put their ideas into practice.

30 The heavens do not, then, give a greater gift to a man, nor can they show a way more glorious than this, and among the many blessings that God has given to your house and Your Holiness in person, the greatest is that he has given you power and material for immortality, and the opportunity of far surpassing in this way the glory of your father and your grandfather. Your Holiness should first of all consider that if the city of Florence is kept in its present conditions, it runs a thousand risks, if accidents happen; even before they happen, Your Holiness has to undergo a thousand troubles such as no man can bear; these troubles His Reverence the Cardinal can tell you of, since he has been in Florence for the past months. These difficulties originate partly with the many citizens who are presumptuous and unbearable in their demands, partly with the many who think they do not live securely with things as they are, and therefore do nothing else than assert the government should be reformed. Some say it should be made freer, some that it should be restricted, and none comes to particulars on how it should be restricted or enlarged. They are all in confusion, and though they do not think they are living securely in the present circumstances, they do not know how they wish to adjust the government, and do not believe anybody who

[19] Cf. the suggestions on honor and glory in *The Prince*, Chap. 19, end, and Chapters 24, par. 1, and 26, par. 1, and the *Discourses on Livy*, I, 10, below.

does know. With their confusion they are enough to disturb any well-settled brain.

31 There are only two ways to get rid of these troubles, one is to be sparing with audiences,[20] and not to give anyone courage to ask, even in an ordinary way, or to speak if he is not asked to do so, as did the Duke of illustrious memory;[21] the other is to organize the state in such a way that it will administer itself, and that Your Holiness needs only to give it an occasional glance. Of these two ways the last would free you from perils and annoyances; the first would free you from annoyances alone.

32 But to turn to the perils which are risked with things as they are, I wish to make a prophecy, namely, that if an accident happens, and the city has not been reorganized, one of two things will happen, or both of them at once: either some unforeseen leader will appear in the midst of confusion and attempt to defend his government with arms and violence, or one party will run to open the hall of the Council and make booty of the other. Whichever of these two things happens—and may God forbid it—Your Holiness may imagine that the many deaths, exiles, and acts of extortion resulting from them will be enough to make the most cruel man—not to mention Your Holiness, for you are full of pity—die of sorrow. There is no other way to escape these ills except to act in such a way that the government of the city may in itself stand firm; and it will always stand firm when every man has a share in it, or when every man knows what he has to do and in whom he can trust, and no citizen of any class will be led to desire revolution either through fear for himself or through ambition.[22]

[20] Savonarola said of the tyrant: "To keep up his reputation, he is very ungenerous in giving audiences" (*Tractate on the Organization and Government of Florence*, book 2, chap. 2). This apparently is the *hard*, opposed to *easy to deal with*, of *The Prince*, Chap. 15.

[21] Presumably Lorenzo de' Medici, Duke of Urbino, representative of his family in Florence from 1513 until his death in 1519, the year Machiavelli composed the present *Discourse*.

In a letter probably written in 1513, Machiavelli spoke of Lorenzo as "liberal and agreeable in audience" (*Opere*, VIII, 40).

[22] Both the ambitious and those desperate through fear appear in *The Prince*, Chap. 19, pars. 3 and 5.

THE PRINCE

NICCOLÒ MACHIAVELLI

TO THE

MAGNIFICENT LORENZO DE' MEDICI [1]

1 As a general rule those who wish to win favor with a prince offer him the things they most value and in which they see that he will take most pleasure; so it is often seen that rulers receive presents of horses, arms, pieces of cloth of gold, precious stones, and similar ornaments worthy of their station. So, in my desire to offer myself to Your Magnificence, with some proof of my obligation to you, I have found nothing among my possessions that I cherish more or value higher than I do my knowledge of the actions of great men, gained from long experience in modern affairs and continual reading on ancient ones. Having for a long time thought over and examined these matters with great diligence, I have finally put them into a little volume, which I send to Your Magnificence.

2 And though I judge this work unworthy to appear in your presence, yet I trust your humanity may cause you to accept it, especially since I can make you no greater gift than to furnish a means of enabling you in a very short time to understand all I have learned in many years and with many discomforts and perils. I have not ornamented this work nor filled it with rhetorical devices, or swelling and magnificent words, or other meretricious finery and extrinsic ornament, such as many use in setting forth and adorning their ideas. I wish that my work may be either without ornament or that it may be made pleasing merely by the variety of the matter and the weight of the subject.[2] I trust it will not be considered presumption for a man of low and humble condition

[1] Machiavelli first intended to dedicate *The Prince* to Giuliano de' Medici, who left Florence for Rome in 1513 and died in 1516. Lorenzo became ruler of Florence, under Pope Leo X, in 1513 and held the post until his death in 1519. A document in Machiavelli's hand, but without date, direction, or signature, gives him virtues such as go to make the good prince (Machiavelli, *Opere*, VIII, 39). Tommasini (II, 76) takes it as genuine; he also quotes various favorable opinions of the time, one of which makes Lorenzo little less able than Cesare Borgia (p. 104). For other references to Lorenzo in the present volume, see the Index.

[2] For remarks on the style see the *Introduction*, pars. 93 and 94.

to dare to examine the conduct of princes and give rules for it; those who draw maps of countries observe the nature of the mountains and the high places from a low position on a plain, and to observe the nature of the plains ascend the high mountains; in like fashion, he who wishes to understand the nature of the peoples must be a prince, and he who wishes to understand that of princes must be one of the people.

3 I beseech Your Magnificence, therefore, to accept this little gift in the spirit in which I offer it. If you peruse and read it diligently you will recognize in it my very strong desire for you to attain the greatness that Fortune and your own good qualities promise you.[3] And if, from the lofty summit on which you stand, Your Magnificence will sometimes turn your eyes to these low places, you will perceive how undeservedly I endure the great and continual malice of Fortune.[4]

[3] Cf. Chap. 26, par. 1.

[4] The same expression is applied to Cesare Borgia in Chap. 7, par. 2.

CHAPTER 1

The Various Kinds of Principates and How They Are Gained

1 All the governments and forms of dominion that have had and now have rule over men have been and are either republican or princely. Princely governments are either hereditary, having been headed by the family of the lord for a long time, or they are new. New principates may be altogether new, as was Milan for Francesco Sforza, or they may be additions to the hereditary state of the ruler who acquires them, as is the kingdom of Naples for the king of Spain. Dominions so gained are either used to living under one prince or to being free; they are conquered with the armed forces of others or with one's own, through either fortune or personal ability.[1]

[1] The Italian word is *virtù,* from the Latin *virtus.* Like the Latin, it may have a moral meaning, but since it more usually indicates worth, excellence, capacity, strength, vigor, and the like, it can hardly be translated by the English word *virtue* as now commonly employed. It is one of Machiavelli's most characteristic words.

CHAPTER 2

On Hereditary Principates [1]

1 I shall omit any discussion of republics, because I have elsewhere dealt with them at length.[2] I shall concern myself only with princely governments, and shall proceed to spin my web about the classes mentioned, and discuss how these princely governments can be managed and maintained.

2 I say, then, that hereditary states, being accustomed to the family of their prince, are maintained with fewer difficulties than new ones, because it is enough for the hereditary ruler merely not to go beyond the customs of his ancestors, and otherwise to deal with accidents by moving slowly and cautiously. This is so true that if such a prince is of ordinary diligence, he will always maintain himself in his position, unless some extraordinary and excessive force deprives him of it; and even if he is deprived of it, he will get it back whenever the conqueror falls into misfortune.[3]

3 We have in Italy, for example, the Duke of Ferrara, whc sustained the assaults of the Venetians in 1484 and of Pope Julius in 1510 for no other reason than that he had long been established in that dominion. For a hereditary prince has fewer causes for doing injury and less necessity for it than a new one; hence it is normal that he will be more loved, and if extraordinary vices do not make him hated, it is reasonable that he will naturally have the good wishes of his people. Moreover, if his government is old and has long been settled, new measures and their causes have been forgotten; for one change always leaves points of attachment for the building of another.

[1] For more on this subject, see **Chap. 19, pars. 9, 15**; **Chap. 24, par. 1.**

[2] In the *Discourses on Livy*.

[3] **Cf. Chap. 24, par. 3.**

CHAPTER 3

On Mixed Principates

1 A new princely government, however, encounters difficulties. And first, if it is not wholly new but a member of a larger unit (so that the whole may be called a mixed principate), changes originate chiefly in a natural difficulty found in all new principalities; namely that men are glad to change their rulers, in the belief that they will better themselves, and this belief makes them take arms against the prince; but they deceive themselves in it, because afterwards they learn from experience that they are worse off. This depends on another natural and normal necessity, which makes it always necessary for a new ruler to harm those over whom he places himself, because he must employ soldiers and inflict various injuries incident to his new acquisition. Hence as a new prince you make enemies of all those you have damaged in occupying your position as ruler,[1] and are not able to keep as friends those who have placed you there, because you cannot satisfy them in the manner they have been looking forward to, and you cannot use strong medicine against them because you are under obligation to them; it is always true, even when one's armies are very powerful, that one who is to enter a province needs the favor of the inhabitants. For these reasons Louis XII, the king of France, quickly occupied Milan and quickly lost it. The forces of Lodovico himself were enough to take it away from him the first time, because the people who had opened the gates of the city, finding themselves deceived in their opinions and in the benefits they had looked forward to, were not able to endure the annoyances caused by the new prince.

2 It is indeed quite true that when a country that has rebelled is acquired for the second time, it is less easily lost, because the ruler, taking his opportunity from the rebellion, is less hesitant in making himself solid by punishing those who failed him, getting at the truth about those he suspects, and strengthening his weakest points. So then, the disturbance Duke Lodovico made on the borders was enough to cause the French king to lose Milan the first time, but if the King was to lose the city a second time he had to have all the world against him and his armies had to be destroyed or driven from Italy. This all resulted from the causes mentioned above. Nevertheless, the city was taken from him both the first time and the second.

3 The general causes of the first loss have been discussed;

[1] Cf. Chap. 6, par. 4.

it now remains to give those of the second, and to see what means of prevention he had, and what one in his condition can do, to enable him to maintain himself in his acquisition better than the king of France did. I say, then, that those states which, when they are gained, are joined to the old dominion of him who gains them, either are of the same region and the same language, or they are not. When they are, it is very easy to hold them, especially when they are not accustomed to independence. In order to have secure possession, it is enough to extirpate the line of the prince who was ruling them, because, when their methods of government are kept up and there is no dissimilarity in customs, men live quietly enough with respect to other things. It can be seen that this has been done in Burgundy, Brittany, Gascony, and Normandy, which have long been under the king of France; and though there is some unlikeness of language, yet the customs are similar, and the peoples can easily tolerate each other. He who acquires such new provinces and wishes to hold them, ought to be attentive to two matters: one is that the race of the old prince be wiped out; the other is that there be no change in laws or taxes,[2] so that in a very short time the new province and the old become one body.

4 But when states are acquired in a region different in language, customs, and laws, there are many difficulties. He who will retain them needs to have great good fortune and great shrewdness. One of the most important and effective devices is that the person who acquires them should go into them to live.[3] This will make his possession more secure and more durable. The Turk has used this method in Greece; if, in addition to all the other methods practised by him to hold that country, he had not gone there to live, he could not possibly have held it. The reason is that, since he lives there, he can see troubles when they arise and can remedy them quickly; but if he is not there, he learns of them when they are already big and there is no remedy for them. In addition, the province cannot be plundered by his officials, and the subjects are pleased by having easy access to their prince; hence they have good cause to love him if they intend to be good, and to fear him if they intend to be otherwise. Any foreigner who wishes to assail that state is therefore more hesitant about it. Hence a prince who lives in a new province can lose it only with the greatest difficulty.

[2] Cf. the *Discourse on Reforming the Government of Florence*, pars. 25, 26. The theme of avoiding violent change is discussed in the *Discourses on Livy*, I, 25.

[3] Cf. Chap. 5, pars. 1, 3, and the Letter of January 31, 1514, par. 6, below.

5 Another excellent remedy is to send colonies into one or two places, to serve as fetters for that state. It is necessary either to do this or to keep there sufficient men-at-arms and infantry. Not much is spent on colonies; they can be sent out and kept up without any expense, or very little; this method damages only those—and they are a very small part of the new state—whose fields and houses are taken away in order to give them to the new inhabitants; those whom the prince damages, since they are scattered and poor, can do no harm, and all the others are undisturbed and uninjured. For this reason the latter are likely to be quiet, and on the other hand they are afraid of doing something wrong, and fear that the same thing may happen to them as to those who have been plundered. I conclude that such colonies are not expensive, are very faithful, and do little damage; those who are harmed are unable to do injury, since they are poor and dispersed, as has been said. From this it may be concluded that men should be either caressed or exterminated, because they can avenge light injuries, but not severe ones. The damage done to a man should be such that there is no fear of revenge. But if a prince keeps men-at-arms in his new province, instead of sending colonies, he will spend much more, since he will consume all the revenues of his state in guarding it; hence his acquisition will cause him loss; and he does much more damage, because he injures the whole state by shifting the encampments of his army. Everybody feels something of this annoyance, and the enemies he makes by it are able to injure him because, if they are beaten, they remain at home.[4] In every way then, this method of protection is useless, but the colonial method is useful.

6 He who goes into a region unlike his own, such as has been spoken of, ought also to make himself head and defender of the neighboring minor rulers of the region, endeavor to weaken the powerful ones, and take precautions against any accident that might cause the entrance of a foreigner as powerful as himself. Those in the province who are discontented, either through too great ambition or through fear, will always try to bring in such a foreigner, as was seen long ago when the Etolians brought the Romans into Greece; in fact the natives of every country the Romans occupied brought them into it. And the course of things is such that as soon as a powerful foreigner enters a land, all the less powerful rulers adhere to him, moved by their envy against the one who has

[4] **They are not destroyed, but still live in the country.**

been in power over them.[5] This is so true that the foreigner has to take no trouble to win the lesser rulers, because at once and all together they willingly unite in one body with the supporters he has gained there. He has only to see to it that they do not grasp too much power and too much authority; then, with his forces and their favor, he can put down those who are powerful, and remain in every way master of that land. And he who does not attend carefully to this matter will quickly lose what he has acquired; and while he holds his territory he will have countless difficulties and troubles within it.

7 The Romans fully observed these requirements in the lands they took; they sent colonies, they sheltered the less powerful men without increasing the latter's power, they weakened the more powerful, and did not allow powerful foreigners to obtain prestige. I think the province of Greece alone will be a sufficient example: the Achaeans and the Aetolians were received; the kingdom of Macedonia was weakened; Antiochus was driven out of Greece; the merits of the Achaeans and the Aetolians did not cause Rome to permit their influence to grow; the persuasions of Philip did not ever induce her to be his friend without lessening his importance; the power of Antiochus could not force her to consent to his having any authority in that province. In fact, the Romans did in these matters what all wise princes ought to do, for they are obliged to take thought not merely about immediate rebellions but about future ones, and to use every effort to forestall them, because if they are foreseen they can easily be remedied, but if they are awaited until they are near at hand, medicine cannot be given in time, because the malady has become incurable. The same thing happens in hectic fever: the physicians say that at the beginning the disease is easy to cure and hard to diagnose, but if it is not diagnosed and treated at the beginning, and a long time elapses, it grows easy to diagnose and hard to cure. So it is in matters of state, for if the ills of a policy are recognized early (something that can be done only by a prudent man), they are soon cured; but when, not being diagnosed early,[6] they are allowed to increase in such fashion that everybody recognizes them, no remedy can then be found.

8 So the Romans, seeing difficulties in advance, always remedied them, and did not let them go on in order to escape a war, because they knew that war could not be avoided but would be deferred to the advantage of others. Hence they

[5] Cf. the conduct predicted for the Italians in the first Letter of December 20, 1514, pars. 8, 10.

[6] Cf. Chap. 25, par. 2.

determined to make war with Philip and Antiochus in Greece in order not to have to make it with them in Italy, yet at that time they were able to escape both wars; but they did not wish to do so. Nor were they ever satisfied with the saying that is always in the mouths of the wise men of our days, about enjoying the benefit the day brings with it,[7] but preferred what they could derive from their own vigor and prudence, because Time sweeps everything before him, and can bring along good as well as evil, and evil as well as good.[8]

9 But let us turn to the King of France and consider whether he has done any of the things mentioned. I will speak of Louis and not of Charles, as of one whose proceedings are better seen because he held territory in Italy for a longer time, and you will see that he has done the opposite to what he should have done in order to hold authority in a region unlike his original dominion.

10 King Louis was brought into Italy by the ambition of the Venetians, who wished to gain for themselves by his coming half the state of Lombardy. I do not desire to blame this decision made by the King; it was necessary because he had no friends in Italy, and more than that, because of the conduct of King Charles, all the gates were locked against him. Hence, if he wished to set out to gain a foothold in the country, he was forced to lay hold of such friendships as he could. This wisely adopted plan would have succeeded, provided he had made no error in his other arrangements. When he acquired Lombardy, then, he regained at once all the prestige Charles had deprived him of: Genoa yielded; the Florentines became his friends; the marquis of Mantua, the duke of Ferrara, Bentivogli, the lady of Forlì, the lords of Faenza, Rimini, Camerino, Piombino, the Lucchese, the Pisans, the Sienese, all appeared before him and said they wished to be his friends. Then the Venetians were able to appreciate the folly of the plan they had adopted; to gain two cities in Lombardy they had made the King lord of a third of Italy.

11 Now consider with how little difficulty the King would have been able to retain his high repute in Italy, if he had observed the rules given above, and kept all his friends secure and protected, for there were many of them, and they were weak and afraid, some of the Church, others of the Venetians; therefore they were under a perpetual necessity of keeping on his side, and through their means he could easily secure himself against

[7] Lazzeri quotes from Filippo de' Nerli (*Commentari*, p. 110) the opinion that Piero Soderini believed that "with patience, enjoying, as it is put, the benefit the day brings with it, he could overcome all difficulties."

[8] Connected with the theme of Fortune, Chap. 25.

the great powers of Italy. But he was no sooner in Milan than he did the opposite, by giving aid to Pope Alexander to enable him to occupy the Romagna. Nor did he understand that through this decision he made himself weak, by depriving himself of his friends and those who had thrown themselves into his arms, and made the Church strong, by adding great temporal power to the spiritual power that gives her so much authority. And having made an initial error, he was obliged to go on, until he was forced to come into Italy to put an end to the ambition of Alexander and keep him from becoming lord of Tuscany. Nor was it enough for him to make the Church great and deprive himself of his friends, but, in his desire for the kingdom of Naples, he divided it with the King of Spain. In this way he gave himself an associate in Italy, though at first he was master there, as if he intended the ambitious men of the country and those who were discontented to have a place for refuge, and though he could have left in that kingdom a king who would be his pensionary, he took him away, to put there one who would be able to expel Louis himself.[9]

12 It is truly very natural and common to desire to gain; and when men do it who are strong enough to succeed, they will always be praised and not blamed; but when they do not have power and all the same set out to gain territory, that is an error and worthy of blame. If the King of France, then, was able to assail Naples with his army, he should have done so; if he was not able to attack the kingdom, he should not have divided it. His division of Lombardy with the Venetians deserves to be excused because with this means he got a foothold in Italy; his later action deserves blame because it cannot be excused on account of the same necessity.

13 Louis, then, made these five errors; he destroyed the lesser powers; he increased the might of one already powerful in Italy; he brought into the land a powerful foreigner; he did not come there to live; he did not place colonies there.

14 And even these errors, so long as he lived, might not have damaged him, if he had not made the sixth one, that of depriving the Venetians of power, because, if he had not made the Church great or brought the King of Spain into Italy, it was reasonable and necessary to weaken the Venetians; but after he had made these first decisions, he never should have consented to their ruin, because, so long as they were powerful, they would have kept all others from attempting any enterprise in Lombardy, either because the Venetians would not have agreed to

[9] Illustrated from the Emperor and Francis I in the Letter of March 15, 1525-6, par. 4, below.

such an enterprise unless they became masters of the province, or because the others would not have desired to take it from France to give it to the Venetians; no one would have had the courage to encounter both of them at once. And if somebody says that King Louis yielded the Romagna to Alexander and the kingdom of Naples to the King of Spain in order to avoid a war, I answer by repeating what I have already said, that one should not let a disorder take its course in order to avoid a war, because it is not avoided, but deferred to your disadvantage. And if somebody should give the excuse that the King had pledged his faith to the Pope to undertake the invasion of the Romagna in return for the dissolution of his marriage and a cardinal's hat for Rouen, I refer for answer to what I shall say later about the faith of princes and how it should be observed.[10] King Louis, then, lost Lombardy through his failure to observe any of the rules observed by others who have taken provinces and wished to keep them. And this is not to be wondered at, but is very ordinary and reasonable.

15 Of this matter I spoke at Nantes with Cardinal Rouen, when Valentino (for so Cesare Borgia, son of Pope Alexander, was popularly called) occupied the Romagna; when Cardinal Rouen said that the Italians did not understand war, I replied that the French did not understand politics, for if they had understood them, they would not have allowed the Church to become so great. And experience shows that France made the Church and Spain great in Italy, and that they then caused the ruin of France. From this can be drawn a general rule, which seldom or never fails: He who makes another powerful ruins himself, for he makes the other so by either shrewdness or force, and both of these qualities are feared by the one who becomes powerful.[11]

[10] Chap. 18.

[11] Cf. the *Capitolo on Ingratitude* 172-83:

When you make a change in rule, the prince you have set up always fears lest you take away what you have given him.

He does not observe to you faith or agreement, because his fear of you is more powerful within him than the obligation he has contracted.

And for as long a time as this fear lasts, he strives to see your race exterminated, and the burial of you and yours.

Hence he who serves denies himself often, and then for his good service gets as a reward miserable life and violent death.

Cf. the *Life of Castruccio Castracani*, par. 65.

CHAPTER 4

Why the Kingdom of Darius Which Alexander Occupied Did Not Break Away from His Successors after the Death of Alexander

1 In view of the difficulties in holding a state newly acquired, one cannot but wonder at the empire of Alexander the Great. He became lord of Asia in a few years; and died when he had scarcely occupied the land. It seems reasonable that all that state should then have rebelled; yet the successors of Alexander maintained themselves in it and had no difficulties in holding it except such as arose among themselves because of their own ambitions. I answer that the principalities of which there is any historical record are managed in two different ways: in the first, one man is prince and all the other officials are slaves, who act as ministers, and aid in governing the kingdom through his grace and permission; in the second type, there are a prince and barons, and the latter hold their positions not through the grace of their lord but through the antiquity of their blood. Such barons have states and subjects of their own, who recognize them as lords and have a natural attachment to them. The ruler has most authority in governments administered by a prince and his slaves, because in all the province nobody is recognized as a superior except himself, and if the people obey any other they think of him as a minister and appointee, and do not feel any special love for him.

2 The examples of these two kinds of government in our times are the Turk and the king of France. The whole monarchial administration of the Turk is controlled by one lord; the others are his servants; and dividing his kingdom into sanjaks, he sends out different administrators and changes and varies them as seems good to him. But the king of France is placed in the midst of a multitude of lords, long established in their positions and accepted and loved by their subjects. They have their privileges, which the king cannot take away except at his peril. One who considers, then, either of these two types of government, will see that the position of the Turk is hard to take away from him, but easy to hold when it is obtained. So, on the other hand, one will observe that in some respects it is easier to take possession of the government of France, but much more difficult to keep it.

3 The causes of the difficulty in conquering the kingdom of the Turk are that it is not possible to be invited to invade the land by the princes of that kingdom, nor to hope that an attempt at conquest will be made easier by the rebellion of the king's officers; this comes from the reasons given above, for since the officials are all slaves and bound to their lord, it is hard to bribe them; and even if they are bribed, not much that is of use can be hoped from them, because they cannot carry the people with them, for the reasons I have given. Therefore he who assails the Turk must of necessity expect to find a united front, and must rely on his own power rather than on the defects of others. But when the Turk is conquered and broken in the field in such a way that he cannot reëstablish his army, there is nothing to be disturbed about except the family of the prince; when that is exterminated,[1] there is nobody to fear, for there is no one else who has credit with the people; and as the conqueror, before his victory, could expect no aid from the king's followers, so afterward he has no reason to fear them.

4 The opposite occurs in kingdoms governed like that of France: you can enter them easily, if you win to your side some baron of the kingdom, because there are always some lords who are discontented and desire revolution; these, for the reasons given, can open you the way to control of the country and make victory easy for you. But afterwards if you wish to maintain your conquest, these conditions will cause you innumerable difficulties, both with those who have aided you and with those you have overcome. Nor is it enough for you to exterminate the family of the prince, because the nobles will still be left to take the lead in new rebellions, and since you can neither satisfy them nor exterminate them, you will lose your position whenever there is an opportunity for revolt.

5 Now if you consider to which type the government of Darius belonged, you will find it like the kingdom of the Turk; and therefore it was necessary for Alexander first to defeat him completely and to take away his power for putting an army in the field; but after the victory, when Darius was dead, control was securely in Alexander's hands, for the reasons discussed above. His successors, if they had been united, would have been able to enjoy it at their ease; and there were no tumults in that kingdom except those they stirred up themselves. But states constituted like France cannot be retained with such quiet. The frequent rebellions of Spain, France, and Greece against the Romans had their cause in the many princely powers in those states, for as long as the memory of them endured, the Roman occupation was uncertain; but when the memory of those powers was blotted out by the long-established might of the Empire, the Romans became secure possessors. Hence when

[1] Cf. Chap. 5, par. 3.

later the Romans fought among themselves, each man was able to carry with him part of those provinces, according to the authority he had obtained within them; and after the families of the ancient lords were wiped out, the provinces recognized only the Romans.

6 When all these things are considered, then, no one should marvel at the ease with which Alexander retained his dominion over Asia, and at the difficulty that many others, such as Pyrrhus and the like, have had in keeping what they have gained. The contrast is not a matter of the great or small prowess of the conqueror but of the difference between the lands they conquered.

CHAPTER 5

The Method of Administering States and Princedoms That, Before They Were Occupied, Lived According to Their Own Laws

1 As I have said,[1] when the states that are acquired are accustomed to live according to their own laws and in liberty, there are three methods by which one may hope to hold them: the first is to ruin them; the second is to go there to live in person; the third is to let them live according to their own laws, taking tribute from them and setting up there an organization composed of a few who will keep the province friendly to you. That organization, being created by the prince, knows that it is not able to exist without his friendship and power, and that it must do everything to sustain him. A city used to living in freedom can be held more easily by means of its own citizens than in any other way, if you intend to preserve it [rather than ruin it].

2 Examples of this are the Spartans and the Romans. The Spartans held Athens and Thebes by setting up there an organization of a few; nevertheless, they lost them. The Romans, to hold Capua, Carthage, and Numantia, dismantled them and did not lose them; they planned to hold Greece as the Spartans had done, making her free and leaving her laws in force, but they were unsuccessful to such an extent that they were obliged to dismantle many cities of that province in order to hold it. In truth there is no secure mode of possessing such cities except ruin. And he who becomes master of a city accustomed to live in freedom and does not dismantle it, may expect to be undone by it, for in rebellion it always has recourse to the name of liberty and its ancient laws, which are never forgotten either by reason of length of time or of benefits bestowed. And if the inhabitants are not disunited or scattered, nothing that can be done or planned will make them forget that name or those laws, and on the slightest occasion they will at once have recourse to them, as the Pisans did a hundred years after they had been reduced to servitude by the Florentines.

3 When cities or provinces are used to living under a prince, and the ruling family is exterminated, the subjects on one hand are used to obedience and on the other have no old prince; so they do not agree to set up one among themselves, and they do not know how to live in freedom; hence they are slow to take arms, and a prince can easily conquer them and establish au-

[1] In Chap. 3.

thority over them.[2] But in republics there is greater life, greater hate, and more desire for vengeance, and the memory of ancient liberty does not and cannot allow them to be quiet; hence the most secure way is to destroy them or to live there.[3]

[2] Cf. *Discourses on Livy,* I, 16, par. 1, below.

[3] Cf. Chap. 3, pars. 4, 13, and the Letter of January 31, 1514-5, pars. 6, 7. The advice that a prince live in his princedom fits the condition of one who is to become lord of one or two Italian cities rather than of one who is to attempt to unify Italy. Was Machiavelli, when he wrote this chapter, still thinking of a limited principality for Giuliano de' Medici rather than of the union of Italy under Lorenzo? Or is he merely recording facts as he had seen them, perhaps with Louis XII, discussed in Chap. 3, still in mind?

CHAPTER 6

ON NEW PRINCIPATES THAT ARE GAINED BY VIGOROUS USE OF ONE'S OWN ARMIES

1 No one should think it strange if in speaking as I shall on princely governments wholly new,[1] and on princes and states, I bring up very great men as examples; men almost always walk in the paths beaten by others, and proceed in their acts by imitation, and yet are not able to follow in every respect the ways of others nor to equal the capacities of those they imitate; therefore a prudent man ought always to follow in the footsteps of great men, and to imitate those who have been especially excellent, in order that his prowess, if it does not equal theirs, at least may give some odor of it.[2] He should act like a prudent archer, who when he sees that the object he wishes to hit is far distant, and knows just what the force of his bow is, directs his arrow much higher than the target, not in order that the arrow may attain that height, but that he may be able, through directing his shot so high, to hit what he aims at.

2 I say, then, as to completely new princely governments, that where there is a new prince, it is more or less difficult to maintain them according as the one who acquired them has more or less ability. And because either prowess or fortune must be assumed when a private citizen becomes a prince, it appears that one or the other of the two should to some extent lessen many of his difficulties; yet nevertheless he who owes least to fortune is in the strongest position. It also makes the problem of such a prince easier that he has no other states and is obliged to make his own residence in his new state.[3] But to come to those who have become princes through their own ability and not through fortune, I say that the most excellent are Moses, Cyrus, Romulus, Theseus, and the like. And though there should be no discussion of Moses, since he was a mere executor of the things he was commanded to do by God, yet he ought to be admired if only for the grace that made him worthy to speak with God. But let us consider Cyrus and the others who have acquired and founded kingdoms: you will find them all admirable; and their actions and individual methods of government, when well considered, will seem not inharmonious with those of Moses, who had so great a teacher. And if you ex-

[1] Chapters 6-9 are especially concerned with new princedoms, and much in following chapters relates to them, as Chap. 13, par. 3; Chap. 19, pars. 8, 12, 13, 18; Chap. 20, pars. 2, 3, 6-8. All look forward to the new prince who shall deliver Italy, Chap. 26.

[2] Cf. Chap. 14, par. 5.

[3] Cf. Chap. 3, par. 4, and the Letter of January 31, 1514-5, par. 6, below.

amine their actions and their lives, it will not appear that they had anything from Fortune other than opportunity, which presented to them matter to which they could give the form they wished;[4] without that opportunity the vigor of their spirits would have been lost, and without that vigor the opportunity would have come in vain.

3 It was, then, necessary for Moses to find the people of Israel in Egypt, enslaved and oppressed by the Egyptians, in order that, to escape from slavery, they should make up their minds to follow him. It was requisite that Romulus should not find room in Alba, and should be exposed at his birth,[5] if he was going to become king of Rome and founder of that nation. It was necessary that Cyrus should find the Persians discontented with the rule of the Medes, and the Medes soft and effeminate after a long peace. Theseus could not have showed his ability if he had not found the Athenians dispersed. These opportunities therefore made these men successful, and their excellent abilities made the opportunities known to them. Hence their native lands gained honor from them and became very prosperous.

4 Those who, like these, become princes in ways requiring personal ability obtain their power with difficulty but hold it with ease; and the difficulties they have in gaining the throne are caused partly by the new laws and methods of government they are forced to introduce in order to give a firm basis to their government and to their own security. It ought to be considered that there is nothing more difficult to plan, more unlikely to succeed with, or more dangerous to manage than to take the lead in introducing new methods of government, because the introducer has as enemies all those who profit from the old methods, and as only lukewarm defenders all those who will profit from the new ones. This lukewarmness results partly from fear of their adversaries, who have the laws on their side, partly from the incredulity of men, who do not really trust a new program unless they learn by experience that it is firmly established. Hence it comes about that whenever those who are hostile have occasion to attack, they do it with strong party-feeling; but the others resist lukewarmly, so that both they and the prince are in danger.

5 If, therefore, anyone wishes to give proper attention to this matter, he must examine whether the innovators stand on their own feet or depend on others, that is, whether, in order to carry on their work, they must make requests, or whether they can

[4] Inert matter is shaped by the spirit.

[5] Cf. *Castruccio Castracani*, par. 4, below.

use compulsion. In the first case they come out badly and do not accomplish anything; but when they depend on themselves and can use force, then they rarely run any risk. For this reason, all armed prophets succeed, and unarmed prophets come to ruin. And in addition to what I have said, the nature of the people is mutable; it is easy to persuade them of anything, but difficult to keep them in that persuasion. Hence the prophet should be so well prepared that when they no longer believe he can make them believe by force. Moses, Cyrus, Theseus, and Romulus could not have made their constitutions respected for very long if they had been disarmed. So in our time it happened to Fra Girolamo Savonarola,[6] who fell in ruin in the midst of his new measures for government when the multitude began not to believe him; he had no means of holding firm those who once had believed nor of making unbelievers believe. Hence such rulers as these have great difficulties in managing their affairs, and in the road leading to supreme power encounter many dangers, which they must overcome with personal prowess. But when they have overcome them and begin to be venerated, and have exterminated those of their own rank who envy them,[7] they remain powerful, secure, honored, and happy.

6 To examples so exalted I wish to add a lesser example, but truly he is not unworthy of comparison with them, and I hope is enough to represent all the others like him. This man is Hiero of Syracuse. He rose from a private station to be prince of Syracuse, nor did he receive anything from Fortune except opportunity, because when the Syracusans were overpowered by their enemies they chose him as their commander, and in that position he conducted himself so well that he deserved to be made prince. And he was of such ability, even in a private station, that he who writes of him says "that he lacked nothing of kingship except the kingdom."[8] He disbanded the old army, and organized a new one; gave up his old alliances and made new ones; and since he had alliances and soldiers who were his own, he was able to erect on such a foundation any edifice he wished to. In short he endured great fatigue in acquisition and little in maintenance.

[6] See the Index.
[7] Cf. Chap. 9, par. 2.
[8] Justin, XXIII, 4.

CHAPTER 7

ON NEW PRINCIPATES THAT ARE OBTAINED THROUGH THE MILITARY POWER OF OTHERS AND FROM FORTUNE [1]

1 Men in private stations who become princes merely through the aid of Fortune, attain their rank with little effort but uphold it with a great deal. They have no difficulty on the road because they fly to their thrones, but all their difficulties come after they have reached their stations. I refer to men who have a place as ruler given to them for money or as a favor from him who gives it, as happened to many Greeks in the cities of Ionia and the Hellespont, where they were made princes by Darius, that they might hold their cities for his security and glory; of the same sort were the emperors who passed from a private station to the imperial throne by bribing the soldiers. Such princes depend merely on the will and fortune (two most uncertain and unstable bases) of those who have set them up; they do not know how to hold their positions and cannot do it. They do not know how because, unless a man possesses great power to think and act, it is not reasonable that after having lived always in a private station he should know how to command; they cannot do it because they do not have forces that are friendly and faithful to them. Positions of authority that come suddenly, like all natural things that spring up and grow quickly, cannot have roots and other parts so well developed that the first bad weather will not destroy them. So those I speak of who suddenly become princes are not wise enough to see that they must at once get ready to keep what Fortune has placed in their laps, and that the foundations others laid before becoming princes, they must lay afterward.

2 I wish to give examples of the two ways of becoming prince I have mentioned—namely, through personal vigor and through the aid of Fortune—that have happened within my memory; they are those of Francesco Sforza and Cesare Borgia.[2] Francesco, through due means and because of his great ability, left a private station to become duke of Milan, and what he had acquired with a thousand difficulties he kept with little effort. On the other hand Cesare Borgia, called by the people Duke Valentino, gained his position as prince with the fortune of his father, and with the same fortune lost it, even though he used every effort and did all the things that a prudent and able man should do to put down his roots in the positions that the arms

[1] Cf. the Letter of January 31, 1514, pars. 5-7, below.

[2] The *Life of Castruccio Castracani* furnishes an example of the first method. For more on Cesare Borgia see the Index.

and fortune of others had granted him. As was said above, he who does not lay foundations early enough, can, if he possesses enough ability, lay them later, though only with difficulty for the architect and peril to the building. If, then, one considers the progress the Duke made, one will see that he laid strong foundations for his future power. I think it is not out of place to consider these, because for my part I do not know what better precepts I could give a new prince than the example of his actions; and if his methods did not bring him success it was not his fault, because his failure sprang from an extraordinary and extreme malice of Fortune.[3]

3 In attempting to make the Duke his son great, Alexander VI encountered many difficulties both present and future. First, he did not see any way in which he could make him lord of any state that was not a state of the Church, and though he wished to take for Caesare the Church's territory of the Romagna, he knew that the Duke of Milan and the Venetians would not consent to it, because Faenza and Rimino were already under the protection of the Venetians. He saw besides that the arms of Italy, especially those he might have availed himself of, were in the hands of men who would naturally fear the greatness of the Pope; therefore he was not able to trust these arms, since they were all in the power of the Orsini and Colonnesi and their associates.[4] Hence it was necessary that existing arrangements should be upset and the dominions of Venice thrown into confusion, if the Pope was to control part of them in security. This was easy because he found that the Venetians, for other reasons, were planning to get the French to return to Italy; so he not merely did not oppose this, but made it easier by dissolving the early marriage of King Louis. So the King marched into Italy with the aid of the Venetians and the consent of Alexander; he was hardly in Milan when the Pope obtained soldiers from him for his enterprise in the Romagna; this undertaking was conceded to him for the sake of the King's reputation.[5]

4 The Duke, having acquired the Romagna and overthrown the Colonnesi, and wishing to keep what he had gained and to proceed further, was impeded by two things: one was that

[3] Fortune appeared on the reverse of one of Cesare's medals, reproduced in E. Rodocanachi's *Historie de Rome, Une Cour Princière au Vatican pendant la Renaissance* (Paris, 1925), pl. 22, and in D. Erskine Muir's *Machiavelli*, p. 150.

[4] Feudal barons of Rome and its vicinity.

[5] Apparently a reference to the King's pledge (Chap. 3, par. 14), which he could not break without injury to his reputation.

The clause is, however, often interpreted to mean that the Romagna yielded to the invaders because of the military reputation of the French.

his forces did not appear faithful; the other was the will of France; that is, he thought the Orsini forces, of which he had availed himself, would leave him in the air, and not merely would hinder him from gaining more, but would take from him what he had already acquired, and that the King also would do the same thing. His suspicions of the Orsini were confirmed when, after the capture of Faenza, he assailed Bologna, for he saw that they were lukewarm in their attack; and as to the King's attitude, the Duke found that out when, after seizing the dukedom of Urbino, he assailed Tuscany; from this attempt the King made him desist. Hence the Duke determined not to depend further on the arms and fortune of others.[6]

5 His first move was to weaken the parties of the Orsini and Colonnesi in Rome, for he won to him all their adherents who were gentlemen, making them his own gentlemen and giving them large pensions; he also honored them, according to their ranks, with military and civil offices, so that in a few months all affection for the Roman families was banished from their hearts and their allegiance turned to the Duke. After this he dispersed the leaders of the house of Colonna and waited for an opportunity to wipe out the chiefs of the Orsini; his opportunity was good and he used it better, for the Orsini, finding out too late that the greatness of the Duke and the Church was their ruin, held a meeting at Magione, in the Perugino; from this came the rebellion of Urbino, the tumults of the Romagna, and innumerable dangers to the Duke, all of which he overcame with the aid of the French. But though he regained his reputation, he no longer relied on the King of France or on other foreign forces; hence, in order not to risk using them, he turned to deceptions. And he understood so well how to dissimulate his purpose that the Orsini themselves were reconciled with him through the mediation of Signor Paulo;[7] in dealing with this man the Duke did not neglect any sort of favor to make him loyal, giving him money, clothing, and horses. As a result, the credulity of the Orsini led them to Sinigaglia, into the hands of the Duke. When these leaders were put out of the way and their partisans had become his friends, he had laid pretty good foundations

[6] Cf. Chap. 6, par. 5; Chap. 17, last par. The topic of self-reliance is frequent in *The Prince*.

[7] On simulation cf. Chap. 18, par. 3. Cesare is called a "very great pretender" in Machiavelli's little work entitled *A Description of the Method Used by Duke Valentino in Killing Vitellozzo Vitelli, Oliverotto da Fermo, the Signor Pagolo and the Duke of Gravina Orsini*. It is sometimes assumed that Machiavelli called this the "bellissimo inganno" (most beautiful deception) of Sinigaglia, but the words occur in Paulus Jovius' *Life of Cesare Borgia*.

for his power, since he had the entire Romagna and the dukedom of Urbino; above all, it appeared to him that he had obtained the friendship of the Romagna and won over all its peoples by allowing them to get a fore-taste of prosperity.

6 And because this method deserves to be noticed and imitated by others, I do not wish to pass over it. When the Duke took Romagna, he found it controlled by lords of little power, who plundered their subjects rather than ruled them justly, and gave them cause for disunion rather than union, so that the province was full of theft, violence, and lawlessness of every sort.[8] Hence he judged it necessary to give the province good administration if he wished to make it peaceful and obedient to the kingly arm. Therefore he set over it Messer Remirro de Orco, a cruel and vigorous man, to whom he gave the most ample power. In a little while Remirro made the region peaceful and united, and gained a great reputation.[9] The Duke then judged that such excessive power was not necessary, for he feared it would become hateful, so he set up in the center of the province a civil court with an excellent president, in which each city had its own lawyer. And because he knew that the past rigor had produced some hatred, he decided to purge the minds of the people and gain them altogether for himself, by showing that if any cruelty had gone on, it did not originate with him but in the harsh nature of his minister. Having taken an opportunity for this, one morning at Cesena he had Remirro placed on the Piazza in two pieces, with a piece of wood and a bloody knife beside him. The savagery of that spectacle caused the people at the same time satisfaction and astonishment.[10]

7 But let us turn back to the point where we left off. I say that the Duke found he was very powerful and in part secured from immediate dangers because he was armed to his liking and had in great part destroyed the forces that, because they were near at hand, were able to damage him. Yet he was still obliged, if he wished to go on with his conquests, to worry about the King of France; he knew that the King, who at last had found out his error, would not support him. He began, therefore, to seek new friendships and to waver in his relations to the King, as in the expedition that the French made to the kingdom of Naples against the Spaniards who besieged Gaeta. His intention was to make himself secure against the French, and he would soon have succeeded in it, if Alexander had lived.

[8] Cf. *Discourses on Livy*, III, 29.

[9] Cf. the Letter of January 31, 1514-5, par. 7, below.

[10] See Gilbert, *Machiavelli's "Prince" and Its Forerunners*, pp. 156-8.

8 And these were his methods of conduct with respect to things of the present. But as to the future, he was obliged to fear, first, that a successor to the papacy would not be friendly to him and would seek to take away what Alexander had given him. Against this he thought to protect himself in four ways: First, by exterminating all the families of those lords he had dispossessed, thus depriving the Pope of opportunity to restore them. Second, by gaining all the gentlemen of Rome, as I have said, in order to be able to hold the Pope in check with them. Third, by making the College of Cardinals his, so far as it was possible. Fourth, by gaining so much power, before the Pope died, that he would of himself be able to resist a first assault. Of these four things, at the death of Alexander he had completed three, and he had almost finished the fourth: of the dispossessed rulers he had killed as many as he was able to catch, and very few escaped; he had gained the Roman gentlemen, and had a strong party in the College of Cardinals; with respect to new territory, he had planned to become lord of Tuscany, and already possessed Perugia and Piombino, and had taken Pisa under his protection. And as soon as he no longer needed to trouble about the King of France (and he was on the verge of not needing to, because the French had already been deprived of the kingdom of Naples by the Spaniards, with the result that each of them was obliged to buy his friendship), he was going to leap into Pisa. After this, Lucca and Siena would be yielding at once, partly through envy of the Florentines, partly through fear; and the Florentines would be standing helpless against him.

9 If he had carried this plan through (and it was to be executed the very year Alexander died) he would have acquired so many forces and such a great reputation, that he would have been master of his own conduct, and no longer dependent on the fortune and forces of others but on his own power and ability to act. But Alexander died five years after Cesare first drew the sword. He left his son with only his control of the Romagna consolidated, with all the others in the air, between two powerful hostile armies, and sick unto death. Yet there was in the Duke such energy and such ability, and he knew so well how men are to be gained or lost, and so strong were the foundations he had laid in such a short time, that if he had not had hostile armies right on him, or if he had been in health, he would have overcome every difficulty. And that his foundations were good can be seen: the Romagna awaited him more than a month; in Rome, though he was but half alive, he was secure; though the Baglioni, the Vitelli, and the Orsini came to Rome, they did nothing against him; even if he could not secure the choice of the pope he wanted, he could at least keep anyone from becoming pope against his will. If only he had been in health at the death of Alexander, everything would have been easy. He said to me on the day when Julius II was made pope that he had thought of what could happen if his father died, and had found a remedy for everything, except that he had never thought that on the death of his father he himself would also be in danger of dying.

10 So when all the actions of the Duke are brought together I do not see how I can censure him; on the contrary, I think I am right in offering him as worthy of imitation to all those who have attained authority through Fortune and by the aid of the armies of others. With his great spirit and lofty intention, he could not have conducted himself other than he did; his designs were thwarted only by the shortness of Alexander's life and his own illness. Any new prince, then, who decides that in his new principality he must protect himself from his enemies, gain friends, win victories either by force or fraud,[11] make himself loved and feared by the people and followed and revered by the soldiers,[12] purge away those who have power or reason to damage him, replace ancient laws and customs with new ones,[13] be severe and kind, magnanimous and liberal,[14] rid himself of a disloyal army and create a new one,[15] maintain the friendship of kings and princes in such a way that they will think him a person they should be glad to favor and hesitate to injure[16]—such a new prince cannot find more stimulating examples than the acts of the Duke.

11 Cesare can be censured only in the election of Julius as pope, and in this he made a bad choice, because, as I have said, though he could not make a pope according to his wishes, he was able to prevent any man from becoming pope; he should never have consented to the choice of any cardinal he had injured, or who, on becoming pope, would have to fear him. For men do injury either through fear or through hate. Those whom he had injured were, among others, San Piero ad Vincula,[17] Colonna, San Giorgio, and Ascanio; every one of

[11] Cf. *Castruccio Castracani*, par. 35, below.

[12] Cf. Chap. 17, pars. 3 ff.

[13] Cf. Chap. 6, par. 4; Chap. 8, par. 5; Chap. 26, par. 3; *Discourses on Livy*, I, 9, below.

[14] Cf. Chap. 16.

[15] Cf. Chap. 6, last par.; Chap. 13, par. 4.

[16] Cf. Chap. 19, par. 4. At the end of his *Discourse on the Method of Treating the People of Valdichiana*, Machiavelli speaks of Cesare as having planned to make himself secure by reason of his own strength, so that his friendship would be an object of desire to other potentates.

[17] Later Pope Julius II.

the others, if he became pope, had to fear him, except Rouen and the Spaniards, the latter because they were allied with him, and Rouen because of the power derived from his connection with the kingdom of France. Therefore the Duke, before everything else, ought to have made a Spaniard pope, and if he could not do so, ought to have agreed that it should be Rouen and not San Piero ad Vincula. He who believes that new benefits make great men forget old injuries, deceives himself.[18] The Duke erred, therefore, in this choice, and it was the cause of his final ruin.

[18] Cf. Chap. 5, last par., and the Letter of April 29, 1513, par. 9, below.

CHAPTER 8

On Those Who Attain Princely Power through Evil Deeds

1 But because a private citizen may become a prince in two ways, which cannot be attributed wholly to Fortune or to ability, it seems to me that these ways should not be omitted, though I can treat of one of them more fully in my work on republics.[1] The two are: first, a man climbs to authority by some criminal and wicked path; or, second, a private citizen by the favor of his fellow citizens becomes prince of his native land.[2] As to the first, it will be set forth by means of two examples, one ancient, the other modern, without other treatment of the merits of this method, because I judge it will be enough to imitate them, if anyone is obliged to.

2 Agathocles the Sicilian, not merely a private citizen but one of low and abject fortune, became king of Syracuse. The son of a potter, he lived wickedly throughout the earlier periods of his life, yet he accompanied his wickedness with such ability of mind and body that, having entered the army, he rose through the various ranks until he became praetor of Syracuse. Being firmly seated in this position, and having determined to become prince and to hold with violence and without obligation to others what had been conceded to him by agreement, and having an understanding about his design with Hamilcar the Carthaginian, who was serving with the armies in Sicily, one morning he gathered the people and the senate of Syracuse, as if it were necessary to settle some public business. At a sign agreed on, he had his soldiers kill all the senators and the richest of the citizens;[3] when they were dead he seized and held power over that city without any popular opposition. And though he was twice defeated by the Carthaginians and finally besieged, not merely was he able to defend the city, but, leaving a great part of his soldiers to resist the siege, he invaded Africa with the rest, and in a short time freed Syracuse from the siege and brought the Carthaginians to dire need; they were obliged to make a treaty with him, to be contented with the possession of Africa, and to leave Sicily to Agathocles.

3 He who considers the actions and life of this man, will

[1] That is, the *Discourses on Livy*, I, 52; III, 8, 34.

[2] See Chap. 9.

[3] Agathocles is condemned because he was selfish, but in the *Discourses on Livy*, I, 9, below, Machiavelli approves similar conduct when engaged in for the good of the state.

see nothing or very little that can be attributed to Fortune, for, as was said above, he became prince, not because of the favor of Fortune but by passing through the various military ranks, which he gained with a thousand troubles and perils; and then he maintained his position with many spirited and dangerous exploits. Yet it cannot be called true prowess to kill his fellow citizens, to betray his friends, to be without faith, without pity, without religion; such courses enable one to gain dominion, but not glory.[4] If one should consider the vigor of Agathocles in entering and issuing from perils, and the greatness of his spirit in enduring and overcoming adversity, there appears no reason why he should have to be judged inferior to any of the most excellent generals. Yet his ferocious cruelty and inhumanity, with innumerable acts of wickedness, do not permit him to be celebrated among the greatest men. It is not possible, then, to attribute to fortune or true prowess what he accomplished without the aid of either.

4 In our times, while Alexander VI was reigning, Liverotto of Fermo, who had been left fatherless in his childhood some years before, was brought up by one of his maternal uncles called Giovanni Fogliani, and in early youth sent to military service under Paulo Vitelli, so that he might learn the profession and attain high rank as a soldier. After Paulo's death he served under Vitellozzo his brother, and in a very short time, because he was intelligent, and vigorous in both body and spirit, he became the first man in the army. But because he thought it servile to obey someone else, he determined, with the aid of some citizens of Fermo who were fonder of servitude than of the liberty of their native city, and with the favor of the Vitelli family, to occupy Fermo. Hence he wrote to Giovanni Fogliani that, since he had been away from home many years, he wished to come to see him and the city, and also to examine his patrimony. And because his only concern was to gain glory he wished to come with dignity, accompanied by a hundred horsemen, his friends and servants, that his fellow citizens might see he had not spent his time for nothing, and he begged his uncle to be so good as to arrange that he should be honorably received by the Firmani, for this would be an honor not only to him, but also to Giovanni, because Liverotto was his foster child. Accordingly Giovanni did not omit any fitting attention to his nephew, and had him ceremoniously received by the Firmani; Liverotto then took

[4] See the *Introduction*, pars. 50-1.

up his lodging in his own houses.[5]

5 After having passed some days there, and attended to secret arrangements necessary for his future wickedness, he made a solemn feast, to which he invited Giovanni Fogliani and all the first citizens of Fermo. And after they had finished the food and all the entertainments usual at such banquets, Liverotto according to his plan began to speak of serious matters and mentioned the greatness of Pope Alexander and Cesare his son, and their undertakings. When Giovanni and the others responded to his discourse, he all at once rose up, saying that these were things to speak of in a more secret place, and retired into a chamber where Giovanni and all the other citizens followed him. No sooner were they seated than soldiers came out from secret places in that room and killed Giovanni and all the others. After that slaughter, Liverotto mounted his horse, rushed through the city, and assailed the supreme magistrates in their palace; in their fear they were obliged to obey him and to set up a government of which he made himself prince.

6 Since all those were dead who were able to injure him if they were discontented, and he provided himself admirably with new regulations both civil and military, he not only was secure in the city of Fermo for the year during which he was prince, but also became an object of dread to all his neighbors. And it would have been as difficult to attack him as it was to attack Agathocles, if he had not allowed himself to be deceived when Cesare Borgia seized the Orsini and Vitelli at Sinigaglia, as was mentioned above. There Liverotto was taken, one year after the parricide he had committed, and strangled along with Vitellozzo, who had been his teacher in both virtues and evil deeds.

7 Anybody can wonder, then, how it was that Agathocles or anyone like him, after innumerable betrayals and cruelties, could live securely for so long a time in his native city and defend himself from his external enemies; moreover, he was never plotted against by his fellow-citizens; yet many others who have employed cruelty have not been able to hold their positions even in peaceful times, not to mention the uncertain times of war. I believe this difference results from the good or bad use of cruelties. Their use can be called good (if the

[5] Guicciardini says that Liverotto "entertained in his house Messer Giovanni Frangiani his uncle, a man of great influence, with a number of the other chief citizens of Fermo" (*History of Florence*, Chap. 26); after the banquet he killed them. This makes clear that the murders were committed in the house of Liverotto, not, as is sometimes understood from *The Prince*, in that of Giovanni.

word *good* can be applied to what is bad) when they are committed at one stroke,[6] and because it is necessary for a ruler to secure himself; yet afterwards he does not continue with them, but takes the opposite course of doing all he can for the profit of his subjects. Cruelties badly used are those which, though few at the beginning, increase with time, rather than disappear. Those who use the first method are able to make some improvement in their condition in the sight of both God and men, as did Agathocles. The others cannot possibly maintain themselves.

8 All this goes to show that anyone who seizes control of a state ought to consider carefully all the injuries he must do, and do them all at one stroke, so that he will not have to undertake new ones every day, but may be able, since he does not repeat them, to give men a feeling of security and gain them to his side by benefiting them. He who does otherwise, either through timidity or bad advice, must always hold his dagger in his hand, and can never rely on his subjects, because the new and continual injuries they suffer do not allow them to feel sure of him. Injuries should all be done together in order that men may taste their bitterness but a short time, and be but little disturbed. Benefits ought to be conferred a little at a time, that their flavor may be tasted better. Above all, a prince ought to live with his subjects in such a way that no accident either favorable or unfavorable can force him to change his policy; if you wait until adversity forces change upon you, you do not have time to do anything bad, and any good you do will be of no use, because it will be looked upon as forced and you will get no gratitude for it.

[6] For severity at one stroke, see *Discourses on Livy*, I, 16, par. 5, below.

CHAPTER 9

ON CIVIC PRINCIPALITY[1]

1 Now I shall deal with the second method,[2] namely, when a private citizen becomes ruler of his native city not through wickedness or other intolerable violence, but with the favor of his fellow citizens. This can be called civic principality. To attain it one does not need pure ability or pure fortune but rather fortunate astuteness. I say that a man rises to such a position as prince with the favor of either the people or the upper classes. For in every city these two opposite parties are found; and the reason is that the people wish not to be dictated to and oppressed by the upper classes, and the upper classes desire to dictate to and oppress the people. From these two opposed longings there grows up in the city one of three results: absolutism, liberty, or license.

2 Absolute rule is brought about either by the people or the upper class, according as one or the other of these parties has opportunity for it. For if the upper class see that they cannot resist the people, they begin to raise the reputation of one of themselves, and make him prince, so that under his shadow they may be able to satisfy their appetites. The people, on the other hand, seeing that they cannot resist the upper class, raise the reputation of one man and make him prince, in order to be defended by his authority. He who becomes ruler with the aid of the great maintains himself with more difficulty than he who becomes ruler with the aid of the people, because the first is in the position of a prince with a good many subjects whom he regards as his equals,[3] and for this reason cannot direct them or manage them as he wishes to. But he who becomes prince with popular favor stands alone, and has no subjects, or at most only a few, who are not ready to obey him. Further, one cannot satisfy the upper class with honor and without injury to others, but it is possible to satisfy the people in that way, because the purpose of the people is more just than that of the upper class, since the latter wish to oppress and the former not to be oppressed.[4] Besides, when the people are unfriendly the prince never can make himself secure, for he has too many against him; but he can secure himself against the upper class, because they are few. The worst that a prince can expect from an unfriendly people is that they will desert him; but when the upper class are hostile

[1] With this chapter cf. the *Discourses on Livy*, I, 16, pars. 5 and 6, below.

[2] See Chap. 8, par. 1.

[3] Cf. Chap. 6, par. 5.

[4] Noteworthy as an argument on purely moral grounds.

he must fear not merely that they will desert him but also that they will act against him, because, since they see farther and are more astute than the populace, they always prepare in advance to save themselves and seek the favor of the man they foresee will conquer. Of necessity the prince must live always with the same people, but he can get on without the same aristocrats, because he can make and unmake them every day and take away and give them prestige as he wishes.[5]

3 To make this matter clearer, I say that the members of the upper class can be considered principally in two ways: either they so conduct themselves in carrying on their affairs that they depend wholly on your fortune, or they do not. Those who depend on you and are not rapacious should be honored and loved; those who do not depend on you are to be examined in two ways. They may act as they do through cowardice and natural weakness of spirit; then you can make use of them, especially of those who are prudent, because in prosperity they increase your reputation, and in adversity you need not fear them. But when they do not depend on you because of craft and for ambitious reasons, it is a sign that they are thinking more of themselves than of you; the prince should take precautions against such men, and fear them as though they were open enemies, because in adversity they will always contribute to his ruin.

4 One who has become prince through the favor of the people ought therefore to keep their friendship; this is easily done, for they demand no more than not to be oppressed. But a man who becomes prince in opposition to the people and with the favor of the upper classes, ought to endeavor before everything else to gain the support of the people; this will be easy for him if he will take them under his protection. And because men feel more obligation to their benefactor when they are well treated by one whom they expect to treat them badly, the people immediately become his well-wishers more than if he had attained his position through their favor. And the prince can gain the people in many ways, on which no fixed rule can be given, because means vary according to conditions, and therefore I omit them. I shall conclude merely that it is necessary for a prince to have the friendship of the people; otherwise he has no resource in adversity.[6]

5 Nabis, prince of the Spartans, underwent a siege by the united forces of all the Greeks and a completely victorious

[5] Cf. Chap. 8, par. 2; Chap. 19, pars. 1, 5; Chap. 24, par. 2.

[6] Machiavelli here speaks wholly from the side of the prince, giving the selfish reasons for good government.

Roman army, and defended against them his native city and his own position. It quite sufficed him, when peril drew near, to secure himself against few,[7] but if the people had been hostile to him, this would not have sufficed. And let no one try to refute this opinion of mine with the trite proverb that he who lays foundations on the populace lays them in the mud. That is true when a private citizen lays such a foundation and allows himself to think that the people will free him when he is overpowered by enemies and the boards of magistrates (in this condition he will often find himself deceived, as were the Gracchi at Rome and Messer Giorgio Scali at Florence); but when he who founds himself on the people is a prince, who has ability to command, is a man of courage, does not get frightened in adversity, does not lack other preparations, and keeps the whole city zealous with his spirit and his wise regulations,[8] he will never find himself deceived by them; it will be evident that he has laid good foundations.

6 Such princely governments are always in danger when they are being changed from the civic type to the absolute, because a civic prince commands either in person or by means of governing boards; in the second case his position is weaker and more perilous than in the first, because he is wholly dependent on the will of those citizens who are at the heads of the governing boards; and they, especially in times of adversity, can with great ease take his position away from him, either by acting against him or by failing to obey him.[9] And in the hour of peril the prince does not have time to seize absolute authority, because the citizens and subjects, since they are accustomed to follow the leadership of the governing boards of the city, are not prepared to obey his orders in the midst of a storm, and in times of doubt he will always suffer from the scarcity of those in whom he is able to trust. For such a prince cannot rely on what he sees in quiet times, when citizens feel they need the administration, because then everybody runs, everybody promises, and, when death is far off, each

[7] According to Livy, XXXIV, 27, he executed eighty selected men.

Savonarola writes of the tyrant: "He always seeks to humble the powerful to make himself secure [*assicurarsi* as in Machiavelli] and therefore he kills or disgraces men who excel, or are rich or noble or talented or possess other good qualities" (*Tractate on the Organization and Government of the City of Florence,* book 2, chap. 2).

For further allusions to securing oneself, see Chap. 3, pars. 2, 11; Chap. 5, last par.; Chap. 8, par. 6; Chap. 10, par. 3; Chap. 24, par. 2; *Discourses on Livy,* I, 16, pars. 4, 5, and 6, below.

[8] Cf. Chap. 10, last sentence.

[9] Machiavelli is thinking of a city governed under republican forms by boards or councils, such as the government of Cosimo in Florence. Cf. the *Discourse on Reforming the Government of Florence,* par. 3, above.

man wishes to die for the ruler;[10] but in times of adversity, when the administration has need of the citizens, then few of them are to be found. And this experience is the more perilous in that it can be gone through but once. Hence a wise prince ought to devise such a government that his citizens, always and in all possible conditions, may have need of his administration and of him; then they will always be faithful.

[10] Cf. Chap. 17, par. 3.

CHAPTER 10

In What Way the Strength of All the Kinds of Princely Government Ought to Be Estimated

1 In examining the nature of these principalities it is necessary to remember another matter: namely, whether a prince has power enough to defend himself with his own forces, if it becomes necessary, or whether he always needs the protection of others. To explain this matter better, I say that I judge a ruler can defend himself with his own forces if he has men enough or money enough to enable him to get together a proper army and fight a battle with anybody who comes to attack him. Likewise, I judge that a prince always needs help from others if he cannot take the field against an enemy, but is obliged to seek refuge behind walls and defend them. As to the first condition, I have already discussed it, and shall speak of it further as is required.[1] As to the second, nothing can be said except that such a prince should be exhorted to fortify and provision the city itself and to take no account of the country round about. And a prince who has properly fortified his city, and has managed his conduct toward his subjects in the way already mentioned and to be further discussed,[2] will always be attacked with great hesitation; because men are always hostile to enterprises in which they see difficulties, and they can see nothing easy about attacking one who has his city well fortified and is not hated by his people.

2 The cities of Germany are wholly free, have little territory, and obey the emperor when they please, and they do not fear him or any other powerful man in the neighborhood, because they are fortified in such a way that every one thinks their capture cannot be other than tedious and difficult. Indeed they have suitable ditches and walls, and plenty of artillery; they always keep in the public magazines enough to drink and eat and burn for a year; and besides this, in order to provide the people with food without exhausting the public funds, they always have for general use enough raw material to give employment for a year at those trades that are the strength and life of the city, and that the people work at for a living. They also hold military exercises in high esteem, and better still, they have many regulations for keeping them up.

3 A prince, then, who has a strong city and does not make himself hated cannot be assailed; and anyone so foolish as to

[1] There has been nothing specifically on this point and nothing follows; perhaps he is thinking of Chap. 6, pars. 5, 6; Chap. 13; Chap. 24, par. 2.

[2] A general reference, chiefly indicating Chaps. 7, 8, 9, 17, 19, and 20.

attempt it would have to retire in disgrace, for the affairs of the world are so variable that it is almost impossible that anyone could keep his army idle a year in order to besiege one city. And if somebody should answer that if the people have their property outside the walls and see it burned up, they will not be patient, and that the long siege and their self-interest will make them forget the prince, I answer that a powerful and spirited prince will overcome all these difficulties, now making his subjects hope that the evil will not last long, now making them fear the cruelty of the enemy, and again skilfully making himself secure against those who seem to him too forward.[3] Besides this, the enemy, according to the usual practice, will probably burn and ruin the surrounding country on their arrival, while the spirits of the people are still warm and intent upon defence; hence the prince should hesitate so much the less, because, even though in a few days the spirits of his subjects cool off, the damage has already been done, and the ills have been suffered and are past remedy; in such conditions the people are still more inclined to unite with their prince, since it appears that he is under obligation to them, because their houses have been burned and their possessions ruined in his defence. And human nature causes men to feel as much obligation when they confer benefits as when they receive them. Hence, after thorough examination one must decide that it will not be difficult for a prudent prince to keep the spirits of his subjects resolute during a siege both early and late, if he does not lack provisions and means of defence.

[3] Cf. Chap. 9, par. 5, on Nabis' method of making himself secure.

CHAPTER 11

On the Principalities of Churchmen[1]

1 It only remains, at present, to discuss ecclesiastical principalities. All the difficulties about these come before one possesses them, because they are gained through either ability or fortune, and are kept without either one, for they are supported by customs that have grown old in the Church, and these are so powerful and of such a sort as to keep princes in power, in whatever way they act and live. These are the only princes who have states and do not defend them, subjects and do not govern them; yet their states are never taken away from them as a result of not being defended; and their subjects do not object because they are not governed; they do not dream of being alienated from the Church, nor can they be. These principalities alone, then, are secure and happy. But since they are protected by higher causes, to which the human mind does not reach, I will omit speaking of them; because, since they are set up and maintained by God, it would be the part of a presumptuous and conceited man to treat them. Nevertheless, someone may ask whence it comes that the Church, in temporal matters, has now attained such greatness; yet before Pope Alexander's time the Italian potentates—not merely those properly called potentates, but every baron and lord, however petty—set a low estimate on the Church in temporal matters. Nevertheless, now a King of France fears her, and she has been able to drive him out of Italy and to ruin the Venetians. Though this matter is well known, it does not seem to me useless to recall quite a portion of it.

2 Before Charles, the King of France, marched into Italy, the region was under the rule of the Pope, the Venetians, the king of Naples, the duke of Milan, and the Florentines. These rulers had to watch against two things especially: one that a foreigner should not enter Italy with an army; the other that no one of themselves should occupy more territory. Those who caused most anxiety were the Pope and the Venetians. To hold the Venetians back, a union of all the others was needed, such as that made for the defence of Ferrara. To keep the Pope down, the barons of Rome were employed, who, being divided into two factions, the Orsini and Colonnesi, always had cause for quarreling with each other; since they stood under

[1] Discussed after Chapter 10 because churchmen "do not defend" their territories. Cf. the two Letters of December 20, 1514, given below. A part of Chap. 19 (par. 18, end) would have been more in place here.

The chapter may be said to deal not with ecclesiastical principates generally, but with the temporal power of the papacy alone, a subject important to any new ruler in Italy. Cf. Chap. 26, par. 2.

the nose of the Pope, with swords in their hands, they kept the pontificate weak and insecure. And though sometimes there happened to be a spirited Pope, such as Sixtus, nevertheless neither fortune nor wisdom was able to rid him of this embarrassment. The cause of this failure was the brevity of life, for in ten years, his average term of office, a pope was scarcely able to put down one of the factions; if, for instance, one pope had almost wiped out the Colonnesi, another pope unfriendly to the Orsini would then appear; he would cause the Colonnesi to regain their power, and would not have time to overthrow the Orsini. For this reason the temporal forces of the Pope received little respect in Italy.

3 Then came Alexander VI, who showed, better than any other pontiff who has ever lived, how much a pope could accomplish with both money and force. With Duke Valentino as an instrument and with the campaign of the French as an opportunity, he accomplished all the things mentioned above among the actions of the Duke.[2] And though his intention was to make, not the Church, but the Duke great, nevertheless what he did contributed in the end to the greatness of the Church, which fell heir to his labors after his death and the overthrow of the Duke.

4 Then came Pope Julius; he found the Church strong, for she had all the Romagna, and the barons of Rome had been crushed and their factions brought to naught by the strokes of Alexander. Julius also found ways that had never been used before Alexander's time for the accumulation of money. He not only followed the steps of Alexander but went beyond, planning to gain Bologna, overthrow the Venetians, and drive the French from Italy; in all these enterprises he succeeded, and with the more glory to him in that it was all to increase the Church and not any private person. He still kept the Orsini and Colonnesi parties in the condition in which he found them; and though they might have had some idea of rebellion, yet two things kept them quiet: one was the greatness of the Church, which terrified them; the other was that they did not have their cardinals, who originate quarrels among them. These parties never remain quiet when they have cardinals, because the latter nourish factions in Rome and outside, and the barons are obliged to defend them; so the ambitions of the prelates cause discords and squabbles among the barons. His Holiness Pope Leo, then, has found the papacy very powerful, and it is to be hoped that, if his predecessors made it great with arms, he will make it very great and worthy of reverence with his benignity and countless other virtues.

[2] In Chap. 7.

CHAPTER 12

THE VARIOUS KINDS OF SOLDIERS AND ESPECIALLY MERCENARIES [1]

1 Having spoken in detail of all the qualities of the different kinds of princely government which in the beginning I set out to discuss, and having considered, in some respects, the causes of their good and ill, and showed the methods with which many have sought to gain and hold them, it now remains for me to survey generally the injuries that each of those mentioned can suffer and their means of defence. We have said above that it is needful for a prince to make his foundations good; otherwise he must certainly come to ruin. The chief foundations of all states, new as well as old or mixed, are good laws and good arms;[2] and because there cannot be good laws where there are not good arms, and where there are good arms there must needs be good laws,[3] I will omit speaking of the laws and speak of the arms.

2 I say, then, that the forces with which a prince defends his state are either his own, or mercenary, or auxiliary, or mixed. Mercenary and auxiliary forces are useless and dangerous; he who bases his government on hireling soldiers will never be solid or secure, because they are disunited, ambitious, without discipline, unfaithful, vigorous among friends, vile among enemies; they have no fear of God or faith with men;[4] your ruin is deferred only so long as an attack on you is deferred; in peace you are plundered by your own soldiers, in war by

[1] On the subjects of this and the following chapter, cf. the Letter of August 26, 1513, pars. 7, 8, below.

[2] Cf. Machiavelli's *First Plan for Organizing National Military Forces in the Florentine Republic:* "All the republics that in times past have been kept up and increased have always had as their principal foundation two things, to wit, justice and arms, in order to be able to control and govern their subjects and to defend themselves from their enemies. The Florentine republic is well founded and provided for the administration of justice with good and holy laws, and lacks only to be well furnished with arms. Yet through long experience and with great expense and peril she has learned how little hope can be placed in men and arms that are foreign and mercenary, because if they are adequate and of high repute, they are unbearable or objects of suspicion, and if they are few and without reputation, they are of no use. Hence the *Signori* have thought it well to arm themselves with their own arms and their own men." Cf. Chap. 26, par. 4, below; the Letter of December 10, 1513, par. 6, below; and that of March 15, 1525-6, par. 7, below.

[3] Cf. *Discourses on Livy,* I, 4, below.

[4] In the *Art of War,* the general speaks on his difficulties with mercenary soldiers because of their lack of religion and, consequently, of faith: "By what God or by what saints can I have them take oaths? By those they worship or by those they blaspheme? I do not know that they worship any of them, but I am sure they blaspheme them all. How can I believe they will observe promises made in the names of those whom they scoff at every hour? How can those who mock at God respect men? What sort of good form can be imprinted on such matter as this?" (Book 7, end). Cf. also the *Discourses on Livy,* I, 11, par. 2, below.

your enemies. The cause of this is that mercenaries do not go to war for love or any reason other than a little pay; that is not enough to make them ready to die for you. They certainly are glad to be your soldiers so long as you do not make war; but when war comes they hope to flee or to go elsewhere. It should not be hard to convince anybody of this, because the present ruin of Italy has been caused by nothing else than the trust that for a long course of years she has put in mercenary armies.[5] In earlier times these forces were of some use to their employers and appeared strong in fighting each other; but when a foreign army came they showed what they were; hence it was possible for Charles, King of France, to take Italy with chalk.[6] He who used to say our sins caused it told the truth,[7] but our sins were not what he believed they were, but those I have spoken of; and because they were the sins of the princes, the princes have been the ones to suffer for them.[8]

3 I wish to show more clearly the calamities caused by hireling armies. Mercenary generals either are men skillful in war or they are not. If they are, you cannot trust them, because they always wish to increase their own power, either by squeezing you, their employer, or by squeezing others contrary to your intention. If such a general is not competent, he usually ruins you. And if someone replies that anybody who has arms in his hands will do this, whether a mercenary or not, I can explain how arms ought to be managed by either a prince or a republic: a prince should go in person and hold the position of general himself;[9] a republic must send its citizens, and when it sends one of them who does not turn out to be a capable man, it should replace him, and if he is capable, it should restrain him by laws in order to keep him within limits. Experience shows that princes acting alone and armed republics make the greatest gains, that hired soldiers never do anything but damage, and that a republic provided with its own arms comes to obey one of its own citizens with more difficulty than one equipped with foreign arms.

4 Rome and Sparta were armed and free for many ages. The Swiss are fully armed and wholly free. Of mercenary arms in antiquity the Carthaginians furnish a good example: they were almost overpowered by their mercenary soldiers at the

[5] An anticipation of Chap. 26, pars. 4, 5.

[6] To indicate the lodgings assigned to his soldiers in the cities he entered. Cf. the *Introduction*, par. 121, above.

[7] Evidently Savonarola.

[8] Cf. Chap. 24, par. 2.

[9] Cf. Chap. 14, Chap. 26, par. 4, and *Castruccio Castracani*, pars. 15 ff., below.

end of the first war with the Romans, even though the Carthaginians had their own citizens as generals. After the death of Epaminondas, the Thebans made Philip of Macedon leader of their soldiers, and after a victory he took their liberty away. The Milanese, after the death of Duke Philip, employed Francesco Sforza against the Venetians, and he, after having defeated his enemies at Caravaggio, joined with them to overpower his employers the Milanese. The elder Sforza, his father, having been employed by Queen Joanna of Naples, suddenly left her disarmed; therefore, in order not to lose her kingdom, she was obliged to throw herself into the arms of the king of Aragon. And if the Venetians and the Florentines have in the past increased their empire with these soldiers, and their generals have not found an opportunity to make themselves their princes, but have defended them, I answer that the Florentines have been favored by Fortune in this matter, because, though they employed generals who were competent and to be feared, some have not conquered; others have had opposition; and still others have turned their ambition elsewhere. The one who did not conquer was Giovanni Acuto; and since he did not conquer, his faith cannot be known; but everybody will admit that the Florentines would have been at his disposal if he had conquered. Sforza always had the Bracceschi against him, and the two watched each other. Francesco employed his ambition in Lombardy; Braccio turned his against the Church and the kingdom of Naples.

5 But let us come to what happened a little while ago. The Florentines made Paulo Vitelli their general; he was a very prudent man who, starting in a humble situation, had attained a very high reputation. Nobody can deny that if he had taken Pisa it would have been necessary for the Florentines to submit to him; because, if he had been employed by their enemies, they would have had no protection, and if they had kept him they would have had to obey him. As to the Venetians, if their career is examined, they will appear to have worked securely and gloriously as long as they made war themselves (before they turned their efforts to land warfare), and acted with the utmost vigor with their own gentlemen and armed people; but when they began to fight on the land, they abandoned this vigorous conduct and adopted the usual custom of Italian wars.[10] In the beginning of their expansion on land, because they did not have much territory and had a high reputation, they did not have to be much afraid of their generals. But when they in-

[10] Cf. the Letter of August 26, 1513, pars. 5, 7, 8, below. The topic is also discussed in the *Art of War*, book 1.

creased their territories, as they did under Carmignola, they had a sample of this error. They saw that he was very capable, for under his leadership they had overcome the Duke of Milan, and on the other hand, they knew that his zeal for the war had grown cold; hence they judged they could no longer succeed under his leadership because he did not wish to conquer, and yet they could not dismiss him without losing what they had gained. Therefore, in order to make themselves secure against him, they were obliged to kill him. Then they had as generals Bartolomeo of Bergamo, Ruberto of San Severino, the Count of Pitigliano, and the like; with these they had to fear not the advantage of the generals but defeat, which actually happened at Vailà, where in one day Venice lost what she had acquired with great labor in eight hundred years.

6 In short, from these arms come slow, late, and slender gains, and swift and astounding losses. And because with these examples I have reached Italy, which has been ruled by hireling soldiers for many years, I wish to go more deeply into the subject, in order that by seeing the origin and development of these armies, a prince may be better able to control them.

7 You must understand, then, that as soon as in modern times the Empire began to be driven out of Italy and the Pope attained greater reputation in temporal matters, Italy was divided into many states, because many of the great cities took arms against their nobles, who, with the favor of the Emperor, had held them in subjection; the Church favored them in order to get prestige in temporal affairs. In many other cities, one of the citizens became prince. Hence, since Italy had fallen into the hands of the Church and of various republics, and the priests and the citizens did not understand arms, they began to employ foreigners. The first who gave reputation to this sort of military service was Alberigo da Conio, a Romagnole. From his school came, among others, Braccio and Sforza, who in their time were the masters of Italy. After these came all those who up to our time have directed such forces. And the effect of their prowess has been that Italy has been overrun by Charles, plundered by Louis, violated by Ferdinand, and insulted by the Swiss.[11] The method they have followed has been, first, to take away the prestige of the infantry in order to increase their own. They did so because, since they were without territory and dependent on their profession, a few infantry would not give them reputation and they could not feed a large number; hence they resorted to horsemen, because with these they could make a living and get honor. Things were brought to such a pass that in an

[11] A suggestion of Chap. 26, especially the last paragraph.

army of twenty thousand soldiers there would not be two thousand infantry. In addition they had used every means to rid themselves and the soldiers of labor and fear, for they did not kill one another in battle, but took each other prisoner without expecting ransom money. At night they did not assault cities, and those in the cities did not attack encampments; they did not make breastworks or ditches around their camps; they did not go on campaigns in the winter. And all these things were permitted by their military regulations, and devised by them, as I have said, to escape labor and peril. The result of their generalship is that Italy is enslaved and insulted.[12]

[12] Cf. Chap. 26.

CHAPTER 13

On Soldiers That Are Auxiliary, Mixed, and A Ruler's Own

1 Auxiliary armies, the other ineffective kind, are those of a powerful ruler whom you ask to come with his army to aid and defend you. Pope Julius recently did this, for, having had an unhappy experience with his mercenaries in his enterprise against Ferrara, he turned to auxiliaries, and made an agreement with Ferdinand, King of Spain, to furnish him aid with his people and armies. These soldiers may be in themselves useful and good, but they are almost always damaging to him who invites them; if they lose, you are undone; if they conquer, you are their prisoner. And though ancient history is full of examples of this, nonetheless I do not wish to give up the recent example of Pope Julius II. No plan could have been less prudent than his: because he wanted Ferrara, he threw himself into the hands of a foreigner. But his good fortune caused a third situation, so that he did not gather the fruit of his bad choice, because, when his auxiliaries were defeated at Ravenna, the Swiss arose to drive away the conquerors; hence, beyond all expectation, his own and that of others, he managed not to become a prisoner to his enemies, who had fled, nor to his auxiliaries, since he had conquered with other arms than theirs. When the Florentines, who had no army of their own, brought ten thousand French to Pisa to capture it, they were in greater danger as a result of this plan than in any other period of their difficulties. The emperor of Constantinople, in order to confront his neighbors, sent ten thousand Turks into Greece; when the war was over they did not care to depart; this was the beginning of the slavery of the Greeks under the infidels.

2 He, then, who wishes not to be able to conquer should make use of such forces, for they are much more dangerous than mercenary ones. Auxiliaries bring swift and certain ruin, for they are all united, and they all yield their obedience to others. But if mercenaries are to do you damage after they have conquered, they need more time and better opportunity, for they do not form a single body, and they are recruited and paid by you; hence a third man whom you may put at their head is not able at once to acquire such authority that he can damage you. In short, in mercenaries laziness is your greatest danger; in auxiliaries, efficiency.

3 Wise princes, then, always have avoided these armies and turned to their own,[1] and have preferred rather to lose with their own forces than to conquer with those of others, believing that a victory acquired with the arms of others is not a true one.

4 I never hesitate to bring forward Cesare Borgia and his actions.[2] This duke entered the Romagna with auxiliary arms, for he led there only French soldiers, with whom he took Imola and Forlì; but since these arms did not appear to him reliable, he turned to mercenaries, thinking there was less peril in them, and employed the Orsini and Vitelli. But since in managing them he found them doubtful and unfaithful and dangerous, he wiped them out and turned to his own arms. And one can easily see what difference there is between the various kinds of soldiers, by considering the difference in the prestige of the Duke in the days when he had the French only, and when he had the Orsini and Vitelli, and in the days when he had his own soldiers and relied on himself. It will be found that his reputation was increasingly greater, and that he was not greatly esteemed until everybody saw that he was sole master of his armies.

5 I do not wish to give up examples that are Italian and modern; yet I cannot omit Hiero of Syracuse, whom I have mentioned above.[3] As I have said, when he was made head of their armies by the Syracusans, he knew at once that their mercenary troops were not effective, because they were soldiers of fortune like our Italians. Since it appeared to him that he could neither keep them nor let them go, he had them all cut to pieces. Afterwards he made war with his own arms and not with those of aliens. I wish also to bring to memory a symbolical story from the Old Testament which is quite to our purpose. When David offered himself to Saul to go to fight with Goliath, the Philistine challenger, Saul armed David with his own armour, in order to give him courage, but when David had it on his back he refused it, saying he could not handle himself well in it, and therefore wished to go to fight his enemy with his sling and his knife.

6 In short, the armour of others either falls from your back, or weighs you down, or constricts you. Charles VII, father of King Louis XI, after he had freed France from the English by means of his good fortune and his ability, recognized this necessity for arming himself with his own arms, and set up in his kingdom the ordinance of men-at-arms and infantry.[4] His son,

[1] See the *Life of Castruccio Castracani,* par. 16, the Letter of August 26, 1513, pars. 7, 8, below, and the *Introduction*, pars. 151 to 163, above. See also the *Art of War,* book 1, and Machiavelli's *First Plan for Establishing National Military Forces in the Florentine Republic.*

[2] An apology for mentioning Cesare after Chaps. 7 and 8.

[3] Chap. 6, last par.

[4] Cf. the Letter of August 26, 1513, par. 8.

King Louis, later gave up the ordinance of infantry and began to hire the Swiss; this error, followed by others, was, as can now be seen from what has happened, the cause of the dangers of that kingdom. The reasons are that by giving a high reputation to the Swiss he lowered that of all his own soldiers; he entirely gave up infantry, and made his men-at-arms dependent on foreign troops, for they have grown used to fighting with the aid of the Swiss, and suppose that they cannot conquer without it. As a result the French are not adequate to fight against the Swiss, and without Swiss they do not risk battle against others. The armies of the king of France, then, have been mixed, partly mercenary and partly his own; such forces as a whole are much better than auxiliary forces alone or mercenaries alone, but much inferior to one's own troops. The example I have given is enough, for the kingdom of France would be unconquerable if the plan of Charles had been developed and retained. But because they have little wisdom, men often begin something in which they see an immediate benefit, but which has hidden in it a poison they do not discover, as I said above about the hectic fever.[5]

7 Therefore the prince who does not recognize the ills of his state when they first appear is not really wise; yet this power of diagnosis is given to few. If you will consider the first cause of the ruin of the Roman empire, you will find that it was only that the Romans began to hire Gothic soldiers, for from that time the forces of the Roman empire began to grow weak, and all the vigor it lost was given to the Goths.

8 I conclude, then, that no prince's position is secure unless he has his own soldiers; on the contrary he is wholly under the sway of Fortune, since in adversity he does not have power to defend himself with confidence. Wise men have always held the opinion expressed in the sententious words: "Nothing is so weak and unstable as a reputation for power not based on force."[6] Your own armies are those composed of your subjects or citizens or dependents;[7] all others are either mercenary or auxiliary. The way to organize your own armies will be easy to learn, if you consider the methods of the four men I have already mentioned, and see how Philip, the father of Alexander the Great, and many republics and princes have armed and organized. In their methods I have complete confidence.

[5] In Chap. 3, par. 7.

[6] Tacitus, *Annals*, XIII, 19.

[7] This explanation looks forward to Chap. 26, par. 4. These were the arms "to his liking" of Cesare Borgia (Chap. 7, par. 7). The prince's "own arms" of the title of Chap. 6 might apparently be mercenaries in a ruler's service, as distinguished from the soldiers of another ruler furnishing him aid according to Chap. 7.

CHAPTER 14

How a Prince Should Act about Military Matters

1 A prince, then, must have no other object and no other thought than war and its methods and conduct, and must not take anything else as his specialty, for this is the only branch of knowledge that is required of him who governs; and it is of such value that it not merely keeps in power those who are born princes, but causes men to rise from humble positions to that rank. On the contrary, it may be seen that princes have often lost their rank when they have thought more on luxuries than on arms. The first cause that makes you lose your position is neglect of the art of war; and the cause that makes you acquire it is skill in that art.[1]

2 Because he had an army, Francesco Sforza rose from a private station to the dukedom of Milan; his sons, because they avoided the hardships of military life, sank from the dukedom to private stations. The reason is that, among the other ills lack of military force brings you, it makes you despised; and that is one of the stigmas from which the prince must guard himself, as will be explained below;[2] for there is no equality between an armed and an unarmed man, and it is not reasonable that an armed man will consent to obey an unarmed one, and that an unarmed man will be secure among armed servants, because when the servant is scornful and the master suspicious, they cannot work well together. Hence, in addition to the other drawbacks I have mentioned, a prince who does not understand military matters cannot be esteemed by his soldiers nor can he trust them.

3 Therefore a ruler must never remove his thoughts from military training, and in time of peace he must labor at it more than in time of war. This he can do in two ways: with his actions and with his mind. As to actions, beyond keeping his soldiers well disciplined and trained, he ought to hunt continually and by means of this sport accustom his body to hardships. Hunting will at the same time aid him in learning the nature of places, and in understanding the elevations of mountains and the descents of valleys, and how the plains lie, and in getting familiar with the nature of rivers and of swamps. To this he should give very careful attention. Such knowledge is useful in two ways: first, the prince teaches himself to understand his country and can see how to defend it, and second, through his understanding of those places and his familiarity with them, he

[1] Cf. Chap. 12, par. 3, and *Castruccio Castracani*, pars. 15 ff., below.

[2] In Chap. 19.

can easily comprehend any other unfamiliar place he is obliged to consider. This he can do because the hills, the valleys, the plains, the rivers, and the swamps of Tuscany, for example, have a certain similarity with those of other provinces, so that through knowing the topography of one province he can easily come to an understanding of others. The prince who lacks skill in this lacks the first qualification a general needs, because this teaches him how to discover his enemy, to select camping-places, to regulate marches, to plan battles, and to besiege towns to his own advantage.

4 Philopoemen, prince of the Achaeans, among other things for which writers praise him, is said in times of peace to have thought only on the methods of war: when he was in the country with his friends he often paused and said to them: "If the enemy were on that hill, and we were here with our army, which of us would have the advantage? how could we advance against them in good order? if we wished to retreat, how should we go about it? if they should retreat, in what manner ought we to follow them?" And he would set before them, as he walked on, all the unexpected events that can happen in an army; he listened to their opinion, and gave his own, and supported it with reasons. Hence, as a result of his continual thought on the subject, it was impossible for any accident of campaigning to take him unprepared.

5 But with respect to the exercise of the mind, the prince should read history, and give attention to the actions of great men related in it, to see how they have conducted themselves in war, and to examine the causes of their victories and defeats, in order to imitate the first and avoid the second; above all he should learn to do as some great men have done in the past, for they have taken for imitation some earlier character who has been praised and lauded, and have always kept his deeds and actions before them.[3] So it is said that Alexander the Great imitated Achilles; Caesar, Alexander; and Scipio, Cyrus. And whoever reads the life of Cyrus written by Xenophon recognizes at once in Scipio's life how much that imitation did for his renown, and how closely he conformed in chastity, affability, humanity, and liberality with what Xenophon has written about Cyrus.

6 A wise prince should practice such habits as these, and never stand idle in times of peace, but should strive to make capital of them, to use in adversity, so that when Fortune grows contrary he may be found ready to resist her.

[3] Cf. Chap. 6, par. 1.

CHAPTER 15

On the Things for Which Men, and Especially Princes, Are Praised or Censured

1 It now remains to see what should be the methods and conduct of a prince in dealing with his subjects and his friends. And because I know that many have written on this topic, I fear that when I too write I shall be thought presumptuous, because, in discussing it, I break away completely from the principles laid down by my predecessors. But since it is my purpose to write something useful to an attentive reader, I think it more effective to go back to the practical truth of the subject than to depend on my fancies about it. And many have imagined republics and principalities that never have been seen or known to exist in reality. For there is such a difference between the way men live and the way they ought to live, that anybody who abandons what is for what ought to be will learn something that will ruin rather than preserve him, because anyone who determines to act in all circumstances the part of a good man must come to ruin among so many who are not good. Hence, if a prince wishes to maintain himself, he must learn how to be not good, and to use that ability or not as is required.

2 Leaving out of account, then, things about an imaginary prince, and considering things that are true, I say that all men, when they are spoken of, and especially princes, because they are set higher, are marked with some of the qualities that bring them either blame or praise. To wit, one man is thought liberal, another stingy (using a Tuscan word, because *avaricious* in our language is still applied to one who desires to get things through violence, but *stingy* we apply to him who refrains too much from using his own property); one is thought open-handed, another grasping; one cruel, the other compassionate; one is a breaker of faith, the other reliable; one is effeminate and cowardly, the other vigorous and spirited; one is philanthropic, the other egotistic; one is lascivious, the other chaste; one is straight-forward, the other crafty; one hard, the other easy to deal with; one is firm, the other unsettled; one is religious, the other unbelieving; and so on.

3 And I know that everybody will admit that it would be very praiseworthy for a prince to possess all of the above-mentioned qualities that are considered good.[1] But since he is not able to have them or to observe them completely, because hu-

[1] An important sentence. The same thing is suggested in the reference to "good examples" in Chap. 24, par. 1. See the *Introduction*, pars. 39-51.

man conditions do not allow him to,[2] it is necessary that he be prudent enough to understand how to avoid getting a bad name because he is given to those vices that will deprive him of his position. He should also, if he can, guard himself from those vices that will not take his place away from him, but if he cannot do it, he can with less anxiety let them go. Moreover, he should not be troubled if he gets a bad name because of vices without which it will be difficult for him to preserve his position. I say this because, if everything is considered, it will be seen that some things seem to be virtuous, but if they are put into practice will be ruinous to him; other things seem to be vices, yet if put into practice will bring the prince security and well-being.

[2] Cf. Chap. 18, par. 5, with its emphasis on what the prince is obliged to do.

CHAPTER 16

On Liberality and Parsimony

1 Beginning, then, with the first of the above-mentioned qualities, I assert that it is good to be thought liberal. Yet liberality, practiced in such a way that you get a reputation for it, is damaging to you, for the following reasons: If you use it wisely and as it ought to be used, it will not become known, and you will not escape being censured for the opposite vice. Hence, if you wish to have men call you liberal, it is necessary not to omit any sort of lavishness. A prince who does this will always be obliged to use up all his property in lavish actions; he will then, if he wishes to keep the name of liberal, be forced to lay heavy taxes on his people and exact money from them, and do everything he can to raise money. This will begin to make his subjects hate him, and as he grows poor he will be little esteemed by anybody. So it comes about that because of this liberality of his, with which he has damaged a large number and been of advantage to but a few, he is affected by every petty annoyance and is in peril from every slight danger. If he recognizes this and wishes to draw back, he quickly gets a bad name for stinginess.

2 Since, then, a prince cannot without harming himself practice this virtue of liberality to such an extent that it will be recognized, he will, if he is prudent, not care about being called stingy. As time goes on he will be thought more and more liberal, for the people will see that because of his economy his income is enough for him, that he can defend himself from those who make war against him, and that he can enter upon undertakings without burdening his people. Such a prince is in the end liberal to all those from whom he takes nothing, and they are numerous; he is stingy to those to whom he does not give, and they are few. In our times we have seen big things done only by those who have been looked on as stingy; the others have utterly failed. Pope Julius II, though he made use of a reputation for liberality to attain the papacy, did not then try to maintain it, because he wished to be able to make war. The present King of France has carried on great wars without laying unusually heavy taxes on his people, merely because his long economy has made provision for heavy expenditures. The present King of Spain, if he had continued liberal, would not have carried on or completed so many undertakings.

3 Therefore a prince ought to care little about getting called stingy, if as a result he does not have to rob his subjects, is able to defend himself, does not become poor and contemptible, and is not obliged to become grasping. For this vice of stinginess is one of those that enables him to rule. Somebody may say: Caesar, by means of his liberality, became emperor, and many others have come to high positions because they have been liberal and have been thought so. I answer: Either you are already prince, or you are on the way to become one. In the first case liberality is dangerous; in the second it is very necessary to be thought liberal. Caesar was one of those who wished to attain dominion over Rome. But if, when he had attained it, he had lived for a long time and had not moderated his expenses, he would have destroyed his authority. Somebody may answer: Many who have been thought very liberal have been princes and done great things with their armies. I answer: The prince spends either his own property and that of his subjects or that of others. In the first case he ought to be frugal; in the second he ought to abstain from no sort of liberality. When he marches with his army and lives on plunder, loot, and ransom, a prince controls the property of others. To him liberality is essential, for without it his soldiers would not follow him. You can be a free giver of what does not belong to you or your subjects, as were Cyrus, Caesar, and Alexander, because to spend the money of others does not decrease your reputation but adds to it. It is only the spending of your own money that hurts you.

4 There is nothing that eats itself up as fast as does liberality, for when you practice it you lose the power to practice it, and become poor and contemptible, or else to escape poverty you become rapacious and therefore are hated. And of all the things against which a prince must guard himself, the first is being an object of contempt and hatred.[1] Liberality leads you to both of these. Hence there is more wisdom in keeping a name for stinginess, which produces a bad reputation without hatred, than in striving for the name of liberal, only to be forced to get the name of rapacious, which brings forth both bad reputation and hatred.

[1] See Chap. 19.

CHAPTER 17

ON CRUELTY AND PITY, AND WHETHER IT IS BETTER TO BE LOVED OR TO BE FEARED, AND *Vice Versa*

1 Coming then to the other qualities already mentioned, I say that every prince should wish to be thought compassionate and not cruel; still, he should be careful not to make a bad use of the pity he feels. Cesare Borgia was considered cruel, yet this cruelty of his pacified the Romagna, united it, and changed its condition to that of peace and loyalty. If the matter is well considered, it will be seen that Cesare was much more compassionate than the people of Florence, for in order to escape the name of cruel they allowed Pistoia to be destroyed. Hence a prince ought not to be troubled by the stigma of cruelty, acquired in keeping his subjects united and faithful. By giving a very few examples of cruelty he can be more truly compassionate than those who through too much compassion allow disturbances to continue, from which arise murders or acts of plunder. Lawless acts are injurious to a large group, but the executions ordered by the prince injure a single person. The new prince, above all other princes, cannot possibly avoid the name of cruel, because new states are full of perils. Dido in Vergil puts it thus: "Hard circumstances and the newness of my realm force me to do such things, and to keep watch and ward over all my lands."[1]

2 All the same, he should be slow in believing and acting, and should make no one afraid of him, his procedure should be so tempered with prudence and humanity that too much confidence does not make him incautious, and too much suspicion does not make him unbearable.

3 All this gives rise to a question for debate: Is it better to be loved than to be feared, or the reverse? I answer that a prince should wish for both.[2] But because it is difficult to reconcile them, I hold that it is much more secure to be feared than to be loved, if one of them must be given up. The reason for my answer is that one must say of men generally that they are ungrateful, mutable, pretenders and dissemblers, prone to avoid danger, thirsty for gain.[3] So long as you benefit them

[1] *Aeneid* I, 563-4.

[2] Cesare Borgia attained it; see Chap. 7, par. 10.

[3] Cf. Chap. 15, par. 1; Chap. 18, par. 3; Chap. 23, last par. In the *Discourses on Livy*, I, 3, Machiavelli writes: "As all those who discuss civil life make clear, and as every history shows with many examples, it is necessary for anybody who organizes a republic and establishes laws in it to assume that all men are wicked, and that they are always going to make use of the malice of their spirits *(Continued on page 146)*

they are all yours; as I said above, they offer you their blood, their property, their lives, their children, when the need for such things is remote. But when need comes upon you, they turn around. So if a prince has relied wholly on their words, and is lacking in other preparations, he falls. For friendships that are gained with money, and not with greatness and nobility of spirit, are deserved but not possessed,[4] and in the nick of time one cannot avail himself of them. Men hesitate less to injure a man who makes himself loved than to injure one who makes himself feared, for their love is held by a chain of obligation, which, because of men's wickedness, is broken on every occasion for the sake of selfish profit; but their fear is secured by a dread of punishment which never fails you.

4 Nevertheless the prince should make himself feared in such a way that, if he does not win love, he escapes hatred. This is possible, for to be feared and not to be hated can easily coexist. In fact it is always possible, if the ruler abstains from the property of his citizens and subjects, and from their women. And if, as sometimes happens, he finds that he must inflict the penalty of death, he should do it when he has proper justification and evident reason. But above all he must refrain from taking property, for men forget the death of a father more quickly than the loss of their patrimony.[5] Further, causes for taking property are never lacking, and he who begins to live on plunder is always finding cause to seize what belongs to others. But on the contrary, reasons for taking life are rarer and fail sooner.

5 But when a prince is with his army and has a great number of soldiers under his command, then above all he must pay no heed to being called cruel, because if he does not have that name he cannot keep his army united or ready for duty. It should be numbered among the wonderful feats of Hannibal that he led to war in foreign lands a large army, made up of

(Concluded from page 145) whenever they have a good opportunity to do so. If their malice remains concealed for a time, there is a hidden cause for it, which, because we have no experience of its opposite, we do not understand. Yet Time, which is said to be the father of every Truth, brings it to light."

[4] Chap. 9, par. 6.

[5] Machiavelli wrote to Giovanni de' Medici soon after the return of the family in 1512, pointing out that an attempt to recover property lost in 1494 and later might be dangerous: "Men feel more sorrow for a farm that is taken away from them than for a brother or a father that is put to death, because sometimes death is forgotten, but property never. The reason is close to the surface, for everyone knows that a brother is not able to rise up again because of a change in government, but there is a possibility of getting back a farm. If this applies to anybody, it applies to the Florentines, because they are commonly more avaricious than generous" (Quoted by Tommasini, *Machiavelli,* I, 601).

countless types of men, yet never suffered from dissension, either among the soldiers or against the general, in either bad or good fortune. His success resulted from nothing else than his inhuman cruelty, which, when added to his numerous other strong qualities, made him respected and terrible in the sight of his soldiers. Yet without his cruelty his other qualities would not have been adequate. So it seems that those writers have not thought very deeply who on one side admire his accomplishment and on the other condemn the chief cause for it.[6]

6 The truth that his other qualities alone would not have been adequate may be learned from Scipio, a man of the most unusual powers not only in his own times but in all ages we know of. When he was in Spain his armies mutinied. This resulted from nothing other than his compassion, which had allowed his soldiers more license than befits military discipline. This fault was censured before the Senate by Fabius Maximus, and Scipio was called by him the corruptor of the Roman soldiery. The Locrians were destroyed by a lieutenant of Scipio's, yet he did not avenge them or punish the disobedience of that lieutenant. This all came from his easy nature, which was so well understood that one who wished to excuse him in the Senate said there were many men who knew better how not to err than how to punish errors. This easy nature would in time have overthrown the fame and glory of Scipio if, in spite of this weakness, he had kept on in independent command. But since he was under the orders of the Senate, this bad quality was not merely concealed but was a glory to him.

7 Returning, then, to the debate on being loved and feared, I conclude that since men love as they please and fear as the prince pleases,[7] a wise prince will evidently rely on what is in his own power and not on what is in the power of another.[8] As I have said, he need only take pains to avoid hatred.

[6] The crowd of Chap. 18, last par., are more consistent in that they approve the means if the end is reached.

[7] Cf. the first Letter of December 20, 1514, par. 15.

[8] Cf. Chap. 9, last par. for something within the prince's own power.

CHAPTER 18

In What Way Faith Should Be Kept By Princes

1 Everybody knows how laudable it is in a prince to keep his faith and to be an honest man and not a trickster.[1] Nevertheless, the experience of our times shows that the princes who have done great things are the ones who have taken little account of their promises and who have known how to addle the brains of men with craft. In the end they have conquered those who have put their reliance on good faith.

2 You must realize, then, that there are two ways to fight. In one kind the laws are used, in the other, force. The first is suitable to man, the second to animals. But because the first often falls short, one has to turn to the second. Hence a prince must know perfectly how to act like a beast and like a man. This truth was covertly taught to princes by ancient authors, who write that Achilles and many other ancient princes were turned over for their up-bringing to Chiron the centaur, that he might keep them under his tuition. To have as teacher one who is half beast and half man means nothing else than that a prince needs to know how to use the qualities of both creatures. The one without the other will not last long.

3 Since, then, it is necessary for a prince to understand how to make good use of the conduct of the animals, he should select among them the fox and the lion, because the lion cannot protect himself from traps, and the fox cannot protect himself from the wolves.[2] So the prince needs to be a fox that he may know how to deal with traps, and a lion that he may frighten the wolves. Those who act like the lion alone do not understand their business. A prudent ruler, therefore, cannot and should not observe faith when such observance is to his disadvantage and the causes that made him give his promise have vanished. If men were all good, this advice would not be good, but since men are wicked and do not keep their promises to you,[3] you likewise do not have to keep yours to them. Lawful reasons to excuse his failure to keep them will never be lacking to a prince. It would be possible to give innumerable modern examples of this and to show many treaties

[1] This is Machiavelli's moral ideal, which the prince is to abandon only when dealing with faithless men who will, if they can, ruin him and his country, as the chapter proceeds to explain. Men ought to be honest (Chap. 15, par. 1) but are not. With the honest, the prince is to be honest (Chap. 22, end).

[2] For the animals differently used, see the Letter of August 26, 1513, par. 1.

[3] Cf. Chap. 15, par. 1; Chap. 17, par. 3; and the Letter of April 29, 1513, par. 8. The world must be dealt with as it is.

and promises that have been made null and void by the faithlessness of princes. And the prince who has best known how to act as a fox has come out best. But one who has this capacity must understand how to keep it covered, and be a skilful pretender and dissembler. Men are so simple and so subject to present needs that he who deceives in this way will always find those who will let themselves be deceived.

4 I do not wish to keep still about one of the recent instances. Alexander VI did nothing else than deceive men, and had no other intention; yet he always found a subject to work on. There never was a man more effective in swearing that things were true, and the greater the oaths with which he made a promise, the less he observed it. Nonetheless his deceptions always succeeded to his wish, because he thoroughly understood this aspect of the world.

5 It is not necessary, then, for a prince really to have all the virtues mentioned above,[4] but it is very necessary to seem to have them. I will even venture to say that they damage a prince who possesses them and always observes them, but if he seems to have them they are useful. I mean that he should seem compassionate, trustworthy, humane, honest, and religious, and actually be so; but yet he should have his mind so trained that, when it is necessary not to practice these virtues, he can change to the opposite, and do it skilfully. It is to be understood that a prince, especially a new prince, cannot observe all the things because of which men are considered good, because he is often obliged, if he wishes to maintain his government, to act contrary to faith, contrary to charity, contrary to humanity, contrary to religion.[5] It is therefore necessary that he have a mind capable of turning in whatever direction the winds of Fortune and the variations of affairs require, and, as I said above,[6] that he should not depart from what is morally right, if he can observe it, but should know how to adopt what is bad, when he is obliged to.

6 A prince, then, should be very careful that there does not issue from his mouth anything that is not full of the abovementioned five qualities. To those who see and hear him he

[4] In Chap. 15, par. 2.

[5] Savonarola observes of the tyrant: "Having set up as his end the position he holds, there is nothing he will not do to maintain it; hence there is no evil he is not prepared to do in the interest of his position, as experience shows, for the tyrant does not hesitate at anything to maintain himself in his place" (*Tractate on the Organization and Government of the City of Florence*, book 2, chap. 2).

Machiavelli, however, has in mind a good prince who rules for the common good; the maintenance of his authority is a high end. Cf. the *Discourses on Livy*, I, 9, below.

[6] Chap. 15, par. 3.

should seem all compassion, all faith, all honesty, all humanity, all religion. There is nothing more necessary to make a show of possessing than this last quality. For men in general judge more by their eyes than by their hands; everybody is fitted to see, few to understand. Everybody sees what you appear to be; few make out what you really are. And these few do not dare to oppose the opinion of the many, who have the majesty of the state to confirm their view. In the actions of all men, and especially those of princes, where there is no court to which to appeal, people think of the outcome. A prince needs only to conquer and to maintain his position. The means he has used will always be judged honorable and will be praised by everybody, because the crowd is always caught by appearance and by the outcome of events,[7] and the crowd is all there is in the world;[8] there is no place for the few when the many have room enough. A certain prince of the present day,[9] whom it is not good to name, preaches nothing else than peace and faith, and is wholly opposed to both of them, and both of them, if he had observed them, would many times have taken from him either his reputation or his throne.

[7] Obviously Machiavelli here condemns the justification of the means by the end, for the reason that the end is specious. The end can justify only when it is genuinely good.

[8] Machiavelli is not here contrasting the people and the upper classes, but the wise and the foolish. In the *Discourses on Livy,* I, 58, he sustains the thesis that the multitude is wiser than a prince.

[9] Ferdinand of Spain, who died January 23, 1516.

CHAPTER 19

On Avoiding Contempt and Hatred

1 But because I have spoken of the more important of the qualities above,[1] I wish to cover the others briefly with this generality. To wit, the prince should give his attention, as is in part explained above,[2] to avoiding the things that make him hateful and contemptible.[3] As long as he escapes them, he will have done his duty, and will find no danger in other injuries to his reputation. Hatred, as I have said,[4] comes upon him chiefly from being rapacious and seizing the property and women of his subjects. He ought to abstain from both of these, for the majority of men live in contentment when they are not deprived of property or honor. Hence the prince has to struggle only with the ambition of the few,[5] which can be restrained in many ways and with ease. Contempt is his portion if he is held to be variable, volatile, effeminate, cowardly, or irresolute. From these a prince should guard himself as from a rock in the sea.[6] He should strive in all his actions to give evident signs of greatness, spirit, gravity, and fortitude.[7] Also in the private affairs of his subjects he should make it understood that his opinion is irrevocable. In short he should keep up such a reputation that nobody thinks of trying to deceive him or outwit him.

2 The prince who makes people hold that opinion has prestige enough. And if a prince has a high reputation, men hesitate to conspire against him and hesitate to attack him, simply because he is supposed to be of high ability and respected by his subjects. For a prince must needs have two kinds of fear: one within his state, because of his subjects; the other without, because of foreign rulers. From these dangers he defends himself with good weapons and good friends. And if his weapons are good, he will always have good friends. Conditions within the state, too, will always remain settled when those without are settled,[8] if they have not already been unsettled by some conspiracy. And when things without are in movement, if he has ruled and lived as I have said,[9] and does

[1] That is, the qualities in the list in Chapter 15, par. 2.

[2] In Chapters 15, 16, 17.

[3] Cf. the two Letters of December 20, 1514, pars. 15 and 2, respectively, below.

[4] In Chap. 17.

[5] The upper classes, Chap. 9.

[6] The same expression is used of hatred in the *Discourses on Livy*, III, 23.

[7] Cf. Chap. 21, par. 2.

[8] For the converse of this, see Chap. 20, par. 10.

[9] Cf. Chap. 10, par. 1.

not fail himself,[10] he will surely repel every attack, as I said Nabis the Spartan did.

3 But with respect to his subjects, when there is no movement without, he has to fear that they will make a secret conspiracy. From this the prince protects himself adequately if he avoids being hated and despised and keeps the people satisfied with him. The latter necessarily follows the former, as was explained above at length.[11] Indeed one of the most potent remedies the prince can have against conspiracies is not to be hated by the majority of his subjects. The reason for this is that a man who conspires always thinks he will please the people by killing the prince; but when he thinks he will offend them by it, he does not pluck up courage to adopt such a plan, because the difficulties that fall to the portion of conspirators are numerous. Experience shows that there have been many conspiracies and that few have come out well.[12] They fail because the conspirator cannot be alone, and he can get companions only from those who, he thinks, are discontented. But as soon as you have revealed your purpose to a malcontent, you have given him an opportunity to become contented, because he evidently can hope to gain every advantage from his knowledge. Such is his position that, seeing on the one hand certain gain, and on the other gain that is uncertain and full of danger, he must needs be a rare friend, or, at any rate, an obstinate enemy of the prince, if he keeps faith with you. To put the thing briefly, I say that on the part of those who conspire there is nothing but fear, jealousy, and the expectation of punishment, which terrifies them. But on the part of the prince are the majesty of his high office, the laws, the power of his friends and his party that protects him. Evidently when the popular good-will is joined to all these things, it is impossible that anybody can be so foolhardy as to conspire against him. Ordinarily the conspirator must be afraid before the execution of his evil deed, but in this case he also has reason to fear after his transgression, because he will have the people against him and therefore cannot hope for any escape.

4 On this subject numerous examples might be given. But I have decided to be content with one alone, which happened in the memory of our fathers. Messer Annibale Bentivogli, grandfather of the present Messer Annibale, prince of Bologna, was murdered by the Canneschi, who conspired against him. He left no heir save Messer Giovanni, who was in the cradle.

[10] Cf. Chap. 9, par. 5, the "spirited" prince of Chap. 10, par. 3, and Chap. 24, par. 1.

[11] Chap. 17, pars. 3 and 4.

[12] Conspiracies are discussed in the longest of the *Discourses on Livy*, namely III, 6.

Yet immediately after that murder, the people rose up and killed all the Canneschi. This act was the result of the popular good-will that the house of the Bentivogli had in those days, as is shown by what followed. After the death of Annibale, no member of the family who could rule the state was left in Bologna. The Bolognese, however, got a hint that there was in Florence a scion of the Bentivogli who had been supposed until then to be the son of a smith. They came to Florence after him and gave him control of their city, which he governed from that time until Messer Giovanni reached an age capable of ruling it.

5 I conclude, therefore, that a prince need not pay much attention to conspiracies when the people are well-disposed to him. But when they are unfriendly and hate him, he must fear everything and everybody. Further, well-organized governments and wise princes have striven with all diligence not to make the upper classes feel desperate, and to satisfy the populace and keep them contented.[13] In fact this is one of the most important matters a prince has to deal with.

6 Among the kingdoms well organized and well governed in our times is France. In this country there are numerous good institutions on which depend the liberty and security of the king. The first of these is the parliament and its authority. He who organized this kingdom set up the parliament because he knew the ambition of the nobles and their arrogance, and judged it necessary that the nobility should have a bit in its mouth to restrain it. On the other hand, he knew the hatred, founded on fear, of the generality of men for the nobles, and intended to secure the position of the latter. Yet he did not wish this to be the special concern of the king, because he wished to relieve the king from the hatred he would arouse among the great if he favored the people, and among the people if he favored the nobles. Therefore he set up a third party as judge, to be the one who, without bringing hatred on the king, should restrain the nobles and favor the people. This institution could not be better or more prudent, nor could there be a stronger cause for the security of the king and the realm. From this can be deduced another important idea: to wit, princes should have things that will bring them hatred done by their agents, but should do in person those that will give pleasure.[14]

[13] Cf. Chap. 9, throughout; Chap. 24, par. 2.

[14] Savonarola said that the tyrant "shows himself as the giver of all the honors and offices that are distributed to the citizens, and endeavors to have everybody realize that they come from him; but lays the responsibility for the punishment of those who do wrong on his boards of magistrates" (*Tractate on the Organization and Government of the City of Florence*, bk. 2, chap. 2). For further parallels see Gilbert, *Machiavelli's "Prince" and Its Forerunners*, pp. 154-6.

Once more I conclude that a prince should esteem the nobles, but should not make himself hated by the populace.

7 It perhaps will seem to many, in view of the lives and deaths of some of the Roman emperors, that they are examples opposed to this opinion of mine, for it is evident that some of them always lived honorably and showed great ability of mind, and nevertheless lost the throne or were killed by some of their followers who conspired against them. Hence, in my desire to answer these objections, I shall discuss the qualities of some of the emperors, and show the causes of their downfalls—not unlike those I have mentioned. In so doing I shall bring under consideration the things most important to those who read about the deeds of those times. I think it will suffice to take all those emperors who came to the throne from the time of Marcus the Philosopher to that of Maximinus. These were Marcus, Commodus his son, Pertinax, Julian, Severus, Antoninus, Caracalla his son, Macrinus, Heliogabalus, Alexander, and Maximinus.

8 First it should be noted that, while in other princedoms the ambition of the upper classes and the pride of the people are the only things to be struggled with, the Roman emperors had a third difficulty. They had to endure the cruelty and avarice of the soldiers. This was so difficult that it caused the ruin of many emperors, for it is hard to satisfy both soldiers and people. The people love quiet, and for that reason love unambitious rulers. The soldiers love a prince of soldierly mind, one who is haughty, cruel, and rapacious; and, in order that they may get double pay and give vent to their avarice and cruelty, they wish him to exercise his vices on the people. For these reasons, those emperors who by nature or art did not have a great reputation—such that through it they could keep both parties in check—always fell. Most of them, especially those who came to the throne as upstarts, knowing the difficulty caused by these two diverse factions, set out to content the soldiers, and thought injury to the people of little importance. Their decision was necessary, because if princes cannot avoid being hated by somebody, they ought to attempt to keep from being hated by the large groups. When they cannot attain this, they should make every effort to escape the hatred of those large groups that are powerful. Hence, those emperors who had need for extraordinary favors because they were new, attached themselves to the soldiers rather than to the people. This policy, however, was useful to them or not according to whether they knew how to keep up their reputation with the troops.

9 From the causes mentioned above it came about that Marcus, Pertinax, and Alexander—men of modest life, lovers of justice, enemies of cruelty, humane, and benignant—all, except Marcus, came to an unhappy end. Marcus alone lived and died honorably, because he succeeded to the empire by hereditary right, and did not have to recognize the rights of the soldiers or of the people. Besides, since this advantage was accompanied by many high qualities that made him respected, he always kept the two parties within their bounds as long as he lived, and was never either hated or despised. But Pertinax was made emperor against the will of the soldiers, who had been accustomed to live licentiously under Commodus. Hence they were not able to endure the honorable life to which Pertinax wished to bring them back. His efforts roused their hatred against him, and to hatred was joined their contempt for him as an old man. As a result he fell in the early days of his administration.

10 It should here be observed that hate is gained through good deeds as well as bad ones. Therefore, as I said above, if a prince wishes to keep his position, he is often obliged not to be good. For if that large body, whether made up of people or soldiers or grandees, whose support you believe you need to maintain yourself, is corrupt, you must feed its humor in order to satisfy it. In such conditions, good deeds are enemies to you. But let us come to Alexander. He was of such goodness that among the other matters for which he is praised is this, that, in the fourteen years during which he held the empire, no one was ever put to death by him without trial. All the same, since he was thought to be under the influence of women, and a man who allowed his mother to govern him, he came to be despised. Then the army plotted against him and killed him.

11 Now considering on the other side the qualities of Commodus, Severus, Antoninus, Caracalla, and Maximinus, you find them very cruel and rapacious. In order to please the soldiers, they did not spare any sort of injury that might be done to the people. All of them, except Severus, came to a wretched end. Severus, however, had so much vigor that by keeping the soldiers friendly, though the people were oppressed by him, he was always able to rule successfully. His ability made him so admirable in the sight of both soldiers and people that the latter continued to be, as it were, amazed and bewildered, and the soldiers respectful and satisfied.

12 Because the actions of Severus were great and worthy of note in a new prince, I wish to show briefly how well he knew how to play the part of the fox and of the lion—whose natures, as I said above,[15] a prince is obliged to imitate. Knowing the sloth of the Emperor Julian, Severus persuaded the army of which he was general in Sclavonia that it would be a good thing to go to Rome to avenge themselves for the death of Pertinax, who had been put to death by the Pretorian soldiers. Under this pretence, and without showing that he aspired to the imperial throne, he directed his army on Rome, and was in Italy before his decision was known. When he arrived in Rome, the Senate, in fear, elected him emperor and put Julian to death. After this beginning, there remained two difficulties for Severus, if he wished to be master of all the empire. One was in Asia, where Pescennius Niger, head of the Asiatic armies, had had himself proclaimed emperor. The other was in the West, where Albinus governed, who also aspired to the throne. Judging it dangerous to show himself hostile to both at once, Severus decided to assail Niger and deceive Albinus. Hence he wrote to the latter that, having been elected emperor by the Senate, he wished to share that dignity with him. He sent him the title of Caesar and, by decree of the Senate, joined him to himself as colleague. Albinus took all this as honestly meant. Severus then defeated and killed Niger, pacified the East, and returned to Rome. There he complained in the Senate that Albinus, not appreciating the benefits he had received, had treacherously sought to kill him, and asserted it was therefore necessary to go to punish his ingratitude. Thereupon he marched against him in France and took from him his territory and his life.

13 So then, anybody who examines his actions in detail will find that he was a very fierce lion and a very crafty fox, and will see him feared and respected by everybody and not hated by his armies. It is not to be wondered at that he, an upstart, was able to hold so great an empire, for his high reputation always protected him from the hatred the people might have conceived for him because of his rapacity.

14 But Antoninus his son was also a man whose excellent qualities made him admirable in the sight of the people and pleasing to the soldiers. He was a soldierly man, able to support the most severe fatigue and one who despised delicate food and every sort of softness; this made him loved by all the armies. Nevertheless his fierceness and cruelty were great and beyond belief, for, after numerous individual murders, he slaughtered a large portion of the inhabitants of Rome and all those of Alexandria. Hence he became most hateful to all

[15] Chap. 18, par. 3.

the world. Finally he began to be feared even by those he had around him; as a result he was slain in the midst of his army by a centurion. In this connection it may be observed that such a death, resulting from the determination of a firm mind, cannot be avoided by a prince. Any man who is not afraid to die can harm you. But indeed the prince should have little fear of that sort of death, for it is very rare. He needs only to restrain himself from doing serious injury to any of those who wait on him, or whom he has around him to carry on the business of his government. Antoninus acted unwisely in this, for he had put to death with disgrace the brother of that centurion and threatened the man himself daily; nevertheless he still kept him in his bodyguard. This was a foolhardy procedure, and fit to ruin him, as it did.[16]

15 But let us come to Commodus. It would have been very easy for him to hold the throne, because, as the son of Marcus, he had it by hereditary right. He needed only to follow the footsteps of his father, for thus he would have satisfied the soldiers and the people. But because he was of a cruel and bestial spirit, he set himself to gaining the favor of the soldiers and making them licentious, in order that he might exercise his rapacity on the people. But on the other hand he did not keep his dignity, but descended often into the arena to fight with gladiators, and did other vile things little befitting the imperial majesty; thus he became contemptible in the sight of the soldiers. So being hated by one party and despised by the other, he was conspired against and killed.

16 It remains for me to tell of the character of Maximinus. He was a very warlike man; so the army, disgusted with the softness of Alexander, of whom I have written above, killed him and chose Maximinus emperor. He did not reign long, because two things made him hateful and contemptible. One of these was that he was of the lowest birth, having once kept sheep in Thrace; this was well known everywhere and detracted greatly from his dignity in the eyes of everybody. The other was that, though at the beginning of his rule he put off going to Rome and entering into the possession of the imperial throne, he yet gave rise to the opinion that he was very cruel, for he exercised many cruelties through his officers in Rome and in other places in the empire. As a result, all the world was moved with disdain for the baseness of his blood, and with hatred through fear of his ferocity. Hence Africa first rebelled, then the Senate with all the people of Rome; and all

[16] "He who is threatened, and sees himself forced by the necessity of either doing or suffering, becomes a man very dangerous to the prince" (*Discourses on Livy*, III, 6).

Italy plotted against him. His own army, which had been fighting against Aquileia and finding the siege difficult, also joined the rebellion, and disgusted by his cruelty and fearing him less because it saw how many were hostile to him, killed him.

17 I do not wish to discuss Heliogabalus or Macrinus or Julian, for being everywhere despised they were quickly overthrown. So I will come to the end of this discussion.

18 I say that the princes of our times are less troubled than the emperors were by the necessity of making their conduct satisfy the soldiers above all others. It is true that they do have to give their troops some consideration, yet it is quickly settled, because none of these princes have armies already formed that have grown old along with the governments and administrations of the provinces, as did the armies of the Roman empire. If, therefore, it was then necessary to satisfy the soldiers rather than the people, it was because the soldiers were more powerful than the people. Now it is more necessary to princes, except the Turk [17] and the Soldan,[18] to satisfy the people rather than the soldiers, for the people are the more powerful. I make an exception of the Turk, who always keeps about him twelve thousand infantry and fifteen thousand cavalry, on whom depend his security and the strength of his kingdom. So it is necessary that, giving second place to any other consideration, that lord should keep the friendship of his soldiers. Since the kingly authority of the Soldan is likewise entirely in the hands of the soldiers, it is needful for him to have them as his friends, without regard for the people. You should observe that this government of the Soldan is unlike all other principates; it is like the Christian papacy,[19] which can be called neither a hereditary principality nor a new one. The sons of the old prince are not heirs and do not carry on a line of princes, but the successor is he who is chosen to that rank by those who have the right to do so. And yet, since this method of government has long been used, it cannot be called a new principality, because it encounters none of the difficulties of new ones. Even if the ruler is new, the institutions of the state are old and arranged to receive him as though he were their hereditary lord.

19 But let us return to our subject. I say that whoever will look carefully at the foregoing discourse will see that hatred or contempt caused the ruin of the emperors I have named. He

[17] The Sultan of Turkey, supported by the Janizaries.

[18] The Sultan of Egypt, sustained by his Mamelukes.

[19] Cf. Chap. 11, par. 1.

will see also the reason why one of them had a happy end and the others miserable ends, even though part of them acted in one way and the others in a contrary manner. For since Pertinax and Alexander were new rulers, it would have been useless and harmful for them to attempt to imitate Marcus, who was on the throne by hereditary right. Likewise it would have been injurious for Caracalla, Commodus, and Maximinus to imitate Severus, because they did not have the vigor that would have enabled them to follow in his footsteps. Therefore a new prince, in a new princely government, is unable to imitate the actions of Marcus, but yet he is not obliged to follow those of Severus. He ought rather to take from Severus those qualities that are necessary for the establishment of his power, and from Marcus those that are suitable to the preservation of a government that for some time has been firmly established, and that will bring it glory.

CHAPTER 20

Whether Fortresses and Other Things That Princes Employ Every Day Are Useful or Useless

1 Some princes, in order to hold their positions securely, have disarmed their subjects. Others have kept their subject territories divided. Some have nourished enmities against themselves. Yet others, by a change in policy, have tried to gain to their side those they suspected at the beginnings of their reigns. Some have built fortresses. Some have dismantled and destroyed them. From all these things it is not possible to educe a final decision, without coming to the particulars of those states where matters like these must be decided. Hence I shall speak in the general manner that the material in itself justifies.

2 It has never been true, then, that a new prince has disarmed his subjects. On the contrary, when he has found them disarmed, he has always armed them, because, when you arm them, their arms become your own; those whom you have suspected become faithful; those who were faithful are kept so, and instead of your subjects they become your partisans. It is impossible to arm all your subjects, yet if you benefit those you arm, you can deal much more securely with those who are left unarmed. The very diversity of procedure which the favored ones see applied to them, binds them to you. The others excuse you, holding it necessary that those should have more favor who undergo the most danger and have the greatest obligation. But when you disarm new subjects you get their ill-will; for you show that you distrust them either for their worthlessness or their lack of fidelity. Either one of these beliefs rouses hatred against you. And because you are not able to remain unarmed, you are obliged to turn to mercenary soldiers, who are of the kind I have explained above.[1] Even if mercenaries were good, they could not be sufficient to defend you from hostile rulers and untrustworthy subjects. Hence, as I have said, a new prince, in a new principate, has always organized armies there. Histories are full of examples of this.

3 But when a prince acquires a new state that he joins as a member to his old one, then it is necessary to disarm the new state, except for those who have been your partisans in gaining it. And even these it is necessary to render soft and effeminate as time and opportunity permit; and you must arrange things in such a way that the arms of your whole state are in the

[1] In Chap. 12.

hands of your own soldiers, who live in your old state close to you.

4 Our old men and those who were thought wise were in the habit of saying that it was necessary to hold Pistoia with parties and Pisa with fortresses. Hence they encouraged dissentions in some cities that were subject to them, in order to retain them more easily. This may have been good policy in those times when Italy was in a way balanced, but I do not believe that it can be given out today as a precept, because I do not believe that divisions ever do any good. On the contrary, when the enemy draws near, divided cities will of necessity soon be lost, because the weaker party will always adhere to the forces outside and the other will not be able to resist.

5 The Venetians, moved, as I believe, by the reasons given above, encouraged the Guelf and Ghibelline parties in the cities subject to them. And though they did not ever let them come to blood, yet they encouraged these differences among them, in order that the citizens, being occupied in their differences, might not unite against their masters. But it may be seen that this did not turn out well, because, when the Venetians were defeated at Vailà, immediately one party among their subjects took courage, and snatched all their empire away from them. In fact such devices indicate weakness on the part of the prince, because in a strong state such divisions are not permitted. They are of value to a ruler only in time of peace, because by their means he can more easily manage his subjects, but in war such an arrangement shows its weakness.[2]

6 There is no doubt that princes become great when they overcome difficulties and opposition. Therefore Fortune avails herself of this, especially when she wishes to bestow greatness on a new prince, who has more need to acquire reputation than a hereditary one. For she causes enemies to rise up against him, and makes him undertake campaigns against them, that he may have an opportunity to conquer them, and rise high by ascending the ladder provided by his enemies. Hence many think that a wise prince, whenever he has opportunity for it, should craftily nourish some hatreds against himself, in order that by overthrowing them he may increase his greatness.

7 Princes, and especially new ones, sometimes find more fidelity and helpfulness in those whom they have distrusted at the beginning of their rule, than in those who at first were at-

[2] The causing of dissentions in the state was a device commonly attributed to tyrants. See the *Discourses on Livy*, II, 2, par. 3, below. Savonarola refers to it in his *Tractate on the Organization of Florence* 2.2. See Gilbert, *Machiavelli's "Prince" and Its Forerunners*, pp. 162-4.

tached to them. Pandolfo Petrucci, prince of Siena, ruled his state more with those he distrusted than with the others. But of this thing it is not possible to speak in general because it varies according to the individual case. I shall say only this. Those men who are unfriendly in the early days of a reign, and are of such a kind that they have need of support if they are to maintain themselves, are always to be gained by the prince with the greatest ease, and they are obliged to serve him faithfully, in proportion as they know it is needful for them to cancel with their deeds the unfavorable opinion he had of them. Hence the prince always derives more profit from them than from those who feel too secure in his service, and as a result neglect his affairs.

8 And because the subject demands it, I do not wish to omit a reminder to princes who have secured a brand new state by means of the favor of persons within it. They should consider well what cause moved those who favored the change to do so. If it is not natural affection for the new ruler, but merely discontent with the government as it was, a prince will succeed in keeping them as his friends only with effort and great difficulty, because it is impossible for him to satisfy them. And if he will examine the cause of this, with the aid of examples derived from ancient and modern affairs, he will see that it is much easier to gain the friendship of the men who had been contented with the earlier government, and therefore were his enemies, than to gain that of those who became his friends and favored his occupation merely because they were not contented.

9 In order to hold their positions more securely, princes have been in the habit of building fortresses,[3] which serve as bridle and bit for those who plan to act against them; princes also wish to have secure places of refuge from sudden assaults. I praise this method, because it has been used from ancient times. Nonetheless, Messer Niccolò Vitelli, in our times, has been seen dismantling two fortresses in Città di Castello, in order to keep that state. Guido Ubaldo, duke of Urbino, when he returned into his dominions after Cesare Borgia had been driven out of them, completely ruined all the fortresses of that province, and believed that without them it would be more difficult for him to lose that territory again. The Bentivogli, when they returned to Bologna, employed similar methods.

10 Fortresses, then, are useful or not according to the times.

[3] The subject of fortresses is discussed in the *Discourses on Livy*, II, 24, and in the *Art of War*, book 7. For the fortress considered from the side of the republic, see the Letter of June 2, 1526, below. Castruccio built one in Lucca (*Castruccio Castracani*, par. 19).

If they benefit you in some circumstances, they will damage you in others. This matter can be considered as follows: a prince who has more fear of the people than of foreigners ought to build fortresses; but he who has more fear of foreigners than of his people should leave them out of his plans. The castle of Milan, which Francesco Sforza built there, has done and will do more damage to the house of Sforza than any other cause of trouble in that state. Therefore not to be hated by the people is the best fortress there is. Even if you have fortresses, and the people hate you, you will not be safe, because, when the people have taken arms, foreigners who will assist them are never lacking.[4] In our times it cannot be seen that fortresses have been of assistance to any prince, except the Countess of Forlì, at the time of the death of Count Girolamo her husband. She was able, by means of her castle, to avoid the popular fury, to await aid from Milan, and to regain the city. Moreover, the conditions of the times were such that foreigners were unable to aid the people. Yet the fortresses were later of little avail even to her, when Cesare Borgia attacked her, and her hostile people united with a foreigner. Therefore, it would have been more secure for her, both early and late, not to have been hated by the people than to have had fortresses. Considering all these things, then, I praise him who builds fortresses and him who does not build them.[5] I blame any prince who, trusting in his castles, thinks it of little importance that his people hate him.

[4] Cf. Chap. 19, pars. 2 and 3.

[5] That is, he praises the prince who adapts his conduct to circumstances, according to Chap. 25.

CHAPTER 21

What Is Necessary to a Prince That He May Be Considered Excellent

1 Nothing gives a prince so much respect as great undertakings and unusual examples of his own ability. In our day we have Ferdinand of Spain.[1] He can be called, as it were, a new king, because, though at the beginning he was weak, he has become the first king of the Christians in fame and glory. If you will consider his actions, you will find them all great and some of them extraordinary. In the beginning of his reign he attacked Granada, and that undertaking was the foundation of his power. In the first place, he carried it on when he was without other occupation and had no fear of being impeded; he used it to occupy the minds of the barons of Castile, who, when they were thinking about that war, did not think of rebelling. By this means he gained reputation and control over them without their realizing it. He was able to support armies with the money of the Church and the people, and, by means of that long war, to lay a foundation for his army, which later did him honor. Besides this, in order to undertake greater enterprises, he availed himself of religion and turned to a pious cruelty, hunting down the Moors and driving them out of his kingdom. Nothing can be more wretched or more unusual than this example of his ability.[2] Cloaked with this same mantle, he attacked Africa; he undertook his enterprise in Italy; and finally he assailed France. And so he has always kept the minds of his subjects in suspense and wonder, and concerned with the outcome of his deeds. And his actions have begun in such a way, one coming from another, that between any two of them, he has never given men time enough to enable them to work quietly against him.

2 It is also to the profit of a prince to give unusual examples of his ability in internal affairs, like those that are related of Messer Bernabò of Milan.[3] I mean when he has an opportunity

[1] Part of the Letter of April 29, 1513, given below, is a preliminary study for this account of Ferdinand.

[2] For similar moral condemnation, see Chap. 8, par. 3, and the *Introduction*, par. 50.

[3] Bernabò Visconti, duke of Milan 1354-85. His extraordinary acts are related by story-tellers and chroniclers. For example, Franco Sacchetti writes that the Duke saw some countrymen digging a grave. Asking about it, he was told that a pilgrim had died leaving no property. The priest and sexton refused to have anything to do with his body because they would not be paid. Summoning them, Bernabò asked: "Are these men telling the truth?" The priest and the sexton shouted together: "Signore, we ought to have what is due us." The Duke answered: "And who can give it to you? Can the dead man who does *(Continued on page 165)*

because someone does something extraordinary, either good or bad, in ordinary life, and the prince takes a method of rewarding or punishing him that will be widely talked of.[4] And above all, a prince should endeavor in all his actions to show that he deserves fame as a great man and one of high mental capacity.

3 A prince is also esteemed when he is a true friend or a true enemy; that is, when without any reservation he shows himself favorable to one ruler and against another. This procedure is always more profitable than to remain neutral, because if two potentates, your neighbors, come to grips, they are such that when one of them conquers, you either will have to be afraid of the conqueror, or you will not. In either of these two cases, it will be better for you to make your policy plain and put up a good fight. In the first of them, if you do not adopt an open policy, you will always be the prey of the conqueror, to the pleasure and satisfaction of him who is conquered. You can give no reason why anybody should protect you and receive you, and will find nobody to do it. The one who conquers does not wish friends whom he suspects and who will not aid him in adversity, and the loser will not receive you because you have not been willing to share his fortunes with arms in your hands.

4 When Antiochus led his army into Greece, summoned there by the Aetolians to drive out the Romans, he sent ambassadors to the Achaeans, who were friends of the Romans, to advise them to remain neutral. On the other side, the Romans tried to persuade them to take arms with them. This matter came up for decision in the council of the Achaeans, where the agent of Antiochus advised them to remain neutral. The Roman legate answered: "As to what the others say about not getting yourselves into the war, nothing is less advantageous to you; without thanks, without dignity, you will be the reward of the victor."[5]

5 It will always come about that he who is not your friend will ask you to be neutral, and he who is friendly to you will

(Concluded from page 164) not have it?" But they replied: "We ought to have our due, no matter who pays it." Then said Bernabò: "And I will give it to you; death is your due. Where is the dead man? Bring him here. Put him in the grave. Seize the priest; throw him in. Where is the sexton? Throw him in. Shovel in the earth." And so he had the priest and the sexton buried with the dead pilgrim, and went on his way. See Vito Vitale, "Bernabò Visconti nella novella e nella cronaca contemporanea," in *Archivio storico lombardo*, series 3, XV (1901), 261-85; and Dorothy Muir, *Milan under the Visconti*, pp. 70-2.

[4] In the *Discourses on Livy*, III, 34, there is a passage similar to this in which words as well as actions are mentioned, and it is said they are in harmony with the common good—something only implied here. Cf. the striking sayings given in *Castruccio Castracani*, pars. 42-77.

[5] Livy, XXXV, 49. Quoted also in the second Letter of December 20, 1514, par. 2.

ask you to come out clearly with arms. Princes of irresolute character, in order to escape the perils of the moment, generally take the way of neutrality, and generally go to smash. But when a prince comes out vigorously in favor of one side, if the one you have joined wins, even though he is powerful and you are at his discretion, he is under obligation to you, and has formed a friendship for you. Moreover, men are never so dishonorable that they will give so great an example of ingratitude as to oppress you. And then victories are never so decided that the victor is not subject to qualifications, and especially with regard to justice. But if the one to whom you adhere loses, you are received by him, he aids you as long as he can, and you are the companion of a fortune that may rise again.

6 In the second case, when those who fight are of such a sort that you do not need to fear whichever one conquers, it is so much the more prudent for you to join your friend, because you go to the ruin of one neighbor with the aid of another who, if he were wise, would protect him. If your ally is victorious he is at your discretion, and it is impossible that with your aid he will not win.

7 Here it may be observed that a prince should be careful not to join company with one more powerful than himself, in order to attack someone, except when necessity constrains him, in the way mentioned above.[6] If your powerful ally conquers, you remain his prisoner. And princes should avoid, as much as they can, being at the discretion of others.[7] The Venetians joined the King of France against the Duke of Milan, when they were able to avoid making that alliance, and it resulted in their ruin. But when such an alliance cannot be avoided (as happened to the Florentines when the Pope and the King of Spain went with their armies to attack Lombardy), then a prince should join in for the reasons I have given.[8] No state should believe it can always make plans certain of success,[9] it should rather expect to make only doubtful ones. For

[6] In the preceding paragraph, where the alliance not to be avoided appears. In the present paragraph the Venetians are said to have entered an unnecessary alliance with a stronger state.

[7] This phrase occurs in the Letter of April 29, 1513, par. 9, and in the first Letter of December 20, 1514, par. 13. Seneca says that "he reaches the heights who does not put his prosperity in the power of another" (*Epistles* 23, 2).

[8] For discussion of alliances and neutrality, see the two Letters of December 20, 1514, given below, and the *Discourse on Reforming the Government of Florence*, par. 11.

[9] This idea is applied to Cesare Borgia at the end of Machiavelli's *On the Method of Treating the People of Valdichiana*. Since the Duke cannot be sure his plans will succeed, he must trust a good part of his cause to Fortune.

the course of human events teaches that man never attempts to avoid one disadvantage without running into another. Prudence, therefore, consists in the power to recognize the nature of disadvantages and to take the less disagreeable as good.[10]

8 A prince should also show himself a lover of excellence by giving preferment to gifted men and honoring those who excel in some art. Besides, he should encourage his citizens by giving them a chance to exercise their functions quietly, in trade and agriculture and every other occupation of man. A citizen should not hesitate to increase his property for fear it will be taken away from him, or to open a new business for fear of taxes.[11] On the contrary the prince should offer rewards to those who undertake to do these things, and to anybody who thinks of improving in any way his city or his dominion. Besides this, at suitable times of the year he should engage the attention of the people with festivals and shows.[12] And because every city is divided into gilds or wards, he should take account of these bodies, meet with them sometimes, and give in person an example of humanity and generosity. At the same time he should always preserve the dignity befitting his rank, for this ought never to be lacking in any circumstances.

[10] This idea is repeated in the two Letters of December 20, 1514, pars. 14 and 7, respectively, below, in the *Discourses on Livy,* I, 6, and 38, and in the *Mandragola,* act. 3, sc. 1.

[11] The prince who brings about this result is working for the common good; cf. the *Discourses on Livy,* II, 2, pars. 2, 9, below.

[12] In language close to that of Machiavelli, Savonarola wrote that the tyrant "engages the attention of the people in shows and festivals" (*Tractate on the Organization and Government of the City of Florence,* book 2, chap. 2).

CHAPTER 22

On the Confidential Servants of Princes

1 The choice of his ministers is of no slight importance to a prince. These men are good or not according to the prudence of the prince. The first method for estimating the brain-power of a ruler is to look at the men he has around him. When they are competent and faithful, the prince can be considered generally wise, because he has been able to recognize capable men and keep them faithful to him. But when his ministers are of a different sort, a good report cannot in any way be given of the prince, because the first error he makes is in this choice.

2 There was nobody who knew that Messer Antonio da Venafro was minister of Pandolfo Petrucci, prince of Siena, who did not think Pandolfo was a very capable man, because he had Antonio as his minister. There are, in fact, three types of brain. One understands things for itself. The second discerns what others understand. The third neither understands for itself nor appreciates others. The first is the best of all; the second is excellent; the third is useless. Hence it must be concluded that if Pandolfo was not in the first class, he was in the second. For whenever a man has judgment sound enough to recognize the good and the evil that some other man does and says, even though he has no great mental power of his own, he recognizes the bad and the good actions of the minister, and rebukes the first and praises the second. Moreover the minister cannot hope to deceive him, and is kept honest.

3 As to the method by which a prince can learn the quality of a minister, there is one way that never fails. When you see the minister thinking more of himself than of you, and in all his acts seeking his own advantage, you can conclude that a person of that sort never will be a good minister, and you will never be able to trust him. A man who has another's well-being in his hand should never think of himself, but of the prince, and should not remember anything that does not pertain to his master.[1] On the other side, the prince, to keep the minister good, should think about him and honor him, make him rich, do him favors, and bestow on him honors and offices. The minister will thus be made to see that he cannot stand without the prince; his many honors will keep him from wishing more honors, his great riches will keep him from wishing more riches, and his many offices will make him fear revolutions. If, then, the ministers, and the princes in their conduct

[1] **Was Machiavelli thinking of his own service to Florence?**

to the ministers, are such as I have suggested, they can have faith in one another.[2] If conditions are otherwise the result will be damaging to both of them.

[2] Since the minister is good, the prince can deal faithfully with him. Contrast his conduct to the wicked, Chap. 18, par. 3.

CHAPTER 23

IN WHAT WAY FLATTERERS ARE TO BE AVOIDED[1]

1 I do not wish to omit an important subject and an error from which princes with difficulty protect themselves,[2] if they are not unusually prudent, or if they are not able to choose well. I refer to flatterers, of whom courts are full. Men are generally so well pleased with their own abilities and so greatly deceived about them that they protect themselves with difficulty from this plague, and when they do endeavor to protect themselves, they run the risk of becoming contemptible, for the reason that there is no way of protecting yourself from flattery except to have men understand that they do not offend you by speaking the truth to you; but when anyone can speak the truth to you, you do not receive proper respect. Hence a prudent prince must adopt a third method. He should choose wise men in his state, and to them alone he should give full power to speak the truth freely, but only on the matters he asks about, and on nothing else. Yet he should ask them about everything, and heed their opinions. Then he should make up his mind in private, at his leisure. With these pieces of advice, and with every one of them, he should conduct himself in such a way that each adviser may know that he will be so much the more in favor in proportion as he speaks more freely. But the prince should not consent to listen to anyone except these advisers, should carry out what he decides on, and should be firm in his decisions. He who does otherwise is either ruined by flatterers, or changes often, because of the varied opinions he listens to. As a result, he receives little respect.

2 I wish to bring up one modern example on this subject. Pre' Luca, one of the ministers of Maximilian, the present emperor, when talking of His Majesty, said he took counsel with nobody, and never acted in anything according to his own wish. This came from a procedure opposite to the aforesaid. The Emperor is a secretive man; he does not communicate his plans to anybody, and does not get advice on them. But when he comes to put them into effect, and they begin to be known and made plain, they begin to be censured by those he has around him. Then, being easily influenced, he is dissuaded from them. From this it comes about that what he plans one day he destroys the next, no one ever understands what is wanted or what the emperor plans to do, and no reliance can be placed on his decisions.

[1] Cf. flattery in *Castruccio Castracani*, par. 44.

[2] An important subject in conventional books of advice to princes, such as Vincent of Beauvais' *De morali principis institutione*.

3 A prince, therefore, should always take advice, but he should do it when he pleases and not when someone else pleases. On the contrary he should not let anyone dare to advise him when he does not ask for advice. But he should be a big asker, and a patient listener to the truth about the things asked. Still further, he should be angry if for any reason anybody should not tell him the truth. Many think that if a prince gives the impression of being prudent, he should be thought so not because of his own natural gifts but because of the good advice he has at hand; but without question they are wrong. For this is a general rule that never fails: a prince who is not wise himself cannot be well advised, unless by chance he gives himself over to one man who entirely directs him, and that man is exceedingly prudent. In this instance the prince surely would be,[3] but such a condition would not last long, because in a short time that tutor of his would take away his throne. As a matter of fact, an unwise prince who asks counsel from more than one man will never receive unified advice, nor will he be able to unify it unaided. Each of the advisers will think about what concerns himself, and the prince will not be able to control them or to understand them. It cannot be otherwise; men are always wicked at bottom, unless they are made good by some compulsion. Hence I conclude that good counsels, whatever their source, necessarily result from the prudence of the ruler, and not the prudence of the ruler from good counsels.

[3] That is, would be well advised.

CHAPTER 24

WHY THE PRINCES OF ITALY HAVE LOST THEIR AUTHORITY

1 The things written above,[1] if they are prudently carried into effect, will make a new prince seem to be an old one, and will immediately make him safer and firmer in his realm than if he had grown old in it.[2] For the actions of a new prince are more closely watched than those of a hereditary one; and when they are seen to show great ability they influence men more and attach them to the prince more closely than ancient blood can, for men are much more impressed with present things than with past ones, and when in the present they find something good, they enjoy it and seek for nothing further. In fact, they will take every means of defending such a prince, if only he does not fail himself in other things.[3] And thus he will secure a double glory:[4] that of having begun a new princedom, and of having enriched and strengthened it with good laws, good arms, and good examples.[5] On the contrary, he is doubly disgraced who, though born a prince, loses his dominion because he is not prudent.

2 And if those lords are examined who have lost their positions in Italy in our times, such as the King of Naples, the Duke of Milan, and others, they will exhibit first a common defect in their armies, for the reasons that have been discussed at length above.[6] Further, it will be seen that some of them either had the people as enemies, or they had the friendship of the people, but had not been able to secure themselves against the upper classes.[7] For realms without these defects are not lost if the prince has strength enough to keep an army in the field.[8] Philip of Macedon, not the father of Alexander but the one who was conquered by Titus Quintus, did not have a large realm, in comparison with the greatness of the Romans and the Greeks who attacked him. Neverthe-

[1] The whole preceding work. [2] Cf. Chap. 2, par. 2.

[3] Cf. Chap. 19, par. 2, and the passages on self-reliance there referred to.

[4] Cf. Chap. 26, par. 1, and the *Discourse on Reforming the Government of Florence*, pars. 29, 30, above.

[5] For the ruler's example, see Gilbert, *Machiavelli's "Prince" and Its Forerunners*, pp. 197-203. The ruler is to exemplify to his people the virtues of Chap. 15, par. 2; it is praiseworthy to possess them (par. 3), and they are to be abandoned only in necessity, and not openly even then (Chap. 18, par. 5). On a dangerous public example, see *Discourses on Livy*, I, 34, par. 2, below. Cf. the *Introduction*, pars. 39 ff.

[6] Chapters 12, 13, 14.

[7] Apparently this does not carry the suggestion of getting rid of them that sometimes accompanies the notion of securing oneself against troublesome persons. Cf. Chap. 9, par. 5.

[8] Cf. Chap. 10, par. 1.

less, because he was a warrior, and knew how to deal with his people and to secure himself against the upper classes, he kept up the war for several years. Even though at the end he lost control of some cities, he nevertheless retained his royal authority.

3 Therefore these princes of ours who have been many years in their positions should blame for the loss of them not Fortune, but their own worthlessness.[9] In good weather they never thought of change (it is a common defect of men not to reckon on a storm when the sea is calm). Hence when times of adversity came, they thought about running away and not about defending themselves; and they hoped that the people, disgusted by the insolence of the conquerors, would call them back.[10] This plan, when there are no others, is good, but it is a bad thing to abandon other resources for this one. A prince should not be willing to fall, just because he believes he will find somebody to set him up again; that may not come about, or if it does, it cannot bring you security, because such an expedient for defence is base and does not depend on yourself. Only those means of security are good, are certain, are lasting, that depend on yourself and your own vigor.[11]

[9] Cf. the Letter of August 26, 1513, last par.

[10] Cf. Chap. 2, par. 2.

[11] The essence of Machiavelli's advice to the prince. Cf., e.g., Chap. 6, par. 5; Chap. 10, par. 1.

CHAPTER 25

The Power of Fortune in Human Affairs, and to What Extent She Should Be Relied on [1]

1 It is not unknown to me that many have been and still are of the opinion that the affairs of this world are so under the direction of Fortune and of God that man's prudence cannot control them; in fact, that man has no resource against them. For this reason many think there is no use in sweating much over such matters, but that one might as well let Chance take control. This opinion has been the more accepted in our times, because of the great changes in the state of the world that have been and now are seen every day, beyond all human surmise. And I myself, when thinking on these things, have now and then in some measure inclined to their view. Nevertheless, because the freedom of the will should not be wholly annulled, I think it may be true that Fortune is arbiter of half of our actions, but that she still leaves the control of the other half, or about that, to us.

2 I liken her to one of those raging streams that, when they go mad, flood the plains, ruin the trees and the buildings, and take away the fields from one bank and put them down on the other. Everybody flees before them; everybody yields to their onrush without being able to resist anywhere. And though this is their nature, it does not cease to be true that, in calm weather, men can make some provision against them with walls and dykes, so that, when the streams swell, their waters will go off through a canal, or their currents will not be so wild and do so much damage. The same is true of Fortune. She shows her power where there is no wise preparation for resisting her, and turns her fury where she knows that no walls and dykes have been made to hold her in. And if you consider Italy—the place where these variations occur and the cause that has set them in motion—you will see that she is a country without dykes and without any wall of defence. If, like Germany, Spain, and France, she had had a sufficient bulwark of military vigor, this flood would not have made the great changes it has, or would not have come at all.

3 And this, I think, is all I need to say on opposing oneself to Fortune, in general. But limiting myself more to particulars, I say that a prince may be seen prospering today and falling in ruin tomorrow, though it does not appear that he has changed in his nature or any of his qualities. I believe

[1] For both general idea and details, such as the figure of the flood, cf. the *Capitolo on Fortune,* and the Letter to Pier Soderini of January 1512-3, below. See also the *Introduction,* pars. 115-120.

this comes, in the first place, from the causes that have been discussed at length in preceding chapters.[2] That is, if a prince bases himself entirely on Fortune, he will fall when she varies. I also believe that a ruler will be successful who adapts his mode of procedure to the quality of the times, and likewise that he will be unsuccessful if the times are out of accord with his procedure. Because it may be seen that in things leading to the end each has before him, namely glory and riches, men proceed differently. One acts with caution, another rashly; one with violence, another with skill; one with patience, another with its opposite; yet with these different methods each one attains his end. Still further, two cautious men will be seen, of whom one comes to his goal, the other does not. Likewise you will see two who succeed with two different methods, one of them being cautious and the other rash. These results are caused by nothing else than the nature of the times, which is or is not in harmony with the procedure of men. It also accounts for what I have mentioned, namely, that two persons, working differently, chance to arrive at the same result; and that of two who work in the same way, one attains his end, but the other does not.

4 On the nature of the times also depends the variability of the best method. If a man conducts himself with caution and patience, times and affairs may come around in such a way that his procedure is good, and he goes on successfully. But if times and circumstances change, he is ruined, because he does not change his method of action. There is no man so prudent as to understand how to fit himself to this condition, either because he is unable to deviate from the course to which nature inclines him, or because, having always prospered by walking in one path, he cannot persuade himself to leave it. So the cautious man, when the time comes to go at a reckless pace, does not know how to do it. Hence he comes to ruin. Yet if he could change his nature with the times and with circumstances, his fortune would not be altered.

5 Pope Julius II proceeded rashly in all his actions, and found the times and circumstances so harmonious with his mode of procedure that he was always so lucky as to succeed.[3] Consider the first enterprise he engaged in, that of Bologna, while Messer Giovanni Bentivogli was still alive. The Venetians were not pleased with it; the King of Spain felt the same way; the Pope was debating such an enterprise with

[2] That is, whenever they have failed in the prudence and industry inculcated throughout *The Prince;* see especially Chap. 24, last par.

[3] For the character of Julius, see the Letter of April 29, 1513, pars. 4, 11, below.

the King of France. Nevertheless, in his courage and rashness Julius personally undertook that expedition. This movement made the King of Spain and the Venetians stand irresolute and motionless, the latter for fear, and the King because of his wish to recover the entire kingdom of Naples. On the other side, the King of France was dragged behind Julius, because the King, seeing that the Pope had moved and wishing to make him a friend in order to put down the Venetians, judged he could not refuse him soldiers without doing him open injury. Julius, then, with his rash movement, attained what no other pontiff, with the utmost human prudence, would have attained. If he had waited to leave Rome until the agreements were fixed and everything arranged, as any other pontiff would have done, he would never have succeeded, for the King of France would have had a thousand excuses, and the others would have raised a thousand fears. I wish to omit his other acts, which are all of the same sort, and all succeeded perfectly. The brevity of his life did not allow him to know anything different. Yet if times had come in which it was necessary to act with caution, they would have ruined him, for he would never have deviated from the methods to which nature inclined him.

6 I conclude, then, that since Fortune is variable and men are set in their ways, they are successful when they are in harmony with Fortune and unsuccessful when they disagree with her. Yet I am of the opinion that it is better to be rash than over-cautious, because Fortune is a woman and, if you wish to keep her down, you must beat her and pound her. It is evident that she allows herself to be overcome by men who treat her in that way rather than by those who proceed coldly. For that reason, like a woman, she is always the friend of young men,[4] because they are less cautious, and more courageous, and command her with more boldness.

[4] The same thing is said in the *Clizia,* IV, i.

CHAPTER 26

An Exhortation to Take Hold of Italy and Restore Her to Liberty from the Barbarbians

1 Having considered all the things discussed above, I have been turning over in my own mind whether at present in Italy the time is ripe for a new prince to win prestige, and whether conditions there give a wise and vigorous ruler occasion to introduce methods that will do him honor,[1] and bring good to the mass of the people of the land.[2] It appears to me that so many things unite for the advantage of a new prince, that I do not know of any time that has ever been more suited for this. And, as I said,[3] if it was necessary to make clear the ability of Moses that the people of Israel should be enslaved in Egypt, and to reveal Cyrus's greatness of mind that the Persians should be oppressed by the Medes, and to demonstrate the excellence of Theseus that the Athenians should be scattered, so at the present time, in order to make known the greatness of an Italian soul, Italy had to be brought down to her present position, to be more a slave than the Hebrews, more a servant than the Persians, more scattered than the Athenians; without head, without government; defeated, plundered, torn asunder, overrun; subject to every sort of disaster.[4]

2 And though before this, certain persons have showed signs from which it could be inferred that they were chosen by God for the redemption of Italy,[5] nevertheless it has afterwards been seen that in the full current of action they have been cast off by Fortune. So Italy remains without life and awaits the man, whoever he may be, who is to heal her wounds, put an end to the plundering of Lombardy and the tribute laid on Tuscany and the kingdom of Naples, and cure her of those sores that have long been suppurating. She may be seen praying God to send some one to redeem her from these cruel and barbarous insults. She is evidently ready and willing to follow a banner, if only some one will raise it. Nor is there at present anyone to be seen in whom she can put more hope than in your illustrious House, because its fortune and vigor, and the favor of God and of the Church, which it now governs,

[1] Cf. Chap. 8, par. 3; Chap. 24, par. 1.

[2] The only clear statement in *The Prince* of the function of the ruler. See *common good* in the Index.

[3] In Chap. 6, par. 3.

[4] In this sentence, with its references to division, Machiavelli implies the idea that dominates this chapter, though it is not baldly stated: that of united Italy. See the *Discourses on Livy*, I, 12, par. 5, below.

[5] See the present chapter, par. 3.

enable it to be the leader in such a redemption. This will not be very difficult, as you will see if you will bring to mind the actions and lives of those I have named above.[6] And though these men were striking exceptions, yet they were men, and each of them had less opportunity than the present gives; their enterprises were not more just than this, nor easier, nor was God their friend more than he is yours. Here justice is complete. "A way is just to those to whom it is necessary, and arms are holy to him who has no hope save in arms." [7] Everything is now fully disposed for the work, and when that is true an undertaking cannot be difficult, if only your House adopts the methods of those I have set forth as examples. Moreover, we have before our eyes extraordinary and unexampled means prepared by God. The sea has been divided. A cloud has guided you on your way. The rock has given forth water. Manna has fallen.[8] Everything has united to make you great. The rest is for you to do. God does not intend to do everything, lest he deprive us of our free will and the share of glory that belongs to us.

3 It is no wonder if no one of the above-named Italians has been able to do what we hope your illustrious House can.[9] Nor is it strange if in the many revolutions and military enterprises of Italy, the martial vigor of the land always appears to be exhausted. This is because the old military customs were not good, and there has been nobody able to find new ones. Yet nothing brings so much honor to a man who rises to new power, as the new laws and new methods he discovers.[10] These things, when they are well founded and have greatness in them, make him revered and worthy of admiration. And in Italy matter is not lacking on which to impress forms of every sort. There is great vigor in the limbs if only it is not lacking in the heads. You may see that in duels and combats between

[6] In the preceding paragraph.

[7] From Livy, *History* 9.1.10. Used in the *History of Florence,* V, 8: "What worse disease can afflict the body of a republic than servitude? What medicine is more necessary than that which frees it from this infirmity? Only those wars are just that are necessary, and those wars are pious apart from which there is no hope. I do not know what necessity can be greater than ours, or what piety can surpass that which rescues one's native land from servitude." The same feeling, though with less assurance, appears in the Letter of March 15, 1525-6, pars. 7, 8, given below.

[8] Exodus 14:17. Note the reference to Moses at the beginning of the chapter.

[9] The "above-named" are thought to be Francesco Sforza and Cesare Borgia; see Chap. 7, par. 2. The direct reference seems to be to the unnamed persons possibly chosen by God to redeem Italy named in the preceding paragraph.

[10] Cf. the *Discourse on Reforming the Government of Florence,* par. 29, and *The Prince,* Chap. 24, par. 1.

small numbers, the Italians have been much superior in force, skill, and intelligence. But when it is a matter of armies, Italians cannot be compared with foreigners. All this comes from the weakness of the heads, because those who know are not obeyed, and each man thinks he knows. Nor up to this time has there been a man able to raise himself so high, through both ability and fortune, that the others would yield to him.[11] The result is that for the past twenty years, in all the wars that have been fought when there has been an army entirely Italian, it has always made a bad showing. Proof of this was given first at the Taro, and then at Alessandria, Capua, Genoa, Vailà, Bologna, and Mestri.

4 If your illustrious House, then, wishes to imitate those excellent men who redeemed their countries, it is necessary, before everything else, to furnish yourself with your own army,[12] as the true foundation of every enterprise.[13] You cannot have more faithful, nor truer, nor better soldiers. And though every individual of these may be good, they become better as a body when they see that they are commanded by their prince,[14] and honored and trusted by him. It is necessary, therefore, that your House should be prepared with such forces, in order that it may be able to defend itself against the foreigners with Italian courage.[15]

5 And though the Swiss and the Spanish infantry are properly estimated as terribly effective, yet both have defects. Hence a third type would be able not merely to oppose them but to feel sure of overcoming them. The fact is that the Spaniards are not able to resist cavalry, and the Swiss have reason to fear infantry, when they meet any as determined in battle as themselves. For this reason it has been seen and will be seen in experience that the Spaniards are unable to resist the French cavalry, and the Swiss are overthrown by Spanish infantry. And though of this last a clear instance has not been observed, yet an approach to it appeared in the battle of Ravenna, when the Spanish infantry met the German battalions, who use the same methods as the Swiss. There the Spanish, through their agility and the assistance given by their

[11] In the Letter of March 15, 1525-6, par. 8, it is hinted that Giovanni of the Black Bands is able to do this. In that of November 1526, par. 4, the division of the generals is blamed for the disasters of Clement VII.

[12] Cf. Chap. 13, pars. 3-8.

[13] The word *foundation* is used in connection with Cesare Borgia in Chap. 7, par. 2; cf. also Chap. 6, last par., and Chap. 12, pars. 1, 2.

[14] On the prince as his own general, see Chap. 12, par. 3.

[15] The word used for *Italian* is the same as that in the quotation from Petrarch that concludes the chapter. It would include the Romans and other early Italians.

shields, got within the points of the spears from below, and slew their enemies in security, while the Germans could find no means of resistance.[16] If the cavalry had not charged the Spanish, they would have annihilated the Germans. It is possible, then, for one who realizes the defects of these two types, to equip infantry in a new manner, so that it can resist cavalry and not be afraid of foot-soldiers; but to gain this end they must have weapons of the right sorts, and adopt varied methods of combat.[17] These are some of the things which, when they are put into service as novelties, give reputation and greatness to a new ruler.

6 This opportunity, then, should not be allowed to pass, in order that after so long a time Italy may see her redeemer.[18] I am unable to express with what love he would be received in all the provinces that have suffered from these foreign deluges; with what thirst for vengeance, what firm faith, what piety, what tears! What gates would be shut against him? what peoples would deny him obedience? what envy would oppose itself to him? what Italian would refuse to follow him? This barbarian rule stinks in every nostril.[19] May your illustrious House, then, undertake this charge with the spirit and the hope with which all just enterprises are taken up, in order that, beneath its ensign, our native land may be ennobled, and, under its auspices, that saying of Petrarch may come true:

> Manhood will take arms against fury, and the combat will be short, because in Italian hearts the ancient valor is not yet dead.[20]

[16] This situation is discussed at length in the *Art of War*, book 2.

[17] Much of the *Art of War* is developed from this sentence.

[18] For this paragraph, see the *Introduction*, pars. 85-9.

[19] In the Letter of May 17, 1526, the barbarian foreigners are "horrible beasts, which have nothing of men except the appearance and the voice."

[20] From Petrarch's patriotic Canzone (VI, 13-6), *My Italy*, in which he also speaks of the northerners as barbarians.

THE LIFE OF CASTRUCCIO CASTRACANI

INTRODUCTION

In 1520 Machiavelli spent in Lucca about three months of the late summer and early autumn. He had gone there on financial business, originally private, which had been taken up by the Florentine state and received personal attention from Cardinal Giulio de' Medici. Since Machiavelli had to negotiate with the Lucchese government, he had practical reasons for learning its nature. This, joined to his ever-present interest in such matters, led him to write a brief exposition of the Luccan constitution, called a *Summary of the Affairs of Lucca.* Evidently his time was not all occupied with matters related to business, for he also wrote and sent to Florence the *Life of Castruccio Castracani of Lucca.* Doubtless Niccolò knew something of this warrior and his part in Tuscan history before going to Lucca, for Giovanni Villani in his *Chronicle* tells much of his wars against Florence. If Machiavelli read this work, he must have had a manuscript, for it was not printed until 1537. It seems likely that in Lucca our author encountered Castruccio's biographer, Niccolò Tegrimi; he surely knew Tegrimi's book, first printed as early as 1496. Some of the material he apparently drew from it is indicated in the notes. He may also have heard legends of the most striking character Lucca had produced. Other chronicles and historical works were laid under contribution, for Machiavelli uses matter found in some of them and not in Villani or Tegrimi; for example, as appears in footnotes 6 and 15, he may have seen the *Storie Pistoresi.*

Legends were, indeed, quite as much to Machiavelli's purpose as facts, and neither of them were his first concern. His *Life of Castruccio* is not a historical work, but a romance with a purpose, that of presenting, for the profit of the reader, an example of governmental and military capacity. The hero is as it were Cesare Borgia before his time, having many of the gifts of the ideal ruler of *The Prince.* Nothing, then, is to be taken as necessarily historical. Castruccio was not a foundling; he was so far from refusing marriage because of his regard for his adopted son that he had a wife and nine children; he did not overthrow Florentine armies at Serravalle and Fucecchio, though he did defeat one at Altopascio; the wise sayings attributed to him were current long before his days. Much indeed is fact, or founded on fact, but all is subordinate to the romance, in which Machiavelli allows himself a freedom that few modern historical novelists have dared to claim.

One of the best analogies is perhaps the *Cyropaedia* or *Education of Cyrus* by Xenophon; in Machiavelli's time this was to be had in both Latin and Italian, and he often alludes to it. As Cicero says, it gives not the literal life of Cyrus, but a picture of government properly carried on.[1] Xenophon's purpose was to present an ideal ruler. He took as his hero one who lived about a century before him, but in a country remote enough to make it credible that strange things would happen there. Machiavelli wrote about two centuries after his hero, but his daring in selecting a Tuscan is such that he can hardly have expected anybody to take his facts seriously. Having given his idea of the prince in his work of that name, he now proceeded to reiterate it for readers not fond of reasoning by throwing it into a form approaching that of the historical novel. He must, however, have as his hero an Italian not too remote, in order to suggest the ruler of his dream, who must begin in Tuscany or Romagna, but whose goal is a united Italy.

THE LIFE OF CASTRUCCIO OF LUCCA, WRITTEN BY NICCOLÒ MACHIAVELLI AND SENT TO ZANOBI BUONDELMONTI AND LUIGI ALAMANNI,[1] HIS DEAR FRIENDS

My dear Zanobi and Luigi,

1 When one considers the matter, it seems remarkable that all or most of those who have done great deeds in this world, and have stood out among the men of their times, have been of humble and obscure ancestors and birth, or at least have been to an unusual extent afflicted by Fortune. All of them have either been exposed to the wild animals, or have had fathers of station so low that they have been ashamed of them and have made themselves out as the children of Jove or of some other god. Since many of these heroes are known to everybody, it would be both boring and unwelcome to the reader to repeat the list of them; hence I omit it as superfluous. I believe the reason for this condition is that Fortune wishes to show the world that she, and not Prudence, makes men great; hence she begins to show her power at a time when Prudence can have no share in the matter, but it must be admitted that all comes from Fortune.[2]

[1] Cicero. Letter to his brother Quintus, 1.1.8,23.

[1] See the *Introduction*, par. 141, above.

[2] For Fortune, see *The Prince*, Chap. 25.

2 Castruccio Castracani of Lucca was, then, one of these, for according to the times in which he lived and the city where he was born, he did great deeds, and yet he did not have a more fortunate or famous origin than other great men have had, as will appear from the narrative of his life. I have wished to tell his story again, since I think I have found in his life many things much worth imitating, both with respect to his native ability and his fortune. And it has seemed fitting to dedicate my narrative to you, because you delight in acts of prowess more than any one else I know.

3 I say, then, that the family of Castracani was counted among the noble families of the city of Lucca, though in our day, according to the course of all worldly things, it has died out. Into this family was born a certain Antonio who, having entered the Church, became a canon of St. Michele of Lucca, and as a mark of respect was called Messer Antonio. He had no relatives except one sister, who married Buonaccorso Cennami; when she was left a widow by Buonaccorso's death, she came to live with her brother, intending not to marry again.

4 Behind his house Messer Antonio had a vineyard, which, because it was bordered by many gardens, could be entered from all sides without much effort. One morning soon after sunrise Mistress Dianora (for that was the name of Messer Antonio's sister) was amusing herself in the vineyard by gathering various herbs to make seasonings, as ladies do. She heard something rustle among the leaves under a vine, and turning toward it, seemed to hear crying. Going in the direction of the sound, she saw among the leaves the hands and face of a baby, who seemed to be asking for help. Partly astonished, partly frightened, and full of compassion and dismay, she took the little boy up, carried him to the house, washed him, dressed him in white clothes such as infants wear, and showed him to Messer Antonio when he came home. When he heard her account and saw the baby, he felt as much wonder and pity as his sister did. They talked over with each other what they ought to do, and determined to bring the boy up, since Messer Antonio was a priest and his sister had no children. So they took a nurse into their house and brought him up with as much love as though he were their own son. When he was baptized, they named him Castruccio after their father.

5 As years went on Castruccio grew more and more attractive, and in everything showed intelligence and prudence. As rapidly as his age permitted, he learned the things Messer Antonio taught him. Since Antonio planned to make him a priest, and in time to turn over to him his canonate and other benefices, he taught the boy with that end in view. But the priest found in his pupil material wholly unadapted to the ecclesiastical temper. As soon as Castruccio reached the age of fourteen he began to get the upper hand of Messer Antonio and lost all fear of Mistress Dianora; so he neglected his religious books and gave his attention to arms. He liked nothing better than handling weapons, and running, leaping, wrestling, and like exercises with other boys. In these sports he showed great power of mind and body, and far surpassed all the others of his age. And whenever he read, no books pleased him except those dealing with war or the deeds of great men. This conduct gave Messer Antonio immeasurable sorrow and trouble.

6 In the city of Lucca there was a gentleman of the family of Guinigi,[3] named Messer Francesco; in riches, elegance, and natural ability he far surpassed everyone else in Lucca. His business was war, and for a long time he had served under the Visconti of Milan. He was a Ghibelline,[4] and was esteemed more than anybody else who belonged to that party in Lucca. When he was in Lucca he was in the habit of meeting every evening and morning with the other citizens in the open gallery of the town hall, which is at the head of the public square of San Michele, the chief square in Lucca. There he often saw Castruccio and the other boys of the neighborhood engaging in the sports I mentioned above. Since he saw that Castruccio not merely beat them but had a sort of kingly authority over them, and that they could be said to love and respect him, Messer Francesco became very eager to know something about the boy. After he had learned the circumstances, he was fired with a still greater desire to take him

[3] An important family which once did rule Lucca. The debt that Machiavelli was attempting to collect in Lucca was owed by a member of the family. There seems to have been no historical connection of the family with Castruccio.

[4] In the time of Dante and Castruccio, Italy was divided into two factions, the Guelfs and the Ghibellines. Generally speaking, the Ghibellines were on the side of the Emperor, who had his usual residence in Germany, and came to Italy only for brief visits. The Guelfs, as their opponents, were on the side of home rule. But the parties tended to become factions in various cities, with no more difference between them than can be found in America between Democrat and Republican. In South Carolina, for example, almost all voters are Democrats, and in parts of New York State, almost all are Republicans. The reasons are historical, and correspond to no personal beliefs at the present time. Something of the sort was true in Italian cities. At their best, the Ghibellines stood for a powerful ruler of Italy who would prevent the local wars that tore the country to pieces; at their worst for oppression by the nobles. The Guelfs at their best stood for liberty; at their worst, for a thousand petty states fighting among themselves and oppressing one another. For a brief account, see Paget Toynbee, *Dante* (London, 1910), pp. 13-58.

into his service. One day, calling Castruccio, he asked him where he would prefer to live: in the house of a gentleman who would teach him to ride and handle weapons, or in the house of a priest where he would hear nothing except holy offices and masses. Messer Francesco realized how pleased Castruccio was to hear horses and arms mentioned; yet the boy was somewhat bashful. But when Messer Francesco encouraged him to speak, he answered that, if it were permitted by his master, nothing could please him more than to drop the studies of a priest and take up those of a soldier. This reply was very pleasing to Messer Francesco, and in a few days he persuaded Messer Antonio to give his permission. The latter was induced to do so more by the nature of the boy than anything else, because he thought he could not restrain his pupil much longer.

7 Therefore Castruccio went from the house of Messer Antonio, the priest, to that of Messer Francesco Guinigi, the soldier of fortune, and in an extraordinarily short time he acquired all the virtues and habits that are demanded of a true gentleman. Above all, he became an excellent horseman, managing the most fiery horses with great skill; in jousts and tournaments, though still only a boy, he was more worth watching than anybody else; in fact, in every action requiring strength or skill, no man was able to surpass him. In addition he possessed good manners, for he showed almost incredible modesty, and never was seen to do a deed or heard to say a word that would cause displeasure. He was respectful to his superiors, modest with his equals, and pleasant to his inferiors. These things made him loved not only by all the family of the Guinigi, but by all the city of Lucca.

8 It happened in those times, when Castruccio was eighteen years old, that the Ghibellines of Pavia were driven out by the Guelfs. Messer Francesco Guinigi was sent to the aid of the Ghibellines by the Visconti of Milan. Castruccio went with him, and was responsible for his whole force. In this expedition Castruccio gave so many signs of his prudence and spirit that nobody else concerned in that undertaking gained from it so good a reputation with everyone as he did. His name became well-known and honored not merely in Pavia but in all Lombardy.

9 On his return to Lucca, with a much higher standing than when he left, he did everything in his power to gain friends, by practicing all the methods that are likely to win men over. When Messer Francesco Guinigi died, leaving a son named

Pagolo, thirteen years old, he made Castruccio guardian of the boy and of his property. For before his death he sent for Castruccio and begged him to agree to bring up Pagolo with the fidelity with which Castruccio himself had been brought up, and to show to the son the gratitude he had not been able to show to the father. When Messer Francesco Guinigi was gone and Castruccio had become Pagolo's guardian, he increased so much in reputation and power that the favor he had in Lucca changed in part to envy, and many slandered him as one who was to be feared because he was trying to make himself tyrant. The chief of these slanderers was Messer Giorgio degli Opizi, head of the Guelf party. He had hoped on the death of Messer Francesco to be the chief man in Lucca, but it seemed to him that Castruccio, by holding the position of guardian, as a result of the favor gained through his virtues, had deprived him of all opportunity for obtaining leadership. For this reason he went about sowing seeds that would deprive Castruccio of popularity. At first Castruccio was angry at this slander; then after a little he became fearful as well, for he thought Messer Giorgio would not stop short of getting him into disrepute with the vicar of King Robert of Naples,[5] who would cause his expulsion from Lucca.

10 At this time the ruler in Pisa was Uguccione della Faggiuola of Arezzo, who first had been appointed general by the Pisans, and then had made himself their ruler. At the court of Uguccione were some Lucchese exiles of the Ghibelline party, with whom Castruccio had negotiations about restoring them to Lucca with Uguccione's help. He also communicated his design to his friends in Lucca, who were not able to endure the power of the Opizi. Therefore, after laying his plans, Castruccio cautiously fortified the tower of the Onesti,[6] and supplied it with munitions and with a store of food, so that, if necessary, he could hold out there a few days. When the appointed night came, he gave the signal to Uguccione, who had come down into the plain between the mountains and Lucca with a large force. Having seen the signal, Uguccione came to the gate of San Piero and set fire to the outer gate.[7] For his part,

[5] Robert I, of the French house of Anjou, ruler of southern Italy. As an independent Italian ruler he was opposed to the Emperor and a supporter of the Guelfs in Tuscany.

[6] The *Storie Pistoresi* for 1314 tells of an attack by the Obizi on Castruccio in the house of the Onesti, which he had fortified (p. 60).

[7] The gate of a medieval or renaissance city was necessarily an elaborate construction with ditches, drawbridges, and various outworks. In this instance the gate seems to have been defended by an outwork, also with its gate. When Uguccione broke through the outer gate he found himself in a narrow space commanded by a tower, which stood above a second gate. Castruccio opened the second gate to allow him to enter the city.

Castruccio raised an alarm within the city, called the people to arms, and forced the gate from within. So Uguccione and his whole force overran the city, and killed Messer Giorgio with his entire family and many of his friends and partisans. The governor was driven out, and the government of the city was changed to suit the wishes of Uguccione; this was a great injury to Lucca, because more than a hundred families were then driven into exile. Of those who escaped, part went to Florence, part to Pistoia; since these cities were ruled by the Guelf party, they became enemies to Uguccione and the Lucchese.

11 Since it seemed to the Florentines and the other Guelfs that the Ghibelline party had obtained too much influence in Tuscany, they agreed to restore the exiles to Lucca. Having raised a large army, they came into the valley of Nievole and occupied Montecatini;[8] then they went on to besiege Montecarlo,[9] in order to have a road to Lucca. Therefore Uguccione, having gathered many soldiers from Pisa and Lucca, and strengthened them with a large force of German cavalry from Lombardy, moved against the Florentine camp. The Florentines, knowing that the enemy were coming, left Montecarlo and took a position between Montecatini and Pescia. Uguccione encamped at the foot of the hill of Montecarlo, about two miles from the enemy. For some days there were skirmishes between the horsemen of the two armies, but because Uguccione was sick, the Pisans and the Lucchese avoided a battle with their enemies.

12 But since the illness of Uguccione grew more serious, he retired to Montecarlo to get well, and left Castruccio in command.[10] This caused the ruin of the Guelfs, because they grew over-confident, thinking that the hostile army was with-

[8] Montecatini di Val di Nievole, on a hill about nine hundred feet above sea-level, six miles from Pistoia, and about a mile north of the main road to Lucca. In a battle near Montecatini, in 1315, the Guelfs were actually defeated by Uguccione. Machiavelli's account puts the battle some six miles southwest of the city. Giovanni Villani, however, says that Uguccione was besieging the place when the Florentine forces came up to the rescue. The River Nievole separated the two armies. Uguccione abandoned the siege, intending to cross the river and retire toward Pisa. This movement resulted in the engagement. Apparently, then, the battle was fought about a mile southeast of the city. Villani represents the Guelfs as making light of Uguccione's army and entering the battle with their forces in bad order. On the other hand, "Uguccione and his soldiers were much afraid, and therefore were on the alert and prudent in leadership" (*Chronicle*, book 9, chap. 71). Villani's information is probably correct; he was an important man in Florence at the time and already engaged on his *Chronicle*.

[9] Montecarlo is a town on a hill rising some four hundred feet above the surrounding country, seven or eight miles east of Lucca.

[10] Tegrimi in his biography of Castruccio (1318C) says that Uguccione was absent and that all the credit for the victory was due to Castruccio, whose wisdom and energy are highly praised.

out a leader. Castruccio knew this and endeavored for some days to nourish their belief, by pretending to be afraid, and allowing nobody to go outside the fortifications of his camp. The Guelfs, on the other hand, became more insolent when they observed his fear, and every day appeared in battle array before the army of Castruccio. He, when he supposed he had given the enemy sufficient confidence, and had learned their habits, determined to join battle with them. First he confirmed the courage of his soldiers with words, and assured them that victory was certain if they were minded to obey his orders.

13 Castruccio had seen how the enemy had put all their best troops in the centre of their line of battle, and the weaker soldiers on its wings. Hence he did just the opposite, for he put on the wings of his army the bravest soldiers he had, and in the centre those of less value. In this order he led his troops out of their encampment. Then when he came in sight of the hostile army, which was insolently marching toward him as usual, he ordered his squadrons in the centre to move slowly, and those on his wings to march rapidly. This command was so well obeyed that when the hand-to-hand conflict began, only the wings of either army were fighting and the battalions in the centre stood still, because the people in Castruccio's centre had remained so far in the rear that those in the centre of the hostile line did not meet them. So the most formidable of Castruccio's soldiers fought with the weakest of the enemy, and the most powerful of the enemy stood still, without being able to injure those opposite them or to give any aid to their own side. Hence the enemy on either wing were put to flight without much trouble. Then those in the centre, seeing themselves deprived of their flanks, fled without having been able to show any of their prowess.[11] The rout and the slaughter were great, because more than ten thousand men were killed, including many leaders and great knights of the Guelf party from all Tuscany, as well as many princes who had come to aid them, such as Piero, brother of King Robert, his nephew, Carlo, and Filippo, the lord of Taranto. On Castruccio's side the loss did not reach three hundred; but among the dead was Uguccione's son, Francesco, a headstrong youth, who was killed in the first charge.[12]

14 This rout gave Castruccio a great name everywhere; so

[11] Castruccio's plan, wholly unhistorical, is like that used by Scipio in a battle against Hasdrubal in Spain. Machiavelli describes it in the *Art of War*, book 4. His account is from Livy, book 23, chaps. 26-9.

[12] This detail is also recorded by Tegrimi (1318DE). Since no reason for it appears, perhaps one may say that here Machiavelli abandoned romance for history.

great, indeed, that Uguccione became so jealous and anxious about his own power, that he thought only of how he might destroy his lieutenant, for it seemed to him that the victory had not given him dominion but had taken it from him.[13] While he was in this frame of mind, and seeking an opportunity to put his thoughts into action with the appearance of justice, it happened that Pier Agnolo Micheli, a man of ability and high reputation, was killed in Lucca, and his murderer took refuge in the house of Castruccio. The officers of the chief of police, going there to arrest him, were repelled by Castruccio, so that the murderer escaped by his aid. When Uguccione, who was then at Pisa, heard of this, he thought he had just cause to punish Castruccio. So, calling Neri, his son, to whom he had given the lordship of Lucca, he directed that, under the pretext of giving Castruccio a banquet, he should seize him and put him to death. Hence Castruccio, going in friendly fashion to the palace of the ruler, and fearing no injury, was first entertained at supper by Neri and then arrested. But fearing that to put him to death without a trial would make the people angry, Neri kept him alive, in order to get clearer instructions from Uguccione on what ought to be done.[14] The latter, condemning the tardiness and cowardice of his son, started from Pisa with four hundred cavalry to go to Lucca to finish the business. But he had not yet reached Bagni San Giuliano,[15] when the Pisans took up arms and killed Uguccione's vicar and his other followers who had remained in Pisa, and made Count Gaddo della Gherardesca their lord. Before Uguccione arrived in Lucca, he heard what had happened in Pisa, but it seemed to him unwise to turn back, because the Lucchese, following the example of the Pisans, might lock their gates against him. But even though he did come into Lucca, the Lucchese, hearing what had happened in Pisa, took the opportunity afforded by their wish to liberate Castruccio, and began to speak without restraint in groups in the public squares, and then to make a disturbance; after that they took up arms, demanding that Castruccio be set free. As a result, Uguccione, for fear of something worse, released him from prison. Whereupon Castruccio at once gathered his friends and with the help of the people attacked Uguccione.

[13] Cf. Castruccio's saying about an old friend and a new enemy, par. 65, below, and *The Prince*, Chap. 3, last sentences.

[14] The details of the banquet, the arrest, and the four hundred horsemen are all from Tegrimi (1319B).

[15] This place is only some five miles from Pisa. According to Tegrimi (1319B), Uguccione had hardly reached the third milestone when the Pisans revolted; the *Storie Pistoresi* (p. 69) makes the distance two miles. The Pisans acted with marvelous promptness.

The latter, seeing he could not help himself, fled with his friends into Lombardy to get help from the Lords della Scala. There he died in poverty.

15 But Castruccio, changed from a prisoner almost into prince of Lucca,[16] succeeded through his friends and the new favor of the people in getting himself made general of their forces for a year. After he had obtained this office, he planned to gain prestige through warfare, by regaining for the Lucchese many towns that had rebelled after the departure of Uguccione. Hence, with the help of the Pisans, with whom he was allied, he went to Serezana;[17] in order to besiege it, he built a fort on the hill above it, which was later walled in by the Florentines and is today called Serezanello;[18] and in two months he took the town. The prestige he gained here enabled him to occupy Massa, Carrara, and Lavenza,[19] and in a short time he became master of all Lunigiana;[20] then, to close the pass that leads from Lombardy into Lunigiana, he besieged Pontriemoli,[21] and took it from Messer Anastagio Palavisini, who was ruler there. When he returned to Lucca from this victory, all the people thronged to welcome him. Since it appeared to him that he need not put off making himself prince, he bribed Pazzino dal Poggio, Pucinello dal Portico, Francesco Boccansacchi, and Cecco Guinigi, who were of high reputation in Lucca, and with their help made himself lord of the city, and was solemnly and by the decision of the people chosen prince.

16 At this time Frederick of Bavaria, king of the Romans, had come to Italy to take the crown of the Empire.[22] Castruccio made himself Frederick's friend and went to meet him with five hundred cavalry, leaving in Lucca as his deputy Pagolo

[16] This is almost quoted from Tegrimi (1319C).

[17] Sarazana, a town of northwestern Tuscany near La Spezia. Remains of its walls are still to be seen.

[18] Sarazanello, a fortress still standing on a hill more than three hundred feet above Sarazana. It is sometimes called the Castle of Castruccio Castracani.

[19] Massa, Carrara, and Avenza are towns of northwestern Tuscany. At Avenza is a tower remaining from the so-called Castle of Castruccio Castracani.

[20] The region of northwestern Tuscany including the cities mentioned and the basin of the River Magra.

[21] Pontremoli, most northern town of Tuscany. The railroad into Emilia (Machiavelli's Lombardy) makes use of the pass referred to. A tower attributed to Castruccio still survives.

[22] Apparently a mistake, though possibly a deliberate substitution, for Louis of Bavaria. Frederick of Austria was chosen Roman Emperor ("king of the Romans") by a minority of the electors in 1314, and Louis was chosen by a majority. War followed, in which Frederick was defeated. Louis went to Rome and was crowned Roman Emperor in 1328. Tegrimi (1320D) says that Castruccio received from Frederick the dignity of counsellor, count, and vicar, and that he was made duke by Louis.

Guinigi, for whom Castruccio, remembering Francesco, had the same feeling as for his own son. Frederick received Castruccio honorably, gave him many privileges, and made him his vicar in Tuscany. And because the Pisans had driven out Gaddo della Gherardesca, and in their fear of him had gone to Frederick for aid, Frederick made Castruccio lord of Pisa; and the Pisans for fear of the Guelf party, and especially of the Florentines, accepted him.

17 Therefore when Frederick returned to Germany and left a governor in Rome, all the Tuscan and Lombard Ghibellines, who belonged to the faction of the Emperor, took refuge with Castruccio, and promised him dominion over their native cities, when restored to them by Castruccio's aid. Among these were Matteo Guidi, Nardo Scolari, Lapo Uberti, Gerozzo Nardi, and Piero Buonaccorsi, all Ghibellines and Florentine exiles. By their help and with his army, Castruccio planned to make himself lord of all Tuscany; and to gain more reputation he allied himself with Messer Matteo Visconti of Milan, and organized military forces in the entire city of Lucca and in all his dominion. And because Lucca had five gates, he divided the surrounding country into five parts, gave the people arms, distributed them under commanders, and provided them with flags.[23] Hence on a sudden alarm he could assemble twenty thousand men, not including those who could come from Pisa to aid him. After he had brought around him these forces and these friends, it happened that Messer Matteo Visconti was assailed by the Guelfs of Piacenza. The latter had driven away the Ghibellines, and King Robert and the Florentines had sent soldiers to aid them in doing it. For this reason Messer Matteo asked Castruccio to help him by attacking the Florentines, so that they would be obliged to call their forces back from Lombardy to defend their own homes. Hence Castruccio with a large army attacked the Valdarno, occupied Fucecchio[24] and San Miniato,[25] and did great damage to the

[23] This account of Castruccio's army made up of his subjects is taken from Tegrimi (1325C). Machiavelli advocated such an army in *The Prince*, Chaps. 13, pars. 3 ff., and 26, par. 4, and himself assisted to raise one for Florence. Possibly the knowledge that Castruccio had followed such a course influenced Machiavelli in choosing him as the hero of his romance of the wise ruler. Machiavelli shows restraint in refraining from developing a subject of such interest to him.

[24] Fucecchio is a town about one-third of a mile north of the Arno between Pisa and Empoli. As Machiavelli remarks farther on (par. 30), it was strongly situated, being on the extreme southwestern spur of Monte Albano. The Usciana (Machiavelli's Gusciana) River flows about a mile to the west, and enters the Arno some half dozen miles beyond. The land along the Usciana was in the middle ages swampy; in fact to the north is the region still called Padule Fucecchio, once a lake. Even now the map of the *Istituto geografico militare* *(Continued to page 192)*

country. Hence the Florentines had to recall their forces. These had scarcely entered Tuscany when Castruccio on his part found it necessary to return to Lucca.

18 The Poggio family was powerful in that city because they had not merely made Castruccio great, but had also made him prince; but as it seemed to them that they were not rewarded according to their merits, they plotted with other families in Lucca to cause a rebellion and drive Castruccio out of the city. Taking an opportunity one morning, they attacked the deputy whom Castruccio had put in charge of the courts there and killed him. But when they wished to go on to raise the people by giving a general alarm, Stefano di Poggio, an aged and peaceful man who had not taken part in the conspiracy, came forward, used his authority to make his family lay down their arms, and offered to be mediator between them and Castruccio to help them in getting what they desired. Therefore they put down their arms, with as little prudence as they had taken them up. Castruccio, hearing of the rebellion, without any loss of time came to Lucca with part of his soldiers, leaving Pagolo Guinigi at the head of the rest. When he found, contrary to his expectations, that the tumult was over, it seemed to him that he had an excellent opportunity for securing his position, so he stationed his armed partisans in all the suitable places. Stefano di Poggio, thinking that Castruccio ought to feel an obligation to him, went to the prince and petitioned not for himself, for he thought he had no need of it, but for the others of his house, and begged that much might be excused because of the youth of the conspirators, and because of Castruccio's old friendship and ties of obligation with their house. The prince replied graciously, and urged him not to worry about it, saying that he was pleased to have found the disorders quieted rather than indignant at the rebellion. He exhorted Stefano to have all the malcontents come before him, saying that he thanked God he had an opportunity to show his clemency and generosity. But when they

(Concluded from page 191) shows no direct road across the valley north of Fucecchio, until one reaches the main road from Pistoia to Lucca; in fact there is no cross communication of any sort until one is about a mile from the Pistoia-Lucca road. But the valley to the west of Fucecchio permitted a road in the middle ages, the Via Francigena, from Rome to Lombardy; it crossed the Arno near Empoli, passed by Fucecchio, and led on to Lucca. It was, then, a place that a ruler would have wished to hold, but the historical Castruccio never took it, though he attempted to in 1323. One of the gates of the town, the Porta S. Andrea, is also called the Porta di Castruccio.

[25] San Miniato al Tedesco, a fortress some two miles south of the Arno, between Empoli and Pisa, to be distinguished from San Miniato at Florence. It was important as commanding both the Via Francigena and the road from Pisa to Florence.

came, under the pledge of Stefano and Castruccio, they and Stefano himself were imprisoned and put to death.[26]

19 In the meantime the Florentines had recovered San Miniato. Hence Castruccio thought it wise to put a stop to that war, for he saw that he was unable to go far away from home until he had made himself secure in Lucca. And having sounded the Florentines about a truce, he easily found out that they were ready for one, because they also were worried and eager to stop the expense of the war. So they made a truce for two years, with the condition that either side should hold what it was then occupying. When Castruccio was rid of this war, under various pretexts and for various reasons, he extirpated all those in Lucca whose ambition made them aspire to the principate, so that he would no longer be in danger of the perils he had earlier run into. He pardoned none of his enemies but exiled them from Lucca and seized their property, and, if he could lay hands on them, took their lives, affirming he knew by experience that none of them could be faithful. And to make himself more secure, he built a fortress in Lucca, getting building material by destroying the towers of those he had exiled and put to death.[27]

20 While Castruccio was suspending hostilities against the Florentines and fortifying himself in Lucca, he did not fail to do what he could, without carrying on open war, to increase his own greatness. He had a great desire to occupy Pistoia, because it seemed to him that if he gained possession of that city he had one foot in Florence; hence in various ways he made all the mountainous country[28] friendly to him; and to the factions in Pistoia he behaved in such a way that both of them trusted him. That city was then divided, as always, into

[26] Machiavelli's remark on Agathocles in *The Prince*, Chap. 8, pars, 2, 3, shows that he would have considered this one of the acts by which a ruler could gain dominion, but not glory. Yet this slaughter, and that mentioned in the next paragraph, show a thorough dealing with a situation that indicated that Castruccio knew how to use cruelty (*Prince*, Chap. 8, par. 7; Chap. 17, par. 1).

Something of the sort is found in Tegrimi (1322A); Machiavelli either adapted it to suit himself, or followed some other historian.

[27] This building of a fortress would indicate that Castruccio did not enjoy the best relations with his subjects, but felt obliged to defend himself against them. See *The Prince*, Chap. 20, last par.

The towers were those built within the city by rich families to secure themselves from their enemies. A number still stand in Lucca, and they are to be seen in other Italian cities, as Bologna and San Gimignano.

The account of the fortress is given by Tegrimi (1323D), who says that three hundred towers were destroyed for material. Villani also tells of the castle (9.154).

[28] Apparently the mountainous country west and northwest of Pistoia. Villani (10.6) tells of operations by Castruccio at two fortified towns, Ravignano and Mammiano.

Whites and Blacks.[29] The chief of the Whites was Bastiano di Possente, and of the Blacks, Jacopo da Gia. Both of these kept up close relations with Castruccio, and each one wished to drive out the other. After many misgivings, both parties took up arms. Jacopo fortified himself at the Florentine gate, Bastiano at the Lucchese gate. Since both of them trusted more in Castruccio than in the Florentines, thinking that he was more active and better prepared for war, both of them secretly sent to him for help. Castruccio promised it to both of them, saying to Jacopo that he would come in person, and to Bastiano that he would send Pagolo Guinigi, his adopted son. After arranging an exact hour with them, he sent Pagolo by the road through Pescia,[30] and went himself by the direct route to Pistoia. At midnight, for so Castruccio and Pagolo had agreed, each of them was at Pistoia, and both were received as friends. When they were in the city, and it seemed to Castruccio that the right time had come, he gave a signal to Pagolo. Then one of them killed Jacopo da Gia, and the other killed Bastiano di Possente. Part of the followers of these men were taken prisoner and part killed, and Castruccio became master of the city without further opposition. He expelled the city council from the palace,[31] and brought the populace to obey him, by canceling many of their old debts, and making many promises. He did the same thing for all the surrounding territory, from which people had for the most part come running to see the new prince. Hence everybody, full of hope, and greatly affected by Castruccio's abilities, felt reassured.

21 It happened in these times that the populace of Rome got unruly because of the high cost of living, saying that it was caused by the absence of the Pope, who was at Avignon,[32] and complaining of the German governors. Hence there were murders and other disorders daily, and Henry, the viceroy of the Emperor,[33] could not check them. Finally he began to fear that the Romans would call in Robert, King of Naples, drive himself out of Rome, and restore the Pope. Having no nearer friend to turn to, Henry sent to Castruccio begging that he

[29] These parties resulted from a split in the Guelf party that dominated Pistoia. Their rivalries led to civil strife in the city. The Florentines tried to suppress it, but succeeded only in bringing the quarrel among themselves. The Whites finally joined the Ghibellines.

[30] Pescia is a little to the north of the direct road from Lucca to Pisa taken by Castruccio himself. Pagolo must have followed a difficult road through the mountains.

[31] The members of the city council or *Signoria* resided in the city hall during their term of office.

[32] From 1309 to 1376 the Popes resided at Avignon, in France, instead of at Rome.

[33] Apparently not a historical character.

would agree not merely to send assistance to Rome, but to come there in person. Castruccio judged that he could not put this off, both because he wished to render due service to the Emperor, and because he thought that he himself would not get on well if the Emperor did not occupy Rome.[34] So he left Pagolo Guinigi at Lucca and went to Rome with six hundred cavalry, where he was received by Henry with the highest honor. In a short time his presence gave so high a reputation to the party of the Emperor that without bloodshed or any sort of violence all the conditions improved. He removed the cause of discontent by getting food by sea from the region of Pisa; and then partly by admonition and partly by punishment, he brought the leaders of Rome to consent to accept the government of Henry. Castruccio was made a senator of Rome and received many other honors from the Roman people. He assumed his position as senator with very great pomp, wearing a brocaded toga, with letters on the front that said: "What now is, God wills." And on the back it said: "What God is to will, will be." [35]

22 Meanwhile the Florentines, who were indignant that in a time of truce Castruccio had made himself master of Pistoia, were considering how they could cause a rebellion there, for they judged that because of his absence this would be easy. Among the Pistojan exiles at Florence were Baldo Cecchi and Jacopo Baldini, both men of influence and quick to take part in any conflict. These made such good arrangements with their friends in Pistoia that, with the aid of the Florentines, they entered the city by night, put to flight the partisans and officers of Castruccio, and killed some of them, thus restoring to the city its liberty. The news of this caused Castruccio much distress and vexation. Taking leave of Henry, he returned to Lucca with his soldiers by forced marches.[36] Hearing of the return of Castruccio, and thinking he would not be likely to rest idle, the Florentines decided to get ahead of him and enter the Valley of Nievole with their soldiers, before he could, thinking that if they occupied that valley, they would block the road by which Castruccio would have to march against Pistoia. So assembling a great army of all the friends of the Guelf party, they moved into the territory of Pistoia. On the other hand Castruccio with his soldiers came to Montecarlo. Learning where the army of the Florentines was, he

[34] Castruccio as a Ghibelline was supported by the imperial power.

[35] This is sometimes interpreted to refer to Castruccio himself, instead of to events in general. Villani (10.59) is one of those who tells of it.

[36] Tegrimi (1333B) makes clear that Castruccio left Louis of Bavaria, not Henry, in Rome when he returned in haste because of a rebellion at Pistoia.

determined not to go to meet them in the plain of Pistoia, nor to await them in the plain of Pescia,[37] but, if he could, to encounter them in the pass at Serravalle. He judged that if he could carry out this plan he would be sure to gain a victory, for he learned that the Florentines had assembled thirty thousand men, and he had chosen from his forces only twelve thousand. And though he trusted in his own preparations and the courage of his troops,[38] yet he feared that if he met the enemy where there was plenty of room, he would be surrounded because of their large numbers.

23 Serravalle is a fortified town between Pescia and Pistoia, on the top of a hill that bounds the Valley of Nievole, not in the pass itself, but above it, two bowshots distant.[39] The place where the the road passes the fortress is narrow but not very steep, because the slope is gentle on both sides of the summit. But the pass is so narrow, especially on the summit where the waters divide, that twenty men drawn up in close order completely block it. In this place Castruccio planned to encounter his enemies, both because his small numbers would have an advantage there, and because the enemy could not be seen before the conflict, for he feared that if his men saw the great numbers of their opponents they would be frightened. Messer Manfred, a German, was lord of the walled town of Serravalle. Before Castruccio became lord of Pistoia, Manfred had been allowed to remain in that town as a place where the Lucchese and the Pistoians had equal rights, and up to this time nobody had had any reason to injure him, because he had promised both sides that he would remain neutral, and make no agreements with either. For this reason, and because he was in a strong place, he had remained there. But under the circumstances, Castruccio was eager to occupy the town. Through his close friendship with one of the inhabitants, he arranged that, the night before the battle was to be fought, this citizen would receive into the town four hundred of

[37] The plain of Pescia, watered by three streams of that name, is between Montecatini and Montecarlo, nearer to the latter; it includes the site of the battle between the Guelfs and Uguccione's army, led by Castruccio, already described. Castruccio did not intend to allow the Florentines to cross the hills separating this plain from that of Pistoia.

[38] Tegrimi (1324E) says that Castruccio "believed victory was to be found not in the number of his soldiers but in their valor." Machiavelli says much the same thing in the *Art of War,* book 7.

[39] The pass of Serravalle is about four miles from Pistoia on the direct road to Lucca. The ordinary road, the *autostrada* (high-speed automobile road), and the railroad go through the pass, the latter by a tunnel some three-quarters of a mile long. The height of the pass on the ordinary road is about 440 feet above sea level. The town of Serravalle is situated about five hundred feet (Machiavelli's two bowshots) from the road and on ground about a hundred and thirty feet higher. Fragments of its fortifications remain.

Castruccio's soldiers and kill Manfred, the lord of Serravalle.

24 Being so prepared, he did not move his army from Montecarlo, in order to encourage the Florentines to march on. These, because they wished to remove the war from Pistoia and bring it into the Valley of Nievole, encamped at the foot of the hill of Serravalle, expecting to march over on the next day. But Castruccio, having taken the town in the night without any noise, left Montecarlo at midnight and in the morning quietly arrived with his army at the foot of the pass of Serravalle. Hence at the same time the Florentines and Castruccio's troops, each on their own side, commenced to climb the slope. Castruccio had ordered his infantry to take the main road, and had sent a band of four hundred horsemen to the left hand toward the town of Serravalle. The Florentines, on the other hand, had sent four hundred horsemen ahead, and then had moved their infantry, and behind them their men at arms. They did not expect to find Castruccio on the hill, because they did not know he had become master of the town. Hence, the Florentine cavalry, on mounting the slope, came unexpectedly upon the infantry of Castruccio, and found themselves so close that they hardly had time to fasten their helmets.[40] Since therefore unprepared soldiers were assailed by those who were ready and in good order, the latter attacked with high spirits and the Florentines resisted with difficulty. To be sure some of them fought well, but when the noise was heard in the remainder of the Florentine army, everything was thrown into confusion. The horsemen were crowded in with the infantry, and the infantry with the cavalry and the baggage train. The road was so narrow that the officers were unable to go either forward or back; so in the confusion nobody knew what he could do or ought to do. Meanwhile the horsemen who were in close conflict with the hostile infantry were killed and thrown into confusion without being able to defend themselves, because the nature of the place was against them. They resisted more from necessity than from courage, because, having the mountains on their flanks, and friends behind and enemies before them, no way for flight stood open.

25 Meanwhile Castruccio, seeing that his soldiers were unable to make the enemy turn back, sent a thousand infantry by the road leading to the town. He had these descend the hill in company with the four hundred cavalry that he had sent earlier, and they struck the flank of the enemy with such violence that the Florentines were unable to resist their charge,

[40] Perhaps meaning "to close their visors," though literally "to lace up their helmets."

but, conquered rather by the nature of the place than by the enemy, began to flee. The flight was begun by those in the rear, toward Pistoia, who scattered over the plain, each one providing for his own safety as best he could.

26 This rout was great and very bloody.[41] Many officers were captured, among whom were Bandino de' Rossi, Francesco Brunelleschi, and Giovanni della Tosa, all Florentine nobles, with many other Tuscans, and many from the kingdom of Naples who had been sent by King Robert to fight on the Florentine side in behalf of the Guelfs.

27 The Pistoians, when they heard of the defeat, lost no time in driving out the faction that was friendly to the Guelfs and gave themselves over to Castruccio. He was not content with this, but occupied Prato and all the fortified towns in the plain on both sides of the Arno, and established himself with his forces in the plain of Peretola, only two miles from Florence, where he remained to divide his spoils and celebrate the victory he had won. In derision of the Florentines he had money coined and held races by horses, men, and harlots.[42] Nor did he fail to attempt to bribe some noble citizen or other to open the gates of Florence at night. But the conspiracy was discovered and Tommaso Lupacci and Lambertuccio Frescobaldi were arrested and beheaded.[43]

28 Bewildered by the rout, the Florentines saw no means by which they could preserve their liberty, and in order to make sure of help, sent ambassadors to Robert, king of Naples, to offer him their city and dominion over it. The King accepted, not so much because of the honor done him by the Florentines, as because he knew how important it was to his authority that the Guelf party should maintain its power in Tuscany. Having agreed with the Florentines that they should pay him two hundred thousand florins a year, he sent to Florence his son Carlo, with four thousand cavalry.

29 Meanwhile the Florentines were in part freed from the troops of Castruccio, because he had been obliged to leave their territories and go to Pisa, to suppress a conspiracy formed against him by Benedetto Lanfranchi, one of the chief men of Pisa. Not being able to endure seeing his native city under the

[41] The battle is Machiavelli's substitute for Altopascio, nearer Lucca, where Castruccio defeated the Florentines in 1325.

[42] Villani (9.322) says that "in order to insult the Florentines still more he had small coins made in Signa with the effigy of the Emperor Otto, and called them *castruccini*." Tegrimi (1322C) also mentions the coining of money.

[43] Villani (9.292) mentions one Florentine traitor, Tommaso di Lippaccio di Messer Lambertuccio Frescobaldo, who escaped. Machiavelli makes him into two. An unnamed knight, apparently a foreigner, his accomplice, was beheaded.

authority of a Lucchese, Benedetto made a conspiracy, with the intention of occupying the citadel, driving out the guard, and killing the partisans of Castruccio. But in such affairs a number of conspirators small enough for secrecy is not large enough for execution. So while Benedetto was seeking to bring more men into his plan, he included one who revealed his designs to Castruccio.[44] This revelation brought infamy to Bonifacio Cerchi and Giovanni Guidi, Florentines who were then in exile at Pisa.[45] As a result Castruccio laid hands on Benedetto, killed him, sent all his relatives into exile, and beheaded many noble citizens. Since it seemed that Pistoia and Pisa were not very faithful to him, Castruccio devoted his thought and effort to making sure of them. This gave the Florentines time to reorganize their troops, and enabled them to await the coming of Carlo. When he came, they determined to lose no time, and gathered a large force by calling to their aid almost all the Guelfs of Italy, so that they brought together a large army, made up of over thirty thousand infantry and ten thousand cavalry. Having debated which they should first attack, Pistoia or Pisa, they decided it was better to attack Pisa, because the recent conspiracy there made success more probable, and such a plan was also more advantageous, in that if they gained Pisa, Pistoia would yield of her own accord.

30 Having marched out with this army at the beginning of May in the year thirteen hundred and twenty-eight, the Florentines quickly occupied Lastra, Signa, Montelupo, and Empoli, and then led their army to San Miniato. Castruccio, on the other hand, learning of the great force the Florentines had brought against him, was not at all frightened, but thought this was the time when Fortune was going to put into his hands dominion over Tuscany, for he believed his enemies would not make a better showing in this attempt on Pisa than they had at Serravalle, and that this time they could have no further hope to reorganize themselves as they did after that battle. So bringing together twenty thousand infantry and four thousand horsemen, he placed himself with his army at Fucecchio, and sent Pagolo Guinigi with five thousand infantry into Pisa. Fucecchio has a site stronger than any other town in the region of Pisa, because it is between the Gusciana and the Arno, and somewhat elevated above the plain.[46] When Castruccio was

[44] Cf. the account of conspiracies in *The Prince,* Chap. 19, pars. 2-5.

[45] Villani (9.230) gives quite a different account, saying that Betto Malepa de' Lanfranchi was a Pisan traitor through whose aid Castruccio attempted to take Pisa. The plot was discovered and Betto beheaded by the Pisans. The revelation was made by one of the Guidi and Bonifazio Cerchi, Florentine rebels who were living in Pisa. Villani (10.13) also tells of a Benedetto Maccaioni de' Lanfranchi, a Pisan rebel, who served with Castruccio.

[46] See par. 17, note 24, above.

stationed there, the enemy could not hinder the coming of provisions from Lucca or from Pisa except by dividing their army into two parts. Neither could they, without great disadvantage, attack him or go toward Pisa. If they attempted the latter, they would be placed between Castruccio's troops and those in Pisa. If they attempted to attack Fucecchio, they would have to cross the Arno, and could do it only with great danger in the presence of the enemy. In order to encourage them to adopt the plan of crossing, Castruccio had not drawn up his forces on the bank of the Arno, but close to the wall of Fucecchio, and had left a good deal of space between the river and the army.

31 The Florentines, having occupied San Miniato, debated what was to be done: whether to go to Pisa or to attack Castruccio. Having compared the difficulty of the two plans, they determined to march against him. The Arno was so low that it could be waded, but not so shallow but what it was necessary for the infantry to go into the water up to their shoulders and the horses up to the saddles. So on the morning of the tenth of June, 1328,[47] the Florentines, ready for battle, had part of their cavalry and a division of ten thousand infantry begin the crossing. Castruccio, who was prepared and on the alert for what he intended to do, assailed them with a brigade of five thousand infantry and three thousand cavalry. He did not give time enough for all the Florentines to emerge from the water before he began the hand to hand conflict.[48] He also directed a thousand light-armed infantry to the bank of the Arno above the fording place and a thousand below. The infantry of the Florentines were impeded by the water and by their arms, and not all of them had climbed out of the river channel. When only a few of the horses had crossed, the bed of the Arno was so broken up that the passage of the others was difficult; many of them, getting into places where the ford seemed bottomless, fell with their riders under them, and many of them were so stuck in the mud that they could not get out. Seeing the difficulty of crossing at that point, the Florentine leaders sent the cavalry higher up the river, to find a bottom that was not spoiled and a place where the channel was better adapted to crossing. To these were opposd the infantry that Castruccio had sent up along the channel. These, lightly

[47] The earlier battles of Castruccio had some sort of historical basis; this one has none whatsoever. Yet Machiavelli is very specific about it, giving here the date, and later the losses to a man.

[48] Machiavelli attributes to Castruccio the wisdom of the good general, of whom he says in the *Art of War*: "Many armies, in attempting to pass over rivers, have been routed by an alert enemy, who has waited until half were on one side and half on the other, and then has attacked them" (book 4).

equipped with round shields and having galley darts[49] in their hands, uttered loud shouts and wounded the horses in the faces and breasts, so that the animals, terrified by the wounds and the shouts, refused to go on and fell down in heaps. The conflict between the soldiers under Castruccio and the Florentines who got across was sharp and terrible. Many fell everywhere. Each man endeavored with all his might to do better than anyone else. Castruccio's men tried to plunge the Florentines into the river again. The Florentines were determined to drive their opponents back, in order to give their comrades behind them a chance to come out of the water and join the fight. This determination was increased by the exhortations of the captains. Castruccio reminded his soldiers that these were the same enemies whom not long before they had conquered at Serravalle. The Florentines reproached their men because many were allowing themselves to be beaten by few. At length Castruccio, seeing that the battle was lasting a long time, that both his men and their adversaries were exhausted, and that there were many wounded and dead on both sides, pushed forward another band of five thousand infantry. When he had led these up to the rear of those who were fighting, he ordered the front line to divide in the middle, and, as though they were fleeing, that half of them should draw off to the right and half of them to the left.[50] When this was done, it gave some space to the Florentines to press forward and gain

[49] Apparently darts like those used in seafights.

[50] The matter of bringing up reserves was one that greatly interested Machiavelli. He condemned the generals of his own time for their failure: "The greatest violation of the correct principles for drawing up an army in order of battle is to give it a single line and limit it to one charge and one fortune. This rises from the loss of the ancient method of receiving one part of the army within another, for without this method the second cannot come to the aid of the first soldiers, nor defend them, nor go into combat in their places" (*Art of War*, book 3). While the fictitious Castruccio does not train his soldiers in the Roman fashion, which Machiavelli admired because of its solution of the problem of the reserve, he does imitate Roman tactics. In the *Art of War* part of the dialogue is as follows: "*Zanobi:* In speaking of the battle of Zama you have reminded me that in the course of the fight Scipio did not have the first line retire through the spaces left in the second, but divided it in the middle and made it draw off to the wings of the army, that it might give place to the second line, when Scipio wanted to send that forward. I wish you could tell me what caused him not to use the normal method. *Fabrizio*: I shall tell you. Hannibal had put the flower of his army in the second line. Hence, in order to oppose it with equal force, Scipio had joined his second and third lines into one, so that the normal intervals in the second line were occupied by the men of the third line, and there was no room for the first line to pass through. For that reason he had them divide and go to the wings of the army, rather than retiring through the second line. But observe that this method of opening the first line to give place to the second cannot be used unless a general has an advantage, because then he has an opportunity to use it, as Scipio did. But if his front line is put to the worse and driven back, he cannot open it without ruining his army" (*Art of War,* book 4).

ground. But when the fresh men came to close conflict with those who were tired out, it did not take them long to drive the Florentines into the river.

32 Between the cavalry of either side there was as yet no advantage, because Castruccio, who knew that his were inferior, had ordered the leaders merely to stand their ground against the enemy, because he hoped to overcome the hostile infantry, and when they were defeated to be able more easily to overthrow the cavalry. This came out according to his plan. For when he saw that the enemy infantry had retreated into the river, he sent the rest of his infantry against the hostile cavalry; the infantry attacked with spears and javelins and Castruccio's cavalry assaulted with still more vigor, so that they put their adversaries to flight.[51] The Florentine leaders, seeing the difficulty their cavalry were having in passing the river, tried to make the infantry cross over farther down stream, in order to attack the forces of Castruccio on the flank. But since the channel was deep and the bank occupied by Castruccio's forces, the attempt was useless.

33 So the army was put to rout, with great glory and honor for Castruccio, for of such a multitude not one-third escaped. Many leaders were captured. Carlo, the son of King Robert, with Michelagnolo Falconi and Taddeo degli Albizzi, Florentine commissioners, escaped to Empoli. The spoil was great and the slaughter very great, as one can reckon it would be in so fierce a conflict, for the Florentines lost twenty thousand, two hundred, and thirty-one, and Castruccio one thousand, five hundred, and seventy.

34 But Fortune, hostile to Castruccio's glory, when it was time to give him life, took it away from him, and interrupted the plans that for a long time he had been intending to put into effect, and which could be broken off only by his death. Castruccio had been exerting himself in the battle all day, and when it was over he stopped, all weary and sweaty, at the gate of Fucecchio, to wait for his soldiers returning from the victory, and to receive them in person and thank them. Moreover, if it should happen that the enemy were able to make any resistance anywhere, he could be prompt in taking some action against it, because he believed it the duty of a good general to be the first to mount his horse and the last to dismount. Being exposed to a wind that often comes at midday from up the Arno, and that almost always brings sickness, he became thoroughly chilled. He paid no attention to this, because he

[51] The passage emphasizes Machiavelli's belief that infantry are the backbone of an army (*Art of War*, books 1 and 2). Yet he provides Castruccio with cavalry and has them take their share in the battle.

was accustomed to discomforts of this sort, but it was the cause of his death. In the following night he was attacked by a very high fever, which continually increased.

35 When all the physicians admitted that his sickness was mortal, and Castruccio realized it, he called for Pagolo Guinigi and spoke to him as follows: "If I had supposed, my son, that Fortune intended to cut off in the middle my path to that glory which so many successful enterprises have promised me, I would have given myself less trouble and would have left you a smaller state, but fewer enemies and less envy.[52] I would have been satisfied with dominion over Lucca and Pisa, and would not have subjugated the Pistoians and angered the Florentines with so many injuries. On the contrary, I would have made both of these peoples my friends, and would certainly have led a quieter life, if not a longer one, and I would have left you a territory smaller, it is true, but unquestionably more secure and solid. But Fortune, who intends to be mistress of all human things, did not, until the present, give me judgment good enough to enable me to understand her nor did she allow me time enough so I could overcome her. You have heard, for many have related it to you and I have never denied it, how I came into the house of your father as a boy, unprovided with all those reasons for hope that ought to exist in every noble heart, and how he brought me up and loved me better than if I had been born of his own blood. Under his instruction I became courageous and capable of attaining the good fortune that you yourself have seen and now see. And because when your father died he committed to my faith you and all his possessions, I have brought you up with as much love and have added to them with as much fidelity as bound me when he died and still binds me. And in order that you might have not merely what your father left you, but also what my fortune and prowess gained, I have never been willing to marry, in order that love for my children might not in any way impede me in showing to your father's family the gratitude I felt myself bound to manifest.

36 "Therefore I leave you a great dominion; with that I am well satisfied. But because I leave it to you while it is weak

[52] Perhaps derived from Aristotle: "Theopompus diminished the power of the kings, but established the kingly office on a more lasting basis, thus making it in a certain sense not less, but greater. There is a story that when his wife once asked him whether he was not ashamed to leave to his sons a royal power which was less than he had inherited from his father, "No, indeed," he replied, "for the power I leave to them will be more lasting" (*Politics* 5. 1313a26-33).

But Machiavelli also may have taken a hint from Tegrimi's account of Castruccio's dying words to his son Henry (1343A).

and insecure, I am greatly grieved. I leave you the city of Lucca, which will never be wholly content to live under your dominion. I leave you Pisa, where the people are naturally variable and full of deception; though this city has had various periods of servitude and grown used to it, yet it will always disdain a Lucchese ruler. I leave you Pistoia, on which you can rely but little, because it is divided, and exasperated against our family by recent injuries. You have as neighbors the Florentines, whom we have angered and injured in a thousand ways but not destroyed; they will be more pleased by the news of my death than they would be by the conquest of Tuscany. You cannot trust in the princes of Milan or in the Emperor, because they are far away, indolent, and slow to give help. Therefore you must hope in nothing but your labor, the memory of my prowess, and the prestige that the present victory will bring you. If you know how to use it prudently, it will help you in making an agreement with the Florentines, for since they are upset by the present rout, they will be glad to meet you half-way. Though I tried to make them my enemies, and thought that through their enmity I could obtain power and glory, you should make every effort to gain them as friends, because their friendship will bring you security and comfort.

37 "It is a thing of great importance in this world to know yourself thoroughly and to be able to estimate correctly the forces of your mind and of your state.[53] He who knows that he is not fit for war should learn how to rule by the arts of peace. It will be well for you to turn yourself to these arts, according to my advice, and in this way to try to secure for yourself the enjoyment of the fruits of my labors and perils. You can easily succeed in this if you will accept my advice as sound. And you will find that you are under obligation to me in two ways: one, that I have left you this kingdom; the other, that I have taught you how to keep it."

38 Then he asked that those citizens of Lucca, Pisa, and Pistoia who were in his army should come before him; after having commended Pagolo Guinigi to them, and made them swear obedience to him, he died. He left behind him a good reputation wherever he was spoken of, and was as much regretted by those who had been his friends as any prince who died in any age. His funeral was of the most honorable sort, and he was buried in San Francesco in Lucca.[54] But Prowess and Fortune were not such good friends to Pagolo Guinigi as to Castruccio, because not long after Castruccio's death Pagolo

[53] Cf. the analysis of one's temperament and circumstances suggested in *The Prince*, chap. 25, pars. 3-5.

[54] A stone with his name is still to be seen there.

lost Pistoia, and soon after Pisa, and he had trouble in maintaining his dominion over Lucca; yet it remained with his house until the time of Pagolo, his great-grandson.

39 Castruccio was, then, as has been shown, a man not merely unusual in his own times, but one who would have been so in many preceding eras. As to his body, he was of more than ordinary height, and his limbs were well proportioned. He had so much charm in his expression and received everybody with so much kindness, that no one who spoke to him ever came away discontented. His hair was inclined to be red, and he had it cut above his ears; and he always went bareheaded in all sorts of weather, even when it rained and snowed.[55]

40 He was pleasant to his friends, terrible to his enemies, just with his subjects, deceitful with foreigners;[56] if he was able to win by fraud he never attempted to win by force, because he said that the victory, not the method of gaining it, brought glory to the victor.[57]

41 Nobody was ever bolder about entering into perils,[58] nor more skilful in escaping from them. He used to say that men should attempt everything, and fear nothing, and that God is a lover of strong men, because it may be seen that he always uses the powerful to punish the weak.

42 He was also marvelous in making answers and in saying sharp things both keenly and pleasingly,[59] and as he did not hesitate to speak to anybody in this way, so he was not angry when some one else did not hesitate to speak in the same way to him. Hence it is reported that he said many sharp things, and heard many with patience.[60]

43 He had bought a partridge for a ducat and a friend censured him for it. But Castruccio said: "You would not have paid more than a soldo for it." When the friend said

[55] A habit of those brought up to the hardships of a military life, according to Machiavelli's *Art of War*, book 1.

[56] Some texts read "deceitful with the deceitful." *Foreigners* seems the better reading, since opposition to *subjects* is lost when it does not appear. For keeping faith with foreign powers, cf. *The Prince*, Chap. 18, and the *Discourses* II, 13. See also Gilbert, *Machiavelli's "Prince" and Its Forerunners*, pp. 123-7.

[57] Cf. *The Prince*, Chap. 7, par. 8.

[58] Cf. Machiavelli's remark on Agathocles, in *The Prince*, Chap. 8, par. 3.

[59] Literally, *urbanely*. For the use of this word and jests that illustrate it, see the *Poetica* (book 6) of Trissino, one of Machiavelli's friends. The passage is translated in Allan H. Gilbert's *Literary Criticism, Plato to Dryden*, New York, 1940, pp. 228-9.

[60] This capacity was attributed to the historical Castruccio by his biographer Tegrimi: "Many things showing weight and sharpness are still extant which he said and wrote to individuals, princes, and republics. There are especially some letters to the Sienese from which anybody can easily estimate the cleverness and readiness of his mind in all circumstances and his wit in making jokes" (1343).

that was true, Castruccio replied: "A ducat is worth much less to me than a soldo to you."[61]

44 There was a flatterer with him, on whom Castruccio spat to show his contempt; but the flatterer said: "Fishermen, in order to take one little fish, let themselves get wet all over in the sea; I certainly can let myself get wet with one spit in order to catch a whale." Castruccio not merely listened with patience but rewarded him.

45 When some one rebuked him because he lived too splendidly, Castruccio said: "If that were a vice, such splendid banquets would not be given in honor of the saints."

46 When he was passing through a street and saw that a youth who was coming out of the house of a harlot blushed deeply at being seen by him, he said: "Don't be ashamed when you come out, but when you go in."

47 When a friend gave him a complicated knot to untie, he said: "You stupid fellow, do you think I should like to untie a thing that gives me so much trouble when it is tied?"

48 Castruccio said to a man who was a philosopher by profession: "You are like dogs, for they always stick close to the man who can give them the best things to eat." The man answered: "No, we are like doctors, for we go to the houses of those who need us most."

49 When he was going from Pisa to Leghorn by sea, and a dangerous tempest arose, which greatly disturbed him, he was rebuked for cowardice by one of his companions, who said that he was afraid of nothing. Castruccio answered that he was not astonished, because each man values his life for what it is worth.

50 When somebody asked him what he needed to do to make himself popular, he said: "When you go to a banquet, see to it that one block of wood doesn't rest on another."

51 When a man boasted that he had read many books, Castruccio said: "It would be better to boast of having remembered a great deal."

52 When someone boasted that he could drink a great deal and not get drunk, he said: "An ox can do the same thing."

53 There was a young woman with whom Castruccio was very intimate. When one of his friends reproached him, saying especially that it was a bad thing for him to let himself

[61] All of the sayings of Castruccio, except as indicated, are from Diogenes Laertius' *Lives and Opinions of Eminent Philosophers*. The first group is from book 2, sections 66-79. Footnotes indicate when Machiavelli begins to draw from other books of the same work. These sayings he modifies to his purpose, as by substituting Italian names for the Greek. He might have read the work in the Latin translation of Ambrosius Traversarius Camaldulensis, printed first at Rome, and in 1475 at Venice.

be taken by a woman, he replied: "You are wrong; I have taken her, and not she me."

54 When someone else rebuked him because he ate too delicate food, he said: "I take it you would not spend so much on it as I do." And when he was told that was the truth, he continued: "Then you are more stingy than I am gluttonous."

55 He was invited to supper by Taddeo Bernardi of Lucca, a very rich man who lived luxuriously. When he arrived, Taddeo showed him a room all hung with silks and with the floor made of small stones, variously arranged in different colors, to represent flowers, branches, and other verdure. Having gathered a good deal of saliva in his mouth, Castruccio spat it in Taddeo's face. Taddeo was annoyed by this, and Castruccio said: "I didn't know where I could spit that would damage you less."

56 After he had been asked how Caesar died, he said: "God grant I may die as he did!"

57 One evening he was in the house of one of his gentlemen, where many ladies were gathered for a party, Castruccio danced and enjoyed himself more than was befitting one of his rank, and one of his friends reproached him for it. But he answered: "He who is thought wise in the daytime will never be held a fool at night." [62]

58 A man came to ask a favor and Castruccio acted as though he didn't hear him. Then the petitioner threw himself on his knees on the floor. Castruccio rebuked him for it and the man answered: "You are the cause of it, because you have ears in your feet." So Castruccio gave him double the favor he was asking.

59 He used to say that the road to hell is an easy one, because the traveler goes downward and with his eyes closed.[63]

60 When a man asked a favor with many needless words, Castruccio said to him: "When you want something from me again, send someone else."

61 Similarly when a man tired him out with a long speech and said at the end: "I have perhaps wearied you with speaking too much," he replied: "You have not, because I haven't heard anything you have said." [64]

62 He used to say of one who had been a handsome boy and was then a handsome man, that he did too much damage: first he took the husbands away from the wives, and then the wives away from the husbands.[65]

[62] The words on the wise man by day and night occur also in Machiavelli's letter to Vettori, January 5, 1513-4.

[63] This and the following saying are from Diogenes Laertius, 4.49-50.

[64] Ibid., 5.20-1.

[65] This and the following saying are from Diogenes Laertius, 4.49-51.

63 He said to an envious man who laughed: "Are you laughing at something good for yourself or something bad for somebody else?"

64 When he was still under the authority of Messer Francesco Guinigi, one of his companions said to him: "What will you take to let me hit you on the head?" "A helmet," answered Castruccio.[66]

65 After he had put to death a citizen of Lucca who had helped him become great, someone told him he had done wrong to kill one of his old friends. But he replied: "You are wrong, I have put to death a new enemy."[67]

66 Castruccio gave great praise to men who planned to take wives and did not actually marry, as well as to those who said they were going on a voyage and did not sail.[68]

67 He said he wondered at men who when they bought a dish of porcelain or glass sounded it to see if it were good, but when they chose their wives were satisfied with merely seeing them.

68 When someone asked him how he wished to be buried when he died, he answered: "With my face downward, because I know that when I am dead this whole country will be turned upside down."[69]

69 When he was asked if he had ever thought of becoming a friar in order to save his soul, he answered that he had not, because it seemed to him strange that Fra Lazzero would be sure of Paradise and Uguccione della Faggiuola would have to go to Hell.

70 When he was asked when one should eat if one wished to remain healthy, he replied: "If a man is rich, when he is hungry; if he is poor, when he can."

71 Seeing a gentlemen who was having his shoes laced up by one of his servants,[70] he said: "I pray God you will also have him feed you."

72 Observing that a man had written on his house in Latin a prayer that God would guard it from the wicked, he said: "He can't go in himself."

[66] Ibid., 6.54.

[67] This saying is from Tegrimi (1326E). Cf. *The Prince*, Chap. 3, end.

[68] Except as indicated, this and the following sayings are from Diogenes Laertius, 6.28-68.

[69] Apparently from Diogenes Laertius, 6.31-2. Something of the sort had, however, long been attributed to Castruccio. Villani (10.86) writes: "A little before his death, when he knew he was going to die, he said to several of his friends: 'I see that I am going to die, and when I am dead, you will see things discombobulated.' This was in his Lucchese dialect and means in more ordinary Italian: 'You will see revolutions.' Or in Lucchese: 'You will see the world upside down.' "

[70] Shoes are not mentioned by Machiavelli, who probably had in mind garments, as doublet and hose, fastened with laces.

73 Passing along a street where there stood a little house that had a large front door, he said: "That house will run away through that door."

74 When he was told how a foreigner had ruined a boy, he said: "He must be from Perugia."

75 When he asked what city had the worst reputation for cheaters and grafters, he was told "Lucca," because everybody there was of that sort of nature, except Buontura.[71]

76 When Castruccio was arguing with the ambassador of the king of Naples about the property of some banished men, and got somewhat angry, the ambassador said to him: "Are you not afraid of the king, then?" He retorted: "Is this king of yours good or wicked?" When the ambassador answered that he was good, Castruccio returned: "Why do you think, then, that I should fear good men?"

77 It would be possible to relate many other things said by him, in all of which wit and gravity would appear, but I think these are enough to show his great qualities.

78 He lived forty-four years, and acted like a prince in both good and bad fortune. There was plenty to remind him of his good fortune, but he wished some reminders also of his bad fortune. Hence the fetters with which he had been chained in prison are still to be seen attached to the tower of his dwelling, where he had put them as continual witnesses to his sufferings.[72] And as in his life he was not inferior to Philip of Macedon the father of Alexander, nor to Scipio of Rome, so he died at the same age as they did; and without any doubt he would have surpassed them both if he had been born not in Lucca but in Macedonia or Rome.

[71] This saying so far as I have observed, is not derived from Diogenes Laertius. It makes use of the words of one of Dante's devils on a sinner from Lucca: "Everybody there is a grafter, except Bonturo" (*Inferno* 21.41).

[72] Probably Machiavelli had seen them, since his contemporary Tegrimi tells the same story (1319C).

CAPITOLO ON FORTUNE[1]

TO GIOVAN BATTISTA SODERINI

1 With what rimes and what verses shall I now sing of the realm of Fortune, and of her prosperous and adverse chances?

4 And how, prone to injury and urgent, as she is judged here below, she assembles all the world at the foot of her throne?

7 Thou art not able to fear, Giovan Battista, nor shouldst thou in any way fear other wounds than her blows;

10 Because this shifting creature often and by habit resists with the greatest vigor where she sees that nature has most vigor.

13 Her natural power overcomes every man; and her rule is ever violent, if great prowess does not overthrow her.

16 Hence I pray thou wilt be content to look a little at these verses of mine, to see if they contain anything worthy of thy notice.

19 And may the cruel goddess meanwhile turn her fierce eyes on me, and read what I now sing of her and her kingdom!

22 And though she sits on high above all, and gives orders and rules violently, may she yet look on him who dares to sing of her dominion!

25 This goddess is called omnipotent by many, because whoever comes into this life feels her power either early or late.

28 She often treads the good under her feet, and raises up the wicked; and if she ever promises you anything, she never carries it out.

31 She turns kingdoms and states upside down, as she wishes, and deprives the just of the good that she gives freely to the unjust.

34 This inconstant goddess and restless divinity often places the unworthy on a throne, to which he who is worthy of it never attains.

37 She arranges the times as suits her; she raises us up, she puts us down, without pity, without law or reason.

40 It never pleases her to favor one person at all seasons, nor does she always afflict him who lies at the very bottom of her wheel.

43 Whose daughter she is or from what family she sprang,

[1] Cf. *The Prince*, Chap. 25, and the Introduction, pars. 115-9.

nobody knows; but it is known for a certainty that even Jove himself fears her power.

46 She seems to rule over a palace open on every side, and she forbids no one to enter it, but the going out again is uncertain.

49 All the world gathers around her, eager to see new things, and full of ambition and full of desires.

52 She stands on the summit, the sight of her is not denied to any man; but in a little time she turns about and moves.

55 This old witch has two faces, the one fierce and the other mild; and from one moment to another, now she does not see you, now she menaces you, now she beseeches.

58 Whoever wishes to enter she receives benignly, but she is angry with him who wishes to go out, and often he is deprived of any way of escape.

61 Within her palace, as many wheels turn about as there are varied ways of climbing to the things every man sets his desire upon.

64 Sighs, blasphemies, and injurious words are heard without ceasing from the lips of those whom Fortune conceals within her bounds.

67 In proportion as they are richer and more powerful, so much the more discourtesy she shows them; so much the less are they acquainted with her favors.

70 For all the evil that comes on men, they impute to her; but if any good comes to a man, he thinks he has it through his own personal virtue.

73 Among that varied and new crowd of fellow servants whom the place closes in, Audacity and Youth make the best showing.

76 Fear may be seen prostrated on the earth, so full of doubts that he does nothing; then Penitence and Envy make war on him.

79 Here Occasion alone amuses herself, and that towsel-haired and simple maiden goes sporting about among the wheels.

82 And the wheels are ever turning, day and night, because it is the will of Heaven (which cannot be resisted) that Laziness and Necessity turn them about.

85 The second puts the world in order again, and the first disorders it. In all seasons and at every hour may be seen how strong and how sufficient Patience is.

88 Usury and Fraud, powerful and rich, enjoy themselves in the crowd; and among these companions Liberality stands ragged and exhausted.

91 Above gates that are never locked may be seen sitting, it is said, Chance and Luck, without eyes and without ears.

94 Power, honor, riches, and health are ready as rewards; for penalty and affliction there are servitude, infamy, sickness, and poverty.

97 With this last group Fortune shows her mad fury; the other she offers to those she loves.

100 Among all those who stand waiting in that place, he follows the luckiest plan who chooses a wheel fitting to her wish;

103 Because, according as they are in harmony with Fortune, the temperaments that make you act are the causes of your good and your ill.

106 Yet you are not able to trust in her, nor to hope to escape her hard bite, and her hard blows, vigorous and hurtful;

109 Because, while you are being brought to the summit of a wheel that then is lucky and good, she is likely to reverse its turn in mid-circle.

112 And since you are not able to change your character, nor to leave the course that heaven has marked out for you, Fortune abandons you in the midst of your journey.

115 Therefore, if this can be understood and fixed in the mind, he who can leap from wheel to wheel will ever be successful and happy;[2]

118 But because the ability to do this is denied by the mysterious power that rules us, our condition changes with the course of Fortune.

121 There is nothing eternal in the world; Fortune wishes it so, and makes herself splendid through it, that her power may be more clearly seen.

124 Therefore we should strive to take her for our star, and as far as we can to accommodate ourselves every hour to her variations.

127 All her palace, within and without, is seen to be deco-

[2] Another method of remaining fortunate is suggested by Machiavelli in the following story of a Florentine who died in 1379: "Piero degli Albizi did not escape on account of the greatness of his house or his long established reputation, for he had been for a long time honored and feared more than any other citizen. For this reason somebody—perhaps one of his friends who wished to make him more humane in his high position, or perhaps one of his enemies who intended to threaten him with the uncertainty of Fortune—when Piero made a banquet for a large number of citizens, sent him a silver cup full of confections, with a nail hidden among them. When this was uncovered and seen by all the guests, it was interpreted as a reminder to nail fast the wheel of Fortune; for since she had brought him to the summit of her wheel, if she continued to turn it around, nothing else could happen but that she would drag him to the bottom. This interpretation was verified first by his ruin, then by his death" (*History of Florence*, III, 19).

rated with paintings giving the stories of those triumphs from which she has gained most honor.

130 In the first panel, painted in many colors, can be seen how once the world was in subjection to the conquering might of Egypt;

133 And how for many long years of peace she held the world subject, and how then was seen what is written of the best things in nature.

136 Next, the Assyrians are seen climbing to the mighty scepter, when Fortune did not wish that the might of Egypt should hold further dominion.

139 After that was seen how smiling Fortune turned herself to the Medes; from the Medes to the Persians; and she crowned the hair of the Greeks with the diadem she took from the Persians.

142 Here may be seen Memphis and Thebes tamed, Babylon, Troy, and Carthage too, Jerusalem, Athens, Sparta, and Rome.[3]

145 Here is shown how splendid they were, noble, rich, powerful; and how at the end Fortune gave them as booty to their enemies.

148 Here may be seen the noble and god-like deeds of the Roman empire; then how all the world fell with its ruins.

151 As a rapid torrent that swells higher and higher as it rushes on, and overthrows everything wherever it turns its course,

154 It adds to one shore and cuts down the other, it shifts its banks, changes its bed to the very bottom, and makes the earth tremble where it passes;

157 So Fortune, in her furious onrush, many times transfers the things of the world now here, now there.

160 If then you turn your eyes further, you will see at one

[3] Machiavelli usually is interested in an individual and particular Fortune; the present passage is more in the spirit of Dante, who writes of Fortune as changing the things of the world "from people to people and from one race to another, . . . for one people rules and the other fades away" (*Inferno* 7.80-2).

On the revolutions of empire Niccolò writes: "The good and evil of the world varies from province to province, as is seen in the information we have on the ancient empires, which varied in good and ill with the variation of their habits, yet the world remained always the same. There was only this difference in it, that while it first established its power in Assyria, it then gave it to Media, later to Persia, and finally sent it into Italy and Rome. And if after the Roman Empire there has been no empire that has lasted and no one place where the world has collected its might, yet nevertheless that vigor is dispersed among many nations where men of courage can be found, such as the kingdom of the French, the kingdom of the Turks, that of the Soldan, and today the peoples of Germany, and earlier there was that Saracen race that accomplished such great things and occupied so much of the world after it destroyed the Eastern Roman Empire" (*Discourses on Livy*, II, pref.).

glance Caesar and Alexander among those who were happy when alive.

163 From this example plainly may be seen how much he pleases Fortune and how acceptable to her is he who strikes her, who thrusts her aside, who hunts her down.

166 Yet nevertheless one of these did not reach the haven he desired, and the other, covered with wounds, was killed at the base of his enemy's statue.

169 Near these are numberless men who that they may fall on the ground with a heavier crash, have climbed the higher with the goddess.

172 Among these lie captive, dead, and ruined, Cyrus and Pompey, though both of them were carried up to the heavens by Fortune.

175 Have you ever seen in any place how an angry eagle rushes along, driven by hunger and fasting?

178 And how it carries a tortoise on high, that the force of the fall may break it, and the eagle feeds upon that dead flesh?

181 So Fortune does not carry anybody on high that he may remain there, but that she may enjoy his ruinous fall and he may weep as he plunges downward.

184 He who looks may also see after these how a person may rise from the humblest rank, and live there with varying chance.

187 One may see, too, how Cicero and Marius tormented her, and how she sometimes increased, sometimes cut off the glorious horns of their fame.

190 Finally it may be seen that, in days gone by, the prosperous have been but few; and these have died before their wheel could turn backward, or in circling around carry them to its lowest point.

THE FAMILIAR LETTERS

Introduction

The Familiar Letters give a view of the last thirty years of their author's life. There are, however, periods from which nothing is preserved, namely 1500-3, 1510-11, 1518-9, 1522. More than half the total, reckoning by pages, comes from 1512 to 1517, the years when he was working on *The Prince* and the *Discourses on Livy;* many of these are addressed to Vettori. A group of three, addressed to Guicciardini, comes in 1521. About a fourth of the total bulk was written in the last three years of his life. Only some ten years, then, are really illuminated by the private correspondence.

The fifteen Letters here presented extend from the beginning to the end of the thirty years. They are chosen primarily to illustrate *The Prince*. The letter to Vettori of December 10, 1513 is our chief external source of information on that work. Many of the others show in more detail his views of subjects discussed there, such as that of April 29, 1513, on Ferdinand of Spain. Others, such as that of April 26, 1527, illuminate the patriotism of its last chapter. Most of them reveal Machiavelli's love for political speculation, even when he knew his information was limited; they also show that even so keen a thinker was not always right. Yet, though realizing that he might be wrong, he was like the political-minded of our day, unable to refrain from speculating on what the rulers of the world intended.

The chief service of the Letters is in enabling us to feel the spirit of the man. Above all they remind us of the rich vein of comedy without which Machiavelli would never have been great. It is the more astonishing that so much of the comic is apparent in letters chosen for the illustration of his political thought. Yet few of them are without a touch at least of the comic spirit. Pope Julius has no scales or yard-stick in his house. Machiavelli is the fox which first feared the lion (Vettori) and at last treated him familiarly. Even the very rack on which he had suffered is touched with comedy. The famous letter on *The Prince* is by contrast with its serious subject the more comic: the picture of the author in his rural surroundings and above all with his piles of cord-wood. The letter from the house of the monks at Carpi is full of laughter, though with such a serious undertone as that of Florence swayed by its preachers. Altogether the correspondence reveals the deep earnestness without which no comic writer is great, and shows the interpenetration of the light and grave that means the insight of a comic poet at work.

SAVONAROLA

March 9, 1497-8.

To Ricciardo Bechi.[1]

1 According to your request, I shall give you full particulars of what has gone on here with respect to the Frate.[2] After delivering the two sermons of which you have already had copies, he preached the Sunday of the Carnival. When he had talked a long time, he invited all his followers to receive the communion in San Marco on the Carnival day. He said he intended to pray that if the things he had predicted did not come from God, God would show a clear sign of it. He did this, as some say, to unite his party and make it stronger to defend him, because he feared that the new *Signoria*, already determined on but not announced, would be adverse to him. Since the members of the *Signoria* were announced on the following Monday, you must have had full particulars of it.[3] The Frate judged that two-thirds of them were hostile to him, and moreover he had received a summons to appear before the Pope, under penalty of interdict, and feared that the new *Signoria* would really wish him to obey. Hence he decided, either on his own initiative or advised by others, to abandon his preaching in Santa Reparata and to go to San Marco. Therefore on Thursday morning, when the new *Signoria* went into office, he said in Santa Reparata merely that, to avoid dissension and to preserve the reverence due to God, he wished to retire, and that the men should come to hear him in San Marco, and that the women should go to San Lorenzo to hear Fra Domenico.[4] Being now in his own house, our Frate began and carried on his preaching with such boldness as to cause no small wonder to his hearers. He had great fear about his own position, believed that the new *Signoria* was rash enough to injure him, and was determined that many citizens should be crushed by his fall. Hence, with words designed to cause terror, and with reasons very convincing to those who did not

[1] Florentine ambassador in Rome. [2] Savonarola. See also the Index.

[3] The Florentine method of choosing the *Signoria* by lot could cause striking changes in policy.

[4] One of Savonarola's most faithful followers; executed with him.

examine them, he began to show that his followers were the best of men, and his adversaries the most wicked; he used every expression he could think of to weaken the opposing party and to strengthen his own. Because I was present, I shall go over some of these things briefly.

2 The text of his first sermon in San Marco was this passage from Exodus: The more the Egyptians afflicted them, the more they multiplied and grew.[5] But before he came to the explanation of these words, he showed for what reason he had retired, and said: Prudence is right conduct in practical matters.[6] Then he said that all men have had and have an end, but different for different persons. "The end of Christians is Christ. That of other men, both past and present, has been and is something else, according to their religion. Since we, then, who are Christians are directed to this end, namely Christ, we ought to preserve his honor with the utmost prudence and regard for the conditions of the time; when these conditions require us to expose our lives for him, we ought to expose them; and when it is time for a man to hide, we ought to hide, as we read of Christ and Saint Paul. And so, he added, we ought to do, and we have done. Thus when it was time to resist the fury of the wicked, we have done it, as on Ascension day,[7] for so the honor of God and the conditions required; now that the honor of God requires that we yield to wrath, we have yielded."

3 After this brief explanation, he said there were two bodies of men: one, which fights on God's side, made up of himself and his followers; the other, which fights on the side of the devil, made up of his adversaries. Then, speaking at greater length, he undertook the exposition of the words of Exodus given above, and said that through tribulations good men grow in two ways, in spirit and in number. They grow in spirit because a man unites himself more closely with God, by overcoming adversity; he becomes stronger because he is nearer his active cause, just as hot water when brought nearer the fire grows hotter because it is nearer its active cause. They also increase in number, because there are three kinds of men: the good, he says, "are those who follow me; then there are the perverse and obstinate, and these are my adversaries." Then there is another kind of men of unrestrained lives, given to pleasures, neither fixed in doing evil nor devoted to doing good, because they do not distinguish one from the other. But since there is some difference in fact between good and perverse,

[5] Exodus 1.12.
[6] Aquinas, *Summa Theologica* 2.2.47.2.
[7] On May 4, 1497, Savonarola's life was in danger during a riot in the Cathedral of the city, which interrupted his sermon.

according to the rule that opposites when placed near one another stand out more clearly,[8] they recognize the malice of the wicked and the simplicity of the good. Therefore they flee from the first and draw near to the second, because everybody naturally flees from what is evil and gladly follows after the good. For this reason the wicked are not to be found in adversity and the good multiply, according to the text: "The more, etc." I am presenting it briefly, because the limit of a letter does not permit a long narrative. He then entered into various discussions, as his custom is, with the purpose of weakening his adversaries still further, and leading up to his next sermon, and said that our discords would cause the rise of a tyrant who would destroy our homes and lay waste our city. And this, he declared, was not contrary to what he had already said, namely that Florence was going to be prosperous and rule over Italy, because in a short time the tyrant would be driven away. With that he finished his sermon.

4 Then the next morning, still expounding Exodus and coming to that passage where it says that Moses killed an Egyptian,[9] he said that the Egyptian means wicked men and Moses the preacher who killed them, by revealing their vices. And he said: "O Egyptian, I wish to give you a dagger thrust." And here he began to examine your books, O priests, and to make such a mess of you as a dog would not eat. Then he added (and this is what he had been moving toward) that he wished to give the Egyptian another heavy blow. And he said that God had told him there was one in Florence who sought to make himself a tyrant, and was working and planning to attain it. This man's wish to drive away the Frate, to excommunicate the Frate, to persecute the Frate meant nothing else than that he wished to play the tyrant. The city should, said the preacher, invoke the laws against this disturber. He said so much about it that men made public guesses and named a man who is as near to being a tyrant as you are to heaven. But since then the *Signoria* has written to the Pope on his behalf, and he sees that he no longer needs to fear his adversaries in Florence. So that whereas he sought at first only to unite his party by making them detest his adversaries and by frightening them with the name of tyrant, now that he no longer needs to do so, he has turned his coat inside out. He now encourages them to favor the movement toward unity that has now begun, and without saying anything more of a tyrant or of the people's wickedness, tries to make them firm against

[8] A rule well known to Renaissance logicians.

[9] Exodus 2, 11-12.

yielding to the Supreme Pontiff. Having turned his teeth on the Pope, he says of him what might be said against the most wicked man you could find. In this way, according to my judgment, he is careful to adapt himself to the times and make his lies plausible.[10]

5 Now what the populace says of this, and what men can hope or fear of it, I will leave to your own judgment, for you are prudent. You can judge it better than I can, because you know completely our various parties, the condition of the times, and, because you are near him, the mind of the Pope. I ask of you only this, that, if it has not been a bore to you to read my letter, you will not think it too much trouble to answer, telling me your opinion of the condition of the times and the feelings of men about our affairs. Farewell.

At Florence, the 9th day of March, 1497 [-8].

Your Niccolò di M. Bernardo Machiavelli.

EUROPEAN POLITICS

June 12, 1506.

To the Honorable Giovanni Ridolfi,[1] Commissioner General against the Pisans, My Patron and Special Benefactor.[2]

Honorable Commissioner:

1 If I have written you no news of late, this letter and those I shall write later may atone for my failure. Letters have come from France from the fifteenth to the thirtieth days of the past month. They say the Emperor and the King of Hungary have reached an agreement, and that the Emperor is giving attention to nothing else than his preparations for coming to Italy. All his army is eager for it, and he has nine thousand infantry and four thousand cavalry; he has also sent to Trent a large part of the artillery he intends to bring with him. Besides, he intends to send to Gonsalvo four thousand infantry. The Archduke has come to terms with the King of Aragon, because they have had a meeting in Galicia; there seems to be close union between them. This is contrary to the expectation of the French, who show themselves displeased with it. The King of England is on good terms with the Archduke, and in the latter's journey to Spain has assisted him with money and with two thousand infantry. The barons of the kingdom of

[10] For adaptation to the times, see *The Prince*, Chap. 25.

[1] Important in Florentine affairs; the civilian director of the war against Pisa.

[2] For the matter of this letter see the Chronological Table, above, and the *Introduction*, pars. 121-35, above.

Naples who are in Spain, that is, the exiled barons who believed they would get back their estates according to the agreements between France and Spain, have not received them again; therefore they have sent a representative to the King of France for fresh aid. The Duke Valentino, a prisoner in Spain, has also sent into France for aid; and the King of Spain has sent his ambassador there, with instructions to favor the Duke and the others. The Pope seeks to employ the Swiss. He also asks men at arms from France, and says he wishes to proceed against Bologna and Perugia. If he will employ a few Swiss and if he will consent to let Bologna alone, the French promise to aid him against Perugia, because they also wish to avenge themselves on Pandolfo Petrucci.[3] But if he wishes to employ a large number of Swiss, the French will hinder him with all their power, because they think he intends something else than Bologna and Perugia, and they suspect that he wishes not to attack those cities, in order to favor the Emperor.

2 The King of France has sent, or is about to send, an ambassador to the Swiss, with a commission. He is called the chief judge of Provence. From Switzerland he will go to Venice and then to Hungary. He will attempt to keep the Swiss firm in their resolution to take wages only from the King, to hold the Venetians firm in their aid, and to disturb the peace between the King of Hungary and the Emperor. The Bailey of Digiuno has returned to court, where he has great favor, because—so it is said—he has a good understanding of German affairs. The King of France is sending M. d'Argenton,[4] with four gentlemen, to the boundaries of Germany, to get away from the Emperor certain German leagues which do not serve the Emperor either with men or with money. The King of France is not observing his obligations to the Emperor according to the last agreement, made by the Cardinal Rouen. Some time ago an ambassador came to court to ask for money and men according to the obligation, but neither one has been given to him; the King dismissed him and said that he will send his ambassador to the Emperor to explain to him, etc. The King of France has given his daughter as wife to M. d'Angoulême, and made all the lords of the kingdom pledge their fidelity to the said Angoulême, if he should die without male children. He has given him as his wife's dower the county of Blois, and 100,000 ducats; and the Queen has given them

[3] See *The Prince*, Chap. 22, par. 2.

[4] Philippe de Commynes, the minister of Louis XI, now in the service of Louis XII. For his possible relation to Machiavelli see Gilbert, *Machiavelli's "Prince" and Its Forerunners*, index, s.v. *Commynes*.

100,000 ducats and the dukedom of Brittany, if she dies without male children. Between the Venetians and the King there has been no new agreement; but they are friendly and keep the old one. The King of France has given a mission to Mgr. di Cisteron, who has been the ambassador of the Pope and is returning to Italy, that he should visit Ferrara, Mantua, Bologna, and Florence, and promise to give them seas and mountains, and keep them well disposed to him when the Emperor enters the country, if indeed he does enter it.

3 These tiding are not enough if I do not also write to you of the comment made on them by some citizens who are very wise. And though in your wisdom you can comment on it as well as they do, I know that their discourse will be pleasing to you. If the news is reliable, it appears to them that the King of the Romans is more likely to pass into Italy than the reverse. They speak as follows: When one sets out to judge if anybody is going to do a thing, it is necessary first to see if he wishes to do it, then what assistance he may have, and what hindrance in doing it. Whether the Emperor wishes to go into Italy or not, all reasons are in favor of his desiring to do so. The first is that he may reasonably desire to crown himself for his own glory, and to pass on that dignity to his son. The other is to recompense himself for the injuries received from the Italians and reacquire the honor he lost in his expedition into Tuscany. It is credible, then, that he wishes to come.

4 Now in order to see who is able to hold back or aid him, it is necessary to consider whom he has at home and who his neighbors are. His subjects in Germany are not well known here. However, he is believed to be more powerful than in the past, since he has overcome the County Palatine and laid taxes on the cities and the lords for their shares of the cost of his expedition into Italy. His neighbors are the Archduke, the King of France, and the King of England. The powers of Italy, where he intends to come, are the Pope, the Venetians, the King of Spain, the Florentines, and others of little weight. If the news is true, it appears that the Archduke, the King of Spain, and the King of England are in accord. And if they are in accord, it follows that they are in agreement with the Emperor, since the Archduke is his son and the two of them have everything in common.

5 As to the Pope, though he treats with the King of France to get soldiers from him, it is apparent that he is more favorable to the affairs of the Emperor; and that is reasonable. The Fortune of France is weary, especially because of what has happened in Italy; that of the Emperor is fresh. This Pope is probably intending to do with the Emperor what Alexander did with the King of France.[5] Of the little states of Italy there is no need to say anything, if the others are in agreement.

6 There remain then to object to his expedition only the greater powers, namely, the French and the Venetians, who should together oppose his coming, but both of them will tread very carefully, for they do not trust one another. And it must be considered that they can oppose the Emperor with force and craft; they will not fail to use every kind of craft and effort to derange his plan, as seems to be done in France, according to the news. But it is likely that craft will not be enough, and that if they have to come to force, they will not be willing to do it. It is hardly credible that the King of France will decide to make war on the Emperor against the wishes of England, the Archduke, and Spain. Nor can it be believed that the Venetians, since they would have to make war in their own country, would wish to do it, for they would always be afraid that the French at a critical moment would abandon them. Hence it is probable that since their craft will not avail to keep him back, they will plan on letting him come, and everybody will try to take care of his own interests. If they have to come to blows with him, they will do it when he has come into Italy, as the Duke of Milan and the Venetians did to King Charles.

7 The Emperor, on the other side, will be content to be allowed to enter the country without opposition, because it will be more to his advantage to make war then than earlier. The reason is that two things cause him to come into Italy: he wishes to get the crown, and to revenge his injuries. If he should make war before he had been crowned, and should be defeated, he could never hope for the crown. But if he should make war after being crowned, even though he should suffer defeat, the crown could not be taken from him, and he would return to Germany with less disgrace. The making of war, whether beyond the Alps or in Italy, need not give him much concern, since he has the friendship of the Pope and all the others who are carried along by his authority. I know that I have written your head off; pardon me. I am under your orders, and if you wish another of these books, let me know.

June 12, 1506. NICCOLÒ MACHIAVELLI, *Secretary.*

[5] Cf. *The Prince*, Chap. 7, pars. 3-5.

FORTUNE AND THE TIMES

January 1512-3.
To Pier Soderini in Ragusa.[1]

1 Your letter presented itself to me in a mask;[2] still, after ten words, I recognized it. I believe your account of the crowds that came to see you in Piombino. I am sure I understand your impediments and those of Philip, because I know that one is offended by little light, the other by too much. January does not trouble me, if only February supports me. I am sorry about Philip's suspicion and I await the end of it in suspense.

2 Your letter was short, and I made it long by re-reading it. It was pleasing to me because it gave me opportunity to do what I hesitated to do, and which you remind me that I should not do; this is the only part I have observed in it that is not to the point. I should wonder at that, if my lot had not shown me so many and so varied things that I am obliged to wonder but little, or to confess that in the course of my reading and practical dealings I have not come to comprehend the actions of men and their methods of procedure.[3]

3 I know you and the compass by which you navigate; if it could be condemned—which is impossible—I could not condemn it, because I see to what port it would have guided you and with what hope it was able to sustain you. Hence I believe that, not according to your mirror, where nothing but prudence is seen, but that of the majority, it is necessary for things to be judged according to the end, which shows how they have been done, and not according to the means, as they are being done.[4] Each man conducts himself according to his fancy. I observe, too, that the same thing results from different methods of procedure, just as one gets to the same place by different paths, and many who work in different ways get to the same end; if any more evidence is needed on this, the actions of this Pope and their results furnish it.[5] There is no use in giving advice or in taking advice, except in the form of a general principle, from anybody; every man should do what his spirit moves him to, and do it with courage.

4 Hannibal and Scipio were equally excellent in military capacity. Yet, in addition, one of them by means of cruelty, perfidy, and lack of religion, kept his army in Italy united,

[1] For Soderini, see the index. As the footnotes suggest, much of *The Prince* was in Machiavelli's mind when he wrote this letter.

[2] In cipher.

[3] Cf. the dedications of *The Prince* and the *Discourses on Livy.*

[4] Cf. *The Prince,* Chap. 18, end.

[5] Pope Julius II. Cf. *The Prince,* Chap. 25, par. 5.

and made himself admired by various peoples, who rebelled against the Romans in order to follow him. The other, by reason of his piety, faith, and religion, gained the same result from the peoples of Spain.[6] Both of them won numerous victories. Further, since it is not customary to cite the Romans as examples, I should like to say that Lorenzo de' Medici disarmed the people in order to hold Florence; Messer Giovanni Bentivogli armed them in order to hold Bologna; the Vitelli in Castello and the present duke of Urbino in his province demolished their fortresses in order to hold those states; Count Francesco and many others built fortresses to make themselves secure of their states.[7] Titus the Emperor believed he would lose his throne on the day when he did not do a good deed to at least one person; some other emperor might believe he would lose it on the day when he accommodated anybody. Many who think over and measure everything succeed in their designs. This Pope, who hasn't a pair of scales or a yard stick in his house, gets by chance—for he has no army—what it would be very hard to obtain with care and the use of force.

5 Such men as these and many others who can be cited on this subject have been seen and can be seen every day either obtaining kingdoms and dominions or falling, according to circumstances; and sometimes the mode of procedure that was praised when it was bringing gain is reviled when it causes loss. Sometimes, when a man suffers loss after long prosperity, he blames nothing in his own conduct, but accuses the heavens and the decisions of the Fates. But why it is that different methods sometimes bring the same benefits and sometimes the same amount of harm, I do not know, but I should be very glad to know. Still, in order to get your opinion, I shall be so bold as to state mine.

6 I believe that as Nature has given men different faces, so she has given them different temperaments and fancies. From this it comes that every man conducts himself according to his temperament and fancy. And because on the other hand the times vary and the conditions of things are different, one man's efforts result just as he wishes them to. He is successful whose way of doing things is fitted to the time; but quite the other way, he is unsuccessful whose actions do not fit in with the times and the conditions of affairs.

7 Hence it can very well happen that two men, working quite differently, come to the same end, because each of them

[6] For cruelty, and the comparison of Hannibal and Scipio, see *The Prince*, Chaps. 8, end, and 17, pars. 5 and 6.

[7] Cf. *The Prince*, Chap. 20, for parallels to many of the ideas of this letter.

is in harmony with his environment, for there are as many types of conditions as there are provinces and states. But because times and things both generally and in detail change frequently, and men do not change their fancies or their methods of working, it comes about that the same man has at one period good fortune, and at another bad fortune.

8 And certainly anyone wise enough to understand the times and the conditions of things, and who fits himself to them, would have good fortune, or would always protect himself from misfortune, and it would seem to be true that the wise man rules the stars and the Fates. But a man so wise as this is never found, because in the first place men are short-sighted, and in the second cannot command their temperaments; as a result Fortune varies, and controls men, and keeps them under her yoke. I believe the examples given above, on which I have based this belief, are enough to establish it; hence I wish one to support the other.

9 Cruelty, perfidy, and irreligion can give reputation to a new ruler in a province where humanity, faith, and religion for a long time have been abandoned. In the same way humanity, faith, and religion are of value where cruelty, perfidy, and irreligion have been in power for a time. The reason is that, just as bitter things disturb the taste and sweet things surfeit it, so men get weary of good and complain of ill. This reason, among others, opened Italy to Hannibal, and Spain to Scipio. And so everybody will fit or not fit the times and the conditions, according to his method of conduct. In that very time a man like Scipio could not have done as well in Italy, and one like Hannibal could not have done as well in Spain, as each man did in his own region.

NICCOLÒ MACHIAVELLI.

A PASSION FOR POLITICS

April 9, 1513.

To Francesco Vettori,[1] the Honorable Ambassador at the Court of the Holy Pontiff, at Rome.

Honorable Ambassador:

1 And I, who was conscious of my color,
Said: "How shall I come if you are fearful,
Whose custom it is to be a comfort in my hesitation?"[2]

[1] Francesco Vettori, to whom Machiavelli addressed twenty-seven of his familiar letters, was Florentine ambassador at Rome when this letter was written. He later held high office in Florence under the Medici.

[2] Dante, *Inferno*, IV, 16-8.

This letter of yours has terrified me more than the rack;[3] and I grieve for every idea you hold that may change me, not in my own estimation—because I am trained not to desire anything further with passion—but in yours. I pray you to imitate the others, who with importunity and craft, rather than with skill and prudence, make places for themselves. With respect to the news of Totto,[4] it displeases me, if it displeases you. I shall not think further of it, and if he is not able to spin around, let him whirl himself. And once for all I say to you that, no matter how many things I have ever asked from you, you do not need to be troubled about them, because I shall not get excited because I do not have them.

2 If you have grown sick of discussing public affairs, because you see things turn out quite differently from anything you had thought of and imagined, you have cause for it; the same thing has happened to me. Yet if I were able to speak with you, you couldn't keep me from filling your head with castles in Spain, because Fortune has decreed that since I cannot discuss silk-making or wool-manufacture, or profits and losses, I have to discuss matters of state. I must either make a vow of silence or talk about that subject.

3 If I were able to get out of Florentine territory,[5] I would come to Rome to knock at the Pope's door; but in the rush for favors my affair stands still because I am not there to push it. I shall wait for September.

4 I understand that the Cardinal de' Soderini has a great deal of business with the Pope. I wish you would advise me, if it seems to you a good idea for me to write him a letter asking him to recommend me to His Holiness; or would it be better for you to do this on my behalf by word of mouth? or would it be better to do neither of them? Tell me in a few words what you think of this.

5 As to the horse, you make me smile by reminding me of it; for you have to pay only when I remember it, and not otherwise.

6 Our archbishop must have died by this time; may God receive his soul and all that pertains to him. Farewell.

Florence, April 9, 1513.

NICCOLÒ MACHIAVELLI, *Formerly Secretary.*

[3] Machiavelli was tortured on the rack in February, after the conspiracy of Boscoli and Capponi against the Medici.

[4] Niccolò Machiavelli's brother.

[5] Soon after the return of the Medici in 1512, Machiavelli was forbidden to leave Florentine territory for a year.

FERDINAND KING OF SPAIN

April 29, 1513.
To Francesco Vettori.
Honorable Ambassador:

1 I never had anything among my greatest joys in which I delighted so much as in your conversation, because I always learned something from it. Imagine, then, how welcome your letter was at a time when I am deprived of every other pleasure, how it lacks nothing but your presence and the sound of your voice. Whenever I have read it—and I have read it many times—I have always forgotten my unhappy state, and appear to be again in the midst of those affairs in which I have fruitlessly labored so hard and spent so much time. And though I have vowed not to think any more of politics or to talk of them, as I have shown by coming to my farm and avoiding conversation, nonetheless, to answer your questions, I am forced to break every vow, because I believe I am more strongly bound by my old friendship with you than by any other obligation I owe to any man, especially when you have done me the honor you have at the end of your letter; to tell the truth, I am a little vain-glorious of it, since it is true that it is not a little thing to be praised by a man who is himself praised.[1] I fear that my ideas will seem not to have their old flavor. But I hope this may be excused because I have deliberately given up these affairs, and in addition do not know any details of the current news. You know how things have to be judged in the dark, and especially such things as these. So what I say will be founded either on your discussion or on my own suppositions, and if the latter are false, I hope the reasons I have already given may excuse me.

2 You wish to know what I think moved the King of Spain to make this truce with the King of France, for when you look at the matter from all sides it seems to you that it is not to his interest. Since, therefore, you think on the one hand that King Ferdinand is wise, and on the other think he has made a mistake, you are obliged to suppose that something important is concealed under his act, which at present neither you nor others understand. And truly your analysis could not be more expert or more prudent, nor do I think anything else can be said on the matter. Yet to act alive and to obey you, I shall say what occurs to me.

3 It seems to me that this uncertainty of yours depends chiefly on your belief in the prudence of the King of Spain. To

[1] Cicero, *Familiar Letters* 5.12.7.

this I answer: I am not able to deny that that king is wise, but all the same he appears to me more crafty [2] and fortunate than wise. I do not intend to review his whole career, but will go directly to the enterprise he last attempted against France in Italy, before the King of England showed his intentions. Even though that undertaking came out well, it seemed to me and still seems to me that without necessity he endangered all his territories.[3] Such an action is very foolhardy in a prince. I say without necessity, as he might have seen from the indications of the preceding year. The Pope had done many injuries to the King of France, attacking his friends and trying to make Genoa rebel. Moreover Ferdinand himself had given France many provocations by sending his soldiers with those of the Church to damage states under French protection. Yet after a victory, when the Pope had been put to flight, and deprived of all his armies, and it was possible to drive him from Rome and the King of Spain from Naples, the King of France did not wish to do so, but preferred a treaty; hence Spain had no reason to fear France. Nor does the explanation that is brought forward for him, namely, that he did it to make sure of Naples, show that he was wise, because the King of France had not turned his attention there, since he was tired out, had many reasons for hesitation, and would continue to have them; the Pope would always be unwilling that Naples should be restored to France, and the French King would always have to respect the Pope and fear the union of the other powers. This was always going to hold him back.

4 Or it may be said that the King of Spain feared that if he did not join the Pope in making war on France, the Pope in anger would join France in making war on him, for the Pope was a passionate man and full of the devil;[4] hence the King of Spain was obliged to join the Pope. But I answer that in those days the King of France would always have been readier to ally himself with Spain than with the Pope, if an alliance with either one of them was possible, for two reasons: first, victory would be more certain and he would not be obliged to go to war for it; second, the French King thought himself greatly injured by the Pope and not by Spain. To revenge himself for that injury and to satisfy the Church by a council, he would always have abandoned the Pope. Hence

[2] The Italian word here is *astuto* (astute). Astuteness is a vice in *The Prince*, Chap. 15, par. 2. For astute conduct by Ferdinand, see The *Prince*, Chap. 16, par. 2; Chap. 18, last par.; Chap. 21, par. 1.

[3] According to the *Art of War*, bk. 3, a general should not risk battle unless he has an advantage or is compelled to fight by necessity.

[4] For the character of Pope Julius II, see *The Prince*, Chap. 25, par. 5.

it seems to me that in those days King Ferdinand could have been either the mediator in a firm peace or the maker of a secure alliance for himself. Nevertheless he passed over all these possibilities and chose war, in which he had to run the risk of losing all his territories in a single battle.[5] He feared that would happen when he lost the day at Ravenna, for immediately after the news of that defeat, he took measures for sending Gonsalvo to Naples, because that kingdom was as good as lost and the kingdom of Castile trembled under him; nor did he have any reason to suppose that the Swiss would avenge him and give him security, and restore him the reputation he had lost, as they did. Altogether, if you consider how all these things were handled, you will see in the King of Spain craft and good fortune rather than wisdom and prudence. When a great man makes one error like that, it is to be presumed that he has made a thousand of them. I do not believe there is anything in his decision that is not apparent, for I am no dreamer, and do not intend to be influenced in this matter by authority without reason. Therefore I conclude that though there is truth in what you say, Ferdinand may have made an error, and planned badly and executed worse.

5 But let us drop this and admit that he is prudent; then we can discuss his plan as that of a wise man. It seems to me that if we intend to make this presupposition and get properly at the truth of the matter, we need to know whether this truce has been made after the death of the Pope and the elevation of the new one,[6] or before, because that would probably make some difference. But since I do not know, I will assume that it was made before Julius died. If, then, I should ask what you think the King of Spain should have done, you would answer what you have already written to me, that is, that he should have made complete peace with the King of France, and given Lombardy back to him, in order to take away from him any reason for leading an army to Italy. In such a way Ferdinand could have made himself secure. To this I answer that in order to discuss this thing well, one must observe that the King of Spain made that attempt against France because he hoped to conquer, and placed more reliance in the Pope, in England, and in the Emperor than, as it turned out, he saw he should have placed there. He thought he could get plenty of money from the Pope. He believed that the Emperor would

[5] Cf. the Venetian loss in the one battle of Vailà, mentioned in *The Prince*, Chap. 12, par. 5.

[6] Julius II died February 20, 1513; Leo X was elevated March 11; the treaty between Louis XII and Ferdinand was on April 1. Time must be allowed for the news to travel.

make a vigorous attack on Burgundy, and that the King of England, being young, rich, and correspondingly eager for glory, would come in great force as soon as he himself had set out. Hence France, both in Italy and at home, would have to receive terms from him. But none of these things came to pass. From the Pope he obtained money at first in small amounts, and at last the Pope not merely did not give him money but every day sought to ruin him, and plotted against him. Nothing has come from the Emperor except the travels of the Bishop of Gurk, slanders, and reproaches. From England he received only weak forces, that did not work well with his own. Hence, if it had not been for the conquest of Navarre, made before France was in the field, both of his armies would have been disgraced, since they would have gained nothing but shame, for one of them never left the forests of Fonterabbia, the other retreated to Pampeluna and had difficulty in defending it. So the King of Spain found himself ruined in the midst of this confusion of friends, from whom he could hope nothing better, but on the contrary he was obliged every day to fear something worse from them, because all of them were every day negotiating for alliance with France.

6 On the other hand, he saw that the King of France could sustain the expense of war, because he was allied with the Venetians, and could hope for aid from the Swiss. Hence he has thought it better to be beforehand with the King of France, as well as he could, rather than to remain in such great uncertainty and confusion, and subject to expense greater than he can bear. For I have learned on good authority that somebody has written from Spain that there is no money there and no way of getting any and that his army there consists of conscripts only, and even they are beginning not to obey him. And I believe that his design in this truce has been either to make his allies recognize their error and make them more eager for the war, since he has promised the ratification, etc., or to get the war away from Spain and relieve himself of so much expense and peril, for if Pampeluna had been taken away from him this spring he would surely have lost Castile.

7 As to affairs in Italy, the King of Spain would be able to rely on his own soldiers, perhaps more than is reasonable; but I think he should put no more dependence than is necessary on the Swiss, the Pope, and the Emperor, and that he should remember that eating may teach the Emperor and the Italians to drink. I believe he did not make a strict agreement with the King of France to give him the dukedom of Milan, both because it was not in his power and because he judged it an act not useful to himself. And I suspect France would not have agreed because he did not trust Ferdinand or his armies, for he would have believed that the King of Spain did not do it for the sake of an alliance with him but for the purpose of nullifying the French alliances with the others.

8 As to the King of Spain, I do not now see that there is any utility in peace for him in any event, because the French king is going to be powerful in Italy no matter how he gets into Lombardy. And even though the Spanish forces were enough to get it for him, if he wished to hold it he would have to send his own there, in large numbers, and they would be enough to rouse the same suspicions in the Italians and in the King of Spain as would be roused by soldiers who came to take it by force. Today no attention is paid to faith and obligations,[7] hence Spain saw no security in them, and on the other side, saw this loss.

9 Ferdinand made peace with France either with the consent of his confederates or without. If he had any thought of making it with their consent, he judged it impossible, because there could be no agreement among the Pope, France, the Venetians, and the Emperor. If then he had to do it against their will, he saw that it would be a clear loss to him, because he would have allied himself with—and thus given power to—a king who, whenever opportunity arose, would have remembered old injuries rather than new benefits.[8] Moreover he would have irritated against himself all other rulers in Italy and outside it, because, since he was the sole provoker of all of them against France, if he then abandoned them, it would be a very great injury. Hence if he had made peace according to your plan, he would have increased the power of the King of France, and been sure to arouse the anger of the confederates, and still could not have felt sure of the faith of France. Yet this faith would have been the only thing on which he could rely. If he made France powerful and the others hostile, it was necessary to take his stand with France; but wise men never place themselves at the discretion of others except through necessity.[9] Hence I conclude he may have made a better decision by making the truce, because that act shows his allies their error; he has made it impossible for them to complain, because they have had time to ratify it; he has got the war away from his own country; he has stirred up new contests and confusion in Italian affairs, where he sees there is yet something to be torn up and a bone to pick. And, as I said

[7] Cf. *The Prince,* Chap. 18.
[8] Cf. *The Prince,* Chap. 7, end.
[9] Cf. *The Prince,* Chap. 21, par. 7.

above, he hopes that eating will teach everyone to drink, and can believe that the Pope, the Emperor, and the Swiss will not be pleased with the greatness of the Venetians and of France in Italy; if they are not strong enough to keep France and Venice from occupying Lombardy, at least with his help they are able to keep the two from going farther. Ferdinand also believes that the Pope for this reason must throw himself into his arms, for he can assume that the Pope will not be able to agree with the Venetians or with their allies on the affairs of the Romagna. Hence he sees that this truce makes the victory of France doubtful, he does not have to trust King Louis, and does not have to fear the alienation of his confederates, because the Emperor and England either will ratify it or will not. If they ratify it, they will do so thinking that this truce is beneficial to all; if they do not ratify it, they will probably become more eager for war, and assail France with larger forces than in the past year. In every one of these instances the King of Spain gets what he is looking for. I say again, then, that the purpose of Spain has been this: either to force the Emperor and England to make war in earnest, or to arrange things to his advantage with other means than arms, by using their reputations. In every other decision he might expect danger, whether he continued the war or made peace. Therefore he took a half-way measure, which could result in either war or peace.

10 If you have observed the plans and methods of this Catholic King, you will be less astonished at this truce. This King, as you know, has risen to his present greatness from a paltry and weak condition, and has always had to carry on his wars with the aid of new states and doubtful subjects. One of the methods of holding new states (and doubtful spirits either come to rest or remain uncertain and irresolute) is for the ruler to raise great expectations of himself, and keep the minds of men always occupied in wondering what end his decisions and enterprises will have.[10] This king has recognized this necessity and used it well. From it resulted his attacks on Africa, the division of the Kingdom of Naples, and all his other various undertakings. Yet he foresaw the end of none of these; for his end is not so much this or that, or a particular victory, as it is to give himself prestige with his people, and keep them in suspense with the multiplicity of his actions. Therefore he has always been a courageous maker of beginnings, and the conclusions of his enterprises are those chance puts before him or necessity teaches; and up to now he has had no reason to

[10] Cf. *The Prince*, Chap. 21, par. 1.

complain of his luck or of his courage. I prove this opinion of mine by the division of the kingdom of Naples he made with France. He must have known that it was certain to cause a war between himself and France, and he was not within a thousand miles of knowing its outcome; he had no reason to believe he would defeat France in Apulia, in Calabria, and at the Garigliano. It was enough for him to begin, in order to get himself the prestige he was seeking, and he hoped either good fortune or skill would enable him to continue. As long as he lives he will always go from labor to labor, without further consideration for the end.

11 I have discussed all these matters on the assumption that Julius was alive; but if the King had learned that Julius was dead and Leo on the throne, I believe he would have done the same thing. If he could not trust Julius because that pope was unstable, violent, mad, and stingy, he cannot expect much from the present pope because of his wisdom. If Ferdinand is prudent he will not remind Pope Leo of connections formed when he was in a subordinate place; then Leo obeyed, but now he commands; then he played another's game, but now his own; then he could gain from war, but now from peace. King Ferdinand should understand that His Holiness does not wish to employ either his money or his armies in wars among Christians unless he is forced to; and I believe that everybody will hesitate to force him.

12 I know that this letter must appear to you a *pastinaca* fish,[11] and not of the flavor you expected. May I be excused because my mind is far away from all these actions, as is proved by my retirement to my farm and withdrawal from every human face, and my ignorance of what is going on in the world. Hence I have to discuss in the dark and have founded everything on the news you have sent me. Therefore I beg that you will excuse me.

I send my regards to everybody and especially to your Paolo, if he has not gone away. Your Friend.
Florence, April 29, 1513. N. M.

[11] "The fish pastinaca, that is, without head and without tail" (Benedetto Varchi, *L'Ercolano*, Sesta Dubitazione, p. 98 in the ed. of Florence, 1570; *Opere*—Trieste, 1859—II, 59.

EUROPEAN AFFAIRS IN RELATION TO ITALY

August 26, 1513.
To Vettori.
Honorable Ambassador:

1 Your letter of the twentieth has disconcerted me, because its arrangement, its many arguments, and all its other qualities so entangled me that at the beginning I was bewildered and confused. And if I had not been a little reassured on rereading it, I would have thrown it away and written to you about something else. But in handling it I have been like the fox when he saw the lion. The first time he was ready to die with fear; the second he stood still behind a bush to look at him; the third he spoke to him. So, reassuring myself by experience with it, I shall answer you.

2 With respect to the state of things in the world, I come to this conclusion about them. We are ruled by princes of such a sort that they have, by nature or accident, the following qualities. We have a wise pope,[1] hence one grave and thoughtful, an emperor who is unstable and uncertain,[2] a king of France prone to anger and timid,[3] a king of Spain stingy and avaricious,[4] a king of England, rich, fiery, and eager for glory;[5] the Swiss are brutal, victorious, and insolent; we Italians are poor, ambitious, and cowardly. I don't know about the other kings. So considering these qualities and current conditions, I believe the friar who said: "Peace, peace, and there will be no peace."[6] I admit to you that every peace is difficult, yours as well as mine. And if you think that mine is more difficult, I do not mind. But I hope you will listen patiently about the matters in which I suspect you deceive yourself, and those in which it seems to me certain that you deceive yourself.

3 I suspect you deceive yourself, first in being too hasty in believing that this King of France is of little importance and that this King of England is very powerful. It does not seem reasonable to me that France should not have more than ten thousand infantry, because even if he does not have Germans he can get many from his own country, and if they are not as well trained as the Germans, they are as well trained as the English. What makes me believe this is that I see that this King of England with so much spirit, so great an army, and

[1] Leo X.
[2] Maximilian I.
[3] Louis XII.
[4] Ferdinand of Aragon. Cf. *The Prince*, Chap. 16, par. 2.
[5] Henry VIII.
[6] Jeremiah 6.14 and Ezechiel 13.10. Perhaps a reference to Savonarola's sermons on Ezechiel, in 1496-7.

so strong a desire to tear things up by the roots, as the Sienese say, has not yet taken Terouenne, a fortified town not stronger than Empoli, at the first attack and at a time when his soldiers were acting with great vigor. This alone is enough to make me fear England less and not estimate France so low. I think that this tardy action by the King of France is a matter of choice and not fear, because he hopes that, if the King of England does not secure good quarters in that region and winter comes on, he will be obliged either to return to his island or to remain in France with danger (I hear that the region is swampy and without a single tree, so that the English must already have suffered a great deal). Hence I believe that it would not be very hard for the Pope and the King of Spain to get rid of England. Besides, it makes me hold to the opinion given above that the King of France has not decided to abandon the Council,[7] because if he were greatly distressed he would need everybody and would try to be on good terms with everybody.

4 I believe the news about the money that the King of England has sent to the Swiss, but I am astonished that it was sent by the hand of the Emperor, who, I believe, would prefer to spend it on his own army and not on the Swiss. And I am not able to adjust myself to the notion that this Emperor is so thoughtless and the rest of Germany so careless that they can suffer the Swiss to attain so high a reputation. And when I see that this has been done, I am afraid to judge the matter, because what has happened is contrary to every judgment that a man can make. I do not see also how it can be that the Swiss have been able to occupy the castle of Milan and have not wished to do it,[8] because it seems to me that if they gained that castle their intention would be carried out, and that they should have done that rather than go to take Burgundy for the Emperor.

5 I believe you completely deceive yourself in the case of the Swiss, and about whether they are to be feared much or little. I feel sure they are very much to be feared. And Casavecchia and many of my friends,[9] with whom I am in the habit of discussing such matters, know how low my estimate of the Venetians has always been, even at the height of their

[7] A council of the Church was held in Pisa, November 5, 1511, and later in Milan. Its purpose was to support the King of France against the Pope.

[8] Cf. the reference to the citadel in *The Prince*, Chap. 20, par. 10. See also the Chronological Table for 1521.

[9] Filippo Casavecchia, a Florentine who held the office of Commissioner at Barga. He is mentioned also in the letter of December 10, 1513, pars. 1 and 7.

power. It has always seemed to me a much greater miracle that they should have acquired that dominion and that they should hold it than that they should lose it. But their ruin was too honorable for them,[10] because what a king of France did could have been done by Duke Valentino or any other general of high reputation who was in Italy in command of fifteen thousand men. What always influenced me was their way of doing, for they get on without generals or soldiers of their own.

6 Now the reasons that prevent me from fearing them make me fear the Swiss. I do not know what Aristotle says about states divided into parts, but I consider well what reasonably can be, what is, and what has been. I remember to have read that the Lucumnians held all Italy to the Alps, until they were driven from Lombardy by the Gauls. If the Aetolians and the Achaeans did not make much progress, it can be charged to their times rather than to themselves, for they had always close at hand a very powerful king of Macedonia, who did not let them get out of their nest, and later they had the Romans. Hence it was more the force of the others than their own government that did not allow them to increase their territory. Or you may hold that the Swiss do not wish to gain new subjects because they do not see that it is to their advantage. They say that now, because they do not see it now, but as I said to you before, things go on little by little, and men are often forced by necessity to do what they did not intend to. The habit of popular governments is to go slowly.[11] If we consider the situation, they already have as tributaries in Italy the Duke of Milan and the Pope. They have made these tributes part of their income, and do not wish to do without them. If sometime a payment is missing, they will look on the failure as rebellion and have recourse to their spears. Then when they have won, they will plan to make themselves sure of their tribute. To do this they will lay more restraints on those they have conquered, and so, little by little, the process will be completed.

7 Do not rely at all on those armies which you say can one day have such effect in Italy,[12] for this is impossible; first, because of the men themselves, for there are several leaders and they are not united, and it does not seem possible to give them

[10] For their overthrow by Louis XII at Vailà in 1509, and their failure to employ their own citizens in war on land, see *The Prince*, Chap. 12, par. 5.

[11] Cf. *Discourses on Livy*, I, 34, par. 2, below.

[12] Vettori had mentioned Ferrara, Mantova, Bartolommeo d'Alviano, and the Colonnesi.

a leader who can keep them united;[13] second, because of the Swiss. And you must remember this, that the best armies are those of states that arm their own people.[14] Only armies like them can resist them. Recall the armies that have gained renown; they are the Romans, the Lacedemonians, the Athenians, the Aetolians, and Achaeans, and the swarms of peoples from beyond the Alps; you will find that those who have done great things have armed their own people, as did Ninus the Assyrians, Cyrus the Persians, Alexander the Macedonians. I find Hannibal and Pyrrhus alone as examples of those who did great things with armies they picked up here and there. The success of these two armies resulted from the extraordinary ability of the leaders, who were of such great reputation that they inspired in those mixed armies the same spirit and discipline that is found in armies raised among one people.

8 If you consider the defeats of the King of France and his victories, you will see that he has conquered when he has had to fight Italians and Spaniards, which have been armies like his own. But now that he has to fight armed peoples, such as the Swiss and the English, he has lost, and is in danger of losing more. And this ruin of the French King has long been foreseen by understanding men, who have based their opinion on his lack of French infantry, and on his having disarmed his subjects.[15] This policy is contrary to every action and every teaching of those who have been thought prudent and great. But this mistake was not made by earlier kings, but by King Louis and his successors. So do not put your trust in Italian arms, unless they are of one sort, like those of Cyrus and Alexander, or unless, though of various sorts, they make one body, like those of Hannibal and Pyrrhus.

9 And as to the divisions and disunions you mention, do not think these will have any effect, so long as the Swiss observe their laws, and they are likely to observe them for some time, because there cannot be now, or appear later, heads that have tails; and heads without tails are quickly destroyed and accomplish little. Those they have put to death are the few, either magistrates or others, who have attempted to favor the French parties in illegal ways, and have been discovered and put to death; they are of no more import in that state over there than a few who are hanged as thieves here.

10 I do not believe, indeed, that they will form an empire as the Romans did, but I believe that they can become masters

[13] Cf. *The Prince,* Chap. 26, par. 3.

[14] Cf. *The Prince,* Chap. 13.

[15] Cf. *The Prince,* Chap. 13, par. 6.

of Italy because of their nearness and our bad methods and despicable habits.[16] Because this alarms me, I should like to remedy it. If France is not equal to it, I see no other remedy for us, and am willing now to begin to weep with you our ruin and slavery; for though they may not come today or tomorrow, they will come in our days. And for this ruin Italy will have to thank Pope Julius and those who make no provision against it—if now it can be provided against. Farewell.

Florence, August 26, 1513. NICCOLÒ MACHIAVELLI.

THE COMPOSITION OF *THE PRINCE*

December 10, 1513.

To Francesco Vettori.

Noble Ambassador:

1 "Divine blessings were never late."[1] I say this because I appeared to have, I do not say lost, but mislaid your favor, since you have been so long a time without writing to me, and I did not know what the cause possibly could be. I paid little attention to all the reasons for it that came into my head except when the fear came to me that you had refrained from writing to me because somebody had written to you that I was not a good guardian of your letters; and I knew that except for Filippo and Pagolo,[2] nobody, so far as I am concerned, had seen them. The last letter I had from you was that of the twenty-third of the past month, from which I learn with great pleasure how regularly and quietly you carry on the business of your public office, and I encourage you to continue so, because a man who gives up his own comfort for that of others loses his own, and the others feel no gratitude to him. And since Fortune wishes to do everything, she wishes you to let her alone, and remain quiet, and not give her trouble, and wait for the time when she will let men do something; and then it will be good for you to undergo more labor, and stir things up more, and for me to leave my farm and say: Here I am. Therefore, though I wish to do you an equal favor, I cannot tell you in this letter anything else than what my life is, and if you judge that you would like to swap it for yours, I am ready to make the exchange.

[16] Cf. *The Prince*, Chap. 24, pars. 2, 3; Chap. 26, par. 3.

[1] Petrarch, *Triumph of Eternity* 13.

[2] Filippo Casavecchia and Pagolo Vettori, brother of Francesco.

2 I am living on my farm, and since my last troubles[3] I have not been in Florence twenty days, putting them all together. Up to now I have been setting snares for thrushes with my own hands; I get up before daylight, prepare my birdlime, and go out with a bundle of cages on my back, so that I look like Geta when he came back from the harbor with the books of Amphitryo,[4] and catch at the least two thrushes and at the most six. So I did all of September; then this trifling diversion, despicable and strange as it is, to my regret failed. What my life is now I shall tell you.

3 In the morning I get up with the sun and go out into a grove that I am having cut; there I remain a couple of hours to look over the work of the past day and kill some time with the woodmen, who always have on hand some dispute either among themselves or among their neighbors. And as to this grove I could tell you a thousand good things that have happened in my dealings with Frosino da Panzano and others who wanted some firewood from it. Frosino in particular sent for several cords of wood without saying anything to me about them, and when he paid for them he wished to keep back ten lire, which he said he won from me four years ago when he beat me at *cricca* in the house of Antonio Guicciardini. I began to raise the devil, and was intending to accuse the drayman who had come for the wood of theft, but Giovanni Machiavelli stepped in between us and got us to agree. Batista Guicciardini, Filippo Ginori, Tommaso del Bene and certain other citizens each agreed to take a cord of wood when the north wind was blowing. I promised all of them and sent a cord to Tommaso, which turned out half a cord at Florence, because his wife, the servants, and his children were all there to pile it up;[5] they looked like Gabburra when on Thursday he and his servants club an ox. Hence, having seen who was getting the profit, I told the others I had no more wood, and all of them have got angry about it, and especially Batista, who puts

[3] His arrest at the time of the conspiracy of Capponi and Boscoli; he was released in March, 1513.

[4] A reference to the *novella* of *Geta and Birria* (from Luigi Russo's note, in his edition of *The Prince*, p. 6).

[5] A perpetual subject of comedy when firewood is sold in piles. A traditional story from western New York in the days when firewood, sold by the cord, was the normal fuel, is as follows: A farmer brought to a widow a cord of wood on bobsleds drawn by two horses. He unloaded the wood and piled it under the purchaser's disapproving eyes, for it was anything but closely packed. When the pile was finished, the farmer remarked that he might have some difficulty in getting his horses and sleds out of the narrow space between the house and the woodpile. Indicating the holes left between the loosely piled sticks of wood, the widow said: "Drive right through the woodpile."

this in the same class as his losses at the sack of Prato.[6]

4 When I leave the grove, I go to a spring, and from there into my aviary. I have a book in my pocket, either Dante or Petrarch or one of the minor poets, as Tibullus, Ovid, and the like. I read about their tender passions and their loves, remember mine, and take pleasure for a while in thinking about them. Then I go along the road to the inn, talk with those who pass by, ask the news of their villages, learn various things, and note the varied tastes and different fancies of men. It gets to be dinner time, and with my troop I eat what food my poor farm and my little property permit. After dinner, I return to the inn; there I usually find the host, a butcher, a miller, and two furnace-tenders. With these fellows I sink into vulgarity for the rest of the day, playing at *cricca* and *trich-tach*; from these games come a thousand quarrels and numberless offensive and insulting words; we often dispute over a penny, and all the same are heard shouting as far as San Casciano. So, involved in these trifles, I keep my brain from getting mouldy, and express the perversity of Fate, for I am willing to have her drive me along this path, to see if she will be ashamed of it.

5 In the evening, I return to my house, and go into my study. At the door I take off the clothes I have worn all day, mud spotted and dirty, and put on regal and courtly garments. Thus appropriately clothed, I enter into the ancient courts of ancient men, where, being lovingly received, I feed on that food which alone is mine, and which I was born for; I am not ashamed to speak with them and to ask the reasons for their actions, and they courteously answer me. For four hours I feel no boredom and forget every worry; I do not fear poverty, and death does not terrify me. I give myself completely over to the ancients. And because Dante says that there is no knowledge unless one retains what one has read,[7] I have written down the profit I have gained from their conversation, and composed a little book *De principatibus*, in which I go as deep as I can into reflections on this subject, debating what a principate is, what the species are, how they are gained, how they are kept, and why they are lost. If ever any of my trifles can please you, this one should not displease you; and to a prince, and especially a new prince, it ought to be welcome. Hence I am dedicating it to His Magnificence Giuliano.[8] Filippo

[6] Batista Guicciardini was *podestà* of Prato when it was sacked by the Spanish forces that brought the Medici back to Florence in 1512. The other men mentioned are of little importance or unknown.

[7] *Paradiso* 5.41-2.

[8] Giuliano de' Medici died March 17, 1516. No copy of *The Prince* with a dedication to Giuliano is known.

Casavecchia has seen it; he will be able to tell you something about the thing in itself and the talks I have had with him, though I am all the time enlarging and repolishing it.[9]

6 You wish, Honorable Ambassador, that I give up my present life and come to enjoy yours with you. I shall do so in any case, but what tempts me now is a certain affair of mine that I can finish inside of six weeks. What makes me hesitate is that the Soderini are there, and if I went to Rome I should be obliged to visit them and talk with them. I fear that at my return I could not hope to dismount at home, but should dismount at the Bargello, because, even though this government has very strong foundations and great security,[10] yet it is new, and therefore suspicious, and there are plenty of wiseacres who, to appear like Pagolo Bertini, would seat others at the dinner table and let me think about paying the bill. I pray you to settle this doubt for me, and then I surely shall come to visit you within the time I have set.

7 I have debated with Filippo[11] about this little work of mine, whether it was wise to give it or not to give it;[12] and if it were wise to give it whether it would be wise to carry it myself or to send it to you. If I do not give it, I fear that, to say the least, it will not be read by Giuliano, and that this Ardinghelli would get honor from this last labor of mine.[13] The pressure of necessity inclines me to give it, because I am wearing myself out, and cannot remain long in my present state without getting so poor that I shall be despised. Then there is my hope that these Medici lords will begin to employ me, even if they begin by making me roll a stone, because if I did not then gain them over to me, I would have only myself to blame. This thing I have written, if it came to be read, would show that I have not been asleep or playing for the fifteen years that I have devoted to the study of the art of the state. Anybody should be glad to get the services of one who has had a great deal of experience at the expense of others. They should not hesitate over my faith, because, since I have always kept my faith, I am not likely to learn how to break it now. He who has been faithful and good for forty-three years, as I have, is hardly able to change his nature, and my poverty is a testimony to both my faith and my goodness.[14]

[9] For comment on the preceding, see the *Introduction*, pars. 76-94.

[10] For a prince's foundations, see *The Prince*, Chap. 7, pars. 2, 5; Chap. 12, par. 1.

[11] Filippo Casavecchia.

[12] To Giuliano de' Medici, to whom Niccolò planned to dedicate *The Prince*.

[13] Piero Ardinghelli, secretary to Leo X.

[14] Cf. the dedication of *The Prince*, and on the faithful public servant, *The Prince*, Chap. 22, end.

8 I hope, then, that you will write to me your opinion on this matter, and I present my respects. I wish you success. December 10, 1513. NICCOLÒ MACHIAVELLI in Florence.

THE TEMPORAL POLICY OF THE POPE: SHALL HE REMAIN NEUTRAL?

December 20, 1514 (first letter).
To Francesco Vettori.

1 You ask me what plan His Holiness, Our Lord,[1] should adopt in order to keep the reputation of the Church such as he found it, if the King of France, with the aid of the King of England and the Venetians, should decide at all costs to regain the state of Milan, and if on the other side the Swiss, the King of Spain, and the Emperor should unite to defend it. This is really your most important question, for all the others depend on this, and if one sets out to explain this, of necessity he explains the others. I believe there has been no question more serious than this in the past twenty years, and I do not know any matter in the past so difficult to understand, so uncertain to estimate, and for which it is so dangerous to select and carry out a policy. Yet, since you compel me to do so, I will enter into the affair, and discuss it faithfully at least, if not adequately.

2 When a prince wishes to know what fortune will attend two states that engage in war, he must first measure the force and the courage of the two. The forces on the side of France and England are those preparations that these kings are said to be making for this conquest, namely to attack the Swiss in Burgundy with twenty thousand men, to assail Milan with a greater number, and with a much greater number to attack Navarre in order to stir up the Spanish states and cause revolutions in them; to put a great fleet on the sea and assail Genoa or the Kingdom of Naples, or any other place that seems to their advantage. These preparations which I mention are possible to these two kings, and necessary if they intend to conquer; hence I presuppose they are truly reported. And though it is implied in your last question and can be imagined that the King of England, displeased with the French King's greatness in Italy, would withdraw his support, I plan to discuss this matter now, because if the King of England abandons him, the whole affair is settled.

[1] Leo X (Giovanni de' Medici).

3 I believe that the reason why the King of England sticks close to the King of France is to revenge himself on the King of Spain for the injuries done him in the war in France. This indignation is reasonable, and I see nothing that is likely to blot it out soon, and to destroy the amity caused by the marriage-alliance contracted between the two kings. The ancient enmity of the English and the French does not influence me, though it influences many, because the people want what the king wants, and it is not true that the king wants what the people want. With respect to the annoyance that the power of France in Italy might cause to England, this would necessarily result from envy or from fear. The King of England would be envious if he had no place in which to get honor, and would have to stand idle. But since he can make himself glorious in Spain, he has no cause for envy. As to fear, you must remember that rulers often gain territory without gaining power; and if you consider carefully, you will see that the King of France when he gains land in Italy will, so far as England is concerned, get position but not power; he could assail that island with as great forces without the states of Italy as with them. And as to any difference that the possession of Milan would make, the King of France would need to fear the more, for he would have a state he could not trust, and it has not been made impossible for the Swiss to move against him with plenty of money. If the Swiss found themselves injured by France, they would be enemies in very truth, and not as they were the other time. And because it could happen that if France gained Milan, England could bring about a rebellion in Castile, the King of England by gaining that province could do more damage to France than France could to him by gaining Milan, for the reasons I have given. Hence I do not see why England in this first rush of the war would need to detach himself from France. Therefore I affirm that these unions and preparations of forces above-mentioned are necessary and possible.

4 There remain the Venetians, who are of the same importance to the forces of these two kings as are the forces of Milan to the other alliance; I judge them few and weak, and to be restrained by half of the soldiers that are in Lombardy. Considering now the defenders of Milan, I see the Swiss fit to assemble two armies strong enough to fight with the French that come into Burgundy, and with those that come into Italy, because if in this matter all the Swiss unite, and the Grisons and the Vaudois unite with the Cantons, they can bring together more than twenty thousand men for each army.

5 As to the Emperor, because I never know what he will do, I do not wish to discuss what he may be able to do now. But if Spain, the Emperor, Milan, and Genoa join together, I do not believe they can exceed fifteen thousand soldiers, because the King of Spain is not able to furnish new forces, when he awaits war at home.

6 As to the sea, I believe that the Genoese and Spain, if they do not lack money, can between them provide a fleet that can for a long time balance in some way that of their adversaries. I think, therefore, that these are the forces of the two.

7 Now when at present I try to see to which side victory is likely to incline, I say that the kings of France and England, because they have plenty of money, can keep their armies in the field a long time. The others, because they are poor, cannot do so. Hence, considering the armies, the organization, and the money of both parties, I believe it can be said that if the battle is fought soon the victory will go to those who now occupy Italy; if the war drags on, the other side will win. It is said, and seems reasonable, that the Swiss realize this difficulty and, in order to come quickly to a battle, plan to meet the French armies in the mountains of Savoy, so that if the French attempt to pass they may be forced to join battle, or if they do not fight, to turn back, because of the difficulty of the country and the lack of provisions. Whether the Swiss can succeed in this can be judged only by one who is well versed both in that region and in the art of war. Nevertheless, I shall say this: I have never read that in ancient times anybody has succeeded in holding mountain passes, but I have read that many have left the passes and awaited the enemy in regions where there was room, because it seemed to them that they could defend themselves better and with less disorder, and would not tempt the fortune of war [in a place where they would have to risk] all their fortune but not all their forces.[2] And though there are some reasons explaining where this idea comes from, I intend to omit them because it is not necessary to discuss them in this connection.

8 When everything is considered then, I see for the alliance on this side the sole hope of fighting a battle quickly—a battle which may be lost. On the part of France, I see that he is also able to win the day, and if he protracts the war, he cannot lose.

[2] The words in brackets are suggested by *Discourses* I, 23, where the defence of mountain passes is discussed at some length. Machiavelli points out that the Swiss did attempt that method in 1515, against Francis I, and that he came into Italy by another road, arriving unexpectedly and so disarranging the Swiss plans that they retired to Milan without a battle. Cf. also the Letter of November 1526, par. 2.

For the party on this side, I see in the management of the war two evident perils, among others. One is that the French by means of their fleet may enter the territory of Genoa or Tuscany through either force or treaty, and as soon as they get there, all the territory of Lombardy will be theirs, and there are many others, some fearful and some malcontent, who will run to them for shelter.[3] As a result, the French, seeing that they are welcome, will be able to delay and overthrow the Swiss at their pleasure. The other danger is that the Cantons that border on Burgundy, on which would fall all the weight of a war carried on in those parts, if they saw it lasting too long, would force the others to make a treaty with France. The example of Charles, Duke of Burgundy, gives me serious fears of this, for by campaigning and plundering in that region he did so much damage that they sent him a blank check, and he would have ruined them completely, if he had not suddenly been forced to fight a battle. And while some hope or fear that possibly the Swiss, showing little fidelity, will change sides and make a treaty with those kings and give the others into their hands, I do not fear this, because the Swiss are now fighting for their ambition, and if they are not compelled by one of the above-mentioned necessities, I think they will be faithful in war.

9 If, then, His Holiness, the Pope, is forced to make a decision and joins the alliance on this side of the Alps, I think victory uncertain for the reasons given above, both because his accession will not make the alliance wholly secure, and because even though it takes away opportunity and prestige from the French, it does not give the others the forces they need if they are to resist the French. The King has a great fleet at sea and the Venetians can provide something; hence, since the Pope's navy has much to guard in all quarters, his forces and yours would hardly suffice. It is possible, to be sure, that His Holiness may avoid immediate danger, when the alliance in Italy attempts to make certain of him, and may find an immediate benefit, since at present he is able to do honor to his friends. If His Holiness takes the side of the King of France, and does it so cautiously that he can without danger await the King, I think the victory certain; for then by means of the fleet he could throw a large army into Tuscany and unite it with his own, and by using the forces the Venetians have in Lombardy he could at once make a great disturbance there. As a result, the Swiss and the Spaniards would not be able to resist two different armies coming from different sides, nor to

[3] Cf. *The Prince*, Chap. 3, par. 10.

defend themselves against the rebellion of the people that would immediately take place. Altogether, I do not see that in this case it would be possible to take the victory from the King.

10 You wish, in addition, to know whether the alliance of the King of France or of the Swiss would be less dangerous to the Pope, if either one of them should succeed because of his friendship. I answer that I believe that just now the faith pledged to the Pope by the Swiss and their allies and friends would be kept, and the promised states turned over to him. On the other hand, he would have to endure the caprices of the conqueror. And because, so far as I can see, there would be no victor save the Swiss, he would have to endure injuries from them. These would soon appear to be of two kinds, namely taking away his money, and taking away his friends; because the money that the Swiss, now that they are making war, say they do not want, you may be sure they will by all means wish when the war is over. They will begin with this tribute, which will be heavy, and to appear honest and for fear of irritating them in the very warmth of their victory, the Pope will not deny it to them. I believe, or rather I am certain, that the Duke of Ferrara, the Lucchese, and the like, will hasten to put themselves under the protection of the Swiss. As soon as they have taken one of them, the liberty of Italy will be done for, because every day with a thousand excuses they will exact tribute and seize booty, they will change the government of states, and what they think they cannot do at present they will await the proper time for. Nor should anybody rely on their not thinking of this, because it is necessary that they think of it, and if they do not think of it, the course of events will compel them to think of it. One acquisition, one victory, gives an appetite for others.

11 No one should think it strange that the Swiss have not openly seized Milan and gone as much farther as they could; their type of government is unlike that of others at home and correspondingly unlike them abroad, and has parallels in all ancient histories. If up to now they have made companions for themselves, in the future they will make for themselves dependents and vassals, not caring to govern them or manage them in detail, but letting it suffice if only they keep on the Swiss side in wars and pay their annual tribute. This condition they will maintain with the prestige of the armies they have at home, and by the punishments they will inflict on those who depart from it. In this way, and quickly, if they sustain this combat, they will give laws to you, to the Pope, and to the other Italian princes. When you see that they take a state under their protection, you may know that the summer is at hand.[4] You may say: There is a remedy for this, because we can unite against them. But I answer that this would be a second error and a second deception, because the union of many heads against one is difficult to make, and difficult to keep together when it is made.

12 As an example I give you the King of France, against whom everybody had united. Then of a sudden the King of Spain made a treaty, the Venetians became his friends, the Swiss attacked him without spirit, the Emperor was no more to be seen, and finally the King of England joined with him. In fact, if the man against whom a coalition is made is of such power that he does not immediately go up in smoke, as the Venetians did, he will always find a remedy in the variety of opinions, as France has done, and as the Venetians apparently would have done if they had been able to continue two months the war they were engaged in. Their weakness, however, could not await the break-up of the coalition, but that would not happen to the Swiss, who would always find, either with France, or with the Emperor or with Spain or with the rulers of Italy, some method either of keeping them from uniting, or, if they did unite, of disjoining them. I know that many will mock at this opinion, and I am so fearful it will become a fact, and believe it so strongly, that if the Swiss succeed in stopping this flood, and we live six years more, I expect to remind you of it.

13 If you wish, then, to know of me what the Pope must fear from the Swiss if they conquer, and he is their ally, I conclude that he should fear that they will demand tribute at once, and that in a short time they will bring about the servitude of the Pope and of all Italy, without hope of redemption. The Swiss can accomplish this because they are a republic, and so well armed that no prince or potentate can be compared with them. But if His Holiness were an ally of the King of France, and should conquer, I believe the King would proceed to observe the conditions, provided they were suitable, and not such as they would be if too great eagerness had caused the Pope to ask too much or the King to grant too much. I believe he would not demand tribute from the Church, but from you Florentines, and he would consider the Church because of his connection with England, and because of the Swiss, who would not all be dead, and because of the King of Spain, for even if the latter were driven out of Naples, he would have to be taken into account, if he remained alive. There-

[4] Matthew 24.32.

fore it would appear reasonable that for his part the King of France would wish the Church to have a high reputation and to be friendly to him, and would have the same feeling for the Venetians. In brief, whichever wins the victory, it seems to me that the Church will have to remain at the discretion of others.[5] Therefore I judge it better for her to be at the discretion of those who will be most reasonable, and whom she has known before, rather than at the discretion of those whose intention she cannot know because she is not well acquainted with them.

14 If that alliance to which Our Lord His Holiness unites himself should lose, I fear that he would be brought to the utmost necessity, and suffer flight, exile, and all that a pope can fear. Hence he should remember that when one is obliged to choose one of two policies, he should, among other things, consider where an unfortunate outcome of either of them can put him, and should always, other things being equal, choose that policy whose results would be less bitter, if it turned out badly.[6] Without a doubt there would be less bitterness in losing with France as an ally than with the others as allies. If His Holiness has the friendship of France, and loses, the power of France remains as his support, and that is enough to keep a pope in high esteem; his Fortune is still such that through the power of that kingdom it can rise again in a thousand ways; he remains in his own territory, in a place where many popes have had their seat. If he is on the other side and loses, he will have to go into Switzerland to die of hunger, or into Germany to be derided, or into Spain to be swindled. Hence it seems there is no comparison between the ills that bad fortune in one policy or the other will bring with it.

15 I do not believe that remaining neutral was ever good policy for anybody in the situation of the Pope,[7] who is less powerful than any of those who are fighting, and possesses territories scattered among those of the combatants. You must understand first of all that it is very necessary to a prince to conduct himself toward his subjects, his allies, and his neighbors in such a way that he does not become either hateful or contemptible, and if he has to let one of these go, he should not be troubled by hatred, but should preserve himself from contempt.[8] Pope Julius never worried about being hated, so long as he was feared and respected; and because of the fear he

[5] Cf. *The Prince,* Chap. 21, par. 7. [6] Cf. *The Prince,* Chap. 21, par. 7.

[7] On neutrality see the following Letter and *The Prince,* Chap. 21, pars. 3-7.

[8] Cf. *The Prince,* Chap. 19

inspired he turned the world upside down and brought the Church where she is now. And I tell you that he who remains neutral will normally be hated by the loser and despised by the conqueror. Moreover, he cannot but fear that every sort of injury will be done to him, and every kind of harm planned for him, as for one for whom people begin to have no regard, esteeming him a useless friend and not a formidable enemy. And justifications for such conduct by the conqueror will not be lacking, when the territories of the neutral are mingled with those of the combatants, because the neutral will be forced to open his gates now to this one, now to that one, to take them into his country, and to provide them with lodging and with food. At the same time everybody will think he is being deceived, and countless things will happen that will cause countless complaints. And even if none of these things happen in the conduct of the war—and that is impossible—they will happen after the victory, because the lesser rulers, and those who are afraid of you, will immediately run to the protection of the conqueror, and give him opportunity to injure you. Somebody may say: It is true that some things may be taken from the neutral, but others can be kept. To this I answer that it is better to lose all one's possessions virtuously than part of them blamably; and it is not possible to lose part of them without letting one's grip of the rest grow shaky. Let anybody consider carefully all the territories of His Holiness, Our Lord, and where they are situated, and who are the minor rulers included within them, and who are concerned in this war. He who does this will decide that His Holiness is one of those whom conditions by no means permit to remain neutral, and that if he does remain neutral he will always have to be hostile to the losing side and to the winning side, and both will wish to damage him, the first that he may get revenge and the second that he may gain something.

16 Then you ask also if, after the Pope has come to an agreement with the Swiss, the Emperor, and the King of Spain, it would be possible for the King of Spain and the Emperor to deceive him and join themselves to France. I believe that an agreement between Spain and France is impossible, and that it cannot be made unless England joins in. England, however, is not able to make an alliance with Spain except against France. Hence France cannot think of such an alliance, because the King of England—a young man and eager for war—can turn his arms nowhere except against Spain or France; and just as peace with France would make him turn his arms against Spain, so peace with Spain would make him invade

France. Therefore, in order not to lose the King of England and not to bring on himself a war with him, and because he has a thousand causes to hate the King of Spain, the King of France will not listen to any suggestion of peace. If he had wished to make it or been able to do so, it would have been made, for the King of Spain could have put before the King of France many plans for doing harm to others. This is so clear that if the Pope should choose the side of Spain, I believe he would have good reason for fearing everything; but if he should choose the side of France, he would feel safe. As to the Emperor, since he is flighty and unstable, any sort of change can be feared from him, whether or not it is to his advantage, for he is a man who has always lived in the midst of changes and fed upon them. If the Venetians should adhere to the party on this side of the Alps, that would be very important, not so much for the additional force they would bring, as that the alliance would be more evidently hostile to France; and if the Pope also joined in, the French would find innumerable difficulties in entering Italy and fixing themselves there. But I do not believe the Venetians will adopt this plan, because I believe they have made more advantageous agreements with France than they could do with the others; and after they have shared the Fortune of France even when she was almost dead, it does not seem reasonable that they should abandon her when she is rising up again. So I fear they are as usual speaking to their own advantage.

17 I conclude then, as the last thing I have to say, that there are more signs of victory on the French side than on the other, that the Pope by joining the French can make their victory certain but cannot do so for the others, that France is less formidable and more endurable as ally and victor than the others, that defeat would be more endurable if he were allied with the French than with the other party, and that he cannot securely remain neutral. For these reasons I think His Holiness, Our Lord, should either join with the French, or should join the others if the Venetians also join them, but not otherwise.

December 20, 1514.

MORE ON NEUTRALITY[1]

December 20, 1514 (second letter).

To the Honorable Francesco Vettori, Florentine Ambassador to the Supreme Pontiff, at Rome.

Honorable Orator:

1 Since you have stirred me up, if I annoy you by writing, you must say: "I must pay for writing to him." I fear it may appear to you that in the reply I made to your letter I passed too quickly over the part that dealt with neutrality; and similarly in what I had to say on what one must fear from the victor, when the party to which one belongs has been defeated. There are many things, on both these subjects, that deserve consideration. Hence I have undertaken to write to you again on the same subject. With respect to neutrality, a policy that seems to be approved by many, I cannot approve it, for I do not remember, either in what I have seen or what I have read, that neutrality has ever shown itself a good thing, but on the contrary has been most pernicious, because it is certain to lose. I intend to remind you of the reasons for this, even though you understand them better than I do.

2 You know that the first business of every prince is to protect himself from being hated and despised, to succeed in avoiding contempt and hatred.[2] As long as he does this well, everything is sure to go well. It is essential for a prince to carry out this purpose in dealing with both his allies and his subjects, for whenever a prince does not avoid contempt, at least, he is ruined. It seems to me that to remain neutral between two who are fighting is to do nothing other than to seek to be hated and despised, because there is always one of these to whom it will appear that, because of benefits you have had from him, or your old friendship with him, you are under obligation to share his fortunes, and when you do not join him, he begins to hate you. The other combatant despises you because he looks on you as timid and of small resolution, and quickly you get the name of a useless friend and an enemy little to be feared. Hence whichever conquers will have no hesitation in injuring you. Titus Livius expresses this idea briefly when he puts into the mouth of Titus Flaminius, who was addressing the Achaeans when Antiochus was trying to induce them to remain neutral, the saying: "Nothing is more remote from your interests; without favor, without dignity, you

[1] Cf. the preceding Letter and *The Prince*, Chap. 21, pars. 3-7.

[2] Cf. *The Prince*, Chap. 19.

will be the booty of the victor."[3]

3 It is also inevitable that, in the management of a war between two such neighbors, numberless causes for hatred against you will come up, because generally a third party is in such a position that he is able in many ways to impede or favor one side or the other. And always, in a short time after the war breaks out, you are brought to such a condition that the declaration that you have not been willing to make openly and graciously, you are obliged to make secretly and against your will. Even if you do not make a declaration, some will believe that you have made one. And even if Fortune were so exceedingly favorable to the neutral that in the course of the war there should arise no just cause for hatred by either of the combatants, it is certain to appear when the war is over, because all those who have been injured by the third party, and all those who fear him, run to the protection of the victor, and give him cause to hate you and quarrel with you.

4 It may be objected that the Pope, because of the reverence felt for his person and because of the authority of the Church,[4] is in another class, and will always have a refuge to which he can escape. I answer that such a reply merits some consideration, and that there is some foundation for it. Nevertheless it cannot be relied on; on the contrary, if I am to try to give good advice, it should not be thought of, because such a hope leads to the adoption of a bad policy. I believe that all the things that have happened can happen again, and I know that popes have been seen fleeing, exiled, and pursued, suffering the utmost misery, just like temporal rulers, and in times when the Church was more revered in spiritual matters than it is today.[5]

5 If His Holiness Our Lord will consider, then, where his territories are situated, who they are who may be fighting with each other, and who they are who can take refuge with the conqueror, I believe that His Holiness will not be able to rest in a neutral policy, and that he will think that in every way it makes more for his advantage to join with one of the opponents. But with respect to speaking at greater length on neutrality than I did before, I have nothing further to say, because I have said everything above.

6 I believe it will appear from the letter I have written to you that I lean toward the King of France, and he who reads it may suspect that affection carried me in that direction. This

[3] Quoted also in *The Prince*, Chap. 21, par. 4.

[4] Cf. *The Prince*, Chap. 11.

[5] Cf. the *Discourses on Livy*, I, 12, par. 4, below, and Father Timoteo in the *Mandragola*.

would displease me, because I strive always to keep my judgment firm, especially in such matters as these, and not to allow myself to be corrupted by empty love of argument, as many do. Hence if I have inclined somewhat toward France, I think I am not in the wrong. Yet I wish to go over again what moves me, as a sort of epilogue to what I have already written.

7 In order to judge which of two powers who are at war with each other is likely to conquer, it is necessary not merely to measure the forces of both of them, but also to see in how many ways victory can come to the one and in how many ways it can come to the other. It seems to me that it can come to the party on this side of the Alps only if they bring on a battle early, and that for the side of France all the other policies are the right ones, as I wrote to you at length. This is the first cause that makes me believe in France more than in the others. Besides, if I am obliged to declare myself a friend to one of the two, and I see that by allying myself with one of them I give him certain victory, and that if I ally myself with the other the victory is in doubt, I believe that it would be better to take what is certain, laying aside every obligation, every interest, every fear, and anything else that does not please me. And I believe that if the Pope allies himself with France, there can be no debate on the matter. If he allies himself to the others, there can be plenty of debate, for the reasons that I have just now written. Still further, wise men, when they do not need to risk everything on one card, are happy not to do so; they try to imagine the worst result a plan can have, and in a choice of evils they decide which is least serious.[6] Because things under the sway of Fortune are always in doubt, wise men are glad to choose the course that will result in least pain, though Fortune does her worst.

8 His Holiness Our Lord has two seats, one in Italy, the other in France.[7] If he allies himself with France he risks the loss of one of them, if with the other side he risks both of them. If he is hostile to France and France wins, he is obliged to follow the fortunes of the other party, and to go into Switzerland to die of hunger, or into Germany to live in despair, or into Spain to be cheated and sold again. If he allies himself with France and loses, France is still left to him, he continues in his own territory, receives the devotion of a kingdom that is a papacy in itself, and is on the side of a prince who has a thousand ways in which he is able to rise up again, either through treaty or war.

9 Farewell. I send my good wishes to you a thousand times.

December 20, 1514.
Florence.

[6] Cf. *The Prince*, Chap. 21, par. 7, and the preceding Letter, par. 14.
[7] At Avignon.

A DOUBLE LETTER: (1) LIGHTMINDEDNESS; (2) THE NEW PRINCE

January 31, 1514-5.

To the Honorable Francesco Vettori, Florentine Ambassador to the Supreme Pontiff, in Rome.

1 The boyish Archer had already many times attempted to wound me in the breast with his arrows, because he takes pleasure in cruelty and in doing injury.

And though his arrows were so sharp and biting that a diamond could not have resisted them, yet they found a resistance so strong that I make little reckoning of all their power.

Hence the Archer, possessed with anger and fury, in order to show his great excellence, changed quiver, changed arrows, and bow.

And he shot an arrow with such violence that now I feel his wounds and confess and acknowledge his power.

2 I do not know how to answer your last letter on lust with any words that appear more to the point than does this sonnet, from which you will see what great effort that little thief Love has made to enchain me. And the chains he has laid on me are so heavy that I am in complete despair of my liberty. I am able to think of no way in which to unchain myself. And even though chance or some other shift of human affairs should open to me a way of escape, it is possible I should not wish to take it. My chains appear to me now pleasant, now light, now heavy, and make such a mixture that I believe I cannot live content in any other sort of life.

3 And because I know how much such thoughts delight you and how pleased you are to see such conditions in life, I am sorry that you are not here to laugh, now at my tears, now at my laughter. And our Donato enjoys all the pleasure you might have.[1] For he and that lady of whom I once talked with you are the only ports and refuges for my boat, which now has been left without rudder and without sail by the unceasing storm. Less than two evenings ago it came to me that I was able to say, as Phoebus did to Daphne:

> O Nymph of Peneus, I pray you, await me; I do not follow you as an enemy. Wait for me, Nymph. In the same way sheep flee from the wolf, the deer from the lion, and thus the doves with trembling wings flee from the eagle, each one from his enemies.[2]

[1] Donato del Corno, a rich Florentine shopkeeper.

[2] Ovid, *Metamorphoses* 1.504-7.

And just as these verses were of little avail to Phoebus, so the same words were of no moment and no use to me when addressed to the lady who was fleeing from me.

4 If anybody should see our letters, honored comrade, and see their diversity, he would wonder greatly, because it would seem to him at one moment that we were serious men, all intent on great matters, and that no thought could enter our heads that was not full of honor and greatness. Then, turning the page, it would seem to him that we were lightminded, inconstant, lascivious, and given to vanity. And this mode of acting, though to some it seems shameful, to me appears praiseworthy, because we are imitating nature, which is variable; and he who imitates nature cannot be rebuked. And though we commonly show this variety in separate letters, I intend to show it this time in a single one, as you will see, if you read the next sheet. Now you may spit.

5 Your Pagolo has been here with the Magnifico,[3] and in the course of some conversation with me on his hopes, said that His Lordship has promised to make him governor of one of those cities of which he is now taking over the rule. Since I have heard, not from Pagolo but from common report, that he is to be lord of Parma, Piacenza, Modena, and Reggio, it seems to me that these cities would form a very strong lordship, and one that could be retained in all conditions, if it were well governed at the beginning. But if anybody hopes to govern it well, it is necessary for him to understand the nature of the problem before him.

6 These new states, when occupied by a new ruler, present numberless difficulties to one who intends to retain them. And if there is difficulty in retaining those who are accustomed to forming one body, such, for example, as the dukedom of Ferrara, there is much more in retaining those that are put together for the first time from new parts, as this of the Lord Giuliano will be, because one part of it has belonged to Milan, another to Ferrara. Therefore, he who becomes ruler of it ought to try to make one body of it, and to accustom the various districts to realize as soon as possible that they form such a body. This can be done in two ways: either by living there himself,[4] or by establishing there a deputy who will be in charge of all of them, in order that the subjects, although of different cities, and divided among various shades of opinion, may begin to feel their allegiance to a single ruler and recognize him as prince. And if His Lordship, wishing as yet to remain in Rome, puts in author-

[3] Giuliano de' Medici.

[4] Cf. *The Prince*, Chap. 3, par. 4; Chap. 5, pars. 1 and 3.

ity one who knows the nature of affairs in his dominion and conditions in the towns, he will lay a firm foundation for this new state.[5] But if he gives every city a separate head, and does not fix his official residence in the province, his state will always be disunited, will yield him no reputation, and will be incapable of revering the prince or fearing him.

7 Duke Valentino, whose deeds I should always imitate if I were a new prince, recognized this need when he made Messer Rimiro President in the Romagna. As a result of this decision, the people were united, in fear of his authority, well disposed to his power, and inclined to trust it. All the love they bore to him—and considering his newness, it was great—resulted from this decision.[6] I believe Lord Giuliano can easily be convinced of this, because it is true. If your Pagolo should succeed in doing so, it would be a step in making himself known not only to His Grace, but to all Italy. Through it he could combine the profit and honor of Lord Giuliano with his own reputation and that of yourself and your house. I have been speaking to him of it; it pleases him, and he will attempt to make use of my idea. I have thought it a good thing to write to you, so that you may know what we have talked of, and be able to pave the way for this plan where it is necessary.

And even when the proud glutton fell he did not forget Mahomet.[7]

8 Our Donato sends his remembrances to you.

January 31, 1514. NICCOLÒ MACHIAVELLI in Florence.

A PREACHER FOR FLORENCE

May 17, 1521.

To the Honorable Francesco Guicciardini,[1] Doctor of Both Civil and Canon Law at Modena, and Kingly Governor Most Worthy and Greatly to Be Honored.

[5] Cf. *The Prince*, Chap. 7, pars. 2 and 6.

[6] See the *Introduction*, pars. 70, 74.

[7] From Luigi Pulci, *Morgante* 1,303-4, not exactly quoted.

[1] Francesco Guicciardini was after Vettori the most frequent of Machiavelli's correspondents; in all, seventeen letters were sent to him. At the time when this letter was written, he was papal governor of Modena. In 1524 he became president of the Romagna, under Clement VII. In 1526 he took charge of the Pope's diplomatic affairs, and later became the Pope's personal representative with the army and in the territory of the Church. His best-known work is his *History of Italy*. Among his other writings are a *Dialogue on the Government of Florence*, *Instructions on the Affairs of Romagna to His Brother Jacopo* (advice to a ruler having some analogy to *The Prince*), and *Political and Civil Recollections* (a series of short, Machiavellian observations on men and things).

Honorable Sir, Greatly to Be Respected:

1 I was sitting in the privy when your messenger arrived, and was just then thinking of the absurdities of this world. I was especially engaged in depicting to myself a preacher who would suit my idea for the place at Florence,[2] and I wanted one who would please me, because I wish to be firmly settled in this as in my other opinions. And because I have never failed that republic, but when I have been able to benefit it have always done my best, if not with deeds, with words, and if not with words, with gestures, I do not intend to fail it in this duty as well. It is true that I know that I am opposed in my ideas on a preacher, as in many things, to the opinion of the citizens. They want one who will teach them the road to Heaven; and I should like to find them one who would show them the best way to the place of torment. Next, they would desire him to be a man prudent, blameless, and frank. But I should like to find one crazier than Ponzo,[3] more crafty than Fra Girolamo,[4] more of a hypocrite than Frate Alberto;[5] for it would seem to me a fine thing, and worthy of the goodness of these days, that all we have experienced from many friars we should experience in one. For I believe that this is the true way to get to Heaven; namely, to learn the way to Hell, in order to avoid it. Seeing, besides this, how much credit is given to a rascal who conceals himself with the cloak of religion, it is easy to conjecture how much credit would be given to a good man who in truth and not in pretence would walk in the muddy road trodden by Saint Francis. My fancy seeming good to me, I have planned to choose Rovaio;[6] and I think that if he is like his brothers and sisters I shall actually do so. I should like it if, when you write to me again, you would give me your opinion of it.

2 I have nothing to do here because I am not able to carry out my commission until the General and the Assessors are chosen;[7] and I am ruminating how I may sow so much dissension among them that here or elsewhere they may do plenty of kicking with their wooden sandals. And if I do not lose my wits, I believe I may succeed. I believe the advice and aid of Your Honor would be very useful. Hence if you would come as far as this, under the color of a pleasure journey, it would not be a bad thing, or if at least you would write to me and

[2] The Wool Gild of Florence had asked Machiavelli to secure a preacher for the coming Lent.

[3] Unknown.

[4] Savonarola.

[5] A wicked friar of Boccaccio's *Decameron,* IV, 2.

[6] A Franciscan friar of a Florentine family.

[7] Machiavelli had been sent by the Florentine government on a mission to the general assembly of the Franciscan order.

suggest a few master strokes. If once a day you send me a servant just for this purpose, as you did today, you will do me several good turns. One is that you will teach me something that fits my circumstances. The other is that you will make me more esteemed by those in the house, when they see that I get frequent messages. And I can tell you that when that arbalester came with the letter and, bowing almost down to the ground, said he was sent especially and in haste, everybody got up with so many bows and so much noise that everything was turned upside down, and several asked me what the news was. And I, to raise my reputation, said that the Emperor was expected at Trent, that the Swiss had called new diets, and that the King of France was minded to go to treat in person with that king, but that his advisers are talking against it. As a result they all stood with open mouths and with their caps in their hands. As I write I have a circle of them around me, and as they see me write at length, they wonder and look on me as inspired. I, to make them wonder more, sometimes hold my pen still and swell up; and then they open their mouths; if they knew what I am writing, they would wonder at it still more.

3 Your Honor knows that these friars say that when a man is confirmed in grace, the devil has no more power to tempt him. Hence I have no fear that these friars may make a hypocrite of me, because I believe I am very well confirmed. As to the lies of the people of Carpi,[8] I should like to enter a contest with all of them, because long ago I trained myself so well that I do not need Francesco Martelli for a servant. For years I have never said what I believed, nor ever believed what I have said; and if it sometimes happens that I tell the truth, I conceal it among so many lies that it is hard to find it.

4 I have not spoken to that governor, because, since I had found lodging, it seemed to me superfluous to speak to him. It is true that this morning in the church I stared at him somewhat, while he was looking at some paintings. His outside appeared to me well-made, and I can believe that the whole corresponds with the part, that he is what he seems to be, and that Telda is not crazy.[9] So if I had had your letter with me, I should have made an attempt to get something out of him. As it is, I have not attempted anything, and tomorrow I expect from you some advice on my affairs. I suppose you will send one of your crossbowmen; but be sure he hurries and gets here

[8] In a letter to which this is a reply Guicciardini had alluded to the air of Carpi as having for many ages made the people liars.

[9] Unknown.

all sweaty, that the crowd may be amazed. By so doing, you will get me respect. And besides, these crossbowmen of yours will get some exercise, and that is a good thing for the horses, in this mild weather.

5 I could write you some other things if I wanted to exhaust my fancy, but I want to keep it as fresh as I can for tomorrow.

6 I send my regards to Your Honor, and may you ever be prosperous.

Carpi, May 17, 1521.

Your most faithful
NICCOLÒ MACHIAVELLI,
Ambassador to the Minor Friars.

WILL FRANCIS I SECURE HIS FREEDOM? GIOVANNI OF THE BLACK BANDS

March 15, 1525-6.

To the Honorable Messer Francesco Guicciardini, etc.

Magnificent and Honorable Messer Francesco:

1 I have delayed writing to you so long that Your Excellency has got ahead of me. The reason for my delay has been that, since peace seemed to be made, I thought you would soon return into the Romagna. Hence I was waiting to address you by word of mouth, since I had my head full of fancies, part of which I poured out to Filippo Strozzi five or six days ago.[1] When I was writing to him about one thing, I got started on something else, and debated three propositions: one, that in spite of the agreement King Francis will not be freed;[2] two, that if the King is set free, he will observe the agreement; three, that he will not observe it. I have not said yet which of these three I believe, but I have decided that whichever comes to pass, Italy must be the scene of war, and for this war I have proposed no remedy. Now having learned your wishes from your letter, I will discuss with you the part of the subject on which I said nothing to him, and so much the more gladly, since you have asked me to do so.

2 If you ask me which of these three things I believe, I am not able to break away from the firm opinion I have always

[1] Important in Florentine affairs. Machiavelli's letters to him have not survived.

[2] From imprisonment in Spain after the battle of Pavia, in 1525.

held, namely, that the King is not going to be set free, because everybody knows that if the King should do what he is able to, the Emperor would find all the roads closed by which he could move toward the high place he has set before himself. I see no cause nor reason strong enough to move the Emperor to let him go. In my opinion, if he lets the King go, it will be either because his council has been bribed—something at which the French are skilful—or because he sees that the Italians and the French kingdom are drawing together, and he thinks he has no opportunity or method for stopping it except the release of the King, and believes that if he does release him, the King will have to keep the agreements. The King ought to have made big promises in this matter, and shown in every way the causes of the hatred he has for the Italians, and other reasons he could bring up to give assurances that he would keep his promises.

3 Nevertheless, all the reasons that may be brought up do not protect the Emperor from being a fool, if the King intends to be wise; but I do not believe he intends to be wise. The first reason is that up to now I have seen that all the bad plans the Emperor has adopted have not injured him, and all the good ones the King has adopted have done him no good. As I have said, it is a bad plan for the Emperor to let the King go, and it is a good one for the King to promise everything to get his freedom. Nonetheless, because the King will keep his word, the plan of the King will turn out bad and that of the Emperor good. I have written to Filippo on the causes that will make him keep it, as follows: he is obliged to leave his sons in prison; if he does not observe it, he will have to burden his kingdom, which is already over-burdened; he will have to exhaust his barons by sending them into Italy; he will at once have to undertake hard tasks, which, to judge from the past, must cause him dread; and he has to do these things to aid the Church and the Venetians, who have aided in his ruin.

4 I have written to you, and write again, that the King has reason for deep hatred against the Spaniards, but that his hatred against the Italians can hardly be much less deep. I know well that it can be said, and said truly, that if because of this hatred he should allow Italy to be ruined, he might then lose his kingdom. But the fact is that he intends to do it, because when he is free he will be between two difficulties: on the one hand that of giving up Burgundy, losing Italy, and living at the discretion of the Emperor; on the other, of avoiding all this by becoming a parricide and breaker of faith. In these above-mentioned difficulties, he would have as allies men unfaithful and unstable, who, if he should win a victory, would for any slight cause make him lose again. Hence I incline to the opinion either that the King will not be freed, or if he is freed he will keep his agreement. The dread of losing his kingdom when Italy is lost will not influence him in the same way as it might influence others, because, as you say, he has a French brain. My second reason for thinking the King will keep his faith is that he will not believe that Italy will go up in smoke, and perhaps will think he can aid her, after she has purged some of her sins. He would also have received his sons again and gained new vigor. And if between the King and the Emperor there were agreements for the division of spoils, so much the more the King should observe his agreement. But so much the more the Emperor would be foolish to put back in Italy one he had driven out of the country, because the King might then drive him out.[3]

5 I am telling you what I think will happen, but I surely am not telling you that I think the King has made a very wise decision, because to put down a power so hateful, so much to be feared, and so dangerous, he ought anew to imperil himself, his sons, and his kingdom.

6 The remedies we have appear to me these: to see that as soon as the King is free he has somebody near him who, with his own authority and persuasions and those of the ruler who has sent him, should make the King forget past things and think on the future; he should show him men assembling from all Italy; he should show him that his plan is certain to succeed if he makes up his mind to be the free king he should desire to be. I believe such persuasions and entreaties would succeed, but I believe deeds would be much more successful.

7 I foresee that however things go we shall have war, and soon, in Italy. Hence it is necessary for Italians to see to it that they have the King of France with them, and if they cannot have him on their side, that they think how they are going to act. It appears to me that in this condition Italians must choose one of two things: they can yield themselves to the discretion of whoever comes, and meet him with money in their hands, and buy themselves off again; or they can really arm themselves and with their arms help themselves as well as they can.[4] For my part, I do not believe that buying themselves

[3] Cf. *The Prince*, Chap. 21, par. 7 and Chap. 3, par. 11.

[4] A people, like a prince, must rely on its own arms; cf. *The Prince*, Chap. 13, pars. 3 ff; Chap. 26, par. 4; Chap. 12, par. 1, with notes, and the Letter of August 26, 1513, pars. 5, 6, on the armed republic of the Swiss.

again and paying money will be enough. If they would be, I should say: Let us rest here, and think of nothing further. But they will not be enough, because either I am wholly blind, or he will take our money first and then our lives. Indeed it will be a sort of vengeance to bring about that he may find us poor and exhausted, if self defense does nothing more than that. Hence I judge that we should not put off arming ourselves, nor await the decision of the King of France, because the Emperor has leaders for his armies, he has them ready, and he can begin war on his own initiative at any time he wishes. It behooves us to get ready, secretly or openly. Otherwise we shall wake up, some morning, all bewildered. I should commend secret preparation.

8 I shall say one thing that will appear to you mad; I shall put a scheme before you that may seem to you foolhardy or ridiculous; yet these times call for plans that are audacious, untried, and strange. You know, and everybody does who is able to think about this world, that the people are fickle and foolish. Yet being as they are, they many times speak of things that ought to be done. A few days ago it was said in Florence that Lord Giovanni de' Medici was raising the flag of a soldier of fortune, to make war where it seemed good to him. This rumor stirred up my mind to think that the people were talking of what ought to be done. I believe everybody believes there is no Italian leader whom the soldiers would more willingly follow, nor for whom the Spaniards have more fear and higher respect. Moreover, everybody thinks that Lord Giovanni is audacious, vigorous, capable of great plans, and able to make important decisions. It would be possible, then, by supporting him secretly, to have him raise his flag, and to put under him as many cavalry and infantry as we can. The Spaniards will think this is some crafty device, and it may be will suspect both the King and the Pope, since Giovanni has been employed by the King. If that came about, it would at once upset the minds of the Spaniards and make them change the plans they have made for ruining Tuscany and the Church without any hindrance. It would be enough to change the opinion of the King, so that he would determine to abandon his agreement and undertake war, for he would see that he is dealing with men who are alive, and who show him deeds as well as inducements. If we must make war, and cannot use this means of defence, I know of no other.

9 And paste this in your hat: if the King is not influenced by arguments and authority, and by things that are actually being done, he will keep his agreement and leave you in the lurch.

Since he has been in Italy several times, and you have acted against him or stood on the sidelines, you cannot expect that he will wish to have the same thing happen to him again.

10 The Barbera is now there.[5] If you can do her any favors, I recommend her to you, because I am more interested in her than in the Emperor.

March 15, 1525.

THE FORTIFICATIONS OF FLORENCE

June 2, 1526.

To Messer Francesco Guicciardini.

1 Though I know that your Luigi[1] has written to you of his opinion about putting the hill of San Miniato within the city wall, yet I do not wish to fail to send you a line about it, because it appears to me a very important matter.[2]

2 The most injurious thing a republic can do is to make within itself a strong place, or one that quickly can be made strong. If you will have brought to you the model that was left in Rome, you will see that, if San Miniato is included and the proposed bastion is made up there, a fortress is built, because the distance from the gate of San Miniato to that of San Niccolò is so short that in one day a hundred men by digging a ditch could make the bastion into a fortress. Hence if ever through some mistaken policy a powerful man should come to

[5] La Barbera was a singer who, with her company, was to present the choruses between the acts of the *Mandragola* in a performance at Faenza; however, the play was not presented. Machiavelli addressed two poems to her.

[1] Luigi Guicciardini, brother of Francesco.

[2] The hill of San Miniato was outside the walls of Florence, yet so near that Pope Clement VII feared the city would not be secure against a besieger who occupied the hill. Hence it was suggested that the walls of the city be extended to include it. Machiavelli objected to this on several grounds. First, he feared that it would make the extent of the walls so great as to weaken the defence. Second, he feared the expense. But most important seems to be the reason given in this letter, namely that the extended portion of the walls could easily be made into a fortress to overawe the city. This could easily be done by making a ditch and wall across the neck connecting the newly fortified portion with the old wall, that is, the space between the gates of San Niccolò and San Miniato. The ditch would have been outside the old wall and parallel to it. Not long after Machiavelli's death Michelangelo become the engineer for the fortification of the city, and proceeded with the fortification of San Miniato. The alternative was the "cutting off" of which Machiavelli speaks, namely that part of the city wall under the hill of San Miniato be moved back, and part of the city left outside it. The excluded houses would then have to be destroyed to permit defence of the new wall.

Florence, as did the King of France in 1494, you would be made slaves without any recourse.[3] If he found the space open, you could not keep him from entering it; and since he could close it up easily, you would not be able to keep him from closing it up. Consider it well, and use all your dexterity to prevent it; advise that cutting off, which is strong and not dangerous; for if the plan of San Miniato is begun, I suspect the cutting off will cause too much indignation.

3 I have written these three letters separately, so that you can use all of them as fits your convenience.

June 2, 1526. NICCOLÒ MACHIAVELLI.

THE MILITARY MISTAKES OF POPE CLEMENT VII

November, 1526.

Dear Bartolomeo:[1]

1 The reason why the Pope started this war before the King of France had sent his soldiers into Italy and acted in Spain according to the agreement, and before all the Swiss had arrived, was the hope he had on account of the people of Milan, and the belief that six thousand Swiss, who had been started out by the Venetians and the Pope at the time of the first disturbances in Milan, would be so prompt that they would join his army at the same time as the Venetians did. And in addition, the Pope believed that the army of the King, if not so nearly ready, would at least be in time to aid in carrying the undertaking to success. To these hopes was joined the need for relief that the Castle of Milan had announced. All these things, then, made the Pope hasten, and gave him such high hopes that he believed the war would end in fifteen days. This hope was strengthened by the capture of Lodi.

2 Well, the armies of the Venetians and the Pope made their junction, but two very important items among those given above were lacking: the Swiss did not come, and the people of Milan were of no moment. Hence when the combined armies appeared before Milan, the people did not rise; and our leaders, lacking the Swiss, did not have courage to re-

[3] In *The Prince*, Chap. 20, Machiavelli discusses the value of a fortress to a prince; here he considers its danger to a republic.

[1] Bartolomeo Cavalcanti wrote several letters to Machiavelli about this time; he esteemed the replies as though they were oracles (Tommasini, II, 856).

main there, and retired to Marignano, whence they did not return to Milan until five thousand Swiss had come. Their arrival, which earlier would have been helpful, was now harmful, because it gave our generals spirit to return to Milan to relieve the Castle, and it was not relieved; yet we were obliged to remain there because, since the first retreat was shameful, no one advised a second one. This caused the enterprise against Cremona to be undertaken with part of the infantry, not with the whole force, as it would have been if on the fall of the Castle the army had still been at Marignano. For these reasons, and also because it was thought easy, the attack on Cremona was feebly made. This was against the rule which says that it is not a wise plan to risk all one's fortune and not all one's forces.[2] Our generals believed, as to the fortress of Cremona, that four thousand soldiers were enough to take it. The weakness of this attack made the city more difficult of capture, because our leaders did not assail the weak points, but merely indicated them. Hence those within the city did not lose these posts, but made them stronger. Moreover, they fixed their minds on resistance. Hence when the Duke of Urbino finally went there, and fourteen thousand surrounded the city, they were not enough. Yet if he had been there at the beginning with the whole army, and had been able to make several attacks at once, he would certainly have taken it in six days. Perhaps the whole enterprise would then have succeeded, because we would have had the prestige of the capture, supported by a very large army, for thirteen thousand Swiss had arrived. For these reasons Milan or Genoa, or perhaps both of them, would have been regained, and our enemies would have had no resource; the troubles at Rome would not have occurred; the enemy's reinforcements would not have been in time, because they have not yet arrived. Yet we have spent fifty days wooing Milan, and the capture of Cremona has come late, when all our affairs have gone to ruin.

3 For our part, then, we have lost this war twice; first, when we went to Milan and did not stay there; second, when we sent, but did not go, to Cremona. The first was caused by the timidity of the Duke, the second by the vanity of all of us, because nobody dared advise a second retreat when it seemed that we had been disgraced by the first one. The Duke, moreover, knew how to do bad things against the wish of all the others, and did not know how to do good things against their wishes. These are the errors that have snatched away

[2] Cf. the first Letter of December 20, 1514, par. 7.

our victory. Snatched it away, I say, because we did not conquer earlier.[3]

4 Yet we might have delayed and not lost the campaign, if our other mistakes had not been added. These also were two. The first was that the Pope did not accumulate money at the time when he could honorably have done it, in the ways used by other popes.[4] The other was that he remained in Rome in such a condition that he could be captured there like a baby, something that has snarled the business up to such an extent that Christ himself could not straighten it out. The Pope has taken his soldiers out of the field, and Messer Francesco is still in the field;[5] today the Duke of Urbino should have arrived there. Many leaders have remained, of many opinions, but all ambitious and unendurable; lacking anybody who knows how to smooth over their factions and keep them united, they make music like dogs.[6] From this comes the utmost confusion in our affairs. Already, the Lord Giovanni does not wish to remain there, and I believe he will go away today.[7] These disorders were normally kept down by the care and diligence of Messer Francesco. Besides this, if money has been coming sparingly from Rome, now it will be entirely lacking. Hence I see little order in our affairs, and if God does not aid us against the south wind, as he has done against the north wind, we have few resources left.

5 As God has hindered the coming of aid from Germany by the ruin of Hungary, so he will need to hinder that from Spain by the ruin of the fleet. In this matter we need to have Juno go to petition Aeolus for us, and promise him Contessa and all the ladies Florence has,[8] if only he will let loose the winds in our favor. And beyond doubt if it were not for the Turk, I believe the Spanish would have come to celebrate All Saints' day with us.[9]

6 Having seen the loss of the Castle, and observed how the Spaniards had established themselves in three or four of these cities and made themselves sure of the people, I judge that this

[3] Machiavelli believed in decision and vigorous execution (*The Prince*, Chaps. 19, pars. 12, 19; 23, par. 1), and knew the value of military celerity: Cesare Borgia, he says, took Urbino "at a single leap" (*First Decennale* 345). See Gilbert, *Machiavelli's "Prince" and Its Forerunners*, pp. 191-5.

[4] For the economy of Pope Julius II see *The Prince*, Chaps. 11, par. 3; 16, par. 2.

[5] Guicciardini.

[6] Cf. *The Prince*, Chap. 26, par. 3.

[7] Giovanni of the Black Bands.

[8] *Aeneid* 1.71-3.

[9] This dates the letter later than October 31, 1526, but earlier than the news of the arrival of the fleet from Spain mentioned in the preceding sentence. The fleet reached Naples on December 1.

war must be a long one, and dangerous because of its length. I think so because I know with what difficulty cities are taken, when there is somebody within who is determined to defend them; and how a province may be taken in one day, while a fortified city requires months and years for its capture, as many ancient histories show us, and in modern times Rhodes and Hungary.[10] For that reason I wrote to Francesco Vettori that I believed the weight of this enterprise could not be supported, except to bring about that the King of France should take it up as his, on our agreement that he should receive Milan; or it might be endured as a diversion, so as to leave the frontiers guarded in the northern states, in order that the Spaniards might not be able to move onward. Meanwhile the Pope should have assailed the kingdom of Naples with all his forces, for I believe he would have been able to take it sooner than he would one of the cities of the north, because in the south he would have found not determined defenders but conquered people to plunder, such as an invader would like to find. Besides, the war would have fed itself, because in addition to the assistance he could have had from the cities he would have had payments of tribute money,[11] and the fatness of the country, which had not been ravaged, would have made them more lasting. Meanwhile the Pope, without new outlay, could have lived securely in Rome; and it would have been seen which the Emperor estimated as more valuable, Lombardy or the kingdom of Naples. If the Pope did not do this, I looked on the war as lost; its length was sure, and in length there are sure perils, either because of lack of money or through other accidents, such as those that have arisen. It seemed to me a strange procedure for the Pope to waste his forces in the field, while the enemy enjoyed himself in the city; and that when our reinforcements came, the enemy should find us worn out, and should ruin us as he had the Admiral and the King.[12]

[10] Cf. *The Prince*, Chap. 10, for the defence of fortresses. Rhodes fell in 1522, after a siege of about six months. After his victory at Mohacs in 1526, Sultan Soliman occupied all of Hungary.

[11] This and the preceding sentence are difficult and emended; see Tommasini, II, 863-4, 1251-3.

[12] Admiral Bonnivet and Francis I, of whom the first was killed and the second taken at Pavia by the imperial forces, led by Charles of Bourbon.

"I LOVE MY NATIVE LAND MORE THAN MY SOUL"

April 16, 1527.
To Francesco Vettori.
Honorable, etc.

1 Monsignor della Motta has been today in the camp of the Imperialists with the final papers of the agreement that has been made in Florence. If Bourbon wishes this truce, he has to keep his army quiet; if he moves it, it is a sign that he does not wish the truce. Hence tomorrow will be decisive for our affairs. For that reason it has been decided here that if he moves tomorrow we shall think of war in earnest, without having a hair that will have further thought of peace; if he does not move, we shall think of peace and abandon all thoughts of war. When this north wind is blowing, it is time for you to set sail. If you decide on war, you must abandon all the habits of peace, in such a way that the allies may go to work without any hesitation; it is now necessary not to waver any more, but to go it like mad, for desperation often finds remedies which choice has been unable to discover.[1] The invaders will come here without any artillery, in a region difficult for an army. Hence if we unite with the forces of the League—which are now ready—the little strength that remains to us, either the enemy will leave this province in disgrace, or they will come to reasonable terms.

2 I love Messer Francesco Guicciardini; I love my native land more than my soul.[2] As a result of the experience that sixty years have given me, I say that I do not believe more difficult negotiations than these were ever attempted, for peace is necessary and war cannot be abandoned, and we have on our hands a prince who is hardly adequate for peace alone or for war alone.[3]

3 I send you my regards.

April 16, 1527. NICCOLÒ MACHIAVELLI in Forlì.

[1] For private desperation see *The Prince*, Chap. 19, par. 5, and the *Discourses on Livy*, I, 5; III, 6. In III, 12, necessity is the "last and most dangerous weapon."

[2] See the *Introduction*, par. 41.

[3] Pope Clement VII.

DISCOURSES ON LIVY

Introduction

It appears that the *Discourses on Livy* were begun earlier than *The Prince* and finished later. They seem to represent much the same state of mind as the more famous work, and give more details on some matters mentioned in it. But their great importance is that they reveal the basis of Machiavelli's theory of government, namely his belief that the purpose and end of the state is to bring about the common good, the well-being of the mass of the citizens.

It is characteristic of Machiavelli that the work from which his general ideas can most easily be derived, and his second most extensive labor, for the *History of Florence* is but ten pages longer, should take the form not of a systematic treatise, but of a running commentary on political and military topics. The three books are somewhat differentiated, the first dealing with affairs within Rome, the second with the extension of the Roman power, and the third with the efforts of individuals at Rome. These limitations, however, are not minutely observed. Not infrequently the effect on the reader is as though Machiavelli turned through Livy and wrote on what occurred to him as he did so. This method gave him opportunity to develop the topics that interested him, and made it unnecessary for him to treat anything he did not care to. The treatment of subjects is uneven; the longest *Discourse* runs to more than twenty-two pages, and the shortest is about one-fourth of a page, in a total of two hundred and seven. The number of parts is one hundred and forty-five in all. Obviously the author appears as a writer of thoughts or reflections on a subject of consuming interest to him.

DISCOURSES ON LIVY, I, 4

That the Discord of the Plebeians and the Roman Senate Made That Republic Free and Powerful

1 I do not wish to omit the discussion of the commotions that disturbed Rome between the deaths of the Tarquins and the creation of the Tribunes; then I shall bring up some things against the opinion of the many who say that Rome was a

tumultuous republic and so full of confusion that if good fortune and military virtue had not supplied her defects, she would have been inferior to any other republic. I cannot deny that fortune and military training were causes of the Roman power; but it seems clear to me that these objectors are not aware that wherever there are good soldiers there must be good government,[1] and it seldom happens that there is not good fortune as well.

2 But let us come to other details about this city. I say of those who condemn the troubles between the nobility and the plebeians, that it seems to me they are blaming the chief causes that kept Rome free, and considering the quarrels and the noise that resulted from those troubles rather than the good effects they caused. Moreover, they are not considering that in every republic there are two opposed factions, that of the people and that of the upper classes; and that all the laws made in favor of liberty result from their discord, as can easily be seen to have happened in Rome; because from the Tarquins to the Gracchi, more than three hundred years, the troubles in Rome rarely caused exile and very rarely led to bloodshed. It is impossible, therefore, to consider those tumults injurious, or to think a republic divided which in so long a time sent into exile by reason of its divisions not more than eight or ten citizens, put to death very few, and levied fines on no large number. Nor can a republic in any way reasonably be called badly constituted where there are so many examples of virtue; such good examples have their origin in good education; good education comes from good laws; good laws come from those tumults which many thoughtlessly blame. If you examine the end of these tumults, you will not find that they produced any exile or violence damaging to the common good, but rather laws and institutions advantageous to the liberty of the city.

3 Someone may say: such methods were extraordinary and almost barbarous, for you see the people making united outcry against the Senate, and the Senate against the people; you see the people running in confusion through the streets, and locking their shops, the plebeians leaving Rome. All these things terrify even him who only reads of them. But I reply that every city ought to have methods with which the people can express their ambition,[2] and especially those cities that intend to make use of the people in important affairs. Among such methods, the city of Rome had this one: when the people

[1] Cf. *The Prince*, Chap. 12, par. 1.

[2] Cf. the *Discourse on Reforming the Government of Florence*, pars. 22, 23.

wished to have a law enacted, either they did some of the things I have mentioned, or they did not consent to be enrolled for war. Hence it was necessary to give the people some satisfaction in order to placate them. The desires of free peoples are seldom harmful to liberty, because they result either from oppression or from a suspicion that the people are likely to be oppressed. When their opinions are false, a resource may be found in the assemblies, where some man of influence gets up and makes a speech showing how they are deceiving themselves. And as Cicero says, though the people are ignorant, they are able to see the truth, and yield easily when something true is told them by a man worthy to be believed.

4 Men ought, then, to be more sparing in their blame for the Roman government, and to consider that all the many good effects the republic produced were brought about only by the very best causes. If disorders caused the creation of the Tribunes, they deserve the greatest praise; for the Tribunes not only gave its proper share to popular administration, but were set up to guard Roman liberty, as will appear in the following chapter.

DISCOURSES ON LIVY, I, 9

That He Who Plans to Give a New Constitution to a State and Make a Complete Reformation of Its Old Laws Must Have Sole Power[1]

1 It may appear to some that I have rushed too far into the midst of Roman history before making any mention of the founders of that state, or of those fundamental laws that relate to religion and military affairs. Therefore, since I do not wish to hold in suspense the minds of those who wish to learn something on this matter, I say that many will judge it a bad example that a founder of a civil society, like Romulus, should first have killed his brother and then been a party to the death of Titus Tatius the Sabine, whom he had chosen as his companion on the throne. It seems that this example would enable citizens to use their prince as a precedent when, through ambition and desire to rule, they injure those who resist their authority. This opinion would be true provided the end for which Romulus committed that homicide is not considered.[2]

[1] This chapter makes clear why Machiavelli could tolerate the idea of a prince in Italy, in spite of his republican sentiments. Cf. the *Discourse on Reforming the Government of Florence*, pars. 12-14.

[2] Homicide for the common good is not a precedent justifying homicide for personal advantage. Similarly the principles of *The Prince*, Chap. 18, apply only to a ruler acting for the common good.

2 This may be taken as a general rule: it never, or very rarely, happens that any state or kingdom is well organized from the beginning, or is completely reorganized and its old laws abandoned, if the organization is not accomplished by one man alone; on the contrary, it is essential that the pattern be given by one man only, and that on his design the reformation should rely. Therefore a prudent organizer of a state, and one who intends to be of service not to himself but to the common good, and not to his own descendants but to the common fatherland, ought to make every effort to have authority, and have it alone.[3]

3 No wise and acute man will ever censure anybody for an extraordinary action he carries out in order to found a kingdom or set up a republic. At least it is fitting that if he blames the action he should excuse its effect; and if it is good, like that of Romulus, he always will excuse it; indeed he who acts violently in order to destroy, not he who is violent in order to restore, should be blamed. He ought, indeed, to be so prudent and virtuous as not to leave the authority he has seized to someone else as an inheritance; for since men are more prone to evil than to good, his successor may use ambitiously what he has used virtuously. Besides this, though one man is best for organizing, the thing organized will not last long if it rests on the shoulders of one man only, but it will last if it is left to the care of many and many have the task of keeping it up.[4] It is true that a large number are not adapted to the first organization of a thing, because they do not know what is best for it, on account of their diverse opinions; but on the other hand, when they have recognized what is good, they do not agree to abandon it. It is clear that Romulus was one of those deserving to be pardoned for the death of his brother and his companion, and that what he did was for the common good, and not by reason of his own ambition, because very soon he established a senate, with which he conferred, and according to the opinion of which he decided. Anyone who carefully considers the authority Romulus kept for himself, will see that he retained nothing except the command of the armies when war had been decided on, and the power of summoning the senate. This was shown later when Rome became free by the expulsion

[3] To work for the common good and one's country is the best thing one can do (see the *Introduction*, pars. 39-51). Hence the highest motives lay an obligation on a man ("ought") to get the sole authority. The new ruler of *The Prince* is under this obligation to the common good, though his duty is seldom made explicit.

[4] This is what Machiavelli hoped the Medici would make possible for Florence, according to the *Discourse on Reforming the Government of Florence*, pars. 24-31.

of the Tarquins; for then the Romans changed no part of their ancient constitution,[5] except that in place of a perpetual king they had two consuls annually. This testifies that all the early fundamental laws of that city had been more in harmony with a free and republican mode of life than with an absolute and tyrannical one.

4 Numerous examples can be given in support of what I have said above, as Moses, Lycurgus, Solon, and other founders of kingdoms and republics, who were able, by appropriating individual authority, to form laws suited to the common good; but I intend to pass them by, as things generally known. I shall bring up just one, not so famous, but worthy to be considered by those who wish to establish good laws. My instance is Agis, king of Sparta; he wished to bring the Spartans back within the limits set by the laws of Lycurgus, because it seemed to him that by partly abandoning them the city had lost much of its ancient vigor, and consequently much of its military power and commanding position; he was killed by the Spartan Ephors at the very outset, as a man who intended to make himself sole ruler. His successor was Cleomenes, in whom the same desire grew up after he encountered traditions and writings about Agis, and from them came to understand the thought and intention of his predecessor. He knew, however, that he could not confer this benefit on his native city unless he came to hold sole authority, and it seemed to him that men are so ambitious that he could not benefit the many against the will of the few. Hence he seized a suitable occasion to kill all the Ephors and anyone else able to oppose him;[6] then he completely restored the laws of Lycurgus. This decision would have been enough to revivify Sparta and give Cleomenes the same reputation Lycurgus had, if it had not been for the power of the Macedonians, and the weakness of the other Greek states. For after his reform he was attacked by the Macedonians and conquered by them because he was himself inferior in force and had no one to whom he could turn for aid. Hence his plan, though well laid and worthy of praise, remained imperfect.

5 Considering all these things then, I conclude that the founder of a state must needs govern alone. Hence Romulus deserves to be excused rather than blamed for the deaths of Remus and Titus Tatius.

[5] Such an easy change Machiavelli believed possible in Florence; see the *Discourse on Reforming the Government of Florence*, par. 28.

[6] His procedure is much like that of the wicked Agathocles of *The Prince*, Chap. 8, pars. 2, 3, but because he acted for the common good and not for selfish reasons, he is praised rather than condemned.

DISCOURSES ON LIVY, I, 10

THE FOUNDERS OF A REPUBLIC OR A KINGDOM DESERVE PRAISE TO THE SAME EXTENT AS THE FOUNDERS OF A DESPOTISM DESERVE INFAMY

1 Among all praiseworthy men those are most praised who have been the heads and founders of religions. Next are those who have founded republics or kingdoms.[1] After them, those are known to fame who as leaders of armies have increased their own dominion or that of their native land. To these are to be added men of letters. And because these men are of several sorts, each of them is famous according to his degree of merit. To other men, in great numbers, some measure of praise is given, as their occupations and their success in them secure it. On the other side, destroyers of religions, wasters of kingdoms and republics, enemies of the virtues, of letters, and of every other art that brings utility and honor to the human race are infamous and worthy to be detested; such men are the irreligious, the oppressive, the ignorant, the worthless, the lazy, and the cowardly. There never will be anyone so silly or so wise, so bad or so good that, if the choice between these two kinds of men is offered to him, he will not praise the kind that deserves praise, and blame the kind that deserves blame. But in spite of this, most men, deceived by a false good and a false glory, allow themselves, either voluntarily or ignorantly, to join the ranks of those who merit blame rather than praise, and though able to establish a republic or a kingdom, to their lasting honor, yet turn aside to absolute rule. They do not understand what great renown, what great glory, what great honor, security, quiet, and satisfaction of mind they abandon by making this decision, and how much infamy, abuse, censure, peril, and disquiet they incur.

2 Those who live in a private station in a republic, or who through fortune or prowess become princes of it, if they read history and get anything of value from the records of the past, cannot possibly, if they are private citizens, wish to do other than live in their native cities rather as Scipios than as Caesars; or if they are princes, they must prefer Agesilaus, Timoleon, and Dion to Nabis, Phalaris, and Dionysius, because they will see that the latter are always strongly censured and the former very much praised. They will see also that Timoleon and the others did not have less authority in their native cities than did Dionysius and Phalaris, and that they had far more security.

[1] The same thought is expressed in the *Discourse on Reforming the Government of Florence*, pars. 29 and 30, in which the Medici are offered the role of founders of a republic.

3 Nor should anybody be deceived by the glory of Caesar, on seeing that he receives the highest praise from the historians, for those who praise him have been bribed by his good fortune, and terrified by the long duration of the Empire, which, since it was ruled in Caesar's name, did not permit literary men to speak freely of him. But he who would like to know what free writers would say of him may read what they say of Catiline. For Caesar is so much the more to be blamed in proportion as he who has done an evil deed is more blameworthy than he who has planned to do it. He may see also with what praises they honor the name of Brutus, for since they are unable to censure Caesar on account of his power, they give honor to his enemy.[2]

4 He who has become prince in a state should also consider that after Rome became an Empire those emperors who lived according to the laws, as good rulers should, deserved much greater praise than those who lived in the opposite way. He will see that Titus, Nerva, Trajan, Hadrian, Antoninus, and Marcus did not need the praetorian soldiers nor the masses of the legions to protect them, because their habits, the good will of the people, and the love of the Senate were their defence.[3] He will see, too, how Caligula, Nero, Vitellius, and the many other wicked emperors did not find the eastern and the western armies enough to protect them against the enemies which their evil habits and their impious lives had raised up against them. If the history of these emperors is well thought over, it will be lesson enough to show any prince the roads to glory or censure, to security or fear. Of the twenty-six emperors from Caesar to Maximinus, sixteen were killed and ten died naturally; and if some of those who were killed were good, as Galba and Pertinax, they were killed because of the corruption their predecessors had left among the soldiers. And if among those who died naturally there was a wicked emperor, like Severus, it happened because of his great good fortune and personal ability, two things that few men have. The reading of this history will also show how a good kingdom can be established, because all the emperors who came to the throne through heredity, except Titus, were bad; those who succeeded through adoption were all good, such as the five from Nerva to Marcus; when the Empire fell to hereditary heirs, it resumed its course toward ruin.[4]

[2] Here Machiavelli as a republican is wholly opposed to Dante, who had Brutus punished in the lowest hell (*Inferno* 34.65) because he murdered Caesar, the divinely guided founder of the Roman Empire.

[3] Cf. *The Prince*, Chap. 20, par. 10.

[4] *The Prince*, Chap. 19, pars. 7-16.

5 A prince, then, may put before himself the times from Nerva to Marcus, and compare them with those before and after; then he can choose in which he would prefer to be born, or in which he would like to rule. In the years when good men ruled, he will see the prince secure in the midst of his secure citizens; the world overflowing with peace and justice; he will see the Senate in full authority, and the public officials honored; the rich citizens enjoying their riches; nobility and virtue respected; he will see everybody quiet and good. On the other hand, all hatred, licentiousness, corruption, and ambition are blotted out; he will see golden days, when each man can hold and defend any opinion he wishes. He will see, in short, the world rejoicing; the prince abounding in reverence and glory, the people in love and security.[5] If after that he will consider briefly the days of the other emperors, he will see them made horrible by wars, torn by seditions, cruel in peace and in war; many princes slain with the sword; civil wars and foreign wars galore; Italy distressed and full of new misfortunes; the cities ruined and plundered. He will see Rome burned, the Capitol laid waste by its citizens, the ancient temples desolate, the ceremonies of religion corrupted, the city full of adulteries; he will behold the sea covered with exiles, the rocks covered with blood. In Rome he will behold countless cruelties come to pass, and nobility, riches, former honors, and above all virtue, counted as capital sins. He will see false accusers rewarded, servants bribed against their master, and freedmen against their former owner, and anyone who lacks enemies suffering injury from his friends.[6] He will then recognize to the utmost what heavy obligations Rome, Italy, and the world owe Caesar.

6 Without question, if he is of woman born, he will be frightened away from the least imitation of these wicked days, and will be fired with a tremendous desire to imitate happy times. Of a truth, if a prince seeks glory in this world, he should desire to possess a corrupt city, not to ruin it completely as did Caesar, but to reform it as did Romulus. Certainly Heaven cannot give men a greater opportunity for glory, nor can men wish for a greater one.[7] And if indeed one who wishes to reform a city finds that he needs to lay aside his place as prince, he deserves some excuse if he does not reform it to

[5] This is what Machiavelli hoped could be brought about by the ruler to whom he addressed *The Prince*.

[6] From Tacitus, *History*, 1, 2.

[7] This is the opportunity that lay open to the Medici, according to Machiavelli's *Discourse on Reforming the Government of Florence*, pars. 29, 30.

keep himself from falling from his position; but if he is able to keep his throne and reform the city, he deserves no excuse. In short, if we consider those to whom Heaven gives such chances, we see that two roads lie open to them: one of these causes them to live in security and renders them glorious after their deaths; the other causes them to live in continual anxiety, and to leave after their deaths an evil reputation that never ceases.

DISCOURSES ON LIVY, I, 11

On the Religion of the Romans

1 Rome had Romulus as her first lawgiver, and as a daughter must recognize that from him she had her birth and education. Yet the Heavens, deciding that the laws of Romulus were not enough for so great an empire, inspired the Roman senate with the thought of electing Numa Pompilius as his successor, in order that anything he had left undone might be attended to by Numa. This king, finding the people very wild, wished to bring them to obey the laws by using the arts of peace. So he turned to religion, as something indispensable to one who wishes to maintain civil organization. He planned this religion in such a way that for many ages God was nowhere so much feared as in that republic. This condition made easier all the undertakings that the Senate or the great men who ruled Rome attempted to carry out. Anybody who will go over a large number of the actions of the people of Rome as a unit, and of many of the Romans by themselves will see that these citizens were much more afraid of breaking their oaths than of breaking the laws, because they had higher respect for the power of God than for that of men. This is proved by the examples of Scipio and Manlius Torquatus. For after Hannibal routed the Romans at Cannae, many citizens assembled, and, in despair of their native land, resolved to abandon Italy and go to Sicily. Scipio heard of this, went to their meeting, and with his naked sword in his hand forced them to swear not to abandon their native city. Lucius Manlius, the father of that Titus Manlius afterwards called Torquatus, was accused of crime by Marcus Pomponius, the Tribune of the People. But before the day for the trial came, Titus went to the house of Marcus, threatened to kill him if he did not swear to withdraw the accusation against Lucius, and compelled him to take the oath. Having taken the oath because he was afraid, Marcus did withdraw

the accusation. Hence those citizens whom love of their native city and its laws could not have kept in Italy, were retained by an oath they were forced to take. And that Tribune laid aside the hate he had for the father, the injury done him by the son, and his own honor, to keep the oath he had taken. These things resulted from nothing other than the religion Numa had introduced into the city.

2 Anybody who carefully studies Roman history will also see how important religion was in making armies obey, in giving spirit to the plebeians, in keeping men good, and in making the wicked ashamed. This is so clear that if there should be any debate about the prince to whom Rome was more under obligation, Romulus or Numa, I believe the first place would at once be given to Numa. If there is religion in a country, it is easy to introduce military virtues;[1] but if there are military habits and not religion, the latter cannot easily be brought in. It is evident that Romulus did not need the authority of God in order to establish the Senate and make other civil and military arrangements. But to Numa divine authority was very necessary, so he pretended to be intimate with a Nymph, who counseled him about the advice he was to give the people. The reason for all this was that he intended to set up new and unaccustomed statutes in the city, and feared that his own authority was not adequate.

3 And truly, no one ever established unusual laws for a people without having recourse to God, for otherwise they would not have been accepted. Many good laws are recognized as such by a prudent man, and yet do not so clearly carry conviction in themselves that anyone else is persuaded to accept them. Hence wise men, who wish to get rid of this difficulty, have recourse to God. Lycurgus did it, and Solon, and many others who have had the same end as they did. The Roman people, then, marveling at the goodness and prudence of Numa, yielded to all his decisions. It is true that because those times were very religious and he was dealing with ignorant people, he found it easy to carry out his designs, and could easily imprint a new form on the people. There is no doubt that at present anybody who wished to set up a republic would find it easier among men in the mountains, where there is no civilization, than among those accustomed to live in cities, where civilization is corrupt; just as a sculptor will more easily get a fine statue from a rough piece of marble than from one badly blocked out by somebody else.

4 Considering everything then, I conclude that the religion

[1] Cf. *The Prince*, Chap. 12, par. 2.

introduced by Numa was one of the first causes of the prosperity of that city; religion caused good laws and customs; good customs caused good fortune; and from good fortune came the successful outcome of undertakings. And as attention to divine worship is the cause of the greatness of states, so contempt for it is the cause of their ruin. Where the fear of God is lacking, a kingdom must go to ruin, unless it is upheld by fear of a prince who supplies the lack of religion. And because princes are short-lived, such a kingdom must pass away as soon as the ability of the ruler passes away. Hence it is that kingdoms depending only on the strength of one man do not last long, because their strength dies with the man, and it is seldom renewed in the next heir, for, as Dante prudently says,

> Infrequently does human probity rise into the branches;
> So He wishes who gives it, that men may call on him.[2]

It does not, then, give security to a republic or a kingdom to have a prince who governs prudently while he is alive; he must be able to arrange that when he dies security will still be maintained. And though rude men are more easily won over to a new order of things or a new opinion, it is not for that reason impossible to convince cultured men and those who think they are not rude. The people of Florence do not think themselves either ignorant or rude, yet Frate Girolamo Savonarola persuaded them that he spoke with God. I do not wish to decide whether this was true or not, because one should speak of so great a man with reverence, but I do say that great numbers believed it without having seen anything unusual to compel their belief. His life, his teaching, and the subject he dealt with were sufficient to make them trust him. Nobody, therefore, should fear that he cannot attain what has been attained by others, because, as I said in my preface,[3] men everywhere are born, live, and die in the same manner.

[2] *Purgatorio,* 7.121-3, not exactly quoted.

[3] In the preface of the First Book he insists that immediate suggestion can be gained from the study of history, though men often make no attempt to gain from it anything other than pleasure, "supposing the imitation of the past not merely difficult but impossible; as though the sky, the sun, the elements, and men are different in motion, arrangement, and power from what they were in ancient times." Cf. also the preface of the Second Book, and Book 3, Discourse 43.

DISCOURSES ON LIVY, I, 12

THE GREAT IMPORTANCE OF TAKING ACCOUNT OF RELIGION, AND THE RUIN OF ITALY BECAUSE SHE LACKS IT THROUGH THE FAULT OF THE ROMAN CHURCH

1 Those princes and republican governments that wish to keep themselves uncorrupted must above everything else keep the ceremonies of their religions uncorrupted, and always respect them, because there can be no clearer sign of the ruin of a land than to see divine worship despised. This is easy to understand when one knows the basis of the religion in which a man is born; for every religion has the basis of its life in some of its important institutions. The life of the Gentile religion was based on the responses of the oracles, and on the teachings of the diviners and soothsayers; all other ceremonies, sacrifices, and rites depended on these, because they easily believed that the God who could predict their future good or future ill could also give it to them. In this originated temples, sacrifices, prayers, and every ceremony in veneration of the gods; this was the reason for the oracle of Delos, the temple of Jupiter Ammon, and other celebrated oracles, which filled the world with admiration and devotion. But when the oracles began to speak to suit the powerful, and this falsity was discovered by the people, men became unbelieving and ready to disturb anything good in the social order. The rulers of a republic or a kingdom ought, then, to preserve the fundamentals of the religion they adhere to. If they do this, it will be easy for them to keep their country religious, and as a result to keep it good and united. And they ought to favor and magnify all happenings that seem to favor religion, even though they think them false. And they ought to do it the more in proportion as they are more prudent and have a better understanding of natural science. And because this method has been practised by wise men, belief in miracles has arisen, and they are of importance even in false religions; indeed prudent rulers aggrandize them, whatever their cause may be, and the authority of these men makes the miracles obtain credence with everybody.

2 There were many of these miracles at Rome. Among them was this: When the Roman soldiers were sacking the city of Veii, some of them entered the temple of Juno, went up to the image of the goddess, and said: "Do you wish to come to Rome?" To some it appeared that the image nodded, and to others that it said "Yes." These soldiers were very religious, as Titus Livius shows by saying that when they entered the temple they were not disorderly but were all devout and reverent. Hence they heard the response to their question which they probably expected. This opinion and belief was favored and added to in every way by Camillus and the other chief men of the city.

3 If the rulers of Christendom had kept their religion in the form in which its founder established it, Christian states and republics would be much more united and more prosperous than they are now. One cannot form a better estimate of the decline of Christianity than by seeing that those people who are nearest to the Roman Church, the head of our religion, have least religion. And anybody who considers the fundamentals of the early Church, and sees how different its practice is at the present time, must decide that, beyond doubt, overthrow or punishment is near at hand.

4 And because many are of the opinion that the well-being of the cities of Italy is derived from the Roman Church, I wish to give the reasons that occur to me on the other side. I will mention two very strong arguments, which, so far as I can see, cannot be refuted. The first is that because of the bad example of the papal court, this land has lost all piety and all religion. This has resulted in numerous troubles and disorders, because, just as every good thing is taken for granted where there is religion, so where it is lacking, the contrary is taken for granted. We Italians, then, are under obligation to the Church and the priests in the first place because we are without religion and vile.

5 But we have a greater obligation to them, which is the second cause of our ruin. This is that the Church has kept this country divided and still keeps it so.[1] And certainly no land was ever united or prosperous if it was not wholly under the rule of one republican government or one prince, as has happened in France and Spain. The cause why Italy has not gained the same position, and has neither a republican administration or a prince to govern her, is the Church alone. Though the Church has her seat here and holds temporal power, yet she has never been so strong or vigorous that she has been able to seize sole authority over Italy and make herself ruler of the land. Yet, on the other hand, she has not been so weak that, when she was afraid of losing her temporal power, she could not bring in some strong man to defend her against anyone in Italy who became too powerful. This was seen long ago in various instances: by means of Charlemagne, she drove out the Lom-

[1] A clear expression of Machiavelli's desire for a united Italy, an idea that underlies *The Prince* but is implied rather than stated even in the last chapter.

bards, who had almost established kingly rule over all Italy; in our times, she deprived the Venetians of power with the aid of the French; later she drove away the French with the help of the Swiss. The Church has not, then, been powerful enough to take possession of Italy, nor has she permitted any one else to possess it; thus she has been the cause that the land has been unable to unite under one ruler.[2] On the contrary, Italy has been ruled by many princes and lords, who have caused such disunion and weakness that she has been the prey not merely of powerful barbarians, but of anybody who assailed her. For this we Italians owe our thanks to the Church, and to nobody else.[3] If anyone should wish to see the truth of this immediately and by certain experience, he would need to be so powerful that he could send the Roman court, with the authority it has in Italy, to live in the provinces of Switzerland. Today the Swiss are the only people who live as the ancients did, as to religion and military customs. But it would be seen that in a short time the wicked habits of the papal court would make more trouble in the land than any other event that could occur there at any time.

DISCOURSES ON LIVY, I, 16

A People Accustomed to Living Under a Prince, if by Some Accident It Becomes Free, Maintains Its Liberty with Difficulty

1 A people accustomed to living under a prince, if by some accident it gains its liberty, as did Rome after the expulsion of the Tarquins, has very great difficulty in preserving it; this is shown by innumerable examples to be read among the narratives of ancient history. A difficulty of this kind is intelligible, because such a people is not other than a wild animal, which, though ferocious and savage by nature, has always been kept in prison and in captivity; but if after a time it is by chance liberated in an open field, it is the booty of the first person who attempts to chain it up again, because it has not learned how to feed itself and does not know the places where it needs to flee for refuge.

2 The same thing happens to a people that has become used

[2] On the Pope as a temporal ruler, cf. the Letters of December 20, 1514, and November 1526, above.

[3] With this and the similar words earlier in the paragraph, compare the obligation of Rome, Italy, and the world to Caesar as stated in the *Discourses*, I, 10, par. 3, above.

to living under the direction of others; since it does not know how to plan for defensive or offensive warfare, and is not acquainted with princes or known to them, it soon submits to another yoke, which generally is heavier than that which a little before it had taken off its neck.[1] There is difficulty in such cases even though the substance of the state has not been corrupted. A people which has been entirely penetrated by corruption is unable not merely for a short time, but for any time at all, to live in freedom, as will be explained below. Therefore our discussions will treat those peoples in which corruption has not grown very great, and where what is good exceeds what is spoiled.

3 Another difficulty must be added to what has been mentioned: that is, the state that becomes free acquires partisan enemies and not partisan friends. All those become partisan enemies who held high rank in the preceding, tyrannical government, and were supported by the riches of the prince. Since the possibility of power is taken away from them, they cannot live in contentment, and are all obliged to try to get back the tyranny, in order to recover their own authority. But, as I have said, partisan friends are not acquired, because a free state bestows honors and rewards for honorable and well-recognized causes, and apart from them gives reward or honor to nobody, and when a man has such honors and benefits as he thinks he merits, he does not admit that he has any obligation to those who have rewarded him. Besides this, the common benefit that is drawn from a free government is not recognized by anybody when it is being enjoyed; I mean such things as the possibility of enjoying freely one's property without fear, not to have any dread about the honor of women or of children, not to have fears for oneself; for nobody ever thinks he is under obligation to one who does not injure him. Therefore, as I said above, a free government and one newly set up comes to have partisan enemies and not partisan friends.

4 If the state wishes to provide against the troubles and disorders that the difficulties I have mentioned bring with them, there is no remedy more powerful, more efficacious, more sure, or more necessary than to kill the sons of Brutus; for, as history shows, they were led to form a conspiracy with the other Roman youth against their native city for no other reason than that they were not able under the consuls to enjoy such unusual advantages as they had under the king; indeed it seemed that the liberty of Rome was servitude to them. He who undertakes to govern a multitude, either according to the

[1] Cf. *The Prince,* Chap. 5, par. 3.

methods of a free state or of a principality, and does not secure himself from those who are enemies of the new order, sets up a state that will be short-lived. It is true that I think those princes unhappy who, to make their positions solid, have to use extraordinary methods, because the multitude are their enemies. He who has the few for his enemies can easily and without many disturbances secure himself, but he who has the body of the people against him can never make himself secure. The more cruelty he uses, the weaker becomes his position as prince. Hence the best recourse he has is to make the people friendly to him.[2]

5 And though this *Discourse* is unlike what I have written above, since here I speak of a prince and there of a republic, yet that I may not have to return to this matter, I wish to speak of it briefly.[3] Therefore speaking of princes who have become tyrants of their native cities—if a prince intends to gain to himself a people who has been unfriendly to him, I say that he ought to examine first the wishes of the people, and he will find that they desire two things: one, to revenge themselves on those who have caused them to fall into slavery; the other, to get their liberty again. The first desire the prince can satisfy completely, the second in part. As to the first, here is an example in point. When Clearchus, tyrant of Heraclea, was in exile, strife arose between the people and the nobles of Heraclea, in which the nobles saw that they were the weaker party. Hence they turned to Clearchus and, making a conspiracy with him, brought him into the city against the popular wish and took away the liberty of the people. Clearchus then found himself between the arrogance of the nobles, whom he was able in no way to content or to control, and the fury of the people, who could not endure the loss of their liberty. Hence he determined with one stroke to free himself from the annoyance of the great and to gain the people to his side.[4] Taking a suitable opportunity, he cut to pieces all the nobles, to the great content of the populace. Thus in this way he gave satisfaction to one of the wishes of the people, that of revenging themselves.

6 But as to the other wish of the people, that of regaining their liberty, since the prince cannot satisfy them, he ought to examine the causes that make them desire to be free. He will

[2] With this and the following paragraphs, cf. *The Prince*, Chap. 9.

[3] The *Discourses* normally deal with republics (*The Prince*, Chap. 2, first sentence). Why did Machiavelli not mention *The Prince* here? Had he not yet written it, or planned to write it? The first reference to it is in Book 2, Discourse 1.

[4] Cf. *The Prince*, Chap. 8, pars. 2, 3, on Agathocles.

find that a small section of them desires to be free in order to have authority, but all the others, who are very numerous, desire liberty in order to live safely. In all republics, however they are organized, not more than forty or fifty citizens rise to positions of authority.[5] Because this is a small number, it is easy to secure yourself against them,[6] either by getting rid of them or by dividing among them so many honors that, in proportion to their rank, they are to a considerable extent contented. The others, for whom it is enough to live in security, are easily satisfied, if the prince makes decrees and laws which provide for both his power and the common safety.[7] If a prince does this and the people see that he does not break such laws in any emergency, they will begin in a short time to live in security and contentment. The kingdom of France is an example of this, for it lives in security for no other reason than that the king is bound by a great number of laws, through which the security of all the people is brought about. He who set up that form of government desired that the king should act as he pleased about military matters and money, but that he should not be able to deal with anything else other than as the laws decreed. A prince, then, or a republican government that does not make itself secure at the beginning of its period of authority, must take the first opportunity to secure itself, as the Romans did. He who lets this opportunity pass will repent too late of not having done what he should.

7 Since, therefore, the Roman people was not yet corrupt when it regained its liberty, it was able to retain it, after killing the sons of Brutus and extirpating the Tarquins, by using all those other methods and plans that have already been discussed. But if the people had been corrupt, neither in Rome nor elsewhere would resources strong enough to maintain liberty have been found, as will be shown in the following chapter.

[5] Cf. Machiavelli's council of Sixty-five, in the *Discourse on Reforming the Government of Florence,* par. 17.

[6] Cf. *The Prince,* Chap. 8, par. 2; and Chap. 9, par. 2.

[7] The idea of the common safety, though implied in *The Prince,* Chap. 9, par. 6, is not expressed there.

DISCOURSES ON LIVY, I, 34

The Dictatorial Authority Was a Benefit and Not an Injury to the Roman Republic; and the Authorities the Citizens Are Deprived of, Not Those They Give with Their Free Votes, Are the Ones Injurious to Free Government

1 Some writers have condemned those Romans who devised in their city the scheme of creating a dictator, as a thing that in time caused tyranny in Rome; these writers allege that the first tyrant of the city ruled it under this title of dictator; and say that if it had not been for that position Caesar would not have been able to make his tyranny seem honorable by the use of any lawful title. But the latter has not been well examined by those who hold this opinion, and has been believed against all reason. It was not the name or the office of dictator that brought Rome to slavery, but it was the power citizens usurped when they remained in authority a long time. If the name of dictator had been lacking in Rome, the tyrants would have taken another, because power easily gets itself a name, but a name does not get power. It can be seen that so long as the dictator was set up according to the laws of the state, and not by his own authority, he always benefited the city. For states are injured by governors that put themselves in power, and authorities that are given in improper ways, not those that come in ordinary ways, as may be seen from what happened in Rome for a long period of time, because no dictator did anything but good to the state. There are obvious reasons for this. First, if you assume that it is possible for a citizen to do injury and seize unusual authority for himself, you must allow him many qualities he cannot have in a republic that is not corrupt: he needs to be very rich and to have many adherents and partisans. Yet he cannot have these things where the laws are observed, and if indeed he could have them, such men are so dangerous that the free vote of the people would not unite to support them. Besides this, the dictator was set up for a limited time and not in perpetuity, and only in order to get rid of the danger that caused his creation. His authority, indeed, extended so far that he could decide by himself on the methods to be used in that urgent need, do anything without consultation, and punish anyone without the victim's having the right of appeal; but he was not able to do anything that would lessen the power of the state, such as taking away the authority of the Senate and the people, or destroying the old constitution of the city and making a new one. Hence, in view of the brief period of the dictatorship, the

limited authority it had, and the uncorrupted condition of the Roman people, it was impossible for the dictator to go beyond his proper bounds and injure the city; in fact, experience shows that he was always helpful.

2 And certainly among the fundamental laws of the Romans, this of the dictatorship deserves to be highly esteemed and to be numbered among those that were the cause of the greatness of their power, because without some such device cities can hardly escape from extraordinary dangers. The normal administrations of republics move but slowly, for no council or board of officers can do everything independently, but in many things one needs the other, and time is required to bring these varying wills into unison;[1] hence their protective measures are very dangerous, if they have to deal with a peril that does not allow time. Therefore republics should have in their constitutions a device like the dictatorship. The Venetian state, which stands high among modern republics, has given authority to a few citizens that in urgent necessity they may, if they agree among themselves, decide immediately, without further consultation. But when a republic has no such method, it must, if it preserves its constitution, be destroyed, or must violate its constitution in order not to be destroyed. And it is not desirable that anything should ever happen in a republic that has to be managed by extraordinary methods. For even if the irregular means have a good effect at that time, nevertheless the example has a bad influence, because the precedent it furnishes for breaking the fundamental laws for a good purpose will then be used as an excuse to break them for a bad purpose.[2] Thus it appears that a republic will never be perfect, if its laws do not provide for everything, and furnish a resource in every accident, and give a means of dealing with it. I say, then, in conclusion, that those republics that in urgent perils cannot have recourse to a dictator or similar authorities, will always be overthrown in serious emergencies.

3 And it is to be noted about this new arrangement how wisely the method of choice was provided for by the Romans. The creation of a dictator was somewhat to the discredit of the consuls, because, though the heads of the city, they had to obey like other men, and it was foreseen that this might cause some irritation among the citizens; hence it was provided that the

[1] The slow motion of republics appears also in the *Discourses*, I, 59, in the Letter of August 26, 1513, par. 5, above, and in the *Discourse on Reforming the Government of Florence*, par. 3, above, where it is pointed out that Cosimo could not move rapidly because he made use of republican machinery.

[2] On examples, see *The Prince*, Chap. 24, par. 1.

power of choosing him should reside in the consuls, in the belief that when such an emergency came that Rome had need of this kingly power, the consuls would be willing to choose a dictator, and since they had chosen him, he would be less displeasing to them, in the same way that wounds and any other evils a man inflicts on himself spontaneously and through choice are much less painful than those inflicted on him by others. Yet in the last days of the republic the Romans, instead of choosing a dictator, were in the habit of giving his authority to the consul, with these words: "Let the consul see to it that no harm comes to the republic."

4 To return to my subject, I conclude that the neighbors of Rome, by seeking to keep her down, forced her to take measures such that she could not merely defend herself, but could use more force, wisdom, and power in attacking them.

DISCOURSES ON LIVY, I, 49

If Those Cities That Have Had a Free Origin, Such as Rome, Have Difficulty in Devising Laws That Will Keep Them Free, Cities That Have Had an Origin Altogether Servile Find It Impossible

1 The course of events in the Roman republic shows how difficult it is in founding a state to arrange in advance for all the laws needed to keep it free. Even though a good many laws were established by Romulus at the beginning, and then by Numa, Tullius Hostilius, and Servius, and finally by the Ten Citizens chosen for the task, nevertheless in the government of that city new necessities were always being discovered, and it was necessary to make new provisions for them. This came about when the Censors were chosen, for the censorship was one of the devices that aided in keeping Rome free, so long as she lived in liberty. Since they were in control of the manners of Rome, they were a very important cause why the Romans were slow in becoming corrupt. It is true that the Romans made an error when they first set up such a magistracy, by giving it a term of five years; but not much later this was corrected by the prudence of Mamercus the dictator, who by a new law reduced their term to eighteen months. The Censors who were then in office took this in such bad part that they deprived Mamercus of his place as senator, an action that was much blamed by both the plebeians and the Senate. And because history does not show that Mamercus was able to protect himself against the Censors, it must be either that the history is defective or that the arrangements of Rome in this matter were not good, because it is not good for a republic to be organized in such a way that a citizen who brings forward a law in harmony with a free way of life can be injured for it without any recourse.

2 But going back to the beginning of this *Discourse*, I say that the creation of this new magistracy indicates that cities that have been free from the beginning and which have governed themselves, like Rome, have had great difficulty in finding good laws whereby to maintain their freedom; if this is true, it is not strange that cities which have had an origin wholly servile find it not merely difficult but impossible to organize themselves in such a way that they can live according to the wishes of the citizens and in peace.

3 The experience of Florence shows this: that city, having been subject to the authority of Rome at the beginning, and having always lived under the control of others, remained for a while in an abject condition and without thinking for herself; then, when there came a chance to show some life, she began to make her own laws; but these laws, being mingled with the old ones, which were bad, could not be good, and so the process has gone on for two hundred years for which there are accurate records, without Florence ever having a government because of which she could properly be called a republic.[1] And this difficulty which has existed there has always existed in all those cities that have had beginnings like hers. And though many times, by public and free votes, full authority has been given to a few citizens to enable them to reform the government, nevertheless they have not organized it for the common benefit, but always to suit their own party;[2] this has produced in the city not order, but greater disorder.

4 To come to a particular example, I say that one of the things the founder of a republic must have in mind is to look closely at the men in whose hands he places the authority of life and death over the citizens. This was well ordered in Rome, because it was commonly possible to appeal to the people, and if something important did occur, in which it was dangerous to put off the execution of judgment in order to permit an appeal, they could have recourse to the dictator, who executed justice immediately; yet they never resorted to that remedy, except when it was necessary. But in Florence and other cities whose origins were like hers, being servile, this authority was placed in

[1] Florence falls between the two groups mentioned in *The Prince*, Chap. 5.

[2] Cf. the *Discourse on Reforming the Government of Florence*, pars. 2 and 4.

the hands of a foreigner, who was sent by the prince to perform this office. When they became free, they still kept this authority in a foreigner, whom they called Captain; this plan was very harmful, because he could easily be bribed by powerful citizens. Later, when this method was changed because of a change in government, they chose eight citizens to fulfill the office of that Captain. This arrangement went from bad to worse, for the reasons given at other times, namely, that the few were always the servants of the few and of those more powerful than themselves.[3]

5 The city of Venice has protected itself against that, for it has ten citizens who are able to punish any citizen without his having the right of appeal. And because they might not be strong enough to punish the powerful, even though they have authority to do it, they have established the Council of Forty, and still more, have arranged that the Council of the *Pregai*, which is their greatest council, should be able to inflict punishment. Hence they have so arranged that when an accuser is not lacking, there is no lack of a judge to hold powerful men in check.

6 We see, then, that even in Rome, which had formed her own constitution with the aid of so many prudent men, every day there came up new reasons why new laws had to be made to preserve free government; it is, therefore, not strange that in other cities, whose beginnings have been more badly regulated, so many difficulties have arisen that they can never be dealt with.

DISCOURSES ON LIVY, II, 2

With What Peoples the Romans Had to Fight, and How Tenaciously These Peoples Defended Their Liberty [with Discussion of the Effects of Christianity]

1 Nothing made it more difficult for the Romans to conquer the peoples around them and parts of the distant provinces than the love that in those times many peoples bore for their freedom, which they defended so tenaciously that they never could have been subjugated except by the utmost prowess.[1] Many examples make plain what perils they underwent to maintain

[3] Cf. the *Discourse on Reforming the Government of Florence*, par. 27.

[1] Cf. *The Prince*, Chap. 5, pars. 1, 2.

and recover their liberty and what vengeance they took on those who had deprived them of it. One can also learn from the reading of history what harm peoples and cities receive from slavery. And whereas in the present day there is but one province that can be said to have free cities in it,[2] in ancient times there were many completely free peoples in all provinces. It is evident that in the times of which I am now speaking the peoples of Italy, from the mountains that separate modern Tuscany and Lombardy to the point of the peninsula, were all free. I refer to the Tuscans, the Romans, the Samnites, and many other peoples who lived in the rest of Italy. No king who ruled there is ever mentioned except those who reigned in Rome and Porsenna the king of Tuscany; history does not tell how the race of the latter was extinguished. Yet it is plain that Tuscany was free in the days when the Romans went to besiege Veii; the country was so fond of her liberty and so greatly hated the name of prince that, after the people of Veii had made a king for their defence and asked aid of the Tuscans against the Romans, the former, after much consultation, determined not to give aid to the Vientines so long as they lived under a king, believing it was not well to defend the country of those who had already submitted themselves to a master.

2 It is easy to see how this love for a free life arises in peoples, because experience shows that cities never have grown in dominion and riches except when they have lived in freedom. Truly it is wonderful to observe what greatness Athens attained in the space of a hundred years, after she liberated herself from the tyranny of Pisistratus. And it is much more wonderful to observe what greatness Rome attained after she liberated herself from her kings. The reason is easy to grasp, because what makes cities great is not individual good but the common good. And beyond doubt this common good is attended to only in republics, because all that advances it is put into execution. Even though it does harm to this or that private person, there are so many whom the said common good benefits, that they are able to go ahead in opposition to the wishes of those few who are injured by it.

3 The contrary happens when there is a prince,[3] for in most instances what benefits him injures the city,[4] and what benefits

[2] Germany. See *The Prince*, Chap. 10, par. 2.

[3] An expression of Machiavelli's normal republicanism. He tended to see the early republics at their best, though he knew that Florence had not actually been one (*Discourses*, I, 49, par. 3, above). The exceptional prince, as a true king rather than a tyrant, may work for the common good (*Discourses*, I, 9, par. 3; 10, pars. 4-6, above), and may be required for such a function as the deliverance of a country from bondage (*The Prince*, Chap. 26).

[4] Here, as frequently, Machiavelli is thinking in terms of the city state.

the city injures him. Hence when a tyranny is set up over a free community, the least evil it can bring to such cities is that they make no more progress and do not increase further in power or wealth; generally, or rather always, it happens that they go backward. And if chance should bring about that a vigorous tyrant appears, who by his spirit and the force of his arms increases his dominions, no advantage comes from it to that city, but only to himself, for he cannot give honors to any of those citizens he tyrannizes over who are valiant and good, unless he is willing to have cause to suspect them. Moreover, he cannot place the cities he acquires under the control of the one he rules or make them tributary to it, because to make this city powerful is not to his advantage, but it is to his interest to keep his territory disunited and to have each city and each province look to him.[5] Hence he alone, and not his native land, profits from his acquisitions. If anybody wishes to confirm this belief with many other reasons, let him read the tractate that Xenophon wrote *On Tyranny*.[6]

4 It is not strange, then, that the ancient peoples pursued tyrants with such great hatred and loved free government, and that the name of liberty was so highly esteemed by them. There was an instance of this when Hieronymous, grandson of Hiero of Syracuse, was killed in Syracuse and the news of his death came to his army, which was not far from Syracuse. At first the soldiers started to raise an uproar and to take arms against his murderers. But when they heard that liberty was being shouted in Syracuse, they were attracted by that word, became quiet, gave up their anger against the tyrannicides, and considered how they could set up a free government in the city. It is not strange, then, that the people take heavy vengeance on those who have snatched their liberty away. There have been many examples of this, of which I intend to give only one, which happened in Corcyra, a city of Greece, in the times of the Peloponnesian war. Greece was then divided into two parties, one of which favored the Athenians, the other the Spartans; as a result many cities were divided among themselves, and one party was devoted to Sparta, the other to Athens. In the city I have mentioned the nobles got the upper hand and took away the liberty of the people; but soon the people with the aid of the Athenians rallied their forces, made captives of all the nobility, and shut them up in a prison that would hold them all. Then they took them out eight or ten at a time, under pretence

[5] Cf. *The Prince*, Chap. 20, par. 4.

[6] Usually known as the *Hiero*. The translation by Petrus Paulus Vergerius, Venice, 1497, was called *De tyrannide*.

of sending them into exile in different places, and put them to death with many cruel punishments. When this was known, those who remained decided it was wise to do all they could to escape that ignominious death. Arming themselves as they could, they fought with those who tried to enter, and defended the entrance of the prison. Thereupon the people, drawn together by the uproar, wrecked the upper part of the building and crushed the nobles in the ruins. Many other similar horrible and striking events followed in that province. Hence it can be seen that the fury of vengeance for liberty that has been taken away is greater than the fury of protection for the liberty somebody is attempting to take away.

5 With these events in mind, I have wondered why in those ancient times the people were lovers of liberty more than in these. I believe the reason is the same as makes the men of the present less courageous, and that, I hold, is the difference between modern and ancient education, founded on the difference between our religion and that of antiquity. Our religion, having showed us the truth and the true way, makes us put a low value on worldly honor. Hence the heathen, who put a high value on it, and made it their highest good, were more vigorous in their actions. This can be deduced from many of their institutions, beginning with the magnificence of their sacrifices, contrasted with the humility of ours, where there is some splendor, more refined than magnificent, but nothing fierce or vigorous. The ancients did not lack pomp and magnificence in their ceremonies, and they added to them the act of sacrifice full of blood and ferocity, for they killed great numbers of animals. This spectacle, being a savage one, made men become similar to it. The ancient religion, besides this, honored as divine only men loaded with worldly glory, such as captains of armies and princes of states.

6 Our religion has given more glory to humble and contemplative men than to active ones. It has, besides, taught that the highest good consists in humility, lowliness, and contempt for human things; ancient religion made it consist in greatness of spirit, strength of body, and in all the other things likely to make men very courageous. If our religion does ask that you possess some courage, it prefers that you be ready to suffer rather than to do a courageous act. It seems, then, that this way of life has made the world feeble, and given it over as a prey to the wicked, who are able to control it in security, since the generality of men, in order to go to Heaven, think more of enduring injuries than of defending themselves against them. But though it may appear that the world has grown effeminate and Heaven has laid aside her arms, the explanation is without doubt to be found in the worthlessness of men, who have interpreted our religion according to sloth and not according to vigor. If they would but remember that our religion permits us to exalt and defend our native land, they would see that she wishes us to love her and honor her and to prepare ourselves to be such that we can defend her.

7 Such education and such false interpretations bring about that today there are not so many republics in the world as in ancient times, and, as a result, the peoples do not now have the love of liberty that they did then. Yet I believe a more important cause is that the Roman Empire with its arms and its greatness destroyed all the republics and all the commonwealths. And though the Empire was afterward liquidated, the cities have not been able to restore themselves or to reorganize their civil life, except in a few places in the Empire. However that may be, in every least part of the world the Romans certainly found a league of republics well armed and fully determined to defend their liberty. This shows that if the Roman people had not possessed rare and extraordinary prowess they would never have been able to conquer them.

8 I wish to give an example of some part of the Empire, and think the instance of the Samnites will be adequate. It seems a wonderful thing, and Titus Livius admits it, that they were so powerful and their arms so effective that after suffering many defeats, ruins of cities, and slaughters in their country, they were able to resist the Romans until the time of Papirius Cursor the consul, son of the first Papirius—a space of forty-six years. This is especially striking because that country, where there were so many cities and so many men, is now almost without inhabitants, but then there was such good organization and such power that the land was unconquerable if it had not been assailed by Roman prowess.

9 It is easy to determine what caused the old excellence and what causes the present bad condition: it all comes from the free life of the past and the slavish life of the present. For as I said just above, all the cities and provinces everywhere that live free make great advances. There are more people in them, because marriages are freer and more desirable to men, since everyone willingly begets such children as he thinks he can bring up, if he has no fear that his patrimony will be taken away from him; moreover he knows that not merely are they born free men and not slaves, but that if they have ability it is possible for them to become the first citizens of the land. Riches increase there to the utmost, both those that come from agriculture and those that come from the arts.[7] For everybody is glad to increase his property and seeks to gain the goods he thinks he can enjoy when he has acquired them. As a result, men compete in bringing about private and public benefits, and both kinds increase wonderfully. The opposite of all this comes about in countries that live in slavery, and in proportion as their servitude is heavy they lose their earlier prosperity. Of all heavy servitudes, that is heaviest which subjects you to a republic; first, because it is more lasting and there is less hope to escape from it; second, because the purpose of the republic is to weaken and exhaust all other bodies to increase its own. This is not done by a prince who overcomes you, unless that prince is some barbarous prince, a destroyer of cultivation and a waster of all the civilization of men, as are the oriental princes. But if he has within him ordinary human principles, he generally has equal affection for all the cities subject to him, and leaves them all their manufactures and almost all their ancient institutions. Hence, if they are not able to prosper as in freedom, they do not go to ruin as do slaves. I refer to the servitude of cities that serve a foreigner, because of subjection to one of their own citizens I have spoken above.[8]

10 Anyone, then, who will take into account all that has been said, will not wonder at the power the Samnites had while they were free, and at the weakness that came upon them when they were in servitude. Titus Livius assures us of it in many places, and especially in his account of the wars of Hannibal, where he shows that when the Samnites were hard pressed by a legion of soldiers at Nola, they sent ambassadors to Hannibal to ask him to rescue them. These ambassadors said in their speech that for a hundred years they had fought the Romans with their own soldiers and their own generals, and often had resisted two consular armies and two consuls, and that now they had fallen so low that they scarcely were able to defend themselves from a small Roman legion stationed in Nola.

[7] A good prince would also strive to bring about this result; see *The Prince*, Chap. 21, last par.

[8] In the *Discourses on Livy*, I, 16, par. 5, above. See *The Prince*, Chaps. 8 and 9.

DISCOURSES ON LIVY, II, 31

How Dangerous It Is to Believe Banished Men[1]

1 It does not seem to me apart from the subject to consider in one of these *Discourses* how dangerous it is to believe those who have been driven out from their native lands, since it is a matter that must be dealt with every day by those who occupy places of authority. I do this especially because I can demonstrate it with a memorable example brought up by Titus Livius in his history, though it is outside his stated bounds. When Alexander the Great went with his army into Asia, Alexander of Epirus, his brother-in-law and uncle, came with soldiers into Italy, summoned by the banished Lucanians, who led him to hope that with their assistance he could occupy that whole province. As a result, though he had come into Italy because of their pledge and the hope they had given him, they put him to death because their fellow-citizens promised to take them back into their native city if they killed him.

2 It should be observed, therefore, how vain the pledges and promises of those who have been exiled from their native land may be. As to their good faith, it must be reckoned that whenever they are able through other means than yours to enter again into their native city, they will leave you and ally themselves with others, notwithstanding any promises they have made you.[2] And as to vain promises and hopes, their desire to return home is so violent that they naturally believe many things that are false, and to these they artfully join many others. Hence, between what they believe and what they tell you they believe, they fill you with such hope that, if you rely on it, you either enter into useless expense or go into an enterprise in which you get badly injured.

3 I hope the example of the aforesaid Alexander, with the addition of Themistocles of Athens, is enough. The latter, when condemned as a rebel, fled into Asia to the court of Darius, where he made such great promises, if the king would go to attack Greece, that Darius undertook the enterprise. When Themistocles could not fulfill the promises he had made, he poisoned himself, either from shame or fear of punishment. And if such a mistake was made by Themistocles, a man of great ability, it can be estimated how much more they err in such

[1] The exile was a frequent figure in Italy for some centuries. See the *Life of Castruccio Castracani*, pars. 10, 11, 17, and 19. Exiles are not mentioned in *The Prince*, though they would often have been found with forces of the foreign enemies mentioned in Chapter 19, par. 2.

[2] Cf. the conduct of conspirators able to make their own peace (*The Prince*, Chap. 19, par. 3).

matters who, having weaker minds, allow themselves to be moved by their desires and passions. In undertaking enterprises on the authority of a banished man, then, a prince should go slowly, because almost always he will at the end suffer shame or very heavy damage.

BIBLIOGRAPHY

The bibliography is obviously only suggestive. Among the Italian titles are a number of works that have been especially helpful to the editor and that form the basis for any study of Machiavelli. The books in English range from the scholarly to the popular. Further bibliography will be found in some of the volumes listed, as in connection with Burd's article in *The Cambridge Modern History,* in Pulver's *Machiavelli,* and above all in Norsa's volume.

Italian Works

Arthur L. Burd
Il Principe di Niccolò Machiavelli. Oxford, 1891.

Francesco Ercole
La Politica di Machiavelli. Rome, 1926.

Machiavelli
Il Principe
con commento storico, filologico e stilistico, a cura di Giuseppe Lisio. Firenze, 1927.

———
Il Principe, edited by Luigi Russo. Firenze, 1931.

———
Lettere. Firenze, 1929.

———
Lettere familiari,
a cura di Cerolamo Lazzeri. Milano, 1923.

———
Opere
Italia, 1813, 8 vols.
This edition was followed in translating the *Discourse on Reforming the Government of Florence.* References to it are in the form VI, 57.

———
Tutte le Opere Storiche e Letterarie,
a cura di Guido Mazzoni e Mario Casella. Firenze, 1929.
This edition was followed in making the translations of all the works it contains.

Achille Norsa
Il Principio della Forza Nel Pensiero Politico di Niccolò Machiavelli.
Seguito da un Contributo Bibliografico, 248 pages.
Milano, 1936.

Savonarola
Prediche E Scritti. Milano, 1930.

Storie Pistoresi (MCCC-MCCCXLVIII)
a cura di Silvio Adrasto Barbi, in Muratori,
Rerum Italicarum Scriptores. Città di Castello, 1907.

Niccolò Tegrimi
Vita Castruccii Antelminelli Lucensis Ducis in Muratori, *Rerum Italicarum Scriptores,* vol. 11, cols. 1308-44. Milan, 1727.

Oreste Tommasini
La Vita e gli Scritti di Niccolò Machiavelli. Rome, 1883-1911.

ENGLISH WORKS

Arthur L. Burd
Florence (II): "Machiavelli," in *The Cambridge Modern History,* I, vi, pp. 190-218.

H. Butterfield
The Statecraft of Machiavelli. London, 1940.

Allan H. Gilbert
Machiavelli's Prince and Its Forerunners. Durham, N. C., 1938.

———
Literary Criticism: Plato to Dryden. New York, 1940.

Ettore Janni
Machiavelli, translated by Marion Enthoven. London, 1930.

George Meredith
An Essay on Comedy, edited by Lane Cooper. New York, 1918.

Dorothy E. Muir
Machiavelli and His Times. New York, 1936.

Sir Charles Oman
A History of the Art of War in the Sixteenth Century. New York, n. d.

Giuseppe Prezzolini
Nicolo Machiavelli the Florentine, trans. by Ralph Roeder. New York, 1928.

Jeffrey Pulver
Machiavelli: The Man, His Work, and His Times. London, 1937.

Ralph Roeder
The Man of the Renaissance.
Four Lawgivers: Savonarola, Machiavelli, Castiglione, Aretino. New York, 1933.

Ferdinand Schevill
History of Florence from the Founding of the City through the Renaissance. New York, 1936.

Pasquale Villari
The Life and Times of Niccolò Machiavelli, translated by Linda Villari. London, n. d.

William Harrison Woodward
Cesare Borgia: a Biography. London, 1913.

INDEX